Register for Free Membership t...

Over the last few years, Syngress has published man..., ...g and critically acclaimed books, including Tom Shinder's *Configu...g ISA Server 2000*, Brian Caswell and Jay Beale's *Snort 2.1 Intrusion Detection*, and Angela Orebaugh and Gilbert Ramirez's *Ethereal Packet Sniffing*. One of the reasons for the success of these books has been our unique **solutions@syngress.com** program. Through this site, we've been able to provide readers a real time extension to the printed book.

As a registered owner of this book, you will qualify for free access to our members-only solutions@syngress.com program. Once you have registered, you will enjoy several benefits, including:

- Four downloadable e-booklets on topics related to the book. Each booklet is approximately 20-30 pages in Adobe PDF format. They have been selected by our editors from other best-selling Syngress books as providing topic coverage that is directly related to the coverage in this book.
- A comprehensive FAQ page that consolidates all of the key points of this book into an easy to search web page, providing you with the concise, easy to access data you need to perform your job.
- A "From the Author" Forum that allows the authors of this book to post timely updates, links to related sites, or additional topic coverage that may have been requested by readers.

Just visit us at **www.syngress.com/solutions** and follow the simple registration process. You will need to have this book with you when you register.

Thank you for giving us the opportunity to serve your needs. And be sure to let us know if there is anything else we can do to make your job easier.

SYNGRESS®

SYNGRESS®

Cyber Spying

Tracking Your Family's (Sometimes) Secret Online Lives

Ted Fair
Michael Nordfelt
Sandra Ring
Eric Cole   Technical Editor

KEY	SERIAL NUMBER
001	HJIRTCV764
002	PO9873D5FG
003	829KM8NJH2
004	BCD4533389
005	CVPLQ6WQ23
006	VBP965T5T5
007	HJJJ863WD3E
008	2987GVTWMK
009	629MP5SDJT
010	IMWQ295T6T

PUBLISHED BY
Syngress Publishing, Inc.
800 Hingham Street
Rockland, MA 02370

Cyber Spying Tracking Your Family's (Sometimes) Secret Online Lives

Printed in the United States of America
1 2 3 4 5 6 7 8 9 0
ISBN: 1-931836-41-8   06-02-06

Publisher: Andrew Williams
Acquisitions Editor: Gary Byrne
Technical Editor: Dr. Eric Cole
Cover Designer: Michael Kavish

Page Layout and Art: Patricia Lupien
Copy Editor: Judy Eby
Indexer: Julie Kawabata

Distributed by O'Reilly Media, Inc. in the United States and Canada.
For information on rights and translations, contact Matt Pedersen, Director of Sales and Rights, at Syngress Publishing; email matt@syngress.com or fax to 781-681-3585.

Acknowledgments

Syngress would like to acknowledge the following people for their kindness and support in making this book possible.

Syngress books are now distributed in the United States and Canada by O'Reilly Media, Inc. The enthusiasm and work ethic at O'Reilly is incredible and we would like to thank everyone there for their time and efforts to bring Syngress books to market: Tim O'Reilly, Laura Baldwin, Mark Brokering, Mike Leonard, Donna Selenko, Bonnie Sheehan, Cindy Davis, Grant Kikkert, Opol Matsutaro, Steve Hazelwood, Mark Wilson, Rick Brown, Leslie Becker, Jill Lothrop, Tim Hinton, Kyle Hart, Sara Winge, C. J. Rayhill, Peter Pardo, Leslie Crandell, Valerie Dow, Regina Aggio, Pascal Honscher, Preston Paull, Susan Thompson, Bruce Stewart, Laura Schmier, Sue Willing, Mark Jacobsen, Betsy Waliszewski, Dawn Mann, Kathryn Barrett, John Chodacki, Rob Bullington, and Aileen Berg.

The incredibly hard working team at Elsevier Science, including Jonathan Bunkell, Ian Seager, Duncan Enright, David Burton, Rosanna Ramacciotti, Robert Fairbrother, Miguel Sanchez, Klaus Beran, Emma Wyatt, Rosie Moss, Chris Hossack, Mark Hunt, and Krista Leppiko, for making certain that our vision remains worldwide in scope.

David Buckland, Marie Chieng, Lucy Chong, Leslie Lim, Audrey Gan, Pang Ai Hua, and Joseph Chan of STP Distributors for the enthusiasm with which they receive our books.

Kwon Sung June at Acorn Publishing for his support.

David Scott, Tricia Wilden, Marilla Burgess, Annette Scott, Andrew Swaffer, Stephen O'Donoghue, Bec Lowe, and Mark Langley of Woodslane for distributing our books throughout Australia, New Zealand, Papua New Guinea, Fiji Tonga, Solomon Islands, and the Cook Islands.

Winston Lim of Global Publishing for his help and support with distribution of Syngress books in the Philippines.

Authors

Ted Fair is deputy director of the Advanced Technology Research Center at The Sytex Group, Inc. (TSGI). Previously, Ted has worked as a software developer and computer systems expert at the Central Intelligence Agency and the National Security Agency. Ted holds a degree from James Madison University and a Master of Science degree in Telecommunications from The George Washington University.

Michael Nordfelt is a senior computer security analyst for the Advanced Technology Research Center at The Sytex Group, Inc. (TSGI). Previously, he spent time at the Central Intelligence Agency researching computer security methods and applications. His work brings him in contact with many different government and commercial organizations from around the world. He holds a degree in computer engineering from Texas A&M University and holds a Master of Science degree in computer science from Virginia Tech. Thanks to Gabriel Ruenes, a freelance artist/animator, for his help with the figures and illustrations in this book.

Sandy Ring is a senior researcher at The Sytex Group, Inc. (TSGI) and the chief scientist at the Pikewerks Corporation. Prior to this position, she worked for the Central Intelligence Agency, operated closely with the National Security Agency, and conducted research at the National Aeronautics and Space Administration's Langley Research Center. She has received many prestigious awards throughout her career, including a Service Medal from the CIA. Sandy's research topics range from autonomic computing to covert communication.

Technical Editor

Dr. Eric Cole is currently chief technology officer (CTO) and chief scientist at The Sytex Group, Inc. (TSGI), specializing in advanced technology research. Eric is a highly sought-after network security consultant and speaker. Eric has consulted for international banks and Fortune 500 companies. He also has advised Venture Capitalist Firms on what start-ups should be funded. He has in-depth knowledge of network security and has come up with creative ways to secure his clients' assets. He is the author of several books, including *Hackers Beware: Defending Your Network from the Wiley Hacker* and *Hiding in Plain Sight*. Eric holds several patents and has written numerous magazine and journal articles. Eric worked for the CIA for more than seven years and has created several successful network security practices. Eric is a member of the Honeynet Project and the CVE Editorial board; both are invited positions. Eric presents at a variety of conferences, including SANS, where he helped create several of the courses. Eric has appeared in interviews on CBS News, "60 Minutes," and CNN.

Contents

Foreword

I am amazed at how much the world has changed in the last 15 years. You grow up hearing that your parents did not have TVs and that they remember when they bought their first car. You cannot believe that they paid only $18,000 for their house and are amazed at how many things have changed over one generation. Like many others, I often wondered what would be the same when I was talking to my children as they get older. Would there really be major differences between what their generation takes for granted and what my generation takes for granted. I often assumed that everything is pretty stable and that you were not going to see many changes. Now that I look back as an older man, I realize how wrong I was. Computers, technology, and the Internet are just a few examples of the many technological advances that have occurred over the last 20 years.

I can just imagine my children asking, what do you mean you did not have computers at the library? How did you look up a book? Are you serious that libraries used to have rows and rows of cards that you would use to find a book? How in the world did you perform research without the Internet? Are you for real telling me that you had to photocopy pages out of books and use that to conduct your research? How did you ever get anything done? How did you communicate from a business standpoint without e-mail? The list could go on and on, and I can imagine my children's amazement over how anyone functioned 20 years ago. This situation is similar to talking with my dad and wondering how he did anything 20 years prior. Whether we like it or not, and whether we realize it or not, the world changes from underneath us.

When I grew up there was no e-commerce; now it is a billion-dollar-plus market. If I needed to purchase something, you would have to go from store to store until you found a store that stocked what you were looking for. Now, you can go to the Internet, purchase something at 9 P.M., and have it by 10 A.M. the next day. Before we even realize it, our world has changed. Now technology is part of our daily routine, and we have no idea how our parents survived without it. The question that pops up a lot is "before e-mail, what did people do all day at work?" Seems naïve, but nonetheless it raises interesting questions.

As the world evolves we must not only embrace the changes, but also clearly understand their attendant danger and risk. Failure to understand, address, and mitigate the risk can be detrimental. This background knowledge and the following two critical points formed the basis for writing this book.

First, do you realize that the current generation of children who are entering school will be the first generation to grow up with personal computers and access to the Internet from birth? I still remember having to type term papers with a typewriter and correct errors with correction fluid. Now I will replace my parents' stories about having to walk barefoot in the snow to school each day with my own story of remembering when I had to type a 30-page report without a monitor. If I made a big mistake on the last line, I had to retype the entire page.

This point is one that concerns me greatly. In most cases, today's middle school and high school children know more about computers than their parents. One of my neighbors was very upset when his oldest child went away to college because now he had no one to fix his computer or show him how to find anything online. I, in turn, was very upset when his oldest child went to college because I became his personal technical support person. Nonetheless, if high school students want to hide something that they are doing, they will have a good chance of succeeding, without their parents knowing about it.

Second, the Internet has created a whole new level of productivity; you no longer have to be face to face to meet, talk, or conspire. Great tools like e-mail, instant messaging, and the Web enable people to communicate from anywhere. In the past, to communicate with someone you either could use mail, which was very slow; meet face to face, which could be prohibitive based on distance; or use the telephone, which is easy to listen in on and track through phone bills. Now there are numerous tools that you can use across the Internet that make it extremely difficult for someone to know what you are doing, or who you're talking to.

The number of people who use the Internet to abduct minors, mislead them, and misguide them is downright sickening. Children, and even adults, jokingly would go to a chat room and play around, thinking that they are just goofing around with other peers. They have no idea that they are being stalked, and if they only knew what could happen based on an innocent conversation, they would turn off their computers and never use them again.

Many people have no idea of the evils that exist across the Internet and problems that answering an innocent-sounding e-mail could cause. Using the techniques in this book to check up on them (aka "spy"), you can learn if they are doing something dangerous, make them aware of it, and help them change their ways. Without the technique of spying, you would not have the knowledge that is needed to help keep your family and loved ones safe.

Just because someone is not aware of a problem, does not mean it doesn't exist. The impact is still there, and if you are not prepared, there is a greater chance that you, or your loved ones will be injured in the process. The Internet has a lot of value and should be a safe place for people to explore. We can make the Internet a safer place for all only by raising awareness and working together.

This book was written to help make the Internet more secure for friends and families; to raise awareness so that people can understand the dangers associated with the Internet; and to help parents keep their children out of trouble.

—*Dr. Eric Cole*
Chief Technology Officer (CTO) and
Chief Scientist at The Sytex Group, Inc.

## Chapter 1

Why Spy?

"A special feature of the structure of our book is the monstrous but perfectly organic part that eavesdropping plays in it."—1958, *A Hero of Our Time*, Vladimir Nabokov

Topics in This Chapter:

- Introduction to Spying

- Pray for Peace, Prepare for War

- Ethics of Spying

- Spying on Spouses

- Spying on Your Children

- When You Should Not Spy

- Real-World Case Study

- Summary

Introduction to Spying

We have worked for quite a variety of places over the last 10 years, from university newspapers to Fortune 500 companies, to NASA, the NSA, and the place where we all met, the CIA. Each place had its own culture and collection of personalities. During our time at these wildly different companies, we discovered a few common traits between what would appear to be an uncategorizable variety of humans. These traits can be simply summed up as man's desire to *snoop*, and man's desire to *stray*. This book aims to satisfy the former and hopefully help to prevent the latter.

These two traits mentioned, the desire to snoop and the desire to stray, aren't exactly what they seem to be at first. We're using them in a slightly different context, so we'll aim to clear up our definitions right now. For the purposes of this book, we refer to snooping as the curiosity to learn more about something you're interested in, not any of the more voyeuristic definitions that can be applied to it. As you read these words, you're probably thinking, "Not Me" I would never snoop on anyone. Before you proceed with condemning us and burning this book, take a second to stop and think about a few things. Have you ever gossiped about someone, ever? Ever gone to your neighbor's open house just to see how they decorated? Ever read an e-mail over someone's shoulder, or quickly glanced at a document on someone's desk? If you answered yes to any of these, like it or not you've definitely snooped at some time in your life. Most of us have done these things and realize that a curiosity about your surroundings and others is part of fundamental human nature. Not snooping at all is ignorance, taking it too far is voyeurism, a balanced approach is intelligence collection, and that is what this book is about.

For the second of the traits that we'll be discussing, straying, our definition of it does not directly correspond with Webster's. We view straying not as literal infidelity, but the desire for any person to investigate their dark side. This can include but is not limited to cheating on a partner, drug or alcohol problems, gambling, gang participation, cheating in school, or almost any other illegal or unethical activity. We define this as "straying" since we feel most people want to and choose to do the right thing. Only occasionally or under the wrong influence do they embark on these activities. Straying isn't always a bad thing either, but if it is your loved one is doing this, it is something you should probably know about. Even if you don't choose to stop or limit this behavior, it is often worth monitoring to ensure that the perpetrators do not harm themselves, you, or others within their lives.

In all of these places we've worked and lived, we've come to realize that there are two fundamental lessons you can almost always count on: the abundance of human drama and results of having, or not having, the right information. These two lessons go hand in hand. Whether you live and work as a roofer in Baltimore,

Domino's Pizza in Alabama, or the Central Intelligence Agency in Washington, D.C., you encounter the same situations over and over. People's spouses cheat, people have divorces, people or their children do drugs, fall in with the wrong crowd, and develop gambling or addiction problems. In every single case we discovered that the individuals who were aware of these issues or had prior knowledge of these events fared much better than those who did not. We've seen people worked over in divorces and parents completely stunned by their children when they failed to notice the problems.

The different aspects of human drama that we've described (divorce, drug use, infidelity, etc.) have been around for a long time. These are the same problems that couples and parents have struggled with for years. The widespread popularity and use of the Internet has added a new twist to these problems. They now can occur faster and easier as people are aided by the wealth of knowledge, instant connectivity, and perceived feeling of anonymity it offers. At one time an individual's social circle consisted of who they lived with, worked with, went to school with and had direct personal contact with. Now, with direct personal contact not longer a necessity, it often consists of dozens of people spread around the world, some of questionable nature. New social circles are now generally an order of magnitude larger, and far more geographically diverse. In addition the relative anonymity of the Internet makes it far more difficult to judge the character or identity of a person's Internet contact. How does one know if that twenty-two-year-old woman they're talking to is really twenty-two, or even a woman?

As a result of this new connectivity the same events that have plagued us for ages are now occurring with the speed and power of the information age. More and more people are using their computers as enabling tools to assist them as they stray. People meet many possible new coconspirators online. In recent years a larger percentage of extramarital affairs have occurred as a result of people first meeting online. Even if the catalyst for the undesirable activity isn't found online, it is quite common to use the expanded connectivity of the Internet to communicate with them. For example in 2003 several gangs in Plano, Texas, coordinated a big brawl using an online chat room. This demonstrates the pervasiveness of the Internet into almost all aspects of life, even such seemingly unlikely ones like gang activity.

During most of our careers we've been in highly technical offices, and worked with highly technical people. These people, like everyone else in the world, had to deal with infidelity, drug use, and other problems. In addition they were also dealing with the influence of computers in these areas. But unlike most of the world, our coworkers had extensive training in computer security, were highly technical, and to put it frankly, quite sneaky. Realizing that technology was brought into play they decided to use their technical background to give them leverage in dealing with these difficult situations. These people would install keystroke loggers, remotely access their computers, and search for digital evidence of the incidents that were affecting them. In most cases simple examination and monitoring yielded surprisingly effective results. Our coworkers got an inside track on what was happening, and armed with this knowledge were more effectively able to confront and handle their challenges. This was especially apparent when they were compared against nontechnical friends, who didn't have the prior knowledge to use their computer as an effective tool for evidence collection. In almost every case those who had performed some rudimentary cyber-sleuthing were a step ahead, less likely to be blindsided, and had a full idea of the big picture. The old mantra has long been held that knowledge is power, and this is a perfect example.

With this book we seek to take the advantages used by our technically gifted coworkers, and extend it out to a larger audience. After observing firsthand how powerful the correct information can be, and how damaging the lack of it is, we want to do what we can to enable everyone to always have as much of the truth as possible. In most cases the steps necessary to collect useful information from a computer are technically simple. Due to the relative obscurity and taboo nature of these methods, they have been largely unknown to the general public. It is time for that to change. In most cases where this type of information is sought the legal, moral, and physical stakes are too high not to take every advantage possible. We don't seek or encourage criminal or unethical behavior. We merely want people who are facing challenges in their life to be empowered to seek the truth.

Pray for Peace, Prepare for War

As previously mentioned, computers now play a large part in most people's lives. Instant and continual connectivity is the hallmark of the information age. With this newfound power people are reaching out and coming in contact with larger groups than previously possible with more traditional methods of socializing. In addition the appearance of anonymity makes many far bolder online than in their real lives. People feel free to explore areas of interest online that they would normally never experiment with in the real world. This combination of apparent anonymity and connectivity can sometimes lead to disastrous results. Over the last five years, as Internet access has become more pervasive, the number of Internet-related and Internet-enabled vices has increased as well. Most apparent are online infidelity, drug activity, and collaboration for other illicit activities.

Figure 1.1 People, Their PCs, and What They Do with Them

If only everyone had labels. Figure 1.1 shows a few people gathering with their laptops to relax, socialize, and go about their business. Unlike this scene, the activities of your family may not be as obvious. Without delving deep into their minds, you may never really know what is going on in their lives. If everyone's actions were as easy to read as in this figure, we likely wouldn't be writing this book. One of the great mysteries of humankind is that unless people tell you, it's difficult to ever really know what they are thinking. An even then, it's impossible to ever truly know that they're telling you the absolute truth. If the labels were left out of Figure 1.1 it would be just another slice of life at a neighborhood coffee shop.

Notice almost everyone in the picture was going about their activity with the aid of a computer. When traditional methods of communication break down, short of mind reading, spying on a computer may be the best way to determine what a person is up to. We feel it is very important for people to be aware of the warning signs and to have an understanding of the true nature of online threats. Not everyone is running off with people they've met online, all kids aren't buying drugs from eBay, and not everyone out there is a dangerous cyber-stalker. Too often the media preys on fear and a lack of understanding to fuel their sensationalism. Since many of these concepts, and computers in general are still somewhat mysterious to the general population, it is easy to prey upon the unknown to build an unreasonable and unrealistic fear. We seek to explain the actual nature of the threats that we are aware of. By no means do we claim to be comprehensive in our knowledge or understanding of all possible cyber-threats. We seek only to present what we know about real threats and their related warning signs. With this book as an introduction, one can study the areas they are interested in deeper to gain a far more comprehensive understanding of their areas of concern.

Notes from the Underground...

Acronyms Your Mother Never Told You About

Acronyms, or *nyms* as they are commonly referred to, are used to make online conversation faster and easier. They are also used to fit in with a crowd and show you speak a certain language. They allow participants to substitute them for longer words or phrases. Most people now are familiar with some of the more common nyms, such as LOL (laughing out loud) and ROFL (rolling on the floor laughing). However, there are few lesser-known nyms that are often used in romance-, sex-, and drug-related discussions. Here are a few of the more interesting nyms we've come across:

- **420** When used as a noun, 420 is referring to marijuana. When used as a verb it refers to the act of smoking marijuana. This supposedly comes from the time 4:20 P.M. on the clock, allegedly the time when most children get high. It also is used to refer to April 20, national smoke out day in drug culture.

- **ASL** Age, sex, location. This nym is often used as the intro statement in most romance chat rooms. People use this, especially when speaking to an ambiguous screen name, to determine if they are interested in further pursuing conversation.

- **Cam2Cam (c2c) Only** This stands for Web cam to Web cam only. This is a common response for people who receive requests from strangers to view their Web cams. This means that they will allow people to view their Web cams only if they receive reciprocation from the requesting party.

- **Cyber** If someone asks if you want to cyber, realize that they are asking for the information age equivalent of phone sex. Cybering is

Continued

the act of typing out sexually explicit situations to a person usually via popular chat programs.

- **IRL** In real life. When people wish to meet outside of the Internet world they are living in, they seek an IRL meeting.

- **ISO** In search of. This is a popular acronym from traditional personals sections in newspapers.

- **NSA** This stands for no strings attached. This is a common acronym on many "casual encounter" message boards. It actually took us a while to figure this one out. When first reading this one, we were thinking "those NSA guys are sluts." After finding out its true meaning, it made a lot more sense.

- **POS** Parent over shoulder. This is usually used by kids when chatting with friends about things they don't want their parents to find out about. This is supposed to be a harmless acronym that signifies that a shift in conversation topic needs to take place.

- **S2R** Send to receive. This is a common response when a person online asks for a copy of your pic, or picture. This response states that you will give a picture only if they send one as well.

Infidelity Online

Online infidelity offers the paradox of being one of the most obvious and hardest to nail down cyber-threats that most people will face. Online infidelity ranges from a relatively innocent chat, to *cybering* (sex talk over the Internet), to in real life (IRL) meetings. Since a cyber-affair can refer to so many different situations we will use the definition given by Dr. Young as reprinted on netaddiction.com [1,2]:

> "Cyber-affairs are generally defined as any romantic or sexual relationship initiated via online communication, predominantly electronic conversations that occur in virtual communities such as chat rooms, interactive games, or newsgroups"

It is important to note that while cyber-affairs start out as online chats, they can eventually lead to real-life relationships or dangerous encounters. While cybering and other online sex talk can be detrimental to a relationship, we feel that a serious line is crossed when both people involved take it into real life. When this occurs it is no different than a traditional affair, except in how it was initiated. This is important since infidelity in the form of a sexual affair has been shown to have an effect in court on divorce settlements and other legal actions.

Cyber-affairs have increased for many reasons. Most apparent is opportunity. The growth of Internet use has increased the total number of people online, leading to an increase in the number of people participating in and looking for extramarital escape. As we had mentioned earlier this is part of expanding social circles. As the number of contacts increases, so does the likely pool of applicants for cyber-affairs and other mischief. It is quite easy to find a sympathetic ear online. Chat is not the only outlet for this; online message boards and dating services are also popular locations for finding partners. Craigslist (www.craigslist.org), a very popular online message board, has an entire section of its personals devoted to casual encounters. It is saddening but not completely unsurprising how many of the ads are from married people seeking one-time relationships. Ads such as these are often accompanied with the infamous NSA (no strings attached) disclaimer. In addition several ads were for sex, but with a "donation" required. Popular rumors indicate that these were really fronted by prostitutes. Here are a few recent personal ads from Craigslist for the Washington, D.C. area.

```
Seeking the unattainable...married or have gf?? - w4m - 22
Reply to: anon-44xxxxxx@craigslist.org
Date: 2004-10-01, 9:05AM EDT
```

```
I am in search of an attractive white male that is taken. Do you need to
live a little? I am very discreet white female hoping to get together with
you and perhaps be your mistress.
```

```
this is in or around MD/DC/VA
it's NOT ok to contact this poster with services or other commercial
interests
```

```
erotic games party - m4mw - 20
Reply to: anon-43xxxxxx@craigslist.org
Date: 2004-09-27, 7:46PM EDT
```

```
Hi everyone,
```

```
I'm currently looking for some young, disease free bisexuals to party with
on Friday or Saturday. This is NOT going to be an orgy, and both men and
women are welcome to come and bring their partners.
```

I've recently discovered a personal fascination with kissing games and other such sexually themed party activities. I would like to get some friendly bi folks together and play a few of these games openly without being judged by homophobes.

Please contact me if any of you are interested in meeting fellow local bi people, playing a few games, killing a few hours, and having a good time.

this is in or around VA
it's NOT ok to contact this poster with services or other commercial interests

ISO strong calves and silky smooth bare feet. - m4w
Reply to: anon-43xxxxxx@craigslist.org
Date: 2004-09-27, 7:20PM EDT

If you are female and enjoy stroking a man with your bare feet, then you're the one I'm seeking to fulfill my foot-play fantasy. I'm looking for a safe, discreet one-time encounter. I'll reciprocate with my tongue. Let's exchange emails and get acquainted. Prefer a woman with red toes ;-)

this is in or around NW DC - Red Line
it's NOT ok to contact this poster with services or other commercial interests

You and me, my office at night - m4w - 30
Reply to: anon-43xxxxxx1@craigslist.org
Date: 2004-09-27, 6:06PM EDT

I've always wanted to have sex in my office. My desk, a conference room, a storage room, anywhere at all. It would have to be sometime after 8:00 PM, preferably next week. I'm in the Ballston area, near metro.

this is in or around Arlington
it's NOT ok to contact this poster with services or other commercial interests

```
Seeking Married Woman - w4m - 35
Reply to: anon-43xxxxxx@craigslist.org
Date: 2004-09-27, 5:44PM EDT
```

I am a married white guy in Northwest who is seeking lots of discretion and lots of fun. I would get a room for several hours in one of DC's classy, upscale hotels. We would get room service and sip champagne. And have great conversation...interested? E-mail me with your description, etc. Marrieds only!

this is in or around NW DC
it's NOT ok to contact this poster with services or other commercial interests

```
ISO open-minded young woman curious about sex - m4w
Reply to: anon-43xxxxxx@craigslist.org
Date: 2004-09-27, 5:02PM EDT
```

People find all sorts of different types of relationships rewarding. I have had great relationships in the past with young women (18-25, generally) and would love to find an open-minded, slender, intelligent young woman who wants to explore her sexuality with an older man who is very comfortable to be with, understanding, patient, fun, and very sexual! Let me show you what real pleasure can be. I'm tall, lean, in great shape. You don't have to be all that experienced yourself. I told you I'm patient; I'll be glad to teach you! Obviously it will be a tremendous turn-on for me to be with you, but I will more than reciprocate by making sure you have a great time.

it's NOT ok to contact this poster with services or other commercial interests

Another leading cause of cyber-affairs is the anonymity the Internet provides. Unlike going to a bar, the chance of accidental discovery remains low until the actual meeting. The perceived ability to remain anonymous decreases the risk involved, which makes the cyber-affair more tempting. Once again after examining the personal ads listed here, you can see all of them were set up for anonymous reply. Without the fear of discovery and persecution most people feel very free to explore the limits of what they can do.

One trend that has popped up over the last few years has been the increase in the number of women participating in extramarital affairs [3]. They are now entering what was once a male dominated field. While there are many factors contributing to this rise in percentage (such as the increase in the number of women in the workforce) the influence of online activity has been shown to be a factor as well. Housewives who stay home can often find what appears to be a compassionate and understanding friend online. People looking for sex online can log on and act interested in the lives of ordinary housewives. The Internet makes the connection of these two unlikely partners exceptionally easy.

One report [4] has results showing that as many as thirty percent of online cyber-affairs (where a married person is flirting) may lead to real affairs. The following lists several of the warning signs that could be indicative of a cyber-affair, or cybersexual addiction [5]:

- Routinely spending significant amounts of time in chat rooms and private messaging with the sole purpose of finding cybersex

- Feeling preoccupied with using the Internet to find online sexual partners

- Frequently using anonymous communication to engage in sexual fantasies not typically carried out in real life

- Anticipating your next on-line session with the expectation that you will find sexual arousal or gratification

- Finding that you frequently move from cybersex to phone sex (or even real-life meetings)

- Hiding your on-line interactions from your significant other

- Feeling guilt or shame from your on-line use

- Accidentally being aroused by cybersex at first, and now find that you actively seek it out when you log on-line

- Less investment with your real-life sexual partner only to prefer cybersex as a primary form of sexual gratification

None of these signs are an iron-clad guarantee of a problem. But they can be indicators. Using these signs and other clues, or possible computer sleuthing can help you determine if there is in fact something going on.

Can You Believe It?

Statistics on Infidelity [6]

The following are some statistics we've gathered relating to infidelity in general and focusing on online infidelity.

"One in 10 respondents said they are addicted to sex and the Internet, according to an online survey of 38,000 Internet users."

— MSNBC.com and Dr. Alvin Cooper

"Results show that respondents devote three hours each week to online sexual exploits. Twenty-five percent have felt that they lost control of their Internet sexual exploits at least once or that they activity caused problems in their lives."

— MSNBC.com and Dr. Alvin Cooper

"Only 46% of men believe that online affairs are adultery."

— *Divorce Magazine*

"Up to 37% of men and 22% of women admit to having affairs. Researchers think the vast majority of millions of people who visit chat rooms, have multiple 'special friends.'"

— Dr. Bob Lanier, askbob.com

"Eighty percent think its Ok to talk with a stranger identified as the opposite sex. Seventy-five percent think it's ok to visit an adult site."

— *Monogamy Myth*, Therapist Peggy Vaughn

"Statistics show more than 72,000 sexually explicit sites on the Web and an estimated 266 new porn sites being added each day. These sites alone generate a revenue of $1 billion each year."

— Harding Institute

Continued

> *"One-third of divorce litigation is caused by online affairs."*
> — "This Is An Internet E-Mergency," The Fortino Group
>
> *"Approximately 70% of time on-line is spent in chat rooms or sending e-mail; of these interactions, the vast majority are romantic in nature."*
> — Dr. Michael Adamse, PhD., coauthor of *Affairs of the Net: The Cybershrinks' Guide to Online Relationships*
>
> *"Because of the anonymity, affordability, and accessibility of Internet sexual resources, the computer can accelerate the transition from "at risk" to "addicted," as well as the progression of sex addition in those with a history of prior sexual compulsivity."*
> — Cooper *et. al.* Survey

Drug Involvement Online

Online drug access is another hot topic we wish to address. For the purposes of this book, when we refer to drugs online we are speaking about drugs that are currently illegal in the United States—marijuana, cocaine, or prescription drugs that have a high likelihood of abuse. We do not mean prescription drugs (such as penicillin) purchased from Canadian and overseas pharmacies. There is a current debate about the legality of those issues, but that is not our concern with this book.

In performing research for this book we decided to investigate several popular Internet drug rumors. The first is that there are several "code words" used to be able to purchase marijuana and other drugs on eBay. These code words were designed to circumvent eBay's very strict policies on illegal items. After extensive searching, and speaking with knowledgeable sources, we came to the conclusion that if there ever were, there are no longer any key words for purchasing drugs on eBay. The second rumor we attempted to address was the fact that there were several Web sites that sold drugs directly to online shoppers. Once again extensive searching failed to yield any positive results. Although we could not successfully find any sites, there are probably some that exist. These may be invitation only sites, to prevent discovery from law enforcement. Keep in mind that most methods of drug distribution are in a state of constant evolution as distributors struggles to evade authorities.

While our searches for well-known illegal drugs came up short, we did find some disturbing sites. Consistent offenders in this category are offshore pharmacies that sold Vicoden, Ritalin, Valium and other prescription pharmaceuticals. While none of these drugs are the ones that are traditionally viewed as illegal, they are all strongly controlled and very susceptible to abuse. In addition we found dozens of sites advertising "legal drugs and drug substitutes" as well as several sites describing in-depth ways for people to build their own drug-like substances. Herbal drug substitutes such as Salvia, Kreton, and peyote cactus are available online. These herbal substitutes are not illegal, but all are on the U.S. Drug Enforcement Agency's "drugs and chemicals of concern" watch list [7]. Many of these herbal drug substitutes have the same side effects as traditional drugs, and can be easily purchased online. Most of the sites offering them had no age or ID checks. While none of this may be as "bad" as buying cocaine online, they all are things people would strongly discourage, or at least want to know that their child or spouse is investigating.

Herbal Alternatives on the Web

Drug-like Substances We Found Online

Word for word these are some items we found for sale online at various sites offering herbal alternatives to traditional drugs. [8]

```
Salvia Divinorum Leaf 1/4 OZ

Now On Sale!

# Ingredients: 100% Salvia Divinorum

# The most potent Psycho Tropic Herb known to Man

# Dried leaves

# Do not ingest!

# Great for meditation & visuals

# Informative page included with every purchase!

# Recommended for use with a butane Torch lighter & waterpipe

# THIS IS THE BEST SALVIA DIVINORUM OR YOUR MONEY BACK!

# For the love of God use in moderation!

Regular Price: $26.97

Sale Price: $18.97!


Club13 KanZak, 10 gram SUPERPACK

Now On Sale!

100% Kanna Mood enlighting herb. Kanna is a herb from Africa that
has been found to have calming/euphoric properties on those [who]
```

Continued

smoke it. USE: If your are feeling lousy, take 2 or 4 hits of KanZak. You will feel great in a few minutes. Effects: Relaxation, a decrease in anxiety & stress for a duration of 4 to 8 hours. A little goes a long way. Do not use if you are taking any medication & read instructions before use. HAPPIER OR YOUR MONEY BACK!

Regular Price: $109.97

Sale Price: $109.97!

High Grade Wild Lettuce Opium 2 OZ

Now On Sale!

Relaxes the mind & body

A pleasantly mild alternative to marijuana

Less harsh to smoke than tobacco or ganja

Nicotine free

Nice effects or your money back!

Regular Price: $29.97

Sale Price: $24.95!

Extra Strength Horny Goat Weed

Horny Goat Weed helps get you in the mood.

How in the mood? Like a 16 year old watching porn!

Works for both women & men

1 Serving per package

Great price for a night of nasty boot knocking!

Product is made by Pro Labs, not Pinnacle as pictured

Your Price: $2.49!

Salvia Divinorum Leaf 1/2 OZ

Organically grown in Oaxacan Mexico

Instructions included

Recommended for use with a waterpipe and butane torch lighter

We purchase Salvia Divinorum directly from the source to get this price to you

This legal product will not show up on drug tests

Highest quality Salvia Divinorum you have ever had or your money back

Your Price: $33.97!

Continued

> Of course, all items were guaranteed to be shipped in a nondescript plain brown box.

Finding Collaborators Online

Even if people are not using the Internet to find new conspirators for their illicit activities, if they are pursing any, it is very likely they are using the Internet in some way for its coordination. Due to its pervasive nature, the Internet is an excellent communication system. It can be much less intrusive, and it is easier to hide communication done with computers than with traditional devices such as telephones. When you have to log on and read e-mail it is much harder for someone to accidentally stumble across anything incriminating. This avoids the problem of the spouse answering the phone when the other participant in the affair calls. Today's computer-literate children often see it as a valuable communication tool as well. They are aware that parents can scrutinize phone bills or caller ID logs, but many are clueless when it comes to tracking e-mail and viewing instant messenger logs. Many teenagers would be reluctant to discuss their sex lives or drug use on the family phone, for fear of being overheard by parents, but often feel uninhibited when e-mailing their friends or chatting about it online.

Not everyone who uses the Internet will participate in these behaviors. Many couples stay faithful their entire lives, and many children never participate in illegal activities. Most people won't have to worry about or deal with these things. Even if you are one of those lucky enough to be confident in your spouse and children's wholesomeness, it is still wise to be aware of the dangers, to understand how they occur, and to know the warning signs. In the words of Flavius Vegetius Renatus "Let him who desires peace prepare for war." Awareness of the dangers and the warning signs costs very little, and can have dramatic and beneficial results.

Ethics of Spying

Perhaps the most difficult decision in the entire process of determining what secrets a person is hiding is determining what steps and remedies are available. Despite lingering suspicions, until positive proof is established that a person is engaged in undesirable and unacceptable activities, the suspicious party could be unnecessarily jeopardizing the relationship. One of the first steps in finding malfeasance is to first determine what you are willing to do in order to uncover what your suspected target is doing. This is where your code of ethics will come in to play.

Ethics are standards of conducts, that guide decisions and actions, based on duties derived from core values. At a young age people develop their ethics and morals from their parents and their environment. A quick glance around you at the people you interact with can easily demonstrate how everyone has their own set of ethics. Even among certain apparently similar demographics—criminals, for instance—there is a set of ethics that they live by; even if those ethics are abhorrent to society at large. This set of ethics and morals guides people in their decision making. Often people will disdain those who make decisions that do not fit within their moral and ethical framework. Each individual has his own code of ethics that he lives by, and staying true to these ethics is very important.

Impacting the Process

For most people, the decision to spy on their loved ones is a very difficult one to make. This decision is wrought with a host of emotional and ethical issues that will pervade the entire process from start to finish. It can very easily start with some basic checking up on someone and quickly proceed to the point of crossing the line. The extremity of the measure a person will undertake in order to prove or disprove their suspicions will be bounded by the ethics and morals that the person has. Some people will quickly come to the decision that everything they will do in pursuit of their suspicions is acceptable, while others will feel that any degree of snooping is outside the boundaries of the relationship. For most people the decision is not as clear-cut, and they will need to determine which steps are acceptable to them, and at what point they will stop. It is very difficult for people to undertake actions, which violate their code of ethics. Often the activities that break a person's ethical code come with deep feelings of guilt, thus it is very important to determine what you are willing to do, and what level of spying you can comfortably live with.

When faced with the possibility of needing to determine what another person is doing, clear boundaries and guidelines must be established ahead of time to prevent unintended consequences. It is fairly easy to establish that certain activities would cross ethical boundaries. For instance installing spyware on a loved one's computer at work would certainly be ethically as well as legally wrong. On the other hand, looking at the contents of a person's pockets while doing laundry would not be violating most people's ethics. It is the activities in between the two extremes that present the ethical dilemma.

Activities that are being hidden from a person can have a profound and lasting effect upon them. In many situations it is far better to have the knowledge to protect yourself and others from long-lasting damage. If parents are trying to determine if an online stalker is targeting their daughter, that relationship has a serious potential to provide long-lasting damage to the child. If spouses are being unfaithful, they have the potential to bring back possible life-threatening diseases to their mates. Most of the activities that people attempt to hide from others are the ones most likely to hurt or damage themselves or others.

The reader now must decide what boundaries they are willing to cross in order to determine what is happening with the other person, and therein lies the ethical dilemma. Normal boundaries may not be sufficient; the information that is hidden may require extreme measures to ascertain. Nobody enjoys (well, a few people do) spying on their loved one, but they must determine if spying is better than the alternative. Each person will have to decide what steps will violate his or her code of ethics. When it comes to violating someone's privacy for a personal or greater good, there is never an easy answer. Some people will have no problems doing this, while others will wrestle with the question. Once a person has decided what they deem is the clear line in the gray area, they can begin to spy.

Breaking the Trust

In every interpersonal relationship there is a level of trust that is built between the two parties. While building trust takes time and effort to achieve, it takes only a single keystroke to rip it all apart. Trust is the cornerstone of any relationship; without it there is very little hope of success. By spying on a spouse you put all pre-existing trust at risk, and open it up to possible irreversible damage. This risk must be understood before the spying process begins.

Some people believe that spying upon their significant others would violate the trust in the relationship. In their minds there are no actions that their partners could commit that would justify spying. Any degree of it would ruin the trust in the relationship. These people would hesitate to take any action that could possibly undermine this trust.

Most people will subconsciously know that something is not right in the relationship. If the other person is hiding activities then they have already destroyed any trust. For example, if someone's spouse is hiding his infidelity from his mate, then he has destroyed the trust. A once-open child hiding disturbing behavior from his parents is another example. Once a person decides to conceal activities because they know that these activities would violate an interpersonal relationship, then they have broken whatever trust existed in that relationship.

Creating a Culture of Mistrust

Spying can create a culture of mistrust between the parties in an interpersonal relationship. Human nature already makes us very distrustful of others and their intentions. It is very easy to take the worst possible interpretation of a set of facts. If a husband feels that his wife does not trust him, this will create strain upon the relationship; it also may lead to the husband doing things to purposefully cause the wife angst. Then this may lead to the wife trusting her husband less. This vicious circle may never be broken and could ultimately cause the relationship to fail. Even though no one initially did anything wrong, the culture of mistrust grew and took over. Once undertaken this cannot be easily broken.

Spying automatically forces mistrust upon a relationship. Even if spying returns no proof of wrongdoing, will the other person ever truly be trusted again? Are people willing to live in a relationship that they feel is only acceptable by constantly checking up on the other individual?

Mistrust does not work in only one direction. Even if initially it is only directed to one aspect, it can quickly consume the entire relationship. Entering into the culture of mistrust can be just as damaging as any activities that would have been hidden. We say this not to dissuade anyone but merely to provide a warning to some of the possible unintended consequences. As the old saying goes "be careful what you wish for, you might just get it."

Our View

In the end we feel that a nuanced approach to the ethical dilemma of spying on loved ones should be taken. The world would be a much better place if people did not do things that would cause harm to their loved ones, and there would be no reason for this book to be written. But sadly this is not the case. So we feel spying is an acceptable solution to certain problems but we caution you to proceed carefully. Before you begin spying ask yourself these questions.

- What is the cause of your suspicions?
- What steps are you willing to take?
- What will satisfy your doubts?
- Are you willing to live with being right?
- Are you willing to live with being wrong?
- What are the consequences to being caught spying?

There are no easy answers to these questions; however answering them will at least provide a guide for further action. We feel that if a person suspects that something is going on then they have the right to ask some questions. If the answers to these questions do not satisfy the feeling, it is acceptable to begin the process of determining what steps you are willing to take. This is the last point at which no boundaries have been crossed. After here the process of spying has begun. If the person is still suspicious and decides to go forward with an investigation, then he should proceed slowly being as unobtrusive as possible.

We feel that an easy and relatively inoffensive first step would be to examine everything that is within the public realm and look at that information. Although this could cause a breakdown of trust within the relationship, the person has not at this point done anything to actively spy on the other person. If the person's suspicions are confirmed, then it is time to determine what additional actions should be considered. We would suggest again that you carefully evaluate your options before taking any action. If additional remedies are needed, then we feel that you should do everything possible to protect yourself without violating the law or your internal ethics.

This book is intended to provide information that can be used ethically. Many things discussed here can also be used in a very unethical and inappropriate manner as well. It is up to the readers to determine if utilizing this information and technology violates their ethics, and their responsibility to stay within the law.

Spying on Spouses

Weddings are one of the happiest days in many people's lives; the day is full of hope and optimism for the future. Everyone toasts the happy couple and the beginning of their lives together. Unfortunately, not all marriages have fairy tale endings. However, people change, and divorce happens. Despite everyone wishing that his or her marriage is in the small percentage that last, this may be hopeless optimism. Figure 1.2 visualizes the percentage of people who reach their respective anniversaries.

Figure 1.2 Percentages of People Who Reach Their Respective Anniversaries [9]

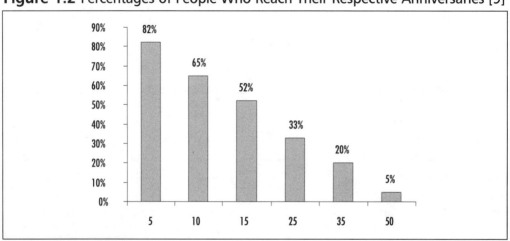

There are many reasons why a marriage fails, and there are no winners when this happens. The marriage contract both explicitly lays out each person's obligations toward the marriage, and in most states, the law is explicit as to what happens in the case of a failed marriage and the resultant divorce. During marriage both partner's assets and liabilities become the responsibility and property of the other. Since each person's actions directly influence the other person, each person has an obligation to be up-front and honest with his or her activities. If people are undertaking activities and hiding them from their spouses, that is a cause of concern. People have a right to know what is going on in their spouse's life, since it may affect them.

It would be naive to think that there are no secrets between a couple, or that it is possible to know what the other person is doing at all hours. However, there is a degree of honesty and trust that must be maintained. Once this has been broken then it is very difficult to build it up again. That is not to say that at any sign of misdoing the spouse loses all rights to privacy, but to serve as a warning to what can happen if the decision to hide something from the spouse is taken. All of the trust can forever be lost from the relationship, even if nothing untold is happening.

The decision to spy on a spouse should never be taken lightly. Once the decision to remove that person's privacy has been made, it cannot be taken back. If the only way to save the marriage is to constantly snoop on the spouse, then there may be something more going on than it appears (and perhaps the marriage is not worth saving). We feel that any step possible short of spying should be taken before actually doing it. There may be other ways to determine what is going on without resorting to snooping. Once the trust in a relationship has been violated, it is not a trivial matter to re-establish it. There will be subtle signs that will be picked up on, that will cause reasons for concern. This will allow a spouse to begin to determine if the hidden behavior is bad enough to cause the need to snoop.

We don't advocate spying on spouses for "fun," or to continually keep tabs on them. Since spying is such a significant undertaking in both resources and potential risk, we feel only very important scenarios warrant spying on your spouse. Those scenarios are questions of fidelity, financial security, liability, and personality disorders.

Infidelity

A leading cause for trouble in a marriage is infidelity by one of the partners. Peggy Vaughan, author of *The Monogamy Myth: A Personal Handbook for Recovering from Affairs*, estimates that 60 percent of men and 40 percent of women will have affairs during their marriages. Since the second party in the affair may not necessarily be married, these affairs are believed to touch 80 percent of all marriages. This enormous percentage should cause great concern, and the warning signs for infidelity should not be ignored. The following are just some warning signs that may be indicators of infidelity [10]:

- Your spouse seems bored. Bored with you, with job, with kids, with hobbies, with life in general
- Your spouse seems to want danger or thrills in his/her life
- There is considerably less intimacy in your relationship. Your sex life is practically nonexistent
- Your spouse has a low self-esteem
- You notice your spouse has a sense of confusion about self
- Your spouse has become lazy, especially around the house
- You can't get your spouse to communicate with you
- Your spouse gets very defensive if you mention infidelity or affairs
- Your spouse is suddenly more attentive than usual
- Your spouse is working longer hours at work, or traveling more than expected
- Your spouse is dressing nicer, looking nicer
- You notice charges on credit card statement that don't make sense
- Your spouse is indifferent to family events like birthdays and holidays
- You find your partner has been lying to you about a variety of things
- Money becomes more of an issue between the two of you
- He/she doesn't want to go anywhere or do anything with you anymore
- You can't even get your spouse to fight with you
- You feel as if you are being avoided
- Your partner abandons religious faith
- Your spouse seems more secretive

If a spouse is showing several of these signs, then some serious questions should be asked. If satisfactory answers are not given then it is time to be proactive. Due to the potential lethality of sexual transmitted diseases, this is not to be taken lightly. One place that evidence of cheating may reside will be on the family computer. Please keep in mind that many of these warning signs can have non-adulterous causes as well. We caution you in many cases to investigate carefully and thoroughly before jumping to any conclusions.

Financial Security

Money issues are another one of the top reasons that marriages face problems. Financial security and arguments about money have driven many marriages to the divorce court. Since a couple's finances are linked, if one spouse is hiding significant financial activity from the other, this is cause for concern. There are many ways to lose fiscal responsibility while using one's computer. These range from responding to spam advertisements for money laundering scams, sports gambling, online gambling, excessive purchases, and Internet sex rooms. All of these activities can cause a financial hardship upon the relationship. Spouses have the right to know how their money is being used, and if their credit is being ruined by the actions of their spouse. It is not unheard of for a malicious spouse to deliberately ruin the couple's finances by spending all of the cash, and maxing out credit cards before leaving the relationship. In addition personal finance software, often with detailed financial records, is stored on most family computers. This software may hold financial clues about your spouse's wrongdoings. Although not the most glamorous reason for snooping on a spouse, financial problems can cause some of the most long-lasting damage even long after the relationship has ended.

Liability

When a couple gets married, the phrase for better or worse is used in the typical ceremony. This is not just for kicks; the liabilities of one spouse are automatically transferred to the other spouse. If one spouse gets sued, the effects will cascade across the marriage. If a husband or wife is engaging in activities that represent a great risk to the couple, both individuals have a right to know what is happening. Since liability resides upon both individuals equally, then both partners have the right to know. If that information is being held outside the purview of the spouse, then spying may be the only way to get to the truth of the matter. For example, if one member of a family is committing an online crime, results of that crime, if caught, could be drastic. The family will immediately lose the computer as it becomes evidence. In addition the entire family will be examined as possible coconspirators. In situations like this ignorance is not a good excuse. Keep this in mind if you feel your spouse is involved in questionable dealings, online or offline.

Multiple Identities

Some people are very good at masking their real selves from their loved ones. They are one person to their family and friends and a completely other person in an online digital identity. These people may suffer from personality disorders that govern their behavior, which can vary dramatically from moment to moment. They choose which behavior they would like people to see, and go to great lengths to hide their "other personality" from family members. It's not uncommon when watching the news to see the friends and family of an accused criminal state how the accused was "the nicest person someone could be." Although this is a worst-case scenario, the Internet does allow people to act how the wish they could in real life, due to the perceived anonymity and moral permissiveness provided. Someone that you know and love could be a completely different person when he is interacting online. Of course, there is a difference between someone merely pretending online, and someone with a serious problem. Only by monitoring people's actions can their true intentions be gleaned.

In extreme cases like this, spying can be a useful means of confirming a suspicion, or tipping you off to someone's problems. However, in cases of multiple identities or personalities, you are often dealing with someone with serious medical problems. These cases should usually be handed off to the proper authorities and be dealt with by true experts. We want the readers of this book to be prepared to find out about infidelity and their kids' drug problems or skipping school. We are not trying to prepare you to pursue the next Ted Bundy.

There is no magic answer as to when it is appropriate to spy on a spouse. Each instance must be taken as a separate case. What may work for one couple may not be an acceptable alternative for others. The decision to snoop should never be taken lightly, and all alternatives ought to be exhausted before taking those steps. Once taken these actions can never be withdrawn; even if no wrongdoing is found, the relationship may never be the same. The decision to snoop will continually get easier; it should be used only as a last resort to protect oneself from the influences of the spouse. Despite wedding vows given in the best intentions, some people do not honor them and will place their spouse unknowingly at risk for their own needs. They will sacrifice their relationship to satisfy other desires. If this is happening self-preservation dictates action.

Spying on Your Children

In the context of this book, spying on your children may be one of the easiest and least morally ambiguous decisions you will make. In fact most parents to some extent or another, naturally spy on their children. Parents want to, and have the right to know whom their children interact with, what they do, and what goes on in their lives when they're not at home. What parent has never picked up a telephone extension, listened up against a door, watched out the window, or casually looked through belongings while cleaning a child's room. Many parents take any action they can to gain insight into their children's lives. We feel all of this is normal, and appropriate. Parental involvement overt and covert, is a necessary element.

But, alas times have changed. The world has turned a bit, and life has sped up with it. While very classic and useful, the techniques mentioned in the previous paragraph may no longer be sufficient. Most kids are proficient computer users, in many cases surpassing their parents. They are often well aware of the latest "fads" for computer use. If there is a new cool way for them to talk to each other, they will most likely be using it. Children under eighteen are some of the fastest adapters and most prolific users of new technology. Instant messaging, texting, e-mail, and blogs are fast replacing traditional and more traceable means of communication. What would have been passed as a note in classroom ten years ago is now text messaged from one cell phone to the next. The household phone doesn't offer nearly the connectivity or flexibility of instant messaging. When it comes to getting in touch, the kids are on the cutting edge, and most parents are left in the wake. In most children's minds the Internet is a "safe" communication and coordination mechanism that their parents do not understand and can never pry into.

Living on the bleeding edge posts an increasing danger to most children. Since they are out there pushing the limits of the Internet, often alone and unguided, they are free to explore almost anything that the net makes possible. In many cases this can be troubling or even dangerous. Even worse, since most children are out there alone, they are without the moral and ethical guidance of their more experienced parents. Instead of learning from the actions and examples of their families, children are led to learn and adapt what they see their peers do. There is often a very wide gap between most traditional family values and morals, and those shown by the millions of online *netizins*. Encountering this ethical chasm, especially young impressionable and alone, can produce confusion, desire, rebellion, and can often lead to trouble.

We break down the types of trouble children can find on the net into two broad classes, old dangers and new dangers. New dangers consist of activities that are relatively new, and would not exist without the Internet. Examples of these are online property theft, hacking, and purchasing schoolwork. Old dangers are new Internet-enabled spins on classic childhood problems. These include drugs, skipping and cheating in school, and bullying. These old dangers are not exactly caused by the Internet, but are made much easier due to its influence. One must understand and be on the lookout for both.

New Dangers

As previously mentioned, new dangers are those that never existed before the Internet. These can include, but are not limited to purchasing schoolwork, intellectual property theft, and criminal hacking. These are all crimes that occur easily, but can also be prevented by watching what happens online.

Cheating on schoolwork has always been a problem. As long as there has been schoolwork, children have been cheating on it. Now, however, the Internet has made it far easier, and much harder to catch. Before a child's group of conspirators was limited to his or her classmates and siblings. Now it has been expanded to include anyone a child can get in touch with across the Internet. We have seen questions about homework being posted on online message boards. These message boards, often set up to discuss topic-specific information such as cars or computer security offer a place where questions can be asked that will reach thousands of eyes. In such places it is not unusual to have an answer within minutes. Now that most school-work is done in electronic format, many former students post all of their previous work, leaving a wealth of material for those who follow. It is also not unheard of to search for answer keys, teachers' manuals, and other resources. While they may furnish the correct answer, they are not what is intended by the original assignment. Finally, there are even some sites such as www.termpaperrelief.com that offer, for a page-by-page fee, to have your papers custom written for you. This capability exploits laziness and makes cheating a trivial task. It takes only a few mouse clicks to obtain a professionally written term paper, all for $14.99 a page.

While using the Internet to find homework solutions can show resourcefulness on the behalf of the child, it comes with its own problems. For one the child is not accomplishing the original task set out by his or her instructors. Instead of learning and solving the problems, children are merely finding the answers to their problems. The true lessons of the work are being bypassed. In addition there is often no guarantee of correctness for what they find online. Anyone can post anything on the Internet, and not all material on the Internet has been edited by fact checkers. By cheating online most children are cheating themselves out of an education.

Online property theft is another issue. Would you approve if you child stole a CD or DVD from the mall? Most parents would never allow that, yet they are blind to a very similar crime occurring on their family computers. File sharing networks such as fasttrack (Kaaza, the first Morpheus), overnet (Edonkey), and Gnutella (shareza, etc), IRC, Warez Web sites and bittorent sites (www.suprnova.org) allow just that. Figure 1.3 shows Edonkey, the current king of peer-to-peer file trading.

Figure 1.3 Edonkey in Action

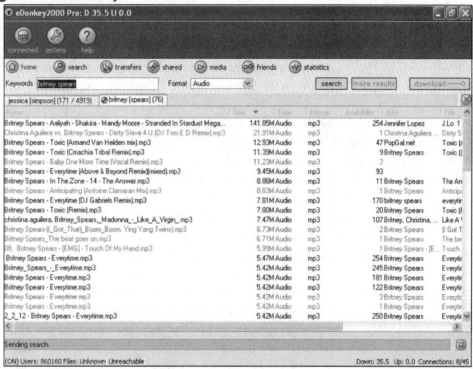

Each of these applications was designed for a perfectly legal and legitimate use, the easy sharing of information. However, realizing the power and perceived anonymity of these networks, many users have turned them into giant networks specializing in the trade of pirated movies, music, software, and pornography. Copyright holders for this shared media argue that they are losing hundreds of millions of dollars in revenue annually due to online piracy. Those downloading would argue that they are not committing theft, merely copyright violation, if that. In their minds stealing the music is no different than taping it from the radio, and that these companies aren't losing any money on them, since they would never buy the music/movie/software anyway. As individuals who both profit from intellectual property, and are outraged at the exorbitant prices for media, we can see both sides of the argument. We can only hope that eventually an acceptable online compromise will develop. Certain ventures like Apple's iTunes have risen to fill the online gap and provide legitimate and cost-effective purchase of online media. However right or wrong, very powerful lobbying organizations such as the RIAA (Recording Industry Artists Association) and MPAA (Motion Picture Artists Association) are filing lawsuits against specific Internet users whome they have deemed are violating their copyrights. Those targeted are often offered a $3000 settlement or the chance to fight it in court against the massive teams of lawyers fielded against them. Many of these targeted are children whose parents often claim ignorance or unawareness of what is occurring on their computer. In fact one of the first and most publicized individuals sued by the RIAA was was a thirteen-year-old girl whose parents were completely unaware that she was sharing music online. Wherever you stand on these issues keep in mind whether a lawsuit is worth the price of a $16.00 hip-hop CD?

The final new danger we wish to present is criminal hacking. While the very definition of the word hacking is surrounded in controversy, for the purpose of this book, we will define it as "any use of a computer to gain unauthorized access or deny legitimate access to another computer system." It is important to monitor your children to ensure that they are not hacking. It is no longer the harmless pastime of computer nerds. New powerful tools and Web sites detailing technique make it accessible to all but the least computer savvy. With these tools and knowledge it is quite easy to cause a lot of damage online. A Denial of Service (DOS) attack on a corporate Web site can result in millions in lost revenue. Breaking into a computer system holding credit cards compromises both the machine and those cards; even if the cards are never used illicitly, the act still causes the expensive need to reissue them. With such high monetary values attached to hacking, it is now a crime that most companies, and the FBI take very seriously.

If your child or spouse is a hacker or computer expert, and you are not, proceed with caution. You must be very careful to gauge your child's level of paranoia. Your child is likely to be more adept than you at spying on people and monitoring computers. Children are already very well aware of most common tools and techniques. The most important advantage you have will be the element of surprise. Hopefully, your children will have little suspicion as to any bugs or monitoring on their home computers, you're a computer newbie after all. In these cases the home computer is ideal for bugging. The hacker or expert will use it almost completely trusting it as a safe and unmonitored computer.

Over the last few years blogging, the process of creating an online Web log or diary, has become extremely popular. Many people, including children, find this a great outlet to pseudo-anonymously vent on the many frustrations they encounter in their day-to-day lives. While searching the Web for information for this book, we came across many different blogs and forums. One disturbing trend we noticed was that many teenagers were baring their souls to complete strangers on these forums, posting about themselves and detailed aspects of their lives, including their sexual activity. While that in itself may be OK, and is a way for people to bond, the worrisome aspect was that many posted in true name, and with their e-mail address as part of the information. This is creating a forum where people can learn all about someone's private life, and with their e-mail address have the beginning of a stalking capability.

Old Dangers

Along with the new dangers, many classic problems have a new spin given to them thanks to the Internet. Drugs, skipping out of class, bullying, and pornography are all problems that have always existed. Now it is even easier to secretly get involved and get away with them.

As we mentioned in the introduction, we feel that the Internet has made it much easier to become involved with illegal drugs. Aside from the fact that one can purchase many controlled drugs such as Valium online there is a huge emerging market of herbal equivalents. Salvia, peyote, and others can easily be bought online along with all the paraphernalia to turn them into legitimate mind-altering substances. Another aspect is the fact that children can use the Internet to connect themselves with people handling and distributing traditional illegal drugs. A quick look at Craigslist shows several people looking for "420" partners. The 420 partners may be a method of finding a drug distributor online. Going down this path presents a twofold danger to children: first, they are involved with illegal drugs, and second, they will be meeting and making themselves vulnerable to a complete stranger. This is very dangerous.

Skipping school, cheating, and bullying are other age-old problems that are receiving new twists due to the power of online collaboration. In the previous section we mentioned how we feel cheating has become a "new danger" due to its now relative ease. Skipping school, gang involvement, and other questionable activities are easier to participate and coordinate due to the Internet. In a couple of instant message clicks a child can have set up plans, a time, and location with a friend all in the time it would have taken him to dial the number if he was using a traditional phone. Bullying has always been a traumatic issue for some children. Now in the virtual world it takes on a new meaning. No longer is someone merely picked on in a lunchroom or school. Bullying can extend into the online domain. There have been several cases of children making "mockery" Web sites, poking fun at their targets, making their comments and available for everyone to see. This can be a big problem regardless of what end of the stick you're on. Bullying can also take place in chat groups or e-mail lists as one child "flames" another with insults and publicly humiliates him or her. If your child is a recipient, this issue needs to be quickly addressed and handled; if your child is the bully, this behavior needs to be stopped immediately to avoid a slander lawsuit in our very litigious society.

Predators

Everything we've mentioned so far relating to how your child can get in trouble online has been something that the child has to willingly do. There are quite a few things children can do to put themselves on the wrong side of right, and the law, and our list is by no means nearly comprehensive. However, there is another fearsome danger, one that you don't have to look for to find; it will find you, the online predator/pedophile. Predators and pedophiles have seemingly always existed and been a deep fear of most parents. Now the anonymity of the Internet has made them even more fearless, and its connectivity opens up their pool of potential prey. Like their predecessor of yesteryear, they still hang around areas of high prey concentration, but instead of playgrounds, schools, and daycare centers, these cyber-pedophiles frequent chat rooms often visited by young children.

To demonstrate how prevalent sexual predators or people at least willing to violate the law are, we created a yahoo messenger account, and made it look like that off a sixteen-year-old girl. Figure 1.4 shows a screenshot of our pseudo-account profile for "Sarah":

Figure 1.4 Profile of a 16-Year-Old Girl Who Was Approached by Multiple Predators

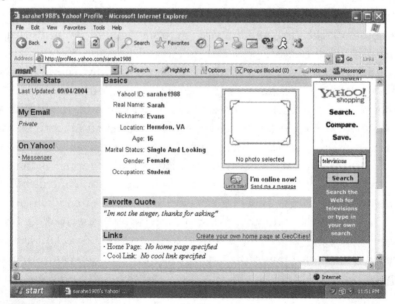

Sarah entered several chat rooms. First on a Friday evening at around 11:00 P.M., entering a local romance for Virginia chat room. Within two minutes she had received four chat invitations from four different men ranging in ages allegedly from 18 to 21. After briefly chatting with each of these men, she had pretty much been asked the same questions, "Do you like older men?" "Do you have a cam?" "Would you let me view it?" The next morning at 9:00 am she entered a different chat room, 15-18xxx. Once again she was bombarded with messages, this time the potential suitors were from far away (the predators in the U.S. must still be asleep), Cyprus and Turkey. The topics they wished to discuss were similar to the previous night, starting with some small talk and then trying to find out my opinions on sex and masturbation. Finally, on a Monday evening she re-entered the Virginia romance chat room. This time it was the most interesting proposition, one person asked within the first few statements if she was interested in a sexual encounter. Even the fact that "Sarah" was 16 and a minor did not seem to affect him.

In the following, we have included part of the conversation resulting from this interaction. The alleged predator's yahoo ID has been changed. We inserted dirtylarry001, a name we control instead of the predator's original ID. In addition the first chat line was cut and pasted from the actual chat window since as of this writing Yahoo Messenger does not archive the first line of any chat. In performing this experiment we did not set out to entrap, expose, or "bust" this or any predator out there. This is a job left to law enforcement. In fact we feel that many vigilante sites that do attempt to expose cyber-predators are violating numerous privacy and slander laws. We merely want to demonstrate the reality of sexual predators in Internet chat rooms. (Please note, some of the material uses strong language and content):

```
dirtylarry001 (1:21:49 PM): Hi, would you like to cyber, or meet later for
some real fun?
sarahe1988 (1:22:09 PM): hi
sarahe1988 (1:22:13 PM): I'm 16
dirtylarry001 (1:22:20 PM): where u live?
sarahe1988 (1:22:23 PM): herndon
sarahe1988 (1:22:24 PM): you?
sarahe1988 (1:22:25 PM): asl?
dirtylarry001 (1:22:39 PM): m/36/richmond
sarahe1988 (1:22:44 PM): ok
sarahe1988 (1:22:52 PM): well I'm f/16/herndon
dirtylarry001 (1:22:54 PM): you ever have sex with an older man?
sarahe1988 (1:23:00 PM): I've never had sex
```

sarahe1988 (1:23:07 PM): do you im every woman on this room asking for cyber?

sarahe1988 (1:24:35 PM): so I'm a virgin and not intersting to you anymore?

dirtylarry001 (1:25:44 PM): virgins are ok

dirtylarry001 (1:25:56 PM): do u want to have sex?

sarahe1988 (1:26:05 PM): with you? I don't even know you

sarahe1988 (1:26:09 PM): do you want to have sex with me?

dirtylarry001 (1:26:19 PM): sure - if you are cute...

sarahe1988 (1:26:26 PM): well I like to think so

dirtylarry001 (1:26:32 PM): got a pic?

sarahe1988 (1:26:48 PM): yeah

sarahe1988 (1:26:49 PM): do you

sarahe1988 (1:26:52 PM): s2r

dirtylarry001 (1:27:08 PM): i dont

sarahe1988 (1:27:22 PM): well

sarahe1988 (1:27:23 PM): ok

sarahe1988 (1:27:29 PM): so you want to meet me or something?

dirtylarry001 (1:27:35 PM): if u want....

sarahe1988 (1:27:44 PM): do you want?

dirtylarry001 (1:27:52 PM): sure - describe your body to me

sarahe1988 (1:28:31 PM): have you been with someone my age before

dirtylarry001 (1:28:41 PM): yeah

sarahe1988 (1:28:42 PM): 5'7" brwn hair, brwn eyes, 120 lbs

sarahe1988 (1:28:44 PM): really

dirtylarry001 (1:28:59 PM): how big are your tits?

sarahe1988 (1:29:31 PM): they're decent

sarahe1988 (1:29:44 PM): 28 B if you must know

sarahe1988 (1:29:50 PM): now you owe me something

dirtylarry001 (1:29:54 PM): how far have you gone with a guy before

sarahe1988 (1:29:59 PM): made out

sarahe1988 (1:31:48 PM): so how far have you gone with a 16 yr old?

dirtylarry001 (1:31:56 PM): and you are willing to let a stranger of the net fuck you?

dirtylarry001 (1:32:54 PM): i have fucked

sarahe1988 (1:33:26 PM): ok

dirtylarry001 (1:33:47 PM): are u alone now?

dirtylarry001 (1:36:03 PM): bye

All of this experimentation leads us to believe that if you are online and you present the right type of profile, those looking for you will find you. All we had to do was sit in a chat room, and apparently this guy was trolling the list of participants looking for those he was interested in. This is a powerful demonstration of the prevalence of Internet predators.

Internet Addiction

And finally online addiction should not be forgotten. In many ways just using the Internet itself can be like a drug. Kids now spend more time in front of the computer than the TV. Even if all the time online is spent in harmless activity, it is important to monitor what goes on. Not paying attention to what your children are doing online is the equivalent of buying 500 channels (including adult ones) and turning your children loose to watch unsupervised. It is important to watch your child and make sure they lead a balanced life. One needs to make sure that the Internet, like most things, is taken in moderation. Failure to do this could lead to a host of social and mental problems.

Tips and Tricks...

Signs of Internet Addiction

The following are several signs of Internet addiction taken from the Illinois Institute for Addiction Recovery's Web site www.addictionrecov.org/intwhat.htm:

- Preoccupation with the Internet. (Thoughts about previous on-line activity or anticipation of the next on-line session)
- Use of the Internet in increasing amounts of time in order to achieve satisfaction
- Repeated, unsuccessful efforts to control, cut back, or stop Internet use
- Feelings of restlessness, moodiness, depression or irritability when attempting to cut down use of the Internet
- On-line longer than originally intended
- Jeopardized or risked loss of significant relationships, job, educational or career opportunities because of Internet use
- Lies to family members, therapist, or others to conceal the extent of involvement with the Internet

Continued

- Use of the Internet as a way to escape from problems or to relieve a dysphoric mood. (e.g., feelings of hopelessness, guilt, anxiety, depression)

For all the reasons listed, and many more, we feel it is definitely appropriate to monitor your children's online activity. Done correctly it can be nonintrusive yet still offer you protection. By knowing what your child does online you can help steer your child down a correct moral and legal path. Monitoring does not have to be a "big brother" activity where you confront your child on every suspicion and raise and environment of mistrust. Instead, it can be a chance to watch your children grow, observe for signs of trouble, and gently guide when necessary. When online most children are entering an adult and dangerous world, often without the maturity and seasoned judgment needed to stay safe. There is always the risk of falling victim to an online predator, many of whom are constantly roaming the Internet searching for new prey. When most parents ask themselves the rhetorical question, "how can I spy on my kids?" they must realize the dangers that exist out there and then ask themselves, "how can I not?"

When You Should Not Spy

Spying is commonly known as the world's second oldest profession, and has been practiced by governments, corporations, and individuals for ages. Spying is the process of gathering knowledge from someone despite his or her intentions to keep the information secret. While there may be no honor among thieves, there are rules among spies. As unlikely as it would seem, most spies have some boundaries that they feel should not be crossed in pursuit of information for their cause. Even among superpowers and governments, there are unwritten rules that are followed in the quest for information supremacy. We mention this because we feel that even you, as an amateur family spy, must follow rules. While you may not have to worry about the Geneva Convention when you are tracking your child's e-mail, you should make sure that you have a very clear idea of what you can and cannot do.

High tech spying used to be an exclusive club; joining required a significant amount of money and expertise. As the technology becomes more integrated into our everyday lives, it is easier for normal people to monitor our activities. While this book demonstrates how to use technology to your advantage, it also illustrates methods that may be abused. In a free society information is not controlled, it is easy to find plans on how to build a bomb from everyday materials on the Internet, or how to defraud people of their life savings. Even if the information can be used for purposes other than what it was intended, the information should still be available. The information provided in the book can be used in the manner intended, but it also carries the capability to be misused. While this is an unfortunate consequence, it is important that people have the information so that they can protect themselves and their families.

There are many situations where it is acceptable to spy upon loved ones, especially when they are placing themselves and your family at risk. In many cases the decision to spy or not to spy is not black and white. There are also some clear lines that never should be crossed. Before any spying should occur several questions should be asked:

- Whom are you planning to spying on?
- Why are you planning on spying?
- What information are you trying to obtain?
- Where will the spying take place?

The answers to these questions play a big part in answering the question should I spy?

Whom Are You Planning to Spy On?

It is very important to start off with a clear target, and be aware of whom you can ethically and legally spy upon. We feel that this is quite clear; for instance, if the person that you want to spy on is not your spouse or one of your kids, then you probably shouldn't be spying on him. This would be stalking. Current technology makes it very easy for people to stalk individuals and prey upon them. There is a wealth of publicly available information that is accessible via the Internet. People can look up phone numbers and quickly get a map to another person's residence. Many instant messaging programs allow for buddy lists to be set up, and it is possible to get a message when a buddy logs in/or out, or any other range of activities. It is very easy and sometimes tempting to use this technology to spy on an individual, but if that individual is not your spouse, or your kids, then you are stalking. This is completely wrong and illegal.

Why Are You Planning on Spying?

The reasons behind the decision to spy must be examined to determine their validity. If the spying is undertaken simply because it is easier than discussing the issues, then the spying should not happen. There will be many reasons for spying upon loved ones, and many people will justify their actions. The reasons for spying must be examined carefully. In every relationship there will be conflict and secrets that must be worked through. Often it is easier to ignore the issues and avoid dealing with them. Spying is one way to avoid difficult discussions and issues, but doing so is not a good solution.

What Information Are You Trying to Obtain?

In order to protect love ones, spying upon them must achieve certain goals. The objective is to find out enough information to answer difficult questions such as, Does my daughter have an eating disorder? Is my husband pursuing an extramarital affair? It is tempting to get a better view of what someone is thinking by examining his or her communications with outside parties. The technology for spying can be used to determine what the husband is e-mailing to a family friend; however, it can also be used to see what he is saying to his boss. It is very easy to extend the scope of spying beyond what is needed to all aspects of someone's life. If the information collected is not intended to protect loved ones but is instead used to intrude on their lives, then the spying should not occur.

Where Will the Spying Take Place

Spying upon people's online activities involves using the computer that they would use to go about their activities. This places a burden upon the person doing the spying as he or she must access that computer. Many people use a variety of computers during the course of the day to do their online activities. Thus, your children may use the computers at school to check their e-mail and the family computer at home in the evening to chat and "fool around." A husband could use his computer at work to coordinate his affair. Despite this, the only computers that should be spied upon are the family computer. It is acceptable to do whatever is needed on the family computer because it is the family's computer. Placing spy tools upon a child's computer at school or a spouse's office computer is acting outside of acceptable ranges. If the spy tools were to be discovered upon the work computer of school computer, whoever put them there could be put at legal risk. Spying should be done only on the home computer.

There are no easy answers in life, and most decisions involving emotions are not cut and dried. It is easy to make rash decisions and to persuade oneself that certain actions are justifiable. Being able to justify answers does not make them correct. Attempting to spy on someone who is not a member of your family, should never be done. Placing spy technology upon machines that are not owned by the family is also out of bounds. Misusing technology to collect information from third parties would also be wrong. Technology allows for an individual to hold a vast amount of power, but this power should not be misused. It would be tempting to use spying as a window into a loved one's life; however, this decision should not be made lightly, and only as a last resort.

Real-World Case Study

In order to illustrate some of the major issues we will deal with we felt it appropriate to include several case studies. All of these are based on real people and situations that we have either heard about our encountered ourselves. Facts, names, jobs, and locations have been changed to protect the identities of those involved. While they may seem only allegorical, they serve to drive home the point that the issues and dangers we discuss are real, and that, sometimes, spying will help you out.

Case Study: Those Who Forget to Erase Their History Must Pay for It

Computers have become one of the most useful communications mechanisms we have. As a result they silently participate and document the many events in our lives. Without discrimination they stoically take part in our adventues of love and hate, happiness and sadness. In this story a CIA historian finds evidence of his wife's infidelity due to her computes accidental disclosure.

Elaboration

"Chris" and "Kelly" were a pair of CIA historians. They met while working together at the agency. During their career they spent a lot of time together working side by side. For many couples this can be the kiss of death; for Chris and Kelly, it made their relationship stronger. The time at work was just more time spent together, which in their minds was just wonderful.

As time went on and the years passed Kelly decided she had career goals of being something other than a historian. It was the late nineties and the dot-com boom was in full swing, paper millionaires were popping up all over the place. For a couple on government salaries in the expensive Washington, D.C. area this was an incredible draw. Kelly left her job at the agency to take a job as a Web developer for a small start-up with long hours, hard work, and hopefully a huge financial reward.

Chris was completely supportive of Kelly's career change. Although he missed having his wife and best friend with him all day, he was excited about the prospect of them becoming wealthy, retiring young, and traveling the world together. He knew her crazy work schedule would be rough and they wouldn't have all of the relationship-building time they were used to, but this job was just temporary really.

They were going to be smart about it; after the IPO and her stock vested, Kelly vowed to leave and spend the rest of her time with her husband basking in the wealth of their Internet millions. Things would be tough for a little bit, but the result would be worth it.

So right away Kelly went from the easy forty-hour-a-week government job to the frenetic pace of a sixty-plus-hour week at an Internet start-up. She liked the job, she liked the work, and she looked forward to the pot of gold at the end of the IPO rainbow. Her office had a great fun environment, free food, free meals, even a place to sleep. Kelly knew somewhere inside that it was all a clever ruse, all of this just to convince employees to stay at work, but she believed. They were all in it together, weren't they? The more they worked, the richer they would be. So Kelly dove into her work. She worked hard at work, often late into the night, and when she wasn't at work, she was still working, or at least thinking about it.

Then right around the year 2000 things started to change. Apparently, the venture capitalists were unhappy at the lack of profit. The company was losing money, and at the risk of losing its funding, Kelly's boss "Jon" made a valiant effort to rally his employees. Yes times were hard, but they were going to change the way people lived their lives. They needed to dig in, work harder, and persevere. When Jon spoke people wanted to believe him. He was like Tom Cruise in *Jerry McGuire*, handsome, charismatic, and to too many of his employees, a visionary. When he smiled at you and asked in his very sincere voice to dig in and work harder, you wanted to work; you saw he believed in the company, and it made you want to believe.

Not wanting to let Jon or her coworkers down, Kelly started to work even harder. If a twelve-hour day wasn't enough, she'd have to do a fourteen, a sixteen, eighteen, or twenty if necessary. She couldn't let everyone down; she couldn't spoil the vision. Chris had been supportive the entire time, but now he was beginning to wonder if Kelly had made the right choice. He had always admired her ambition and work ethic, but she was becoming a different person than the woman he knew and loved. Yes, they wanted a good life, but at what cost? He realized that they hadn't been as happy as they were since the time they had worked together at the agency. One night, Chris asked his wife to quit her job and come back to work with him. Instead of the expected response, he was met with outrage. "Did he realize what she was working on?," "Didn't he want to retire early, want a nice house, want to be rich," "I work my butt off for us and that's all the thanks I get" were the responses he got. Kelly, angry and upset, stormed out of the house and went to the place she where she could at least get something done while she cooled down, her office.

When she got in, it was almost one o'clock in the morning and the place was empty, except for one office, Jon's. Kelly decided to drop in and say hi. Jon definitely looked like he had seen better days. He looked tired, had circles under his eyes, needed to shave, and there were coffee cups and fast food wrappers everywhere. "Well how's it going Kelly?" he asked, and like a waterfall she opened up and let flow everything—how she was tired and stressed and overworked, and worse, how the one man whom she thought really understood her didn't. After hearing it all Jon nodded his head and agreed; he knew what it was like. He was going through the same thing; in fact, his wife had just gone on an extended visit to stay with her mom. Some people just couldn't understand; he guessed. If you're not in this company, you just can't get it. Kelly couldn't disagree with him and couldn't pull herself out of his office. She stayed there for another hour just talking with him, feeling close to someone for the first time in months. What happened next can be left to the reader's imagination, but that night was the beginning of the affair.

After that night work took on a new meaning for Kelly. It was still her job, and still something she loved and believed in, but it was also a chance for her to see Jon. Over the next three months they met repeatedly. Kelly was always wary of discovery by her husband even though she was very cautious. They only met away from other people who knew them, they didn't talk more than normal at the office, and most important, Jon was never to call her at home. E-mail and instant messaging became their preferred method of communication since it was quiet and effective.

While Kelly's life was picking up, Chris's was getting worse. He had felt distant from her since she had started her new job. Now their sex life was suffering, too. They hadn't been together in over two months. Chris was beginning to wonder if all those jokes about marriage were true. He knew Kelly spent a lot of time at work, but he couldn't fathom her cheating. But she was staying even later now, sometimes not even coming home, and she didn't seem to mind. She didn't want to talk about what went on as much anymore either; she was either too busy, or "didn't want to think about it right now."

Then one morning everything changed. Chris was in the shower and Kelly was at her computer. She noticed Jon logged onto his instant messenger and then buzzed her.

```
Bigmoney4all: Are you there?
Kelly1971: Yes
Bigmoney4all: I miss you
Kelly1971: I miss you too, but I'll see you at work
Bigmoney4all: I want to call you, I want to hear your voice
Kelly1971: You know you can't do that
```

Right then the phone rang. She closed the instant messaging window and ran out to get the phone. When she picked up the phone she heard Tom's voice (her friend and Chris's carpool partner). "Hey, Kelly, we haven't talked in a while; how are things going?"

Meanwhile Chris had finished his shower. He heard Kelly on the phone in the other room and though wondered who it was, walked into the bedroom to get his clothes. Passing by the computer, he glanced and saw an instant messaging window sitting there:

`Bigmoney4all: So are we still on for tonight after work?`

Chris stopped dead in his tracks. Thousands of thoughts raced through his head, he quickly steadied himself and typed:

`Kelly1971: Yes`

After a few anxious seconds later he received:

`Bigmoney4all: And your husband?`
`Kelly1971: What about him?`
`Bigmoney4all: He still doesn't know about us does he?`
`Kelly1971: No, not yet`

That moment Kelly walked into the room, "Hey Chris that was Tom he won't be able to make it ….. oh no," she noticed Chris was staring at her computer. Once again the details are left to the reader. But this was the moment of clarity for Chris, where he learned that his wife was having an affair. It explained a lot to him. Everything he had feared but dismissed had just been proven on her computer screen.

So a divorce ensued. It was amicable, or at least as much as a divorce can be. Chris and Kelly sold the house, divided the proceeds and each went their separate ways. It could have been much worse, but the situation had set the tone. Virginia, where they both lived is a state that is very tough on the adultery laws, and Chris now had proof of it. He wouldn't owe Kelly anything above and beyond what they had accumulated together. The settlements were fair, but could have been much worse for Chris had he not learned about what was happening and prepared himself for this scenario.

Analysis

Chris found out about Kelly's infidelity due to a simple slip up. Had she locked her screen he may never have been the wiser. But due to a little low-tech computer snooping, he was able to figure out what was going on. Chris probably never would have looked at Kelly's screen, if he hadn't already been suspicious. He had come from the CIA, he understood the value of personal privacy. However he felt something was wrong, and he looked for clues wherever he could. Kelly's affair was very typical, it occurred at work, and with someone she spent a lot of time and was under a lot of pressure with. She didn't meet her partner on the Internet but she did use it as a communication mechanism. She had thought it would be safer than the phone, and when she rushed off in fear that the protocol was broken, she made her fatal mistake. Chris didn't employ elaborate technical measures to spy on Kelly; he didn't need them. His senses and other clues led him to know something was wrong, and his casual observation gave him all the evidence he needed. The moment he typed back in response to the instant messages, he crossed the line. At that point he very well could have been answering to any one of Kelly's friends for any reason. If he had been wrong, the relationship still might have ended, with his spying giving Kelly a perfect excuse to drop him. So all in all spying is a serious and dangerous game. The consequences are almost always high. It is definitely something that each person must understand and be prepared for all outcomes.

Summary

This chapter served as an explanation of the book and an introduction into the world of spying to discover your family's secret lives. It discussed many of the possible illicit and somewhat scary activities they can become involved with online. We also approached several of the ethical issues and scenarios where spying may not be the most appropriate action. So far we've covered the following important concepts:

- ☑ Being informed of potential situations beforehand almost always offers an advantage when dealing with them.

- ☑ We present our definition of snooping and straying. These are the fact that most people are inherently curious about their loved ones, and that many people have a tendency to occasionally visit their dark sides.

- ☑ The Internet has become an awesome communication mechanism. E-mail, instant messaging, Web browsing, and blogging have enlarged the social circle that most people have.

- ☑ People are still people and do the same activities they always have, cheating, gambling, lying, abusing drugs … and so on. Now they have the power of the Internet to enable their activites, and put them in touch with new partners in crime.

- ☑ Spying on your family can be a VERY touchy subject; one must take time to consider the many implications it could have.

- ☑ The damage done by spying may sometimes exceed the damage done by the act you're trying to catch.

- ☑ When dealing with spouses, infidelity, financial security, liability and multiple identities are all scenarios that may have a significant Internet component. When any of these are suspected it may be time to examine computer usage.

- ☑ Drug use, cheating in school, online theft, and pornography are all typical uses of computers that parents may wish to monitor and prevent their children from doing.

- ☑ Stalkers, pedophiles, and other very shady characters exist out on the Internet. They hunt for their prey where it gathers and apply clever techniques to seduce them.

- ☑ Internet addiction itself can be a dangerous problem. It is important to keep an eye on computer usage and look for its warning signs.

☑ Quite a few situations exist where it is clearly not appropriate to monitor someone's computer usage. It is very important that potential cyber-sleuths understand these and avoid them.

☑ The case study shows how the Internet played a part in one person's affair. It also showcased how technical measures allowed the cheated partner to discover what was happening, and prevail in a court of law.

Hopefully this chapter has brought to light the many potential issues involved with spying on your family. The following chapters will take you first through some of the psychology and concepts behind spying, and then the mechanics of it. Keep in mind the many dangers and rewards involved and proceed with caution, you may learn more than you ever wanted to know.

References

Endnotes

[1] K. S. Young "The Evaluation and Treatment of Internet Addiction" in *Innovations in Clinical Practice: A Source Book*, L. VandeCreek and T. Jackson, eds. (Sarasota, FL: Professional Resource Press, 1999a) Vol. 17, 1–13

[2] K. S. Young, James O'Mara, and Jennifer Buchanan. "Cybersex and Infidelity Online: Implications for Evaluation and Treatment," Netaddiction.com, Sept. 24, 2004, www.netaddiction.com/articles/cyberaffairs.htm

[3] Newsweek, July 12, 2004

[4] Cathy Keen, "UF Study: Online Dating Virtually Irresistible to Some Married Folks," University of Florida, Gainesville; Sept. 24, 2004, www.napa.ufl.edu/2003news/internetinfidelity.htm

[5] "What Is Cybersexual Addiction?" The Center for Online Addiction, September 24, 2004, www.netaddiction.com/cybersexual_addiction.htm

[6] Infidelity Check, Sept. 24, 2004, www.infidelitycheck.org/statistics.htm

[7] "Herbal craze puts drug users on a legal high," Guardian Unlimited, Sept. 24, 2004, www.guardian.co.uk/drugs/Story/0,2763,1278595,00.html

[8] "Herbal Blends," Club13.com, Sept. 24, 2004, www.club13.com/products.cfm?pid=12

[9] "U.S. Divorce Statistics," *Divorce Magazine*, Sept. 24, 2004, www.divorcemag.com/statistics/statsUS.shtml

[10] Sheri and Bob Stritof, "Warning Signs of Cheating Spouses," About, Inc.; Sept. 24, 2004, http://marriage.about.com/cs/infidelity/a/infidelsigns.htm

## Chapter 2

Spying Basics

"Trust, but verify" — President Ronald Reagan

Topics in this Chapter:

- **Goals of Spying**

- **Psychology of Spying**

- **Spying Methodology**

- **Using Overt Monitoring as a Deterrent**

- **Using Covert Spying to Observe Behavior**

- **Demonstration**

- **Case Study: Dangers of Misinterpretation and Distrust**

- **Summary**

Introduction

Imagine two separate scenarios. In the first scenario, you order a drink at a coffee shop. The barista politely takes your order and sets your change down next to the "tips" jar. She then heads to the backroom for another bag of espresso beans. There is no one else in the store, and you are all alone. Do you take all of the change or leave some for a tip?

Now imagine that you are waiting in line behind two of your coworkers, both of whom put all of their change into the "tips" jar following their order. They have received their coffees and are now watching you as you collect your change.

Look at Figure 2.1. Would you be more inclined to leave all of your change now that the others are watching you? Would it make a difference if those watching have left their change? Would it make a difference if those watching are colleagues as opposed to strangers? What if it is your boss versus your peer?

Figure 2.1 Public "Tip Jars" Provoke a Social Pressure to Give Money When Others Are Observing You

For some, this is deemed an *intimidation* tactic. Experiments have shown that when people think they are being observed, their behavior changes based on who is observing them. Michael Lynn, an associate professor of consumer behavior at Cornell University's School of Hotel Administration, has researched this topic extensively over the past 20 years. He suggests that people tip primarily to avoid social disapproval. His research found that the amount of the tip had very little to do with the quality of the service. In particular, he estimates that quality attributes to roughly only four percent of the variance.

Take a restaurant, for example. Have you ever thought about the pressure to leave a "customary" 15 to 20 percent tip? Whom do you generally leave the tip for? In most cases, it is the waiter or waitress with whom you interacted the most. What about the chef who prepared your meal? You never saw him, so perhaps you did not feel social pressure to leave a tip. Tips are left for people to whom you feel a "connection." Many experiments show that waiters and waitresses who write simple things such as "have a nice day," or draw a smiley face on the bill receive larger tips. The server does something nice for the customer, and the customer reciprocates.

What does this have to do with spying on your family? A great deal, when your intent is to modify their behavior by spying, rather than just catch them "in the act." In particular, this chapter explores the social pressure from a lack of privacy and ties psychological aspects such as this into the activity of spying. In addition, this chapter outlines the goals of spying, explores the use of active surveillance as a deterrent, investigates some of the emotional effects of spying, and touches on the legality of monitoring others. The moral of this story is that spying is a powerful technique that can be used to gather information on those that have done wrong. At the same time, it is a dangerous weapon that should only be used as a last resort. Honesty, trust, and communication are relationship builders; spying is based on deception, cynicism, and secrecy. Take this into account before you pursue any act of surveillance.

Goals of Spying

Historically, the goal of spying has been to collect information from targets without their knowledge. This information is useful in that the target doesn't think you have it, and doesn't realize when you do have it. It is the closest you can come to reading someone's mind. For the purpose of this book, we extend our definition of spying to include all types of monitoring. In addition to information collection, spying can be used as a technique for monitoring and modifying people's behavior. The primary goal of spying is to improve your position in a situation either by controlling behavior or using the information to give yourself an unexpected advantage.

Information collection plays a part in every multiparty interaction. When two groups come together there are primarily three levels of information exchange: active and inactive (both overt) and covert. Active information is any information that you receive via request from another party. This information is always voluntarily given. Inactive information is the information actively gleaned from nonvoluntary factors such as facial expression, mannerisms, tone of voice, and other relatively apparent clues. Although this information is not voluntarily given, it is not concealed either, and it is apparent for all those who would collect it. Finally, covert information is the information you glean by other methods consisting of those activities traditionally associated with spying. Information collected by covert methods may not be obvious and is definitely not voluntarily given by the monitored party. Covert information plays a critical part in obtaining the big picture of any interaction. Without it, you have only what you observed or inferred from the interaction. Covert information gives you what is unseen and in many cases helps round out the big picture. Voluntary, involuntary, and covert information round out the information puzzle.

Imagine that you are quizzing your spouse about a former love. What your spouse offers to tell you in response to your questions is one part of the information puzzle, the overt and active information. You now have the information that your spouse is willing to disclose on the subject. When talking with your spouse, you also pay attention to facial expressions and tone of voice. This offers another piece of the puzzle. Your spouse's nonverbal clues—i.e., smiling or frowning or appearing happy or sad—are involuntary factors that round out what you overtly know. If you search your spouse's diary for entries about the former love, you are covertly collecting information. This action may give you a completely different view of the topic. Now you have access to information that your spouse feels is secret and not being observed. In many cases, this is the most truthful version of the story. The overt and covert information all combine to flesh out the big picture.

Notes from the Underground...

Spy Terminology

- **Canary Trap** A technique in which artificial or incorrect information is deliberately fed out to help determine the source of an information leak.

Continued

- **Cipher** A type of simple encryption in which letters or numbers are substituted for each other to secretly hide a message.

- **Concealment Device** A device used to hide objects such as surveillance equipment or secret messages.

- **Covert** A method of doing something secretly.

- **Legend** A cover story used to explain a situation if caught.

- **Listening Post (LP)** The place where covertly collected information is sent. This comes from the world of audio surveillance devices. Most of these bugs send their recorded audio back to a literal listening post. In most of the cases discussed here, the listening post and spying device are the PC.

- **Mark** The target of an effort (usually the person spied upon).

- **Overt** A method of doing something openly.

Behavior modification can be another result of the spying process and is usually achieved by revealing a capability to monitor activity. The resulting effect can be a deterrent, such as the case of police cameras in public areas. It can also be used to complicate a subject's activities. If concerned about being monitored, people being spied on may adapt additional behaviors as the knowledge of being monitored drives them to a new level of caution. The additional complexity of trying to avoid monitoring techniques may drive them away or complicate the process they were originally embarking on. In these cases it is not the actual covert collection of information, but the overt knowledge that someone may have the capability to watch them that can be played upon to modify bad behavior.

When the two end goals of spying are carefully executed, they can be used to place people in a much stronger position than they would be without spying. They now have new information, or have modified the behavior of their target in such a way that a sense of control has been established. Being able to obtain covert information or to modify behavior puts one in a position of enormous advantage.

Can You Believe It?

Social Spotlight Effect

Do you think everyone notices you when you accidentally stumble while walking over a break in a sidewalk? Probably only a few people would notice you; people appreciably overestimate how much they are in the spotlight. A group of psychologists at Cornell University conducted a series of experiments to demonstrate this point and to identify the magnitude of these discrepancies.

In one case, researchers asked skiers to estimate how many people on the ski lifts watched them as they skied. These skiers exaggerated the percentages of those on the lifts who were watching them. Similarly, researchers conducted an experiment with a student sitting alone at a table in a busy college cafeteria. The student felt self-conscious about having many people observing his social isolation, yet few even noticed him.

As Thomas Gilovich, a leading researcher in this field, said, "Nobody has gone broke or lost an election by underestimating that people believe social acts have consequences. Everything we've done suggests that fear of social shunning may keep some people, and even some politicians, from taking certain stands that they are afraid will result in people shunning them."

Researchers also studied how critical observers can be of mistakes. They found that observers were more likely to pass harsh criticism when they couldn't apply the individual's perspective to themselves. However, if the observer and the individual made the same mistake, they were less critical.

An interesting example of this occurred in November 1999, when presidential candidate George W. Bush was given a pop quiz on foreign policy during a television interview. He was asked to name the political leaders of Chechnya, India, Pakistan, and Taiwan. Bush answered only one of the four correctly. Numerous political surveys and psychological experiments followed that supported the theory that Bush's poor performance had little effect on the opinion of viewers who also did not know the answers. Only those who were knowledgeable of the correct answers tended to criticize his mistakes.

Will this knowledge change our behavior? Kenneth Savitsky, one of the leaders in these experiments, remarked, "I'm a researcher in this area, and I'm often afraid to go outside if I feel that my jacket doesn't look right or that my pants aren't pressed properly." He was probably joking, but even if people are aware of their hypersensitivity, it is still difficult for them to adjust their behavior.

Psychology of Spying

As the old saying goes, "Monkey see, monkey do." The change in your decision to leave a tip at a coffee bar may be influenced by the actions and perceived importance of those around you (whether conscious or not). This is an example of how social environments affect behavior. Changes brought about by these conditions are commonly referred to as the *chameleon* effect. In an article titled "The chameleon effect: The preception-behavior link and social interaction" (Journal of Personality and Social Psychology, 76, 893-910, 1999), researchers T.L. Chartrand and J.A. Bargh define this as:

> *"nonconscious mimicry of the postures, mannerisms, facial expressions, and other behaviors of one's interaction partners, such that one's behavior passively and unintentionally changes to match that of others in one's current social environment."*

In other words, the person surrounded by a group practicing a behavior is likely to adopt that behavior even if he or she would not normally do so when alone.

Now apply this perception-behavior link to something deemed "forbidden" with assumed consequences. If children are instructed not to smoke, are they more likely to do it in private when no one is around, or in plain site of their parents? Common sense says that they are aware of cause and effect and will choose not to smoke around someone who will object and punish them.

The same is true with an adulterous husband. Rather than taking his illicit lover to the family's favorite restaurant where he is likely to be observed and recognized, he'll go to great strides to schedule dinner on the other side of town. Great care will be taken to minimize the risk of being discovered. Like it or not, the social pressure of monitoring (or fear of being caught) plays a principal role in how many individuals behave.

Computers and the Internet complicate the chameleon effect because people have a sense of privacy and anonymity when using them. They provide a new area that falls somewhere between complete privacy and the fully observable behavior of the real world. Figure 2.2 illustrates the trade-off between social pressure and privacy ranging from the freedom to "think" thoughts without social feedback to the slightly less private Internet to the real world, which is largely composed of social observation and very little privacy.

Figure 2.2 Privacy Diagram

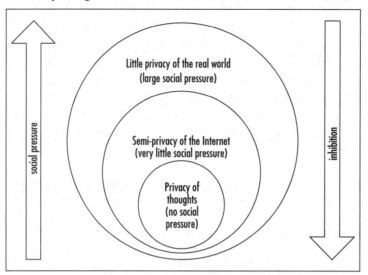

Little privacy of the real world
(large social pressure)

Semi-privacy of the Internet
(very little social pressure)

Privacy of
thoughts
(no social
pressure)

social pressure

inhibition

Are you Self-Conscious?

Barry Manilow T-shirt Experiment

Researchers at Cornell University conducted an experiment in which 109 students were each asked to wear a Barry Manilow T-shirt into a room full of their peers.

The students felt self-conscious about wearing the T-shirt knowing that he was not the most popular artist on campus, and they estimated that at least half of the observers noticed their choice in clothing.

However, they overestimated; only one-quarter of the observers noticed on average. Follow-up experiments yielded results that show that this exaggeration is commonly up to six times the percentage of the true observers.

As the remainder of this book will demonstrate, unless specific actions are taken to ensure it, privacy on the Internet is based on a false sense of security. In these circumstances, observation is not as publicly advertised, and therefore, it does not play as large of a role in decision making.

Spying Methodology

Spying can be broken down into two basic categories: overt and covert. Overt spying is analogous to surveillance and advertised monitoring. It is the police officer patrolling a neighborhood, the surveillance camera above the bank's automatic teller machine (ATM), and the phone call you make to ensure that your son is home promptly after school lets out. Whether you are aware of it or not, you participate in overt monitoring every waking minute of your life.

> *"He looked about his surroundings. They had become so familiar to him that, without realizing it, he was beginning to take on some of the mannerisms of the people who lived there."*
>
> – Georges Simenon, *Maigret and the Toy Village*

> *"The briefing had said, 'Don't speak'... but while the crowd acknowledged people's need to hurry it demanded at the least some slight apology for breaking the etiquette of the rush hour."*
>
> – Gerald Seymour, *Harry's Game*

Covert spying is what "spymaster" authors John Le Carré, Gerald Seymour, and Ian Fleming are famous for writing about. However, in real life, mystery and intrigue may not be what you want to experience.

Spying on others, especially family members, can be a stressful and emotional event. Under such circumstances, it is very easy to allow emotions to control decisions, which can then lead to mistakes. As discussed previously, the consequences of mistakes can sometimes be worse than the crime. As we have learned, in stressful and emotional situations it is good to have a well-defined plan and a backup plan. When the stress takes hold, a well-practiced plan becomes instinctual; the true value of a contingency plan is apparent when it is actually used.

To approach the task of spying methodically like a professional, it is a good idea to develop a strategy that can be used to evaluate and plan most spying sessions. A method we developed, called SLEUTH, consists of six steps to help you walk through a mission; evaluate scenarios and risk; and execute and examine your results. The SLEUTH methodology corresponds to:

1. **S**etting goals

2. **L**aying out a strategy

3. **E**valuating and understanding risk

4. **U**sing best judgment to execute the plan

5. **T**aking in observations and results

6. **H**andling the scenario using your results

Setting Goals

The first step in spying is to determine what your objectives will be. Rarely is it useful to run blindly into a spying mission. Although it may occur occasionally, it is good to set a well-defined goal before you begin. For example, a solid goal would be "to prove your wife's infidelity," and a not well-defined goal would be, "I know my wife is up to something. I need to find out." Both would involve the same type of work, but the first gives a clear goal, whereas the second is like a "fishing trip," where you hope to turn up something. With a solid goal, you can either prove your hypothesis or determine that it is outside your technical skill to discover. Even when there is no solid end result, it is important to have a clear quitting point. It is generally better to concede at a certain point and realize that either nothing is going on or your target is hiding his actions beyond your ability to find out. Failing to have a well-established stopping point can result in an endless quest that may eventually result in an obsession with collecting information.

Goals, as we describe them, are not necessarily conclusive decisions, but ways of measuring progress and accomplishment. For example, if you want to keep an eye on your teenager, you won't necessarily set a goal such as "prove he smokes marijuana." Searching only for drug-related material may cause you to bypass other useful clues about other activities you may have an interest in. In this situation, a better goal may be to monitor your teenager's e-mail and chat, looking for anything that may endanger him or her.

Laying Out a Strategy

Laying out a strategy is a critical step in every spying operation. Even if you skip setting goals (which is not recommended), do not skip this step. Proceeding with any operation without a plan is a bad idea. A well-designed, strategy will give you a path to take and alternative routes to follow toward reaching your objective.

Before laying out a plan of action carefully assess your situation. Study and understand your target and the layout of the environment you will be operating in.

In the scope of this book it boils down to understanding spouses' or children's personalities, how they use their computers, and in some cases how they have their computer set up. Do they e-mail a lot? Chat? Does their computer have a password? Try to learn as much as possible beforehand so that you can take everything you know into account when designing your strategy. This will minimize unexpected surprises and the amount of "on-the-fly" decisions that have to be made.

As you plan for different scenarios, look for possible failure points. When you reach one of these critical points, try to find all of the possible causes of failure. Think about what you can do to minimize your chances of failure at those times. Whenever possible, make a backup plan. Determine what you will do if your normal plan is diverted. Planning for failures and extraordinary situations is what separates a good strategy from a great strategy. It is not so much the plan, but how you handle things when they don't go according to plan that matters. The goal of a good strategy is to eliminate last-minute decisions. When you are dealing with emotionally volatile issues, it is important to proceed based on study and research. When things go wrong, emotions can come into play that drive you to follow paths that, if viewed from a logical perspective, may be incorrect. A strategy can ensure that you have a predeveloped plan, hopefully made at a time when the "big picture" was viewed free of situational complications. If done well, a good strategy will help increase the chances of success with most spying operations.

Evaluating and Understanding Risk

Risk plays a central role in any spying operation. It is very important to be aware of the different risks posed and to determine their possible effects. When planning any operation, you must carefully balance the possible risk and consequence versus the potential reward.

From walking across the street to playing with live rattlesnakes, risk is present in almost everything we do. We make quick mental trade-offs between risk and reward and then choose our course of action. In many cases, when the risk is understood, steps can be taken to minimize it. For example, when crossing the street we can decrease our personal risk by crossing at a crosswalk and waiting until there are no cars approaching. In some activities, such as playing with rattlesnakes, not much can be done to reduce the risk to an acceptable level. Those are the activities we will choose to avoid after considering the risk versus reward trade-off. This same trade-off and risk minimization principle should also apply to spying on family members. Take careful consideration of the risk factors involved. Evaluate each risk factor for severity. Is it a big risk? Can you live with the consequences? Can anything be done to minimize risk?

Risk is an extremely important factor to consider when spying on someone. Many complex issues come into play when spying on a family member because there are many levels and types of risk. At a high level there is the risk of being discovered, which would put an end to your current operation and possibly tip off your target. At a deeper level, spying may be placing your relationship with your target in jeopardy. In searching for a possible problem, you may be seriously risking the integrity of the relationship. Think very carefully about all of the issues involved. Only when you understand them and their possible consequences should you proceed to spy.

Using Best Judgment to Execute the Plan

The goals are set, the plan is made, and the risk is understood; now it is time to spy. Using your best judgment, begin to execute the strategy you have prepared and outlined. Even though you have planned every step very carefully, situations will arise where judgment calls must be made. As the plan is executed, keep in mind the end goal, the strategy devised, and the risk involved. Use those three factors to guide any decisions that must be made. If done cautiously and carefully, execution of the strategy will yield the most reward.

Take in Observations and Results

As you spy, information will begin to pour in. It may not always be what you want or expect, but most of it will have some value. Store and analyze all of it. This collected information can usually be broken down into three primary groups: operations intelligence, targeted intelligence, and chaff, or useless information.

It is important to securely collect and store both types of useful information. If the information you obtain is not stored securely, you risk its discovery, which can lead to a compromise of both your capability and your activity. Once you feel that either of those has been compromised, you can no longer trust the value of the intelligence. Targets may operate in a manner specifically designed to thwart your collection efforts.

Operational intelligence increases your ability to continue, maintain, and possibly expand your spying activities. An example of operational information is discovering that your spouse leaves his or her laptop on with an open e-mail program every morning while he or she showers. Now you have a new window of opportunity to look for information that can possibly help lead you deeper into the information jungle in search of your goals. While operational intelligence may be more "dry" and less interesting than your targeted information, do not neglect it. If you do not plan on using it immediately, store it. Once you have executed all of the paths of your strategy, the operation intelligence you've gleaned may open up new avenues to explore.

Targeted intelligence is the information you are looking for, the material that will help you realize your goal. Sometimes this information presents itself as a "smoking gun" that gives direct evidence of your suspicions. Usually, however, it is a loosely correlated collection of clues. These clues make sense only when they are collected and viewed as an aggregate.

Because targeted intelligence can be difficult to locate, it is necessary to closely examine and analyze the information you initially discern as chaff, which can hold potential clues. For example, before you discard a series of e-mails consisting of forwards, recipes, or sports scores, reexamine them for a hidden meaning. Do the recipes make sense? Are the forwards changed dramatically from the ones on the Internet? Do the sports scores correspond to real-life events? It is not unusual for a clever adversary to use innocent looking information to disguise a communication channel. This technique, known as *steganography*, is a mainstay in many secret methods of communication. Spies, terrorists, and a host of other characters, both good and evil, use it as a method of slipping their information "under the radar."

Handling the Situation Using Your Results

Now that you have some information, it is time to use it to work toward reaching your goal. At this time, we'll assume that you have material that describes some aspect of your target that they do not wish to make public and that they do not know you have. What you do with this information depends on your goal. It can be useful for confrontation, or as a lead-in into an area where more spying can be done. You might have just enough information to steer your interactions in a new direction. Regardless of the specifics, careful analysis and use of the information is the final stage of the spying process.

Using Overt Monitoring as a Deterrent

Behavioral changes associated with active spying, or monitoring, are psychological phenomena that scientists believe date back to human hunter/gatherer days. Studies have demonstrated that people are hypersensitive to the social spotlight when they believe they are being watched. Imagine your comfort level when you are being interviewed for a job in a closed conference room with no windows versus a conference room with a large one-way glass and a video camera focused on you. In the closed room you are able to judge the importance and reaction of those watching you, but in the surveillance room you cannot, and you fear the opinions of those behind the glass.

This hypersensitivity is believed to have helped early man coexist in small group settings. At this time, isolation even for a matter of days could mean death to those dependent on their groups. It was of utmost importance to peacefully coexist within the group. Today, group coexistence is not necessary, yet we still overestimate what others observe about us and change our behavior because of it.

Overcautiousness leads us to try and adopt what we believe is acceptable by those observing us. There is an innate desire to please that makes us want to please the observer. For example, it is unlikely that someone would pursue an affair using e-mail if he or she thought that each message were being monitored by a spouse. However, there are some cases (imagine an ornery teenager) where the observed people might choose behavior they feel will deliberately upset their observer.

Surveillance as a Deterrent First and Observer Second

Rather than using monitoring to "catch" someone in the act, overt monitoring can be used as a deterrent. A classic example of this is the use of police cameras, which are typically mounted high on poles and aimed at suspicious street corners. Supporters of this system claim it has a dramatic effect on street crime. However, it should be noted that there are mixed statistics on their effectiveness; they provide observation evidence, but it is difficult to estimate how many crimes they actually prevent.

In September 2002, Madelyne Toogood and her 4-year-old daughter finished shopping at Kohl's department store in Mishawaka, Indiana. Toogood placed her daughter in the back of her SUV, appeared to scan the parking lot for observers, and then repeatedly hit the young girl. This act was caught on a parking lot surveillance camera similar to the one pictured in Figure 2.3.

If you look at the video footage, it appears as if Toogood looked for people who might see her, but she never looked up for cameras. The question is: if she had seen the camera would she have still done it? If so, would she have done it in the parking lot, or would she have waited until she was out of sight? Also, how many people have ever intended to commit a crime like this, but then realized they were being observed prior to doing it? This is a difficult (if not impossible) statistic to measure. The knowledge that they might be being watched influences the decisions that people make.

Figure 2.3 Surveillance Camera

When it comes to computers, there is little public knowledge of the ease of monitoring. Police cameras have been granted widespread media attention, but little has been said about the collection and monitoring conducted by Internet service providers, Web-based e-mail services, and Web site tracking. All of these are entities that perform some type of monitoring. If people were as aware of this as they were of police cameras, would they be as willing to participate in some of the more unsavory behavior that occurs online?

Can You Believe It?

Who Uses Police Cameras, and Do They Deter Crime?

You may be monitored more than you expect. The following list is not all inclusive; according to industry estimates there are approximately 2 million video surveillance systems in the U.S. Police cameras are used throughout most cities to actively monitor in an attempt to deter crime and catch criminals. The verdict is still out on their success.

- **Baltimore** Sixteen cameras are used to scan the downtown streets and sidewalks 24 hours a day.

- **Chicago** Thirty cameras that are mounted on poles have been used to scan for crime since 2002.

- **Memphis** Twelve cameras have been used in the business district since 1996.

Continued

- **NYC** In 1998, numerous police cameras were installed throughout the city starting with public housing developments, Grand Central Station, and Washington Square Park.
- **Tacoma, WA** In 1993, Tacoma was the first city to use surveillance to publicly deter crime by mounting cameras on top of light poles in high crime areas.

Very few people are aware of the fact that in July 2004, a 2-to-1 decision by a panel of the U.S. Court of Appeals for the 1st Circuit in Massachusetts proclaimed that any company providing e-mail service has the right to copy and read any message bound for its customers. This means that e-mail is not afforded the same expectation of privacy as a telephone call or in-person conversation. For a law enforcement officer to gain access to e-mail, only a search warrant is required. This compares with a wiretap order needed to record a telephone line, which is far more difficult to acquire. Some see this as a loss of privacy, and other see it as a means of deterring illegal behavior on the Internet.

When it comes to your family, children who have been instructed not to participate in illicit activities will likely not do so if they feel their parents are monitoring their behavior. For example, many Internet protection groups urge parents to place computers accessible by children in the "family" room versus behind the closed doors of their bedroom. This reinforces the notion that the child is subject to monitoring and that his or her behavior may be observed by an objecting parent.

While this monitoring may seem excessive to privacy advocates, it also represents one method of parental involvement. One of the big criticisms of the Columbine tragedy was that the parents of Eric Harris and Dylan Klebold allegedly had little involvement in their sons' personal lives. For example, it was reported that the boys openly communicated their deadly interests on their Web site, yet the parents remained unaware. Complaints about the Web site were made to local police more than one year prior to the school incident by concerned parents whose children were listed as targets of violence on this page. No one at the time could have predicted the extent of this tragedy. One may wonder, what could have been done to deter this event? Would things have been different if the parents were more aware of what their children were doing in the secrecy of their rooms? Would things have been different if Harris's parents were aware of this Web site, and aware that in his room he had a gun? Although the parents slept the evening before the attack, the two boys made a video and in it Harris imagined that his parents would say, "If only we had checked his room. If only we had asked more questions."

There is a benefit to being aware of what your children are involved in, especially if you fear they are in trouble and more traditional methods of communication have failed in the past. For young children, this is easy because they communicate openly with their parents. For teenagers who become reclusive and withdrawn, this becomes more difficult. There are many options and techniques to try to become more involved.

One such option is to tell your children directly that you are aware of what they are doing at home and on the Internet. This is accomplished through open monitoring or "advertised" surveillance. This is analogous to posting a sign in front of your home that says it is protected by a security device. Maintaining a home surveillance system helps protect you against burglars, but advertising the fact that you have one may prevent the need for the system altogether. Figure 2.4 shows an example security sign that might make some believe that a location is actually protected by a real security system. Some people post the signs in their yard without actually having the alarm system installed.

Figure 2.4 Advertising Surveillance Sometimes Is Just as Effective as Implementing It

The same is hoped to be true with monitoring on the Internet (especially when it comes to children). Overtly conducting surveillance may help protect you from hurtful events, but depending on the circumstances, merely advertising the threat of monitoring may be just as effective. A quick search on *www.google.com* for the phrase "my parents don't know" brings attention to this. The search alone brings up thousands of hits. On one Web site uncovered during this search (*www.oasismag.com*) the question is asked:

"How many of your parents know that you post here?"

Overwhelmingly, the response was that (1) they do not know and (2) the children feel that if they did know there would be repercussions. Some of the responses to the question are listed here:

"Naw, my parents don't know. If they did my computer would be gone, I'd be banned from the Internet for... well, as long as they have power over me, lol. I'd get a long rant about how I'm completely without morals and wondering where they went wrong. I just delete the history and cookie files on my computer before I go to bed so they can't track it."

"They don't know. If they did my mom or dad would freak. They don't like the idea that I can open up on the Internet but not to them."

"I know every so often when my dad comes in to talk to me he reads whatever it is that I've written or am reading or something like that, but I never told him I write stuff about my life online. He has no knowledge whatsoever about his computer or computers in general, and wouldn't know something like this even existed."

This is just a sample of many instances in which children indicate that their parents are not aware of what they do, and that they feel comfortable doing this because there is no indication that they will be caught.

NOTE

The Web site *www.dotgov.gov* greets visitors with this threat:
   Warning! *Use of this site is restricted!*
   This computer system is for the use of the United States Government. Unauthorized access, or access which exceeds authorized access is punishable under 18 USC 1030.
   Users have to click on the **Agree** button to continue. This threat is a powerful deterrent that is used to attempt to prevent misuse rather than merely recording and prosecuting against it.

Explore More...

Mini Case Study: Deterrents

The following story demonstrates some of the psychology involved in spying and its deterrent effects, and is a universal scenario that most people can identify with.

When I was a kid, I like most kids, would do things that made my parents mad. I'd stay out too late, sneak out of the house, skip class to smoke cigarettes, and run around town without their permission. Like most amateur wrongdoers, I was occasionally caught, and when I was, I fell victim to several of my parent's clever methods at dealing with the situation.

Being caught hammered in the fact that they were always one step ahead of me. First, they would never confront me immediately after I did something. They would wait a day or two before bringing it up. After this had occurred a couple of times, I could never be sure once I'd done something wrong if I had actually gotten away with it. I might have, or I could just be in my parents waiting period where they lulled me into a false sense of security. Sometimes they would wait weeks before dropping the dime and revealing their hand.

A second method of theirs was slightly less insidious, but just as painful. When they did catch me doing something wrong, they would never tell me how. I was always left wondering how they found out. Did I slip up, did my friends or their parents sell me out, or did my parents have some secret monitoring capability I didn't know of? These tricks definitely had a powerful deterrent effect, and they usually made me think twice before I'd consider doing something they wouldn't approve of. They allowed my parents to keep the edge in information superiority longer than they would have otherwise.

Explore More...

The Polygraph as a Deterrent

Many employees of the Central Intelligence Agency (CIA) have a common response when asked to partake in questionable activities: "No, I can't. I have my poly coming up soon!" It is not that the desire to commit crime is rampant among employees, but rather it is a testament to the deterrent power of the polygraph test. Polygraph tests instill fear in most people who are subjected to them as a requirement for continued employment. This fear extends from decisions they make in their daily lives down to the actual event in which they confess everything from taking a pen home to cutting in line in the company cafeteria.

It is often speculated that polygraph tests keep innocent people innocent. We can speak only from the experience of behaviors that we have observed personally.

The polygraph works by measuring the physiological changes in a person when they are confronted with questions related to a topic. The assumption is that when the subject attempts to deceive the administrator of the test, the natural interaction between the mind and body will cause physiological stresses to be visible. These stresses include changes in respiration, increases in skin response, and changes in blood pressure.

An employee's fear is an example of overt monitoring advertisement to deter "forbidden" behavior. In this case, the monitoring actually occurs after the fact, but it demonstrates the same common purpose: to notify individuals that their actions will become known by others and that consequences will be applied if they step out of bounds.

Most reliability studies estimate that the polygraph is at least 90 percent or more accurate in detecting deception. From what we have observed, the remaining 10 percent probably instills more fear than the 90 percent accuracy rate. Those subjected to the polygraph know that it is not perfect, and often fear that *thoughts* versus *actions* of "forbidden" activities may be misconstrued in that fuzzy area of inaccuracy. Perhaps this adds to the fear of the polygraph and, as a lucky side effect, actually increases its ability to deter behavior *around* the line and not just actions that cross it.

Problems with Overt Spying

While overt spying has the potential of helping to avoid problems down the road, it is naïve to think that it is without problems. Three of the biggest issues are:

- Overt spying advertises *where, when*, and *what* you are monitoring.

- Monitoring explicitly indicates your lack of trust in someone.

- You have to deal with the "rules-are-made-to-be-broken" attitude.

Each of these concerns is addressed in detail in the following sections.

Smile for the Camera

There is a reason why most inspections are called "surprise" inspections, and why crime tends to decrease in areas that introduce visible police surveillance cameras. People change when they think someone is observing them. Would you spend the extra 20 minutes at the coffee machine talking about last night's football game or your fantasy "Survivor" picks if your boss was watching you? Probably not, but chances are high that you would do it once your boss left the area.

When you overtly spy, you are indicating exactly where, when, and what you intend to monitor. Unless the people involved explicitly want to upset you, they are not going to partake in the "forbidden" behavior while you are monitoring them. Maybe this convinces people to think twice about what they were about to do, or maybe it simply makes them temporarily suppress their desire. Be forewarned that overt spying may cause the person wanting to commit the act to evolve and adopt more covert techniques and conduct the behavior out of your sight.

A classic example of this in the intelligence world is observed through the eyes of overhead surveillance cameras. Nearly everyone has seen the overhead photos of the missiles from the Cuban missile crisis (see Figure 2.5). This photograph, along with many others, is from the Dino A. Brugioni collection at the National Security Archive. Brugioni was a CIA officer responsible for "all source" intelligence during the time of this crisis. Brugioni has also written a book titled *Photo Fakery* where he discusses how actions can be taken to mislead the viewers of the photographs when those being watched are aware of their surveillance. During the Cold War, for example, the Soviets were known to build "fake" tanks and ships to try and misrepresent their locations, capabilities, and intent. In addition, items that were deemed to be sensitive or "forbidden" were covered with reflective materials such as chicken wire to hide what was secretly placed underneath.

Figure 2.5 Overhead Surveillance from November 1962 Capturing the Image of Soviet Missiles Being Loaded at Mariel Port

The same tactics are applied to the Internet world when people identify that they are under surveillance. Take the acronym POS as an example. In the world of instant messages and chat, it means, "parent over shoulder" and is used to indicate that the subject should be changed immediately because someone is monitoring the conversation that is likely to object.

A husband who knows his wife is spying on the home e-mail accounts may sign up for secret Web mail accounts, which are far more difficult to monitor. In reality, if the objective of the wife is to collect evidence for court proceedings, it would be better not to give away the fact that she is monitoring the home e-mail. In this case, covert spying is far more appropriate. As Sun Tzu once said:

> *"When capable, feign incapacity, when active, inactivity. When near, make it appear that you are far away, when far away, that you are near."*

Otherwise, you are revealing your true capability (as the Russians did in 1962). By doing this, the spouse who intends to cheat regardless of the fear of monitoring may be driven to adopt sneakier techniques to prevent being caught.

There are a number of defensive tactics that can prevent someone else from monitoring you. Providing someone intent on doing something with the knowledge of how they will be monitored can drive them to use advanced techniques that you cannot detect. When this occurs, the overt monitoring method has had the opposite effect than was intended.

Explore More...

Mini Case Study: Secrecy

The following story shows that sometimes it is better not to broadcast your capability because it may drive your opponent to develop even better techniques to beat it.

I grew up in a fairly rough part of town. Crime was pretty much an everyday occurrence that everyone lived with and accepted. One year, my parents bought a brand-new Suburban and decided to protect their highly desirable vehicle from thieves by installing a car alarm in it. After the alarm was installed, I went with my mom to the shop to pick up the car. Along with the remotes, the shop worker handed us two stickers proclaiming the alarm brand. "Shouldn't we put those on the car?" my mom asked. "I wouldn't if I were you" was the response. Not willing to let it go, my mom brought up the point, "But they're a deterrent, aren't they? That's what I'd always heard."

"Look lady, in most places they would be, but here the thieves are a little better than that, heck most of them probably work in alarm shops just like mine. If you show them exactly what alarm you have, they have all the time in the world to look into their bag of tricks to see what they can do to beat it. It's better to let them find out the hard way that there's an alarm there. It's a lot harder to figure out what you're up against when the pressure's on."

Much in the way the sticker advertising the alarm gave the thieves a good idea of what they were up against, overt spying can give your targets a clear picture of exactly what they need to overcome. Wily targets of overt spying can soon build up a clever routine to accomplish whatever they want all the while appearing to be perfectly innocent toward the surveillance system. Depending on the skill of your mark, it may sometimes be better to hide your hand and never reveal your full capability.

Detriment of Distrust and Avoidance

A second side effect of overt monitoring is that the mere act of doing so displays a lack of trust and an invasion of privacy toward an individual. At times, this can be more destructive than the behavior they were first suspected of committing. The previous chapter addressed the ethics of spying in general, and its impact on a relationship. Rather than revisiting that, we now want to address the social impact of being "watched." Privacy is sacred, and when it is taken away there is bound to be resentment, whether it is within your family, your neighborhood, or across an entire country.

Outrage from constant monitoring can be seen everywhere from users furious about TiVo reporting that people rewatched the exposure of Janet Jackson's breast during the half-time performance of the 2004 Super Bowl three times more than any other section of the broadcast, to grocery shoppers upset with purchase-tracking "discount cards," or protestors such as the Surveillance Camera Players (*www.not-bored.org/the-scp.html*) upset with the broad use of closed circuit video surveillance cameras.

In another parody by the Surveillance Camera Players, posters were purposely displayed in front of cameras to act out scenes from George Orwell's novel, *1984*.

Apply this to computers. Imagine how you would feel if your wife said that she wanted to install monitoring software to observe which Web sites you visit and whom you chat with because she fears that you are having an affair. This would probably be a death sentence for your marriage. This is partially because a marriage is a *partnership*; both parties are assumed to be operating in the best interest of the collective marriage. In the case of overt surveillance, one party demonstrates blatant distrust for the other, and attempts to forcibly dominate in an authoritative manner by setting limits on what can and cannot be done by the spouse. For a marriage to succeed, trust and partnership are critical.

This is in contrast with the relationship between a child and a parent. As children grow, they test the limits of parental boundaries. An attempt to participate in an activity that is not endorsed by a parent is part of growing up. Over time, children change from dependent toddlers that are "put to bed" at 8 P.M. every evening to independent decision makers who choose when to wake and sleep. Marriages that are marked with constant attempts to participate in "forbidden" behavior are not operating in an effective manner.

Romeo and Juliet Meet the Fonz

Some personalities thrive on the satisfaction of doing something against the will of others. Instead of adhering to the limits set forth by others, they may instead purposefully conduct the "forbidden" behavior as a form of protest. We know this sounds silly, but think about your dog for a moment. Every dog that we have had in our lives does the same thing: if you push them while they are standing up in one direction, they push back in the opposite direction! The same can be seen in people too (especially teenagers). With their newfound independence comes the desire to be their own leaders. This means that they may not agree with the rules that mom and dad have set. In addition, some children go through phases in which they are constantly questioning authority and attempting to break the rules. In some cases, this is because they are seeking more attention (even if it is negative), and in others it is simply their way of "growing up."

Doing something "taboo" can also be fun for adults. We are all curious, and a certain amount of excitement comes with the thought of breaking the rules (and getting away with it). For example, take the classic love story, *Romeo and Juliet*. They were forbidden to be together, which fueled their love even more.

Why Not?

We once knew a married man who was having an affair. When asked what prompted his decision, his response was, "Why not?" Because he worked for the government, he was always traveling. He explained that for the past five years his wife had accused him of cheating during every business trip even though the thought had never crossed his mind.

These constant unfounded accusations wore on him, and at some point he began cheating. "I was already being punished for it, so why not actually do it?" he said. It is hard to say if he would have started without the continual display of distrust, but it is obvious that it did not help his situation. First, it planted the idea in his head, and second, it lowered the expectations of his relationship.

Using Covert Spying to Observe Behavior

Covert spying is the secretive collection of information, which is frequently used by private detectives to gather evidence on everything from suspected adultery to insurance fraud and child custody battles. Unlike active spying where the goal is to deter and manage behavior, covert spying is used to collect information that catches the target in the act. Covert spying is done without the person's knowledge, and steps are taken to conceal the spying from that person. This is usually how Hollywood portrays spying.

A person should have absolutely no indication that they are being covertly spied on. It is expected that they will be less inhibited and will not take extreme measures to hide their behavior as they would if they were being actively monitored. One advantage to active spying is that you know that the other person is aware of your activities. If you are silently spying on someone, it is difficult to know if they are even aware of you. You can never be sure if something or someone has tipped them off. Someone who suspects they are being spied on can create a canary trap by appearing to perform a behavior that would cause the observer to reveal himself. People who discover that they are being passively monitored can cause a lot of frustration by never revealing that they've discovered the game, which may send their pursuers on countless wild goose chases. The people spied upon may also be much angrier than usual if they were caught by someone using active spying techniques.

Be prepared for what you may find out. Imagine that your wonderful husband is also a terrific father. He takes care of you and your family, and is supportive of your job. You are still as in love with him today as the day you married each other. Nonetheless, you have the feeling that he is up to something. He is acting more perfect than normal, giving you more attention, dressing nicer, and spending extra time in the gym. You fear that he may have met someone. Do you really want to know the truth? Is he just flirting, or is he doing more? Is it worth ending your seemingly perfect relationship?

Problems with Covert Spying

Covert spying presents several problems. The biggest issues involved with covert spying are:

- It is a more involved procedure.
- You will never know if your target has discovered you.
- Presenting evidence obtained through covert spying reveals your capability.

Each of these issues is discussed in depth in the following sections.

Involvement of Procedure

Unlike overt spying, which involves a monitoring capability only, covert spying requires the capability to monitor and to disguise monitoring, and the opportunity to install your capabilities. This is a much more involved procedure than presented by most overt spying methodologies. For example, if it is your corporate policy to monitor employees' keystrokes, you only need to locate the appropriate keystroke logging software. Its presence is made known, and all employees must have it installed on their computers. However, if you want to covertly monitor an employee's machine, the operation becomes more complex. You must find an appropriate keystroke logger, one that has enough capability to be installed in such a manner that it avoids most reasonable efforts at detection. Finally, you must find the opportunity to install this keystroke-monitoring capability on your target's machine without his knowledge.

While these obstacles can be difficult, they are not insurmountable. In fact, the very challenges of covertness and installation are the excitement that many real-life spies crave. The careful development of capability and careful planning for opportunity can make the procedures much more achievable.

Target's Awareness of Your Capability

When you spy overtly, you may never know everything your target knows, but you have a good starting point. You can immediately assume that they are fully aware of all of the capabilities that you have disclosed to them. Now that a covert aspect is in play, your target will ideally be completely unaware of your capability.

While it is hopeful to expect, it is also very naïve. Dumb luck also plays a big part. An electrician replacing wiring may discover a listening device that was planted behind a wall. Even the best-laid plans can be upset by random chance. This factor increases the risk on all operations.

Discovery is possible at any time; therefore, it is impossible to know if the target has discovered your capability. Adversaries who discover they are being spied on may react in many different ways. Changing or concealing their behavior is one possibility. Or, the targets may adjust their behavior to mislead those monitoring them, in which case, most of the information the spy obtained is no longer valid, and the results they developed using this information is flawed.

Presentation of Evidence Reveals Capability

A new danger arises when all of the evidence is collected and the spy wants to use it as evidence of the target's wrongdoings. Possession of the different types of evidence could lead to a revelation of the spy's capabilities. Once targets have been presented with documentation of their activities, they begin to figure out how they were spied on. Using the information they are presented with, they can evaluate the collection capability deployed against them. In cases where the spy wishes to maintain his capabilities in the future, this may not be desired.

The U.S. is often faced with this challenge. When presenting satellite information to the United Nations, the press, and other organizations, it often has to obscure the image as to not reveal the full extent of its capabilities. At other times, the U.S. has had to withhold evidence of other countries' wrongdoings to protect its sources.

Demonstration

You must be careful that your covert spying is not realized and changed into overt spying against your intentions. Such was the case with FBI spy Robert Hanssen. Luckily, by the time he observed the surveillance, it was too late and enough evidence had already been gathered against him. His resignation letter demonstrates how the "threat" of spying is capable of altering someone's behavior.

Explore More...

Robert Hanssen Spy Case

The Robert Hanssen spy case demonstrates the effects of both covert and overt (or known) spying on illicit behavior. For as long as 20 years, Hanssen had been selling secrets to the Russians. Once the FBI suspected his involvement, it began covertly monitoring his telephone and other communications. From that it was on to him. As his letter indicates, he believed that he was being watched. As a result, Hanssen decided to cease his illegal activity. Little did he know that at this point it was too late; he had already been caught.

Hanssen's resignation letter to his Russian "handlers":

Dear Friends:

I thank you for your assistance these many years. It seems, however, that my greatest utility to you has come to an end, and it is time to seclude myself from active service.

I have been promoted to a higher do-nothing Senior Executive job outside of regular access to informaiton (sic) within the counterintelligence program. I am being isolated. Further, I believe I detected repeated bursting radio signal

Continued

> *emanations from my vehicle. The knowledge of their existence is sufficient. Amusing the games children play.*
>
> *Something has aroused the sleeping tiger. Perhaps you know better than I. Life is full of its ups and downs.*
>
> *I will be in contact next year, same time, same place. Perhaps the correlation of forces and circumstance then will have improved.*
>
> *Your friend,*
>
> *Ramon Garcia*
>
> Robert Hanssen was arrested and on July 6, 2001. He pled guilty to 15 counts of espionage and conspiracy charges in exchange for federal prosecutors not to seek the death penalty. He was sentenced to life in prison without parole on May 10, 2002.

Spy versus Spy

How do you decide whether you should overtly or covertly spy on someone? For the most part it comes down to two factors:

- What is your end objective?
- Who are you spying on?

When you want to deter a behavior, overt spying is more effective. If your prime objective is to collect evidence, then covert spying will be the most successful. Overt spying tends to work well with children, while covert spying works better with adults. Table 2.1 helps distinguish additional differences between the two.

Table 2.1 Table for Determining When Different Types of Spying Are Most Appropriate

	Overt	Covert
Do you want to collect information?		X
Do you want to modify behavior?	X	
Deterrence is the best policy.	X	
Catch them in the act!		X
Does your target always try to get around things?		X
Do you feel your target has a "secret life?"		X
Does your target generally follow the rules?	X	

Revealing Your Hand

Now that you understand the benefits and weaknesses of overt and covert spying, we address how to deal with the realization that someone in your family is secretly doing something that he or she knows you would object to. The question is: *What do you do now?*

Events that are time critical like child abuse, underage sex, or drug abuse should obviously be dealt with immediately. Waiting could cause further incidents and irreparable damage. However, sometimes the situation is less critical, and more of an "awakening" to you. In cases such as this, your capability to monitor may be more important than the actual deed, or what you have evidence of to date. You may be better served not to react immediately, but to instead monitor so that you are aware of the big picture and the extent of the problem.

We realize that this is difficult. You catch your wife exchanging sexually explicit e-mails with someone and you are suddenly overtaken with rage. You want to let her know immediately that you are aware of what she is doing. You are furious. You want her to stop. But, maybe there is more to it? That "someone" is a coworker, her boss. Maybe this goes beyond e-mails and to an affair. The finances are not what they seem; she was given a raise one year ago and her full paychecks are not going into the family account like you thought they were. Her business trips have been weekend visits to the beach with her lover. They are building a house there, together. Slowly she has been hiding money from you and diverting it to this. She is planning on leaving you, but she first wants to collect all that she can from you. You need to know the entire breadth and depth of the problem before you come up with a solution. If you had approached her at the start, you may not have realized the true challenge that you were about to face. In fact, approaching her from the beginning would place you at more of a disadvantage, as she would be better prepared to end the relationship.

Learning all of this gives you the ability to make a much more solid and well thought-out decision. This is the exact same reason why intelligence organizations slowly and methodically collect information. Their job is not just to "catch" other countries in the act of committing atrocious crimes; it is also to arm policymakers with all of the necessary information to make well-founded decisions.

A perfect real-life example of when to reveal your hand can be seen when you examine how the police operate when investigating organized crime figures. Often, these figures are very closely monitored and watched. In many cases, evidence of crimes ranging from misdemeanors to felonies is observed. The police will often not arrest or prosecute their target until they feel that enough evidence has been gathered for them to develop an iron-clad case. Once they make their move, their capability is revealed. This also alerts the mark that they have been the target of an investigation. If the bust is made too early the police lose both the element of surprise and the possible covertness of their spying methodology. Use this example when considering the possibility of revealing your hand.

Of course, there may never be a situation where you must reveal your hand, such as when you feel that the information collected is enough to point you to obvious clues that you can pass off as your capability. Sometimes a guilty feeling target will confess and not even inquire about how you found out. Other times you may not feel the need to ever confront your target. Since revealing can be an emotional and potentially dangerous situation, think carefully and do it cautiously.

The Benefit of Patience Taught by the Enigma

In the late 1920s, the German military adopted a new cryptographic machine called the *Wehrmacht Enigma*, as shown in Figure 2.6. Communications encrypted by it were thought to be unreadable by the Allies. In its early stages they were, but over time they could be monitored. Polish mathematicians Marian Rejewski, Jerzy Rozycki, and Henryk Zygalski made initial breaks to the code with help from Hans-Thilo Schmidt, an employee of the German cryptographic agency. On July 25, 1939, the fear of a German invasion led the Poles to share their breakthroughs with the British and French forces. This energized a surge to break more of the encryption by the Brits.

Figure 2.6 German Enigma Machine

Mathematicians Alan Turning and Gordon Welchman from Cambridge University conceived the design for a machine capable of reading the encrypted traffic. This design was taken to Harold "Doc" Keen, who was an engineer at British Tabulating Machines. Doc was hired to turn their design into a reality. Refinement and construction of this machine took many months. In 1940, it became operational and was dubbed the "Bombe."

The Bombe, as shown in Figure 2.7, was successful against German Air Force and Army Enigma traffic, but it lacked the ability to consistently break German Navy traffic. The Navy operators adhered to strict security procedures, and their machines contained three additional rotors.

This lack of monitoring capability allowed the German U-boats (submarines) to rule the waters. Admiral Doenitz, the commander of the U-boat fleet, was very strategic in his operations. Once one submarine spotted a ship that belonged to the Allies, it alerted all of the other nearby submarines with messages encrypted by the Enigma. This coordinated attack was virtually unstoppable by the lone ship.

Figure 2.7 The Bombe Encryption Breaking Machine

In May 1941, the tables turned. British forces captured the German submarine U-110. The crew of the captured U-boat was so terrified by what they felt was impending death that they abandoned the ship and jumped overboard. The result was that their encryption equipment was left completely intact with the proper daily settings in place. In addition, secrets such as codebooks and instruction manuals were left behind.

At this point, the British had an important decision to make. Do they break news of the capture and ability to read traffic, or did they wait to reveal their hand at a later date? As history tells us, they chose wisely to wait. They went through great strides to make it appear as if the submarine had sunk to the bottom of the ocean before it could have been boarded by anyone. Finally, the British could read the Navy traffic. They were able to quickly take measures that enabled their ships to travel the seas without being attacked by the U-boats. Because they did not want the Germans to fear that their encryption had been broken, they purposefully sent aerial reconnaissance to suspected areas to help misdirect concerns over the failed attacks. This disguise campaign was known as Ultra, and it was backed by deceptive excuses for any action based on intelligence gathered from the Enigma. If nothing could be done to misdirect attention to the investigative source of an action, then it was not acted upon.

The benefit of this intelligence is often claimed to have shortened the war by at least one year. Intelligence aided the Allies in the Battle of the Atlantic. It contributed to the Italian defeat at Capa Matapan, assisted the British in El Alamein in Western Egypt, helped in the hunt for the battleship Bismarck, and provided intelligence from messages between Adolf Hitler and General Günther von Kluge during the campaign in France. In this case, patience paid off far more for the Allies than revealing their capability and knowledge of the first "offense" would have.

Faults and Consequences

The following story of a wrongly accused victim demonstrates how facts can be misrepresented and how undeserved distrust can be devastating. At the start of the "Russian mole" investigation that ultimately led to the arrest and prosecution of Robert Hanssen, a 28-year-old CIA employee was escorted into an unexpected meeting where she was told:

> *"Please sit down, we have some bad news for you… your father is a spy. He's working for the Russians."*

At the same time, her father, who had been an agency veteran for nearly 20 years, was being accused of espionage. These accusations led to the CIA officer being suspended for 21 months and to unrecoverable embarrassment. The FBI agents interrogated the accused officer's children, sisters, coworkers, and friends. The agent warned one of the sisters that if she did not cooperate, the FBI would go to the nursing home and question her 84-year-old mother. The allegations of spying against this officer were prompted by a suspect jogging map, and the unfortunate coincidence that he had access to the same information and lived on the same street as the real spy, Robert Hanssen.

John Moustakes, the lawyer for the wrongly accused CIA officer, wrote the following in a letter to the then FBI director Louis Freeh, requesting a formal apology:

"The corrosive effects of the FBI's wrongful and indiscriminate accusations are incalculable and pervasive... The investigation has been emotionally devastating to both him and his family... To cause my client to live one more day than necessary as the suspect in the nation's most damaging espionage case was reprehensible. But to delay longer still the exoneration to which he is manifestly entitled is unforgivable... This experience left indelible personal scars that will never fully heal and a cloud that will continue to mar his impressive career unless it is explicitly dispelled. Under the circumstances, our request is at the very low end of what fairness and decency require."

Frustrated by their lack of willingness to publicly apologize, the accused officer spoke out in a telephone interview with the *Courant*

"They had gotten it so wrong, for so long. They drove at me to the exclusion of all others. Some of the people there got medals for this investigation, for God's sake."

This is a real-life example of how information can be easily misinterpreted and false accusations can be made that hurt otherwise innocent and uninvolved people.

Are the consequences of being caught spying worse than the activities you are trying to catch your spouse or child doing? In some cases they are. Take a perfectly healthy relationship as an example. Pressure and stress at work can cause many of the same characteristics that "how to tell if your spouse is cheating on you" Web sites claim are sure-fire signals. Acting on these accidental signals with spying can cause more harm than good.

Imagine that a husband is putting in some extra hours at work because he has heard that holiday layoffs are right around the corner. He does not want to draw attention to the situation because his wife is pregnant and has recently quit her job. He is suddenly under tremendous stress trying to (1) ensure that he does not lose his job, (2) develop a suitable plan in case he does, and (3) cope with the sudden increased pressure of being the sole provider for an entire family.

Due to these circumstances, his behavior may closely resemble an affair: working late nights, being withdrawn, dressing "nicer" (job interviews), and participating in secret phone conversations about his situation to friends and potential employers. His pregnant wife is likely to be self-conscious because of her physical condition and the lack of "closeness" with her husband due to his recent stress. Because of this, she may be more apt to jump to conclusions and assume that he is cheating on her because she is pregnant. Furthermore, she may choose to back up this gut feeling by using monitoring software. If she does and her husband finds out, it could mean the end of their relationship before their first child is even born.

In the wife's eyes she was the victim, and many companies that sell monitoring software push sales with comments such as, "He started the affair and broke all trust. Monitoring will only prove his guilt!" However, the husband was innocent. Instead, he was the victim of his wife breaking the trust within the relationship. Spying has consequences and breaking trust in relationships is just one of them.

Spying on your children can also have unintended consequences and can provide a mixture of results. Once the decision to spy has occurred, there are only a couple of possible outcomes: the spying produced results that confirm the suspicions, or the suspicions were found to be untrue. Both parties can either continue the relationship, or intervention may be required.

There is another outcome that provides much more in the way of long-term consequences. If a parent is caught spying on their child, their relationship may change for the worse. The child, who expects some monitoring of their actions by their parents, will feel that their privacy has been violated. Many will feel that if their parents are going to treat them like a criminal, they might as well be one. Getting caught spying may cause the child to withdraw further from the parents.

The consequences of spying cannot be determined before the actions are begun. The possible consequences should be thought of and then a determination made as to whether the worst consequence is better than not spying at all. Different people will take being spied on in different ways; however, every relationship will change forever once spying occurs. Whether it changes for the positive or the negative will depend on the existing relationship and the results of the spying. In order to successfully spy on a person, you must be willing to sacrifice the existing relationship.

Liability

We are not lawyers and the legal aspect of spying is not a black and white subject. What is legal for video capture is not legal for audio capture. While keystroke capturing may be legal against your children, in many instances it is not legal against your spouse. Files and e-mails located on the hard drive of your computer may be read, but the privacy of those stored remotely elsewhere may be protected. Before you do anything, you should familiarize yourself with all state and federal laws associated with the surveillance and monitoring of others. If in doubt, consult a lawyer for expert advice.

On the topic of legal allowance and liability, three different situations must be addressed: the monitoring of keystrokes, the capturing and viewing of files and/or e-mail, and the capturing and monitoring of voice and video.

First, a Word About Companies

Federal law is aimed more at protecting employers while state law protects employees. The Electronic Communications Privacy Act (ECPA) allows a company to monitor an employee's e-mail if one of the following requirements is met:

- One of the parties has given consent.
- There is a legitimate business reason.
- The company needs to protect itself.

To better protect employees, legislators proposed the Notice of Electronic Monitoring Act in July 2000. This act was intended to require employers to notify all new employees that e-mail was subject to monitoring, and enforce an annual notification of the same declaration. This act has not been passed, but written policies established by companies that provide this type of notice can help prevent litigation related to privacy claims.

Monitoring of Keystrokes

On the surface, the legality of installing a keylogger and collecting keystrokes seems cut and dry. Most law clearly indicates that it is legal if the computer is owned by you, or if the owner provides consent to being monitored. So, what exactly does "owned by you" mean?

It means that if you run a company, and an employee is using a computer that was purchased by the company, you can create a policy that allows you to monitor their activities on it. Likewise, as a parent, you are assumed to "own" the computer that your child uses and you can therefore legally install monitoring software. Where it gets touchy is when you want to monitor your spouse. If you are the owner of the computer, it may be legal, but if your spouse is the owner, their privacy may be protected.

Capturing and Viewing Files and/or E-mail

Similar to keystroke capturing, the prime factor in the legality of file and e-mail monitoring is the ownership of the computer. As briefly discussed previously in this chapter, there is a difference between e-mail that is in transmission versus e-mail that is stored. Federal wiretapping law states that e-mail being actively transmitted (i.e., across a wire) is protected against the wiretapping law. However, when e-mail passes across computers it is temporarily (or permanently if it is the end user) stored. A number of court cases have ruled that this temporarily stored copy of the e-mail may be monitored. For example, in the United States v. Mark L. Simmons, the court ruled that the monitoring of personal e-mail at work did not violate any federal wiretapping laws. This ruling was because the e-mail was viewed from a storage device and not as it was being transmitted.

Transmitted e-mail is a different case. Most cases have permitted it if there is a proper policy in place. For example, in Bourke v. Nissan, the court ruled in favor of Nissan who fired two employees for sending sexually explicit e-mails back and forth. In Smyth v. Pillsbury Company, an employee was fired for sending threatening e-mail that included comments such as "kill the backstabbing bastards" and references to the holiday party as the "Jim Jones Kool-Aid affair." This employee sued on the grounds that his personal privacy was violated, but lost. In the city of Scottsdale, a police department learned the hard way that even though monitoring was allowed, actions they took based on the monitoring were excessive. An officer that had just been promoted sent an e-mail to a female co-worker asking if she would sleep with him now that he had been promoted. The recipient was a good friend and took the e-mail as a joke, but the department removed his name from the promotion list and eventually fired him over the event. The officer sued and was awarded $300,000.00 in damages. The award was based on the action of removing him from the promotion list and eventual firing and had nothing to do with the actual monitoring of the e-mail. However, it serves as a lesson to be cautions of actions taken based on potentially misinterpreted information that is collected through monitoring.

When applied to your spouse, if e-mail is stored locally on a hard drive that is accessible to the family, then you can access it. If your spouse instead uses a Web-based e-mail account that is password protected, you may have legal issues with accessing it (even if you know the user name and password).

Voice and Video Capturing

It is legal in all 50 states to record video with a hidden camera in your home. Audio, however, is a different story. It is against the law to record speech without consent from both parties in California, Connecticut, Delaware, Florida, Hawaii, Illinois, Louisiana, Maryland, Massachusetts, Montana, Nevada, New Hampshire, Oregon, Pennsylvania, and Washington. This means that if you live in these states, cameras are okay as long as you disable the microphone on them.

To prevent against litigation, many experts recommend that in cases such as "nanny-cams" you obtain written permission from the nanny prior to recording.

Note that this changes the monitoring from covert to active, which means that it is intended to be more of a deterrent than an evidence "catcher." In the case of potential child abuse, however, active is what you want. Merely capturing the act afterward assists the parents in pressing charges against the nanny, but it does not stop the child from being abused.

Case Study: Dangers of Misinterpretation and Distrust

Interpreting a situation wrongly can be as dangerous (if not more) than leaving the event to its natural course. One of the biggest risks is that you reveal your hand and toss unscrupulous accusations against an innocent family member. By doing this, you damage their trust in you, their feelings of personal privacy, and their self-image because you demonstrate that you "expect" them to do that type of behavior. When such behavior is against a spouse it is hurtful, but when it is against an impressionable young child it may be irreversible, as demonstrated in the following case study.

Elaboration

Jeremy was a quiet and independent 15-year-old who lived with his parents and younger sister, Emily, on the outskirts of New York City. His family was always close and loving. This past fall, Jeremy's sister enrolled in kindergarten and his mother returned to the work force. Trained originally as a nurse, she accepted a job with the local hospital. Because she just recently started, she was only offered a position working evening hours. She hesitantly accepted because the family needed the money; college was right around the corner for Jeremy.

Working evening hours took a toll on everyone. The family was used to the mother being around and taking care of the daily problems. Likewise, the mother felt less involved with everyone's lives. There were no more "family" dinners around the table, and the children were responsible for ensuring that their homework was completed and baths were taken every night on their own.

Jeremy's father helped as needed, but in the past most of this was done by his wife so it was a difficult role for him to jump right into. Thankfully they found an energetic babysitter in the neighborhood named Amy to help fill in the gaps. Both Jeremy and Emily adored Amy, and she helped them with homework and listened to their daily problems.

Although Jeremy's father honored the relationship with his wife, the mother could not help but feel a little jealousy between herself and Amy. She felt as if her lines of communication between her children and her husband were limited to a few brief moments in the afternoon before she headed off to work. She kept promising herself that soon she would be promoted and transferred to a daytime position.

Six months went by and before she knew it, it was winter already. In this short period of time she had really started to lose touch with her family, mainly Jeremy who was in the height of his "teenage" years. One Saturday afternoon, she was gathering Jeremy's laundry and came across a small bag of pills in his room. Immediately her head began spinning. Being a nurse and a mother, she knew the dangers of drugs and feared seeing Jeremy arrive in the Emergency Room from an overdose.

Suddenly, all of the events over the past several months began making sense. Jeremy had been more withdrawn and quiet than usual, he had not been hanging around his old friends as much, and his grades in school had been dropping. She brought the bag to her husband, who was equally surprised and concerned. Never having been faced with this type of challenge before, they had a difficult time deciding how to handle it. They knew as quiet as Jeremy was, confronting him directly would be painful.

They were correct. As soon as Jeremy returned home from spending the day with one of his new friends, they asked him how involved he was with drugs, and who got him involved. He became upset and insisted that his parents were wrongly accusing him. They had anticipated this type of reaction and stood firm in insisting that he talk with them. Jeremy became frustrated, refused, and retreated to his room. Suddenly, all lines of communication between Jeremy and his parents were cut. He would not talk to them, and they were so angry that all they could do was yell and insist that he admit his guilt. This went on for a week, and his parents decided to take action to find out what was going on. Like many teenagers, Jeremy spent a good deal of his time at home on the computer chatting with friends on AOL's Instant Messenger (IM). Jeremy's father was a software developer and was very knowledgeable about computers. He decided to install some monitoring software on Jeremy's computer. In addition, because most of Jeremy's time was spent in his room with the door closed, they decided to install a camera in there to record what he was doing. They openly told Jeremy that he was being monitored. This angered Jeremy more and caused him to push away from his family even further, and spend more time away.

After one week, the monitoring recorded something noteworthy. The babysitter, Amy, who was unaware of the camera, entered Jeremy's room in the evening while the father was gone and Emily was having dinner. Both parents watched as they observed her removing drugs from her purse and taking them. Suddenly, they felt terrible. They realized that Jeremy was indeed telling the truth when he proclaimed his innocence and that the drugs never did belong to him. Instead of solving a problem with the confrontation and monitoring, they had created one. They managed to drive Jeremy away from them and surround him with feelings that his own family distrusted him.

Analysis

The combination of the mother's insecurity of not being home, and the misinterpretation of what was found led the parents to jump to conclusions. They assumed the worst and visibly displayed their distrust of Jeremy. Furthermore, rather than giving him the benefit of the doubt in their minds, they had already decided that he was guilty based on what they observed. This caused them to further demonstrate their distrust for him by installing active monitoring capabilities. This humiliated and alienated Jeremy. In his case, he was an innocent victim that never committed any "forbidden" behavior, yet he was treated as if he had. The damage to his relationship with his parents was just as bad as if the drugs had indeed belonged to him.

You expect your family to be your strongest supporters. Monitoring suggests distrust, and without a valid cause can cause more problems than solve them.

Summary

This chapter explored the purpose and use of different types of spying, addressed the consequences of each, and touched on legal aspects associated with monitoring. The following are ten key points that we want you to walk away with after reading this:

☑ There are two types of spying: active monitoring in which you declare your intentions and covert spying in which you secretly watch someone.

☑ Active monitoring can be a useful deterrent for children and in the work environment, but it is not recommended in husband/wife relationships, which should operate more like a partnership.

☑ Active monitoring can cause feelings of distrust and resentment against the observer by those being watched.

☑ Those being actively monitored that are determined to commit the action will likely evolve to adopt sneakier methods outside of the view of the observer.

☑ Covert spying is similar to the tactics used by intelligence organizations and is used to "catch" someone in the act of an undesirable behavior rather than prevent it from occurring.

☑ Covert spying can be helpful to "prove" or gather evidence against problems such as drug use, underage sex, and adultery when they are already highly suspected to exist.

☑ Both covert and overt spying can lead to misinterpretations of evidence and wrongly accused victims.

☑ Ill-founded accusations and feelings of mistrust can be more damaging to a relationship than the act that the spying was intended to expose.

☑ Parents can use monitoring software to help protect their children from online abuse.

☑ An employer can install spy software on computers they own as long as they have the necessary policies in place that declare this loss of privacy.

## Chapter 3

Technology Overview: Computer Basics

"If you know the enemy and know yourself, you need not fear the result of a hundred battles."
—Sun Tzu, *The Art of War*

Topics in this Chapter

- Hardware

- Software

- Summary

Introduction

Would you try to assemble a complex device without the instruction book, or work on a car without knowing where all the parts are? Most people wouldn't consider embarking on a difficult task without having at least some idea of what they are doing. Because this book covers the sometimes daunting task of using your computer as a spying tool, this and the next chapter provide a crash course on computer and network technology.

Before you can begin to use your computer for spying, you must have a basic understanding of how it works. Don't expect to become a computer guru overnight. Home PCs are very complicated machines and becoming even more so; however, the basics have not changed much since IBM introduced its first PC back in the 1980s. An introductory level of understanding is all that is needed to get you through the concepts taught in this book.

To provide the best description of what computers are and how they work, this chapter is broken into two parts: *hardware* and *software*. The hardware section covers the physical computer itself, including all of its connections and parts. Some spying done at the hardware level may require connecting new pieces of hardware to a computer. Some techniques involve studying a computer for evidence, which requires you to be able to physically disassemble and reassemble it. For these reasons, it is important to understand the basics of how things work together.

Software is the collective name for programs that run on a computer. The first and most fundamental piece of software everyone encounters is the operating system (OS). In most cases, the OS is a variant of Microsoft Windows. Next is a class of software known as *device drivers*. Device drivers can be thought of as a cross between the OS and the user applications; they plug into the OS and allow it to use different pieces of hardware.

The last category of software is referred to as *user applications*, or *programs*. Most of the software discussed in this book falls under this category. Internet Explorer, Notepad, and Solitaire are all examples of user applications.

A working knowledge of and familiarity with computer hardware and software can prepare you for using it as a spy device. Only by really understanding what everything does can you truly and safely exploit it. Having a big picture of how software and hardware work and interact will allow you to determine the appropriate location and technique for spying with your computer.

Hardware

Hardware is the first part of a computer a person encounters. Hardware can be broken into two main sections: *interface components* and *non-interface components*. Interface components are the parts used to interact with the computer, including but not limited to keyboards, mice, trackballs, printers, monitors, scanners, speakers, Webcams, and microphones. Non-interface components are the "brains" or guts of the computer. They are usually housed in the case and consist of the motherboard, the central processing unit (CPU), the memory, the hard drive, the sound, the video, and the network cards. There is also a special class of hardware referred to as *connectors*, the methods by which the interface devices are connected either to each other or to non-interface devices. Examples of connector types are Universal Serial Bus (USB), serial cable, network cable, and firewire.

Non-interface Components

Non-interface components are the parts of the computer that make up its working body and that are not involved in interacting with users. Most computer parts are non-interface components, and they range from the computer's CPU and memory, to its case and disk drives. Although you may never have to deal with CPUs and memory, you will probably use disk drives, optical drives, and other types of media. Understanding the non-interface components will give you the big picture of how a computer is put together and how it works.

Cases

Most non-interface components are housed in the computer's case. Cases for computers range in size and shape. Desktop cases were once popular, but are now being replaced by tower-style cases. There are other unusual cases as well, such as the Mini-ATX. Figure 3.1 shows some popular models.

Figure 3.1 Common PC Cases

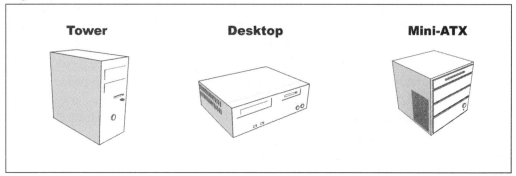

CPUs

The CPU is the "brain" of a computer, the core component. For example, when someone refers to his or her computer as a "2.4-gigahertz Pentium IV," he or she is is actually referring to the CPU. People use CPU as both a measure and a description of their computer.

In the PC market there are two primary CPU vendors: Applied Micro Devices (AMD) and Intel. Intel was the original developer of the 80x86 microprocessors, the distant ancestor of all current CPUs. AMD, which started out developing popular and generally lower cost clone microprocessors, has begun to introduce many innovative designs of its own. For the most part, and for the scope of this book, the processor involved does not matter; the software will run on either kind of processor.

Tips and Tricks…

Clearing Up the Terminology

When mentioning PCs we are referring to IBM-compatible machines. Although they are functionally personal computers, machines by Apple are not covered in this book. Apple produces a line of computers called Macintosh, or "Macs." Some of their popular models include the IMac, the PowerMac, the IBook, and the PowerBook. These computers run on an entirely different line of processors that are built by Motorola. Macs are very powerful and easy to use, but they do not have the market penetration of Intel- or AMD-based machines running Windows. Most techniques described in this book are geared toward Intel/AMD-based PCs and will not work on Macs.

The CPU performs most of the processing that occurs on a computer. A CPU's speed is measured in gigahertz (GHz), which refers to one billion cycles per second. On a historical note, at one time most CPU speeds were measured in megahertz, meaning one million cycles per second. Now, however, most CPU speeds are 1 GHz or greater. As you might expect, faster CPUs perform better than slower ones.

CPUs may also have onboard memory called "cache," which helps them to quickly access frequently needed data. The types of cache are named depending on their distance from the CPU. The L1 case is closest to the CPU and is the cache that can be accessed most quickly. The L2 cache is slightly farther away, but can still be accessed relatively quickly.

Main Memory

Main memory is often referred to simply "as memory." Here, we maintain the distinction of "main memory" to differentiate it from the memory on video cards or other devices. Usually, when people refer to having 512MB of memory, they are referring to main memory. The main memory is the memory a computer uses to load programs and perform other functions related to processing data and communicating with hardware devices. This type of memory is usually composed of random access memory (RAM), meaning that any section can be accessed independently. Another characteristic of RAM is that the data is only stored there for as long as the memory is powered up. For example, when a computer is shut down and the memory loses power, all of the data stored there is lost unless it has been saved to some type of permanent storage such as a hard drive. It is best to make sure that any data you want is saved before you turn off the computer's power. On the flipside, if someone is discovered unexpectedly while using his or her computer, he or she can hide incriminating data by quickly turning off the machine's power. Understanding the difference between what is in main memory and what is not is important when spying and is discussed in more depth later in this book.

Hard Drives

Hard disks, also known as hard drives, are the closets of the computer world; no matter how big the hard drive is, it is never big enough. These devices are used for the permanent storage of programs and data. Unlike RAM, hard disks maintain the information stored on them, even when the computer is powered off. Anything written to a hard disk can be viewed at a later date. Items that are deleted from hard disks can also be recovered given enough time and technology. Hard disks can usually be taken from one computer and read by another relatively easily. Many interesting spying techniques have arisen around exploiting hard disks and their unique properties. Although most hard drives reside inside the computer case, there are external hard drives that connect via USB or firewire. These portable hard drives are popular and are frequently used to hide data. Figure 3.2 shows a typical internal hard drive and the cables used to connect it to a computer.

Figure 3.2 An Internal Hard Drive and ATA Cable for Connecting It to the Motherboard of the PC

It is not uncommon for people to get their hard drive size and amount of main memory mixed up. Both are measured in the same units (kilobytes, megabytes, gigabytes, and so on). When looking at specifications for a computer, the hard drive is almost always an order of magnitude larger than the main memory. Current standards include 256 MB to 1 gigabyte (GB) of memory and 30 to 200 GB of hard drive space.

Tips and Tricks...

Measuring Storage

Main memory and hard drives both use the same units of measurement when describing their size because computers work on bits (1s and 0s) of information. Large amounts of bits are grouped into logical units of storage.

- A bit is a 1 or a 0.
- A byte is a collection of 8 bits (e.g., 0110011).
- A kilobyte (KB) is a collection of 1,024 bytes.
- A megabyte (MB) is a collection of 1,024 KB.
- A gigabyte (GB) is 1,024 MB.

You may find it unusual that a KB is 1,024 and not 1,000 bytes (after all a kilogram is 1,000 grams). Because computers have only two fundamental values, 1 and 0, everything is calculated in powers of 2, which is why a byte is 8 bits and a KB and larger are multiples of 1,024.

- To calculate 8 bits use $2^3 = 8$
- To get the measurement for KB, MB, and GB use $2^{10} = 1,024$

Video Cards

Video cards are the devices used by the computer to generate the images you see on your monitor. Over the last few years they have become increasingly complex and powerful. Modern video cards now boast their own microprocessors and large amounts of memory. Some modern video cards can even support multiple monitors. Several clever hackers and programmers have developed stand-alone programs that are run completely on modern video cards. While there is a possibility that future video cards will have some spying potential, they are not important for the scope of this book.

Sound Cards

Sound cards are used to produce the sound effects that software applications generate. At one time, sound cards produced poor quality sound. Modern cards are capable of producing very high quality surround sound to support multimedia and the latest games. These cards usually have connectors for speakers, a line out for additional speakers, and a microphone. In addition, some of the higher end sound cards have fiber-optic connectors for high-end digital receivers. Sound cards are an interesting, essential part of the computing experience, but there are very few spying techniques that exploit them.

Modems

Modems are devices used for computer networking. They allow computers to communicate using standard telephone lines. They convert computer data into analog signals that can be transmitted on the phone lines, received by remote computers, and converted back into digital data. Modems can be internal or external to the computer case. Most modems are internal to the case, although external modems are still available. Although similar sounding, cable modems are a completely different technology and not related to traditional phone modems.

Network Cards

Network cards are also used for computer communication. They use network cables, such as Category 5 (Cat-5), Category 6 (Cat-6), fiber optic, or Ethernet, for communication. They offer a speed increase of 10 to 1,000 over traditional modems. Network cards can be used to connect two computers or a small group of computers, or to connect a computer to a broadband adapter (cable or Digital Subscriber Line [DSL] modem).

Motherboards

A motherboard is the hardware that ties everything together: the CPU, the main memory, the video card, the network card, the sound card, and so on. It also usually has connectors for the hard drives, the compact disc (CD), and the digital versatile disk (DVD) drives as well as most of the external connectors. Many modern motherboards have sound cards, video cards, and network cards integrated into them.

Optical Drives

Optical drives are the means by which a computer can read a CD or a DVD. They are a popular means of distributing software because they can hold vast amounts of data. Optical drives are also used to play CDs and DVDs. Special versions of these drives, such as CD-R/RW or DVD+-R/RW, allow users to write (or burn as it's commonly called) data to blank CD and DVD media to create their own custom CDs and DVDs. Figure 3.3 shows a standard CD-RW drive.

Figure 3.3 An Internal Optical Drive

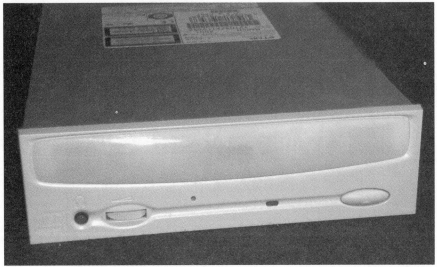

Different optical media have different storage sizes. CDs can hold between 650 and 700 MB of data. Once, this was enough for most programs; entire hard drives could be backed up to them. This storage has been eclipsed by DVDs, which can hold between 4 and 9 GB of data. Even this impressive number looks small when stacked up against the gargantuan storage capacity (160 to 350 GB) of most modern hard drives.

Floppy Drives

A floppy drive is a legacy device that was once used for backup and to transfer data between machines. Many modern computers still come with floppy drives. In the past, software applications came loaded onto floppy drives, and they were also used for data transfer and to make emergency boot disks. Now, they are used mostly for emergency boot disks. Floppy drives hold only 1.44 MB of data at best. Their capacity is almost useless because modern applications and even data take up much more space. A digital picture taken with a medium- to high-quality camera takes up between 1 and 2 MB, almost too big for a floppy. New technologies such as USB drives and cheap blank digital media have rendered the floppy drive all but obsolete. Figure 3.4 shows a traditional internal floppy drive.

Figure 3.4 A 3.5″ Floppy Drive

USB Drives

USB drives are the modern replacement for floppy drives. They are small devices, about the size of a key chain, that hold between 64 and 512 MB of data. They are smaller, much faster, and in many ways more durable than floppy drives. When hooked up to a computer through the USB interface, a USB drive can be used just like an additional hard drive. A small 256-MB USB drive is pictured in Figure 3.5).

USB drives are very useful. Their low cost, small size, high-storage capacities, and almost universal compatibility make them excellent spying tools. You can plug one into almost any modern computer, and it will be instantly recognized. If you plan on taking files from a computer, or will be attacking a computer you have only limited access to, we strongly recommend that you purchase one. A USB drive will allow you to quickly and covertly take copies of files from a targeted computer, which can then be viewed by you elsewhere at your leisure.

Figure 3.5. A Portable USB Drive

Memory Cards

These small media are possible floppy replacements that are popular in digital cameras, portable media players, personal digital assistants (PDAs), and other devices. There are several different types of memory cards available, with some of the most popular being smart media, compact flash, memory sticks, and secure digital (SD) media. Memory cards can hold between 8 MB and 1 GB of data and are useful for transferring data and storing it in small, easily concealable devices. Figure 3.6 shows some examples of popular memory cards.

Figure 3.6 Several Popular Memory Cards: Smart Media, Sony Memory Stick, Compact Flash, and SD Memory

Table 3.1 summarizes the various components discussed and their use in spying.

Table 3.1 Summary of Non-interface Hardware Components

Hardware	Useful for Spying	Not Useful for Spying
CPU		X
Main Memory		X
Hard Drive	X	
Video Card		X
Sound Card		X
Modems	X	
Network Cards	X	
Motherboards		X
Optical Drives	X	
Floppy Drives	X (but not likely)	
USB Drives	X	
Memory Cards	X	

Connectors

Connectors are the means by which the interface and non-interface components communicate. Next to interface components, these are the parts of a computer that you deal with the most. It is important to have a good working knowledge of connectors because they will play several roles in your spying game.

PS/2

A PS/2 is a small circular connector that is commonly used to connect keyboards and mice to the computer. On most computers, they are color-coded, with the keyboard connector shaded purple and the mouse shaded green. In the future, this is the location where we will apply hardware keystroke loggers. Figure 3.7 shows typical PS/2 ports. Next to each port is an icon representing the device that should be plugged in there.

Figure 3.7 PS/2 Ports for Keyboard and Mouse Connectivity

USB

The USB is one of the most popular standards for connecting peripherals to computers. This type of connection is plug-and-play, meaning that devices connected to the USB "announce" their presence to the computer so that it can configure them without any interaction from anyone. Before plug-and-play became widely accepted, installing peripheral devices was a much more difficult and manual process. Now, most USB devices are automatically configured. There are two standards of USB, 1.1 and 2.0, with 2.0 being faster and offering some other minor advantages. For all intents and purposes, it won't matter which version of USB you are dealing with unless you need a high speed and high bandwidth device. USB is now used for connecting everything from printers, to scanners, keyboards, mice, digital cameras, Webcams, and so on. In addition, there are also devices called USB hubs that are small boxes with several USB ports on them. Some modern monitors have USB hubs built into them. Most USB ports can be recognized by the common USB symbol, as shown in Figure 3.8.

Figure 3.8 Symbol for USB Connectivity and Some USB Ports

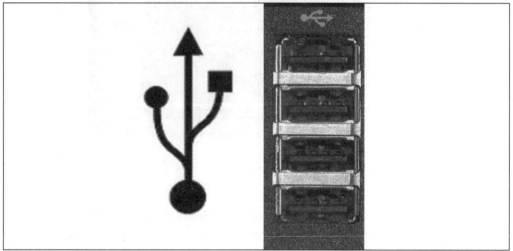

Firewire

Firewire also goes by the names Institute of Electrical and Electronic Engineers (IEEE) 394 and Ilink (used by Sony). It is very similar to USB in that it supports plug-and-play, and devices plugged into a firewire port "announce" themselves to the computer (Figure 3.9). There are two types of common firewire ports: a small non-powered one and a larger one that can be used to power external devices. Most laptops have the smaller one, and firewire-enabled desktops have both. Firewire offers a faster connection and more bandwidth than USB. As a result, firewire ports are commonly used for connecting devices that transfer large amounts of data such as digital video cameras and other video devices, external hard drives, and the Apple iPod.

Figure 3.9 Firewire Symbol and Connectors

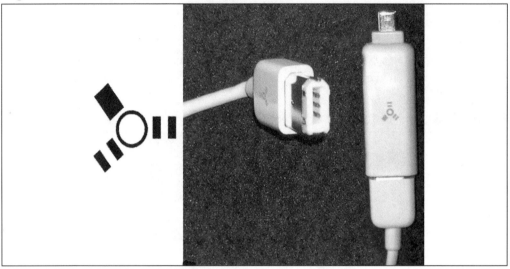

Modem and Network Ports

Modem and network ports are used for connecting modems and network cards to networks either directly via network cable or through phone lines. While they appear similar, and phone cable will fit in either connector, they are actually very different and won't work with the wrong cable or in the wrong connector. Most computers label the modem and network ports with the diagrams shown in Figure 3.10.

Figure 3.10 Modem vs Network Port Labels

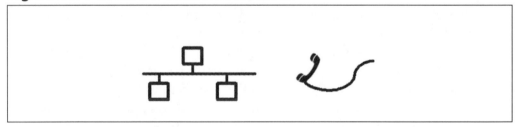

If the port isn't clearly labeled, look into it and find the small wires. A modem will have two or four wires, and a network port will have eight. Figure 3.11 shows a closeup of network and modem ports.

Figure 3.11 Modems vs. Network Ports

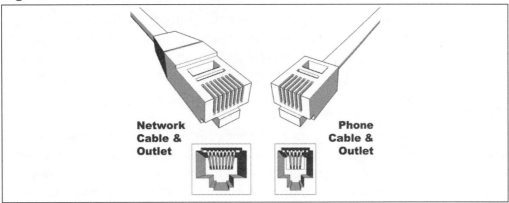

Serial and Parallel Ports

Serial and parallel ports are rarely used on modern computers. Yet most computers still include them. Prior to USB, most printers used the parallel port to communicate with the machine and the mouse, external modems, and some early Webcams used a serial port. Figure 3.12 shows one parallel and two serial ports.

Figure 3.12 Parallel and Serial Ports

Interface Components

Interface components are the parts of the computer you will be dealing with the most. It is likely that you are already familiar with most interface components. What you may not know is how they can be subverted for spying purposes. Following are reviews of the most popular ones and a description of their spy potential, if any.

Monitors

The monitor is the primary output device for a computer, and probably what you interface with the most. Advanced techniques allow people to reconstruct an image from a monitor from the electromagnetic waves it emanates. Since this technology is very expensive and difficult, it is only mentioned for completeness and will not be further discussed in the book.

Keyboards

The keyboard is perhaps the most important interface component of a computer. Almost everything a user enters passes through the keyboard. This will become a point of interest in future chapters. Keyboards can be connected to a machine in one of three ways: a USB connection either directly to the machine or through a USB hub, a PS2 (most common) connection directly to the machine, or the outdated AT interface (very rare). Figure 3.13 shows the three types of connectors. It is important to know which method of connection you should use in your specific case, because it may come into play when selecting hardware-based spying devices for keyboards.

Figure 3.13 Three Types of Keyboard Connectors: AT, PS2, and USB

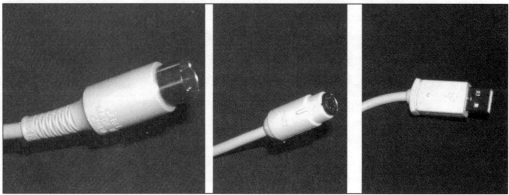

Mice

Another important input device is the mouse. Most mice connect to the computer either through a PS2 or USB connector. Unfortunately, even though the mouse is used a lot, its design does not make it easy to subvert and spy with.

Microphone

Like traditional microphones, a PC microphone is used to capture sound and send it to the computer. They are used for different games, Internet Protocol (IP) telephony, and many chat programs. It is also not uncommon to use one in conjunction with a Webcam. In some cases, microphones may be remotely activated for use as a listening device. Most microphones connect to a special connector on the sound card. Figure 3.14 shows a couple of PC microphones and highlights the connector they use.

Figure 3.14 PC Microphones (The Inset Highlights the Connector for Interfacing to the Sound Card.)

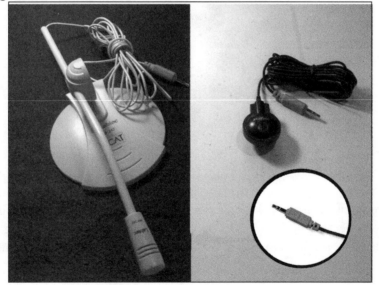

Webcams

Webcams are small cameras that are used to capture video images and then send them to a PC. These devices have increased in popularity due to a drop in price and an increase in the amount of broadband high-speed Internet-wired homes. Webcams are used for videoconferencing, monitoring, and other streaming video uses. Some have built-in microphones that can also be used with a separate microphone. Most

Webcams are attached to the computer via a USB or firewire interface. Some of the more advanced commercial Webcams communicate via the network or through wireless technology. These advanced Webcams are usually self-contained computers that stream the video of a network link to a remote computer. There are several potential spying uses for Webcams when they are combined with microphones. Figure 3.15 shows an example of a Webcam.

Figure 3.15 A Typical Webcam (Notice That It Has a USB Interface.)

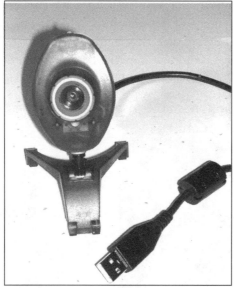

Scanners

Scanners are input devices used to convert printed images into digital images. Before digital cameras became popular, many people used scanners for converting their pictures into digital images. Scanners are usually connected to computers using USB cables.

Printers

As you would expect, printers are used for printing documents. A printer is useful for spying only when someone leaves interesting material sitting on it by accident. Most modern printers connect to a PC with a USB cable, although many still use a parallel port cable.

Laptops

Laptops are machines where all of the components, interface and non–interface, are housed together in one transportable case. They are designed to be more portable than regular computers; they even come with the monitor attached. Laptops are generally more difficult to open up and manipulate than traditional desktop machines. Certain hardware spying devices won't work on laptops. In addition, they sometimes come with extra built-in security features. Most of the software spying techniques we discuss are effective for laptops.

Software

The other half of the computer puzzle is the software, which *programs*, or instructs, the hardware on how to perform the "magic" of the computer. It is the computer code or collection of programs that is executed on the hardware. As previously mentioned, software is broken up into three major categories: the operating system, the programs, and the device drivers.

Operating Systems

The OS is a program or collection of programs used to control and manage the hardware and to run other programs. The OS keeps each individual program from having to learn different hardware specifics. It forms a standard base for all programs, which end up running on a variety of different hardware combinations. When the computer is turned on, the operating system is loaded. After it is loaded, the users can run whatever programs they prefer.

Common Operating Systems

Microsoft makes the operating systems that run on the majority of home computers; they are usually some variation of Microsoft Windows. Like it or hate it, you will probably be dealing with it the most. Nearly all PCs are sold with Windows preinstalled, so you will have little choice in selection and installation. However, it is important to note that Microsoft Windows comes in several varieties with various differences that may affect your capability to spy.

Windows 9x Family

The Windows 9x series consists of Windows 95, Windows 98, and Windows ME (Windows Millennium). Windows 95 (also known as Windows 4.0) was the groundbreaking version of Microsoft Windows that had well-integrated network and multimedia capabilities and could natively run 32-bit programs. Its interface was a dramatic departure from previous Windows and supposedly much easier for people to use. Windows 98 and Window ME were basically upgrades to the Windows 95 platform that offered bug fixes, USB, and other advanced hardware support. Currently, Microsoft no longer supports any of these operating systems, although there are still many computers running them.

Windows NT Family

Windows NT was Microsoft's attempt at the complete development of a server and enterprise OS. When first designed, NT stood for "New Technology." Windows NT's first really famous version was NT 4.0, which debuted in July 1996. NT 4.0 was primarily a server OS but still had the Windows 95 interface. NT 4.0 was incredibly successful and is still supported by Microsoft. Its first successor was Windows 2000, which is now one of the most popular business operating systems in use. The successor to Windows 2000 is Windows 2003. Because most of these operating systems were designed for the business or enterprise environment, it is unlikely that you will encounter any of them.

Windows XP

Windows XP is Microsoft's currently produced and supported desktop OS. It has been in production since December 2001 and is scheduled to be used until 2006. Windows XP is a combination of the 9x and NT families and adds many usability and functionality improvements over previous versions of Windows. There are two different types of Windows XP operating systems: Home and Professional. They are almost identical except that Windows XP Professional has support for multiple processors, remote access, encrypting files systems, group and user policies, and other business-related functionality. Microsoft claims that Windows XP is the most popular desktop OS. For those reasons, in this book we assume that all techniques are being applied against a Windows XP machine. When they do differ, we will point out how they must be changed and whether they can to be applied to Windows NT and 9x machines.

Linux

Linux is a free OS distributed under the GNU public license that was created by Linus Torvalds as a hobby when he was a student at the University of Helsinki in Finland. He started in 1991, and released Version 1.0 of the Linux kernel in 1994. This free OS is available from many different free and commercial vendors, each of which modifies it and updates it to suit its clientele. It runs on the same types of hardware as Microsoft Windows and has become the number two OS for desktop users. Although you may encounter this OS occasionally, most of the techniques for exploiting it are beyond the scope of this book.

MacOS

MacOS Version 10, commonly known as OSX, is another popular desktop OS. It runs on Apple computers including the IMac, the PowerMac, the IBook, and the Powerbook. The theory for exploiting Macs is the same as that for PCs, but most of the hardware and software is completely different. So Macintosh computers are not covered in this book.

Device Drivers

These special pieces of software help the OS communicate with the hardware. They are the only pieces of software that are generally specific to the make and model of the hardware used in the computer. Because drivers are vendor-specific and offer little benefit to spying, they are not addressed in this book.

Application Software

Any other software that is not part of the OS or is not a device driver falls under the "application software" category. Most programs that users run are standard application software, such as Microsoft Word, Internet Explorer (there is some debate on this because it is very tightly integrated into the Windows operating system), and AOL Instant Messenger. Many of the techniques in this book involve installing, removing, and modifying different pieces of application software.

Operating System Concepts

The following concepts are important to know before exploiting a PC. These concepts are universal and generally apply to all of the operating systems listed in the previous section. This does not attempt to be a complete background on OS concepts.

Files

Data is stored on hard disks as blocks of ones and zeros. Computers can access the hard disks and read the data. In order to make sense of the data, the OS organizes it into files. Files are logical collections of data. For example, a Microsoft Word document is a file and so is a grocery list, a database, and a picture. Most of the information you want is stored as a file. Files are arranged in a hierarchical manner. At the top of the hierarchy is the disk drive, which in most Windows machines is the C drive. Disk drives then contain many folders (also known as directories) and files. Each folder is a special file, acting much like a folder in a filing cabinet in that they hold files and other folders. Figure 3.16 illustrates the relationship between disk drives, folders, and files.

Figure 3.16 Relationship between Disk Drives, Folders, and Files on a Computer's Hard Drive

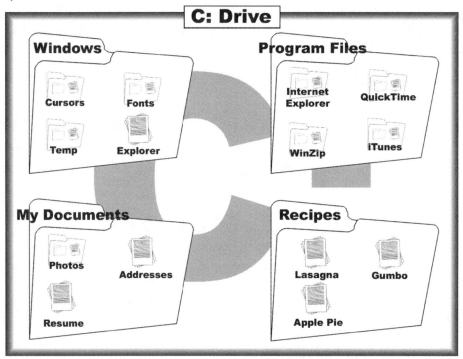

In order to understand the data in most files, you will need an application capable of viewing that file. If a hard disk is considered a filing cabinet, then the computer's files are the contents of the cabinet.

Processes

Whenever a program is run, it becomes a process. A process is an image in memory of a program and different information about it that the OS needs to control the process. In addition to processes that users run, there are also processes that run all the time that have been started by or are part of the OS.

Users

Most modern operating systems are designed to accommodate multiple users, and some allow multiple simultaneous users. Users are the people who use a computer system. They generally have a name and a password. Computers keep track of user's names and passwords and then assign them "property." This property consists of a user's files, lists of the different programs they can run, things they are allowed to do, and lists of the different user's configurations for shared programs. Most systems also a have a "superuser," the primary user who has control over the system. On Linux the superuser is named "root," and on Windows the account is named "Administrator." When spying on a computer it is very important to know which user you are and which you are after, because it will affect what you are allowed to do.

Permissions

Permissions are how an OS determines what users are allowed to do. Permissions can be applied to files and programs to keep users from reading each other's files or changing the permission on files. Superusers generally have permission to change other permissions and run all programs. The permissions and OS security that uses them prevent user "Joe" from reading user "Sue's" files while allowing him to read his own files. However, the "Administrator" is allowed to read both "Joe's" and "Sue's" files. When spying on a computer, it is important to be aware of what permissions you have, and what permissions you will need to get the information you want. Having Administrator access enables you to access the most data (this subject is covered later in Chapter 5).

Summary

This chapter gave an overview of the basic hardware and software of a typical PC. It started by describing interface and non–interface hardware and the different ways they can be connected. Next, it described various operating systems and some of the concepts involved. Different types of software are covered as well as some fundamental OS concepts. This chapter addressed the following key concepts:

- ☑ Hardware is the physical components of the computer.

- ☑ A working knowledge of the different types of interface, non–interface, and connection hardware.

- ☑ Software refers to the programs that run on the hardware.

- ☑ A working knowledge of the difference between an OS, device drivers, and application software.

- ☑ A basic understanding of the OS concepts of files, processes, users, and permissions.

All of the fundamentals covered here are built upon in the following chapters, as we discover the many different ways these basic components of a computer can be subverted for spying. Armed with this knowledge, you can make an educated plan of attack against your target by utilizing your awareness of the environment (the target's PC) that you will be operating in.

## Chapter 4

Network Basics

"There are some mysteries where you don't know the answers, there are others where you don't even know the questions." — Anonymous

Topics in this Chapter:

- **Network Basics**

- **Network Traffic**

- **Summary**

Introduction

The miniaturization and versatility of computers have allowed them to pervade everyday life. While amazing on their own, one of the most powerful things about computers is their ability to link together to make a more capable entity. One positive effect of the Internet revolution is the continuing expansion of the Internet to home users. A few years ago, very few people were connected to the Internet. Now, most people wouldn't dream of not being connected to it. The quality of Internet connections has also increased. According to *www.nwfusion.com*, in July 2004, there were 63 million broadband users and 61.3 million dial-up users.

This dependence on the Internet will play very strongly into how you plan to spy on someone. Once the decision has been made to spy on a loved one, a certain amount of prerequisite knowledge is required to proceed in an intelligent manner. This chapter presents information that will enable you to understand how your computer connects and communicates with other computers via the Internet. Typical setups for home networks and their components are also discussed. This chapter also explains the different types of traffic that computers use to communicate. Finally, it discusses some of the popular Internet-enabled applications that are used. This chapter completes the basic knowledge that you will need throughout the rest of the book.

Network Basics

A computer network is a collection of computers set up in a manner that allows them to communicate with each other. Imagine that each computer is a house and a neighborhood is like a local area network (LAN). Next, bring in a powerful and universal communication system such as mail. With mail, any house in the world can communicate with any other house regardless of distance. Communication is also the basis of a network; if computers can't pass information between each other, there is no network. The following sections explain several fundamental concepts that enable networks to be formed.

IP Address

Every house has an address; when sending a letter between houses, the envelope is marked with the destination and sending address. Likewise, when two computers communicate, they are identified by their Internet Protocol (IP) address. Every computer connected to the Internet via dial-up or broadband is assigned an IP address in the format *x.x.x.x*, where "*x*" is any number between 0 and 255 (e.g., 10.1.1.33).

Computers in a specific network usually have the same first set of numbers, which is analogous to every house in a neighborhood having the same zip code.

Most IP addresses are public and Internet routable, meaning that if you know the IP address of a machine, you can send data directly to it. There is also a special class of IP addresses called *private* or *non-routable* that are usually in the form 10.*x.x.x* and 192.168.*x.x*. The actual ranges are:

- 10.0.0.0 to 10.255.255.255

- 172.16.0.0 to 172.31.255.255

- 192.168.0.0 to 192.168.255.255

- 169.254.0.0 to 169.254.255.255

These private IP addresses are usually used for small networks and LANs that are either not connected or have only one or two points of connection to the Internet. Machines that have private IP addresses cannot have packets sent directly to them from other computers on the Internet. This is an important distinction to understand, as the type of address your target machine has may affect how you spy on it. Most computers connected directly to a cable or Digital Subscriber Line (DSL) modem or that use dial-up accounts, have a public IP address. In contrast, most computers connected to a broadband router have private IP addresses.

Explore More...

Network Address Translation

When a machine has a non-routable internal IP address, it must connect to another computer in order to access the Internet. This other machine performs Network Address Translation (NAT) so that the internal computer can communicate with the outside world. In many home networks, the router that is connected to the cable modem or DSL performs this task. Routers that are used for NAT have two IP addresses: a public routable address for communicating with other machines on the Internet and a private routable address for communicating with machines on its local private network. The router takes all of the packets destined for the outside network and replaces the sender's IP address with its own routable IP address. If the router does not replace the IP address, the packet will be dropped at the next machine it reaches. The router keeps track of the traffic and when packets are returned from the outside network, the router rewrites the destination address to the address of the internal computer that ini-

Continued

tiated the connection. Thus, NAT allows many computers on an internal network to share a single routable IP address. This is how an entire family can share cable modem connectivity simultaneously, and how businesses can share a small range of IP addresses for their entire business network.

Ports

Computers can run many different applications at the same time. People can sit at home and simultaneously check their e-mail, browse the Web, and instant message. Computers use ports to determine which application they are communicating with. There is a reserved port for most of the common Internet applications. For example, web uses port 80, and e-mail traditionally uses port 25. A port refers to a number that a computer connects to when it accesses a specific application or service. A port ranges in value from 0 through 65,535. A port and an IP address together is the fully qualified information that a computer needs to connect to another computer. Therefore, a port can be thought of as an extension of the IP address. For example, in IP address 192.168.100.1:2323, ":2323" refers to the port. Once data has reached an IP address, a port helps it to reach the appropriate program. A simple analogy is of a large apartment building. Each apartment shares the same street address, but is differentiated by the apartment number. Ports are like the apartment numbers: all of the communication is sent to the computer, which sorts the traffic by port, much like the mailman who puts all of the mail into separate mailboxes.

It would be difficult to determine what traffic goes with what program if every application ran on the same port. Likewise, if standards were not set to distinguish which traffic should use which port, it would be difficult for two computers to communicate. To facilitate ease of use, ports 1 through 1,024 are reserved and standardized for different classes of applications. For example, most Web servers are run on port 80, America Online (AOL) Instant Messaging uses port 5190, and e-mail often uses port 25. Using the apartment analogy: if every apartment building's superintendent resides in Unit 1, mail for the supervisor would always be addressed to Unit 1, allowing you to send mail without having to ask for the address. Ports are an important concept to understand, because they help differentiate between the types of traffic passing through a machine.

Notes from the Underground...

Ports of Interest

We previously mentioned that standard applications run on standard ports and listed a few of the most popular and interesting ones. Why is this important? In later chapters when we begin examining network traffic for interesting data, we can use our knowledge of common ports to help zero in on traffic of interest. Because many modern high-speed networks produce an enormous amount of traffic, not knowing these popular ports would make looking at network traffic overwhelming.

- File Transfer Protocol (FTP): 21
- Simple Mail Transfer Protocol (SMTP) (Mail): 25
- Web: 80
- Post Office Protocol (POP): 110
- Secure Sockets Layer (SSL) (Secure web): 443
- Secure SMTP 465
- Secure POP: 995
- AOL Instant Messaging 5190
- Internet Relay Chat: 6667

Domain Name System

Although IP addresses are technically very useful, they still have some problems. Nobody wants to remember to type in 64.236.16.116 when they want to read *www.cnn.com*. The solution to this complex numbering system is the Domain Name System (DNS). DNS maps IP addresses to domain names. A domain name is the name by which most people know Internet services. For example, *www.hotmail.com*, *www.cnn.com*, and *www.whitehouse.gov* are all domain names that are much easier to remember than their respective IP addresses. When a user types a domain name into a computer, the computer asks the DNS for an IP address matching that domain name and the DNS server responds with the correct registered IP address. This allows people to remember names instead of IP addresses when using the Internet.

DNSes consist of dedicated servers that hold IP addresses and their corresponding domain names. Because there are so many possible IP addresses, it is impossible for one machine to hold all Internet addresses and corresponding domain names. To handle this, DNS servers are arranged in a hierarchy. When a request for a DNS address can't be fulfilled by one server, that server sends a request to the server above it. This request passes up the system until it encounters a machine that has the result (see Figure 4.1). Servers cache frequently requested IP addresses and their corresponding domain names, which is similar to directory assistance for the public telephone system. If a person wants to dial the local power company but does not know the number, they can call Directory Assistance who will respond with the correct telephone number. If the person requests an out-of-area number, Directory Assistance transfers the call to the proper directory assistance location.

Figure 4.1 DNS Request

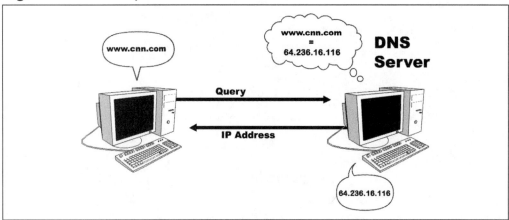

Local Area Networks

A LAN is defined as a group of computers or devices that are interconnected such that any device can communicate with any other device (see Figure 4.2). In keeping with our housing analogy, imagine a large apartment building in a complex with many other apartment buildings all connected by walkways. Many corporations run their own LANs. A person's home setup that is comprised of multiple computers connected together is also considered a LAN. A LAN may be, but is not necessarily, connected to the Internet.

Figure 4.2 A LAN with a Shared Printer

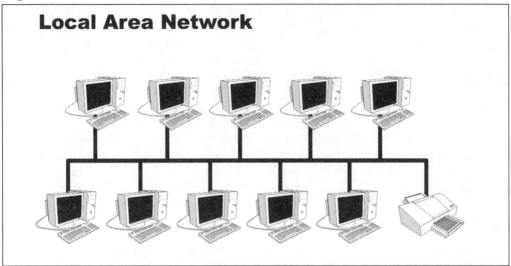

Internet

The Internet is made up of thousands of interconnected networks. There are all kinds of services and communications taking place on the Internet, including Web services (browsing), e-mail, and instant messaging. Voice over IP (VoIP) technology allows people to make telephone calls while using the Internet. The number of uses for the Internet is huge, and will continue growing as people discover innovative ways to take advantage of its size and power.

Tips and Tricks...

Measuring Bandwidth

Like memory and hard disks, bandwidth data is sent to a computer network in streams of 1s and 0s. Modems can use multiple voltages and represent more than two values, however, all of the theory and naming is designed to assume 1s and 0s. Bits are grouped together once again to describe bandwidth of certain networks.

- A bit is a 1 or a 0
- Bytes are largely ignored

Continued

- A kilobit or Kb is a collection of 1,000 bits
- A megabit or MB is a collection of 1,000 Kbs
- A gigabit or GB is 1,000 MBs

Instead of staying with powers of 2, in networking we go back to powers of 10. The bandwidth of modems is often measured in Kb per second (Kbps), while faster Ethernet networks are measured in megabits per second (Mbps) and gigabits per second (Gbps).

If you find the difference between megabytes and megabits confusing, don't worry about it. Most people, including a lot of computer professionals, gloss over the differences. There are not very many places, except maybe on computer science exams, where knowing the difference matters.

Packets

When two computers attempt to communicate with each other they send the information in packets. Packets are like letters sent using the mail system. A packet is the simplest form of communication between two computers. It is comprised of a string of 1s and 0s formatted so that the group of binary data can find its way across the Internet to its specific destination machine. All higher forms of communication are built upon the packet system. There are many different protocols that use packets, but all packets are fundamentally the same.

A packet has a header section and a data section. Once again, this is like a letter, which has an envelope (the header) and correspondence (data). The header of the packet contains the information needed to send it to the correct computer, including the sending computer's IP address and the destination computer's IP address. Also included in the header is the port that the packet is intended to go to. The data portion of the packet contains the data that is to be sent. If the data is too large it will be broken into many smaller packets, similar to sending a very long correspondence in multiple letters to a friend.

Understanding what a packet is and its role in communications is fundamental in being able to determine a computer's use.

Explore More…

The Traveling Packet

The network traffic created by a single Web page Hypertext Transfer Protocol (HTTP) request travels farther across the globe than most people travel in a lifetime. For example, take a visit to the Web site *www.newzealand.com*. The request begins in Alexandria, VA, USA and takes the following path (depending on network congestion):

```
1  ge-4-4-rr01.alexandria.va.dc02.comcast.net

2  srp-8-1-ar01.arlington.va.dc02.comcast.net

3  pos-6-0-cr01.ritchieroad.md.core.comcast.net

4  12.126.168.9

6  tbr1-p012201.wswdc.ip.att.net

7  tbr1-cl4.sl9mo.ip.att.net

8  tbr1-cl2.sffca.ip.att.net

9  gbr1-p10.sffca.ip.att.net

10 gar1-p360.sffca.ip.att.net

11 sffca201lr1-pos21.ip.att.net

12 ausydn1102cr1-5-1-1.au.ip.att.net

13 ausydn1101cr1-3-0.au.ip.att.net

14 nzacld1101er2-11-0-0-4.nz.ip.att.net

15 auck1br1-3-0-0.au.nz.ip.att.

16 nzlapak1.nz.ip.att.net

17 www.newzealand.com
```

After leaving the local network, the packet travels to Arlington, Virginia, Maryland, and Washington, D.C., shoots over to St. Lewis, Missouri, bounces around in San Francisco, California, and then zips across the Pacific Ocean to Sydney, Australia. Following the short layover in Australia, it finally ends up at its destination in New Zealand. That is quite an amazing voyage for one small packet.

Home Networks

Many people have multiple computers set up at home as a home network. They may have a desktop system, a kid's computer, and a laptop from work all connected to the Internet. Each home user must have a way to access the Internet, including dial-up access, cable modem, or DSL. Sometimes people have several computers sharing an Internet connection; these computers form a home network. Some home networks are connected and held together by wireless protocols. Over the past couple of years there has been an explosion in the number of wireless networks. Most new laptops include built-in wireless connectivity. Some very enthusiastic home users incorporate technologies into their homes that are usually reserved for corporate networks. Regardless of its individual components, a home network is comprised of the computers and other devices such as printers that the owner wishes to connect together.

Dial-Up

Approximately 61 million people connect to the Internet through dial-up access. Home users connect through a modem to a dial-up provider. A modem is a device that allows a computer to transmit data over analog phone lines. The modem takes the digital data and converts it into analog data that it passes through the phone line. Likewise, it receives an analog signal from the other computer and converts it back to a digital signal for the computer to interpret.

Historically, dialing up using services such as Prodigy and CompuServe was the only way that home users could connect to the Internet. AOL is currently the most popular dial-up provider in the U.S., but there are also many local dial-up providers that people use.

While relatively cheap and pervasive (all you need is a normal phone line), dial-up Internet access is not without its drawbacks. Originally, people connected through at a 14.4Kbps maximum speed. As technology has progressed, the design of modems has allowed for increasing speeds. Currently, there are 56.6Kbps modems available for purchase. However, the actual speed at which people receive data depends on a variety of factors. Because modems use copper phone lines, the quality of the phone line impacts the speed of the connection. Even the fastest modems at 56K would, in an ideal world, take about one minute to transmit 1MB of data (1MB is about the size of a normal photo taken with a medium quality digital camera).

Dial-up is slowly being surpassed by higher speed connection mechanisms in part due to the ever-increasing amount of information that a Web page displays. The pictures and graphics that are imbedded in many Web pages increase the download time, making it difficult to surf via dial-up. Despite dial-up's popularity loss, there will always be a segment of the population that prefers its lower cost.

Cable Modems and Digital Subscriber Line

Many people have given up dial-up access in favor of a broadband connection such as cable and DSL. Broadband offers higher bandwidth than dial up and, as a result, changes the Internet experience for many people. Using a broadband service transforms accessing the Internet from a time-consuming task to a task requiring no effort. It also allows people to download at high speed, enabling them to use file-sharing tools such as *Kazaa*. It has also become more common for Web sites to have specific broadband content such as streaming video that help enrich the Internet experience.

DSL technology allows for the high-speed transfer of data over normal phone lines. Most DSL subscribers have an asynchronous connection, which means they can download from their Internet Service Provider (ISP) faster than they can upload (send) information. A user's DSL speed depends on their distance from their ISP. While speeds may vary, DSL connections are usually capable of about 1.5 Mbps .

A cable modem is another popular type of broadband access. The home user is provided with a cable modem, which is similar to a telephone modem. The difference is that the signal is broadcast over the cable line and the cable modem is always connected. A cable modem is capable of 1 Mbps or greater speed. Cable modem connections have become increasingly popular.

Hubs and Switches

Hubs and switches are devices used to connect computers together. With few exceptions, computers must be connected at a hub or a switch (see Figure 4.2). Networks need a common device to transmit and receive all of the packets from one location to another, and hubs and switches do just that. They are the hardware that moves the packets from one machine to another.

While hubs and switches appear to be structurally similar and have the same end result, they are functionally different. Both devices are usually small plastic or metal boxes with several network ports in them. (When using ports in the context of switches, hubs, and routers, we mean physical ports, not the data ports referred to earlier). They both usually need power from an external supply and both of them allow connected computers to "see" and communicate with each other. Hubs, however, use the "broadcast" mechanism for transmitting data to all of their connected computers; switches learn the location and route packets from one port to another.

When a computer connected to a hub wants to send data to another computer, it transmits the data onto the network. The hub sees that a computer on one port is transmitting a data packet, takes the packet, and broadcasts it out to every other port.

As a result, all of the traffic on a network connected by a hub goes to each computer. Figure 4.3 demonstrates this concept.

Figure 4.3 A Hub Broadcasting Packet

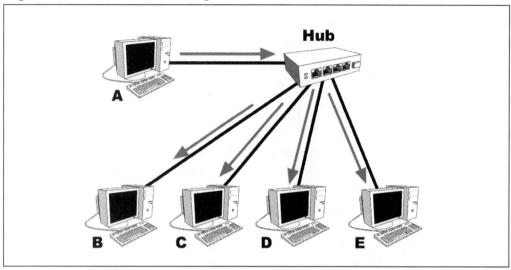

While the broadcast method is effective for transmitting data, more efficient and more secure methods of network connectivity have emerged. Switches are very similar to hubs and appear to function pretty much the same. Internally, though, switches behave very differently. When two computers "talk," one of the first steps is for a computer to make a special packet called an Address Resolution Protocol (ARP) request. This packet is sent out asking any computer that sees it if it is the computer that is about to receive data. The purpose of this ARP packet is to find the first place the packet needs to be sent (in a LAN this is the same as the destination computer) and get the low-level information that the sender needs to build future packets correctly. Switches look for these ARP requests, and when they see one, they record the port number and the low-level address of the sending computer in a table. They then broadcast the ARP request out to every port with a computer on it. When a response comes back from the destination computer, the switch also records its port number and low-level address in the table. Now, all future communication between the two computers is sent directly through the switch without being broadcast on every port. As more computers talk, the switch learns where they are and can build a table describing the network. As a result of this perceived direct connectivity, each port only has packets on it that are destined for computers connected to it. Figure 4.4 illustrates this concept.

Figure 4.4 How a Switch Works

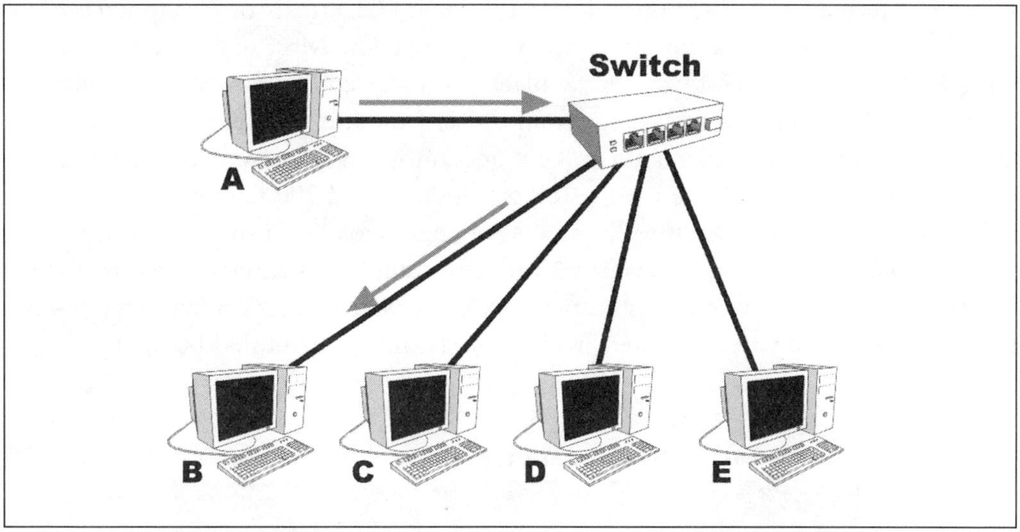

Broadband Routers

One of the great things about broadband is that it usually offers enough bandwidth for multiple computers. As a result, many people share their broadband connection with multiple computers in their homes. Some operating systems such as Microsoft Windows 2000 allow for Internet connection sharing; however, many people opt to use specialized hardware for the task since it is easier to set up. Electronics stores such as BestBuy sell broadband routers that take the connection from the Internet and allow the user to plug into multiple computers. The broadband router splits the Internet connection among many computers, which allows those computers to talk to each other.

A broadband router consists of two parts: a hub or switch that the internal network devices are plugged into, and a router. Both of these parts are usually housed within the same case. The router connects the external network (from the ISP via the cable or DSL modem) to the internal network. It is responsible for passing traffic to and from the Internet, thus allowing the user to split their broadband connection. In this way, a user can have multiple devices connected to the Internet at the same time. This is the primary method that many people use to set up their home network.

Wireless Routers

In the past several years there has been an explosion in the amount of wireless Internet traffic. Previously, computers were connected to each other via Ethernet cable (wired); wireless technology transmits packets through the air. Wireless Internet, referred to as Wi-Fi or by its formal name 802.11(a, b, or g), allows computers to be on a network without a physical connection. Most new laptops come with Wi-Fi built in, and adaptors are available for older computers. Wireless routers provide access within a limited range from the access point. As the distance increases from the router, the signal strength and connection speed decrease. The typical distance at which service can be used is 150 feet indoors and 300 feet outdoors[2], which is usually enough for most homes. Many new broadband routers also have wireless capability built in, allowing the wireless router to function as three separate pieces of hardware: a router, an Ethernet hub, and a wireless access point. Figure 4.5 shows two example wireless routers, which can usually be identified by their antennas.

Figure 4.5 Two Different Wireless Routers

Wi-Fi routers are generally insecure by default; they allow anyone to access and connect through them. While this makes it easy for individuals to plug in and use their routers, it also allows other people to use their Internet connectivity. The people on their network can now access their resources as if they're wired directly into their house. This is usually not a good idea. While it is not covered in this book, there are many resources available on securing a wireless network.

Typical Home Network Setups

Now that the all of the main components of a typical home network are known, they can be put together to enable users to fully harness their computers. Although many people have their own unique home network configured to their exact needs, a typical home network is used as an example throughout this book. A typical home network connects the ISP through a cable modem or DSL connection. Dial-up access can be, but is generally not, used to share a connection. The ISP connection is run into a broadband router. This broadband router also has the functionality of a wireless router. Most home desktops are connected to the broadband router via Ethernet cable. The printers and other peripherals are connected to the main family computer for them to share. All members of the family share this main computer. The wireless router will allow members of the family to use laptops at home to connect out. Figure 4.6 shows a typical home network setup.

Figure 4.6 Diagram of a Typical Home Network

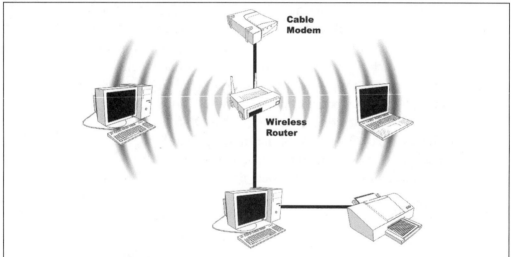

Network Traffic

Computer hardware and software are very useful and powerful when connected together. Now that we know what the pieces are and their functions, we can delve deeper into networks and how they function. The following sections explore the different types of packets and ways of capturing and examining them. They also investigate the mechanisms used to prevent people from examining your network traffic and determining what information you are passing.

Types of Traffic

At any given time, most networks have many different packets residing on them. The packets on a network, referred to as "traffic," come in many different varieties. The distinct packet types provide different functionality that is used to transmit the information. One class of packets, referred to as low-level packets, are special packets that are usually broadcast to everyone and used primarily for network setup and maintenance. The ARP requests and replies mentioned in the section on switches are a good example of low-level packets. IP packets are another class of packets, ones that are usually part of machine-to-machine communication and very likely to contain data that a spy would love to have. The majority of traffic that captured and examined in this book is IP traffic. Web browsers, e-mail clients, Instant Messaging, and chat rooms transmit their data through different IP packet types.

IP traffic can then be broken down into two main classes of packet: user datagram protocol (UDP) and transmission control protocol (TCP). UDP is a connectionless protocol, which means that UDP packets are sent from one machine to the next without confirmation or guaranteed reliability. In addition, there is no promise that packets sent via UDP will arrive at their destination in the same order they were transmitted. When a UDP packet is sent to a target address there is no guarantee it will every reach the target, and there is no automatic confirmation that it ever got there. Because there is very little overhead, UDP is generally faster than TCP, and is used by a lot of games as the protocol of choice. Outside the gaming world, the only other service that relies on UDP is DNS.

TCP is the other popular means of transmitting data through IP packets. Unlike UDP, TCP is a connection-oriented protocol, which means that when two machines want to communicate using TCP they must first initiate a sequence of packets to establish the connection, which is called a three-way handshake. After the connection is established, the receiving computer acknowledges every packet that is sent. As a result, TCP guarantees an in-order delivery of packets. This reliability comes at a cost, as both machines are required to do more work for each connection versus the relative ease of a UDP transmission. However, it seems that most applications desire this reliability. Many popular protocols and applications such as Web browsing, e-mail, and most Instant Messenger clients use TCP as their preferred method of data transmission.

TCP and UDP packets may appear to be more confusing and complicated than they actually are. Imagine that you want to send a copy of a book to a friend. They agree that, since it would be too expensive to mail all at once, you can break it up and send each chapter individually. This book also does not have individual chapter markings, so if they get out of order your friend would not read the entire book the way it was intended. You and your friend decide to send the chapters through the mail with a return receipt. The first chapter is sent to your friend, who signs for the package, and a couple of days later the return receipt arrives. You now know that your friend has the first chapter. The second chapter is sent the exact same way, and you wait for the return receipt. After receiving the second receipt, you send the third chapter, but no return receipt arrives. After a period of time, you assume that the chapter is lost and try to send a copy of the third chapter again. This chapter arrives successfully, as does every subsequent chapter. This is the equivalent of using TCP for transferring your data. TCP is used when data must be guaranteed to arrive.

UDP is used for many streaming media applications. Imagine you own a small mail order company with your own catalog. Every week you send a new catalog to your customers. It would be prohibitively expensive to send the catalog via First Class mail with registered receipt. After all, you are sending one catalog a week to the customer, so if one or two get lost, it is not a big deal. It is also not important to you if they aren't delivered promptly; a couple of days delay is not a big deal as long as they arrive close to the original due date. As a business owner, you decide to send your catalog via Fourth Class mail, which allows you to send the catalog to your customers with as little cost to you as possible. UDP is that Fourth Class mail. Figure 4.7 graphically illustrates the differences between TCP and UDP. In TCP, every packet is received in order and acknowledged. With UDP, most packets get there, although there is nothing to keep some from getting lost or arriving out of order.

Figure 4.7 The Top Session Is Done via a TCP Connection with Guaranteed and In-order Delivery

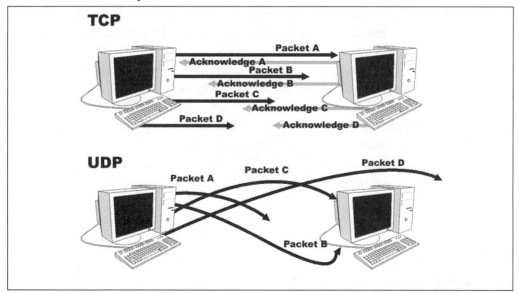

Sniffing

Sniffing is the act of collecting packets from a network connection using either a special application or a piece of hardware called a *sniffer*. A sniffer takes a copy of and displays all of the traffic a network card sees. When implemented correctly, a sniffer is completely passive, having no effect on the traffic. Except for the fact that it takes processing time and memory, a sniffer should have no effect on its host computer. Ethereal, Ettercap, and Packetyzer (discussed further in Chapter 5) are some popular sniffers that allow for traffic collection, analysis, and TCP stream reconstruction. Traffic collection refers to the sniffer's ability to receive a copy of network traffic. Traffic analysis is the sniffer's ability to break out relevant fields (such as IP address) from the captured packets. A sniffer with good traffic analysis capabilities can easily be display specified fields within the packet. It will also be able to recognize many different types of packets. Some even have the capability to analyze proprietary packet types. TCP stream reconstruction is the process by which a sniffer captures and reconstructs an entire TCP stream so that the user can see and analyze the traffic in an easy-to-understand manner. Some sniffers allow for almost complete stream reconstruction. They can pull out the data that is being passed within the traffic. This allows reconstruction of the sequence of mail commands that is passed between a mail host and a client, thus enabling debugging of the higher level protocols. For instance, SMTP could be debugged with the help of a sniffer. Sniffing is done for many reasons, with two of the most common being network performance analysis (boring) and spying. Sniffing will be used as a tool to further our spying capability.

By 1999, most LANs were held together by hubs. As explained earlier, hubs are broadcast devices. Any traffic that goes through one port of a hub is broadcast to all of them. Every computer connected to a hub receives all of the traffic on the network. It is up to the network card to discard traffic not meant for it. The network card is responsible for picking the traffic sent to it. Most network cards have a special mode called *promiscuous* mode. When placed in this mode, a network card accepts *all* traffic it receives. As a result, when sniffing on a network held together by a hub, one user can see the traffic destined for everyone. Most network connections and the data in them are in plaintext, which has significant security implications. Lots of data today still flies across the network in plain sight. For example, e-mail (unless you explicitly encrypt it) is completely viewable if the packets containing it are captured (see Figure 4.8).

Figure 4.8 E-mail Captured with a Packet Sniffer

The prevalence of switches over hubs makes sniffing an entire network much more difficult. Sniffing will still yield a lot of information about what is going in and out of your computer, but it is no longer the "grab everything around" capability that it once was. This is both good and bad. Good because it offers more security, and bad because it will make spying more difficult. No longer can you merely sniff from another machine; you have to install your sniffers on the target machine. There are certain advanced attacks that allow you to coerce switches into acting like hubs, but these attacks are generally more difficult to perform and easy to catch. Finally, there are certain broadband routers that while advertising a switched network actually broadcast all of their traffic as if they were hubs. We won't mention the offending vendors; rather, we leave it up to you to always test and see what you can get on your network.

Encryption

Encryption is a daunting and complex topic to many people and some readers may think that they won't be able to understand it. In fact, encryption constantly used in the world, and many people use it without even realizing it. Encryption mechanisms have been around for centuries; the ancient Romans used a form of it to protect their messages. It is not necessary to understand the inner workings of an encryption algorithm, merely to know what is happening and why.

Encryption is used to provide a variety of assurances to a communications medium. There are many different types of encryption that are used for distinct purposes. It can be used to guarantee that only the intended individuals can read a message and it can also be used to assure someone that the sender really did send the message. Differing methods of encryption can provide the following:

- **Confidentially** Assuring that only the person sending the message and the intended recipients can read the message.

- **Integrity** Assuring that the message that was sent was not altered, added to, or changed.

- **Authentication** Determining that the sender of the message was indeed the sender, not someone posing as that individual.

- **Nonrepudiation** Allows the recipient of the message to prove that it was the sender who sent the message; the sender will not be able claim that they did not send the message.

Encryption is the process of transforming data so that it is unreadable and no longer resembles its original form. It takes plaintext (the original data) and converts it into ciphertext, which is what is sent to the recipient. The encryption process usually starts with data and an encryption key. The data and key are then placed into a mathematical function that produces encrypted data (ciphertext). Except for possibly size, the encrypted data no longer resembles the original data. The mathematic functions are carefully chosen so that they cannot easily be reversed without having the key. The current American Encryption Standard (AES) algorithm, Rjindall, uses a very long key and is believed to be strong enough such that it would take all of the computers in the world thousands of years to break.

Explore More...

Encryption Strength

A common method of comparing encryption strength is in the key length. Data encryption standard (DES) originally used a 40-bit key. That is 2^{40} possible key combinations. The current AES can use up to a 256-bit key, which produces 2^{256} distinct combinations. This makes it much harder to break the encryption via brute force. To break encryption using brute force, all possible key combinations are tried until the correct key is found. As shown, using AES makes it much more

Continued

difficult to brute-force a key. This is important due to the ever-increasing speed of modern computers that are reaching speeds that were once thought unreachable. An encryption mechanism with a small key that was safe five years ago might not be safe now.

Data is generally most vulnerable at two distinct times: in transit, and in storage. Data in storage is usually data that is sitting on a CD, a USB drive, a floppy, hard disk, or other storage medium. If it is non-encrypted, anyone can copy the data and view it at a later time. Data in transit is data that is being sent between two locations such as between storage and a CPU or between two different computers on a network. Transitional data is vulnerable to being collected (by a sniffer) and analyzed. If the data is encrypted either when it is stored or in transit, it is significantly more difficult to analyze. Unless the person capturing the encrypted data has the key, they will not be able study, view, or otherwise make sense of it. Figure 4.9 demonstrates encryption at work.

Figure 4.9 Encryption at Work

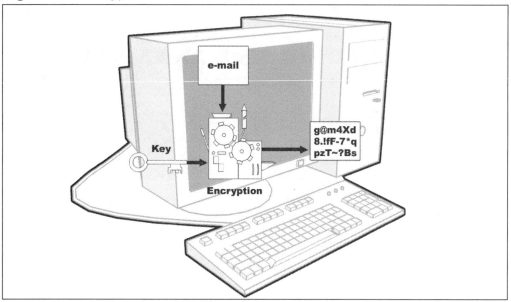

One example of a popular encryption package is Secure Socket Layer (SSL), which has become a standard for encryption. While initially designed to secure Web browsing, it is now used with several popular protocols to provide a layer of encryption and enhanced security. For example, both SMTP (outgoing e-mail) and POP (incoming e-mail) can be wrapped in SSL. When that is done, any e-mail that passes between the e-mail client and the server is encrypted. This makes it extremely difficult for someone sniffing the line between the client and the server to determine the contents of the e-mail.

Many Web sites use encryption when logging in or in e-commerce. Internet Explorer displays a lock icon on the bottom of the screen if the connection is using SSL. Mozilla Firefox, another Web browser, also displays a lock in the bottom left of the application when SSL is being used. They use encryption to prevent third parties from intercepting passwords and account numbers.

SSL is a means of encrypting an entire connection. While its useful, it has several drawbacks. For one, both sites communicating must have SSL enabled, which is not always the case. However, there exists a method of encrypting data called public key cryptography (commonly referred to as PGP), which can be used in almost every online transaction. (Pretty Good Privacy or PGP is actually a product, but it has become so strongly associated with public key cryptography that the terms are often interchanged.) PGP, or its free cousin GPG, are commonly used to encrypt e-mail and other types of data. PGP is also useful for protecting stored data. Figure 4.10 shows a packet captured while encrypted with PGP.

Figure 4.10 Packet Capture of E-mail Encrypted with PGP

Encryption is a powerful technology. Used correctly it can make data extremely secure. If you encounter encrypted data in your sleuthing, do not waste time trying to break it; if it was done right you won't be able to. Instead, think of what encryption is for: to protect data that may be discovered in transit or storage. Remember that the encrypted data was at one time unencrypted, and in order to be used, will have to be decrypted. Don't give up, but shift your focus to when and where you can get what you need. Instead of attacking the encryption, try to get the data when it's vulnerable, and unencrypted.

How Network Technology Is Used

Most people use computer networks and the Internet for one of three main purposes: communication, transactions, and entertainment. We view communication as all of the processes by which a person actively communicates with another. Examples of this are e-mail and instant messaging, which are the modern equivalents of letters and walkie-talkies and are very pervasive, and very powerful. These applications are two of the foundations of the Internet and the most popular uses for it. They have become so popular that in some demographics they are replacing traditional methods of communication.

Transactions are another common use for networks. When we refer to transactions we are describing primarily e-commerce and online banking. Once again, these are information-age twists on two very traditional areas. Both of these are significant parts of people's lives; knowing what goes on regarding a person and their transactions can give a good idea of what a person is going through at any given time.

Finally, many people use the Internet as a source of entertainment. This can be casual Web browsing, reading the news online, downloading movies, listening to Internet radio, or watching Web casts of interesting events. High-speed Internet access and fast computers have combined many normally disjointed aspects of a person's life into one unified location—their computer.

As a spy, it is very important for you to grasp the depth of the Internet's penetration into most people's lives. Since so much is done through the Internet, you have a location where you can look for many clues about a person's life. Complete access to a person's Internet activity can give you a thorough picture of them. You will know with whom and about what they communicate. You will know some of what they buy, and you may learn about their financial situation by looking at their bank and retirement accounts. You can learn what they are interested in, what they read about, what they are researching, and what they are looking to buy. You will get a glimpse of what they enjoy by the images, music, and movies they look at.

Taking all that into account, it is very easy to see how total information awareness for an individual can be extremely useful. All that passes through a computer can build a complete picture of a person, and may help uncover any mysteries you are concerned with. In most cases, even in the best of situations you will not have complete and total access to everything a person does online. It is important to maximize what you can obtain, study it carefully, and treat it like one piece of a very complex puzzle.

Summary

This chapter gave a very brief yet broad overview of computer networks. As shown, a home network comprises many different components that allow for a multitude of configurations and options. It included the following key points:

☑ Networks are like neighborhoods, but instead of houses they are computers that are grouped together to communicate.

☑ Many people connect their home network to the Internet via dial-up services, DSLs, or cable modems. Cable modems and DSLs are considered to be broadband access; that is, they offer higher bandwidth than the traditional dial-up capability.

☑ An IP address is what identifies a computer on a network. There are both public and private IP addresses.

☑ A port identifies an application so that the computer can tell which program to send data to.

☑ Packets are the building blocks upon which communication protocols are based.

☑ Hubs and switches hold most home networks together. Hubs broadcast data to all connected machines and switches transmit data only to the destination computer.

☑ Users with broadband connections often use broadband routers to enable multiple computers to access the Internet. Some broadband routers have Wi-Fi built in. While Wi-Fi is a very convenient way of connecting, it is often not the most secure.

☑ There are two primary types of IP traffic: UDP and TCP. UDP is connectionless and unreliable and TCP is connection oriented and reliable. Most interesting network applications use TCP.

☑ Sniffing is the process of collecting and analyzing traffic from the network.

☑ Encryption allows people to protect their data in transit and storage.

☑ Network technology has enabled many new trends such as e-mail, Web browsing, and e-commerce that have affected our lives and the economy.

☑ Total information awareness gives you a good picture of someone's life. However, you will probably never have total awareness, so treat everything you discover like a piece of a puzzle.

References

[1] *www.nwfusion.com/net.worker/news/2004/0818netrabroad.html?net&code=nlnet-flash520*

[2] *http://compnetworking.about.com/cs/wirelessproducts/f/wifirange.htm encryption: Applied Cryptography*; Bruce Schneier; 1996; John Wiley and Sons

## Chapter 5

Taking Control

"All right, look, this is real simple. Whatever miles we put on it, we'll take off."

"How?"

"We'll drive home backwards." — Ferris Bueller

Topics in this Chapter:

- **Basic Skills**
- **Software You Will Use**
- **Mastering Your Domain**
- **Summary**

Introduction

Before going to war, a general (or at least a good one) sets goals, carefully trains his forces, studies his enemies, assesses his capabilities, and executes his plans. Just as a general should take these steps in preparation for a lengthy campaign, you too should follow a well-thought-out strategy as you begin to spy on others. This chapter discusses some of the first steps toward becoming a cyber-spy. By the end of this chapter, you should have a good understanding of how the SLEUTH methodology (see Chapter 2) can help you develop a professional spying strategy that will improve your chances of success. You will learn how to assess your home computer and network layout, and how to develop a plan that allows you to take full advantage of the SLEUTH methodology in order to meet your goals.

The previous two chapters discussed the fundamentals of cyber-spying; now we introduce a few "tricks" that everyone should know when using a computer for cyber-spying. Following this is a section describing the usage and installation of software that is useful for spying.

Finally, this chapter concludes with "Mastering Your Domain," which is about taking charge of your home computer. To spy effectively, it is important to have knowledge of your surroundings and as much control as possible. Mastering your domain takes that spy fundamental and helps you apply it to your home computer and network. In this chapter, we introduce you to several types of software and hardware that can be used for spying (most of this spy software was actually designed for other purposes). The techniques and tools described here will have you well on your way to becoming a powerful cyber-spy.

Cover Your Tracks

Covering your tracks is a critical skill in all types of spying. It is especially important when dealing with computers, because they can meticulously log just about every action you take without your knowledge. As you exert control over different computer systems, you will generally run across two types of users: those who use default settings and environments, and those who painstakingly customize their environments to their liking. The latter will probably notice any small change you make to a system, and both will notice major changes. Because you may not know what type of user you are dealing with or what they might notice, it is wise to make as few permanent changes as possible. Record the changes you make, and when you have concluded spying, work backwards and undo them whenever possible. This step will give you the lowest profile and minimize your chances of being caught. In the words of Verbal "Keyser Soze" Kint, "The greatest trick the devil ever pulled was convincing people he didn't exist." Removing evidence of what you have done prevents them from being able to effectively follow your maneuvers. This book offers different tips and tricks that can be used for covering your tracks.

Basic Skills

This section covers some basic skills that are critical to cyber-spying. These skills may seem obvious to many advanced computer users, so if you feel comfortable around a computer feel free to skip this section. During the evolution of Microsoft Windows, many features have been added to mask the inner working of the operating system from users. These features help most users make the computer a simpler and friendlier device, but it can also slow down cyber-spies. The computer skills covered in this section are all fundamentals that you will need for investigating and spying on other people's computers.

Running Explorer

Explorer is Microsoft's graphical file browser. It is used to gain a visual representation of all of the files and directories (folders) stored on a computer. Because we will be looking for a lot of files and using the file system to mask our tracks, Explorer will be a key component in many future exercises. Depending on the operating system installed on your computer, there may or may not be a menu item to launch Explorer. Regardless of its presence, Explorer can be launched from the **Run** box in the Start menu. This will work regardless of operating system, from Windows 95 to Windows XP.

There are four steps for launching explorer from the **Run** box:

1. Click the **Start** button on the task bar on the bottom left-hand corner of the screen.
2. Select **Run** (Figure 5.1).
3. Type **explorer.exe** in the Run dialogue box.
4. Click the **OK** button (Figure 5.2).

Figure 5.1 Selecting the Run Button on the Start Menu

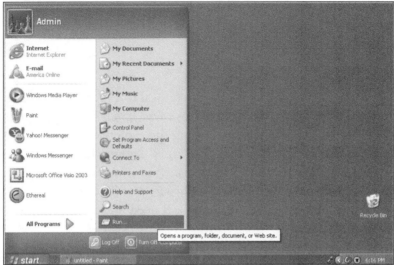

Figure 5.2 Running explorer.exe

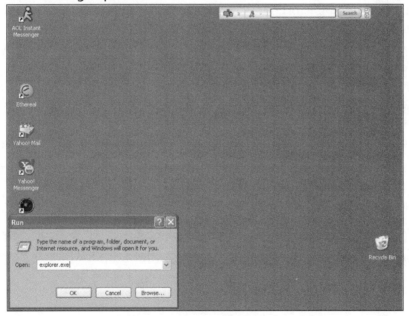

A window similar to the one shown in Figure 5.3 appears.

Figure 5.3 Explorer Running

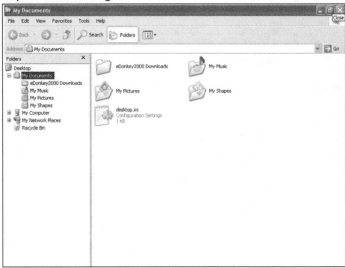

Anything but the oldest systems will show the My Documents folder. Use this to examine all of the files in your computer. Some of the items you should see are a Desktop folder, which contains your windows desktop; a My Documents folder; and most importantly, a My Computer folder. There will be other items such as a My Network folder, but we are not concerned with those. For now, let's examine the My Computer folder more closely.

Upon clicking on it, several other icons appear such as a C: drive, a floppy (or A:) drive (if you have one), and an optical drive that can be any letter from D: onward. The type of drive will be denoted by its icon or explained more verbosely in the right-hand pane of Explorer. Figure 5.4 shows a typical setup.

Figure 5.4 Inside My Computer

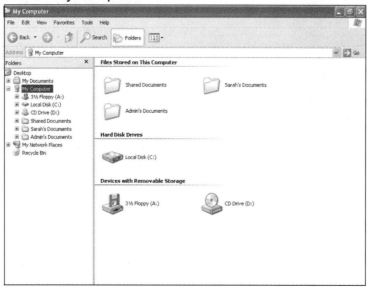

The icon of prime interest is the C: drive, which represents the primary hard drive where all of your software and data is stored.

NOTE

You should be aware that some computers have more than one hard drive installed. Do not get confused if you see this; simply treat each hard drive icon as a separate drive, executing the steps we discuss on each. Figure 5.5 shows *explorer.exe* open on a computer with two hard drives. Notice that they are not consecutively named; one is C: and one is Z:.

Figure 5.5 Computer with Two Hard Drives

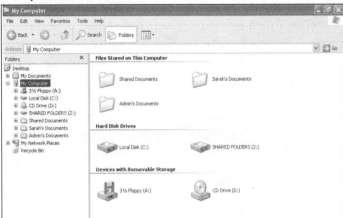

Click on the C drive icon labeled **Local Disk (C:)**. You will see a screen similar to that in Figure 5.6. If you see a different screen (see Figure 5.7), someone else has already purposely changed the viewing permissions on the system files. This may indicate that your adversary is attempting to hide something from you, that they are attempting to snoop on you, or that they are computer savvy (like you will be after reading this book). Regardless of why this setting was changed, the fact remains that it was, so proceed through the rest of the techniques in the book with caution.

Figure 5.6 Show Files Warning

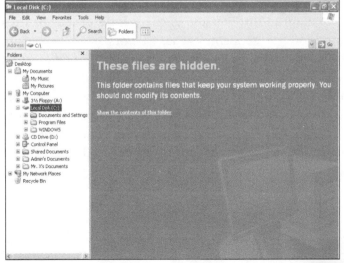

This is a standard warning that shows whenever you view many system folders. Because of the way files and the access to them are laid out, there is little reason for most users to view things such as the C: drive. However, as cyber-spies you are not most users; therefore, it is time for you to click the **show files** button on the far left-hand side of the screen. This step enables you to see what files are stored there. Now your screen should look something like Figure 5.7.

Figure 5.7 C: Drive without Warning

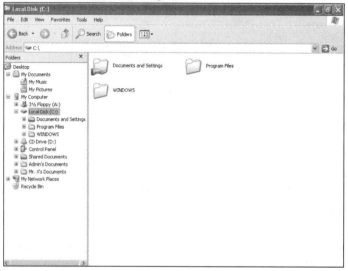

Next, we enable a setting to allow you to see hidden and system files, which will give you a complete view of your file system. This is an important setting to enable, because it is trivial to target a file *hidden* in Windows. In addition, when changing this setting, we recommend that you also uncheck **hide extensions for known file types**, which will allow you to identify what type of data a file contains. Many different tricks can be done with extensions to disguise files as different types. This helps alleviate and prevents some of those tricks. These settings can be found by clicking on **Tools | Options** in Explorer's menu. Then select the **View** tab. The three items of interest are **Show hidden files and folders**, **Hide extensions for known file types**, and **Hide protected operating system files (Recommended)**. The last one gives you a warning; read it and click **yes**. Apply the suggested settings and your dialogue box should look like Figure 5.8.

Figure 5.8 Settings for Making Many Files Visible

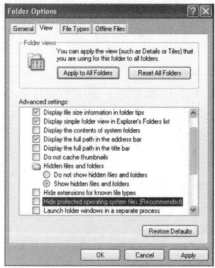

After clicking **OK**, your Explorer window should resemble Figure 5.9. Notice how many new items are visible. It's amazing what you can find when you know how to look. It is very important that these Explorer settings be applied every time you look at a computer. Failure to do so could result in your overlooking important information.

WARNING

Before changing these settings, make sure you document how they were initially set so that you can undo your steps.

Figure 5.9 Previously Hidden Items Now Visible

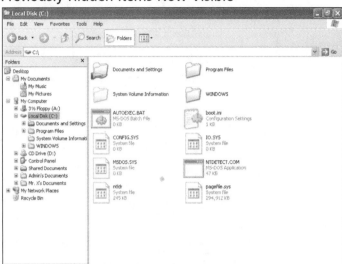

Opening a Command Prompt

The command prompt is another little-used program that comes bundled with all versions of Windows. It is useful because it allows you to run several programs that require command prompts, and it allows you to use several different software packages that must be started from a command prompt. Some users may find it a bit confusing, but mastering the command prompt is a necessity for spying.

A command prompt can be started from the **Run** item on the Start menu. In the same way Explorer was launched, click **Run** and then enter **cmd.exe** (Windows 2000, XP), **command.exe** (Windows 95, 98, ME, or 2000), or **command.com** (Windows 2000, XP) to start the program.

Cmd.exe has the same functionality as **command.com,** and it also has several additional features, such as command history (i.e., you can scroll though previous commands with the arrow keys). Once the command prompt is launched, you will get a window similar to the one shown in Figure 5.10. When you are in this window you can enter commands at the C:\> prompt followed by **Enter** to execute them.

Figure 5.10 Command.com Window

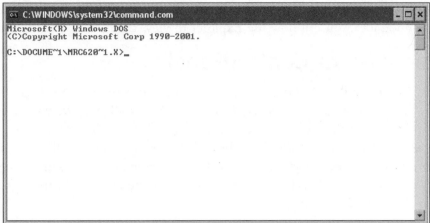

Unpacking an Archive to a Folder

Several of the tools we offer on our Web site come as zipped archives. In Windows XP, these files can be viewed with Explorer as if they are normal directories. If you don't have Windows XP, or even if you do, we suggest a third-party tool for viewing archives, such as IZArc, which is a free and powerful archive tool. Other options are 7-Zip (*www.7-zip.org*), WinZip (www.winzip.com), and WinRAR (*www.rarlab.com*). All of these tools generally have support for many archive types.

Once your third-party archive tool is installed, double-clicking on an archive will open the tool. From there you can click on **Extract**, as shown in Figure 5.11.

Figure 5.11 Extracting an Archive Using IZArc

Now select a directory in which to store your extracted files. Feel free to create a new directory at this time. Giving it an inconspicuous name such as "program settings" is a good idea. You can now use Explorer to view the files.

Classic View of Control Panel

Windows ME and XP both group the Control Panel's capabilities into "logical" groups, which is known as the *Category View* of the Control Panel. We will be referring to and accessing the Control Panel frequently, so for the purposes of this chapter we use the phrase *Classic View* where all of the items are in a single group, thus allowing you to see everything on that Control Panel. To put Control Panel in Classic View mode, click **Start | Control Panel**. A window should appear, as shown in Figure 5.12.

Figure 5.12 Control Panel Context View

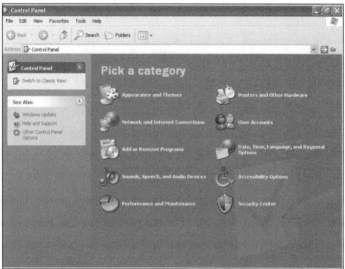

If it looks different it may already be in Classic View. Assuming it is in Context View, click on the item on the left-hand side of the screen labeled **Switch to Classic View**. It will now resemble the control panel shown in Figure 5.13.

Figure 5.13 Control Panel in Classic View

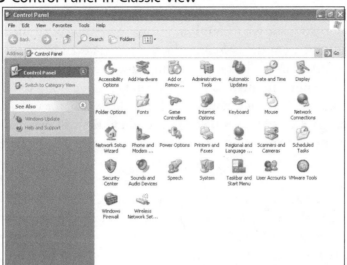

In Windows ME, Classic View is accessed by clicking on the **View All Options** link on the left-hand side of the screen.

Because you may be installing software on a target machine, it would be wise to do it as covertly as possible. One simple step you can use is Microsoft's built-in ability to "hide" files. Once you've installed your software and know which file or folder you want to hide, find and select it in Explorer and then right-click on the file and select **Properties**. In the resulting dialogue box (Figure 5.14) select **Hidden**, which should be at the bottom of the dialogue box.

Figure 5.14 File Properties Dialogue

Depending on your settings, the file or folder will now become less opaque (Explorer with our recommended settings) or disappear (Explorer's default settings). This is an easy way to mask your files from normal users. A second method of file hiding has to be done from the command line, but offers even more powerful options. To hide files from the command prompt, use the **attrib.exe** command. **Attrib.exe** is a system utility used to set file attributes. In addition to a hidden attribute, you can also give files a system attribute. The syntax for using **attrib.exe** is **C:\>attrib.exe +h +s <file to hide>**. The resulting file will now have hidden and system attributes set. You can reset these values using the **C:\>attrib.exe –h –s <hidden file>** command.

With the system attribute set, you have several extra advantages besides just hiding the file from Explorer. Being able to view system files is a totally different option on Explorer; a user would have to change two default options in order to be able to view your files. In addition, if the system attribute is set, the hidden property cannot be removed from the file by using Explorer; the system attribute has to be removed first with **attrib.exe**.

The nice thing about built-in hidden and system attributes for files is that programs can execute normally even when they are in a hidden folder or system folder.

Uninstalling Software

Uninstalling software can be very tricky; however, it is a necessity, as some items in this section require the newest version of a library, which means that you have to uninstall any previous ones. In addition, after you are done spying and you've collected the information you need, you should uninstall your spy tools.

Uninstallation is done from an add/remove software dialogue box that is found in the Control Panel. To do this, select **Start** | **Control Panel** | **Add or Remove Programs**. If an add/remove software option does not exist, switch the Control Panel to Classic View, as described in the previous section. Once you select and click on the add/remove software icon, you will see a dialogue box similar to the one shown in Figure 5.15.

Figure 5.15 Add/Remove Software Dialogue

Each item in the dialogue box represents an installed program. They are all alphabetized. When you select a program, you are usually given usage information and the option to uninstall it. Uninstallation consists of simply clicking a button.

Some programs don't come with an uninstall option in the Control Panel, and they can be deleted the same way that a word document is deleted. Find the executable on your computer using the Explorer bar; it is most likely in a folder in the *C:\Program Files* folder. Delete the entire folder and the program is gone. Ensure that all of the files associated with the program are deleted. All programs created by this company will be put in that folder.

Running regedit

Microsoft Windows has many different settings that are modified in the different menus and in the control panel. However, these settings only scratch the surface of the many options that can be configured. Since Windows 95, the operating system has stored most of its settings and other information in a group of files collectively called the *registry*. The registry consists of *system.dat* and *user.dat* files that make up most of the thousands of configuration options that control the look and behavior of the operating system. The registry data is in binary format, and cannot be viewed or modified with standard tools. However, Microsoft does provide a tool for viewing and editing the registry named *regedit*.

Unlike most standard Windows accessories, there are no Start menu icons for launching **regedit**; you must know that the program exists. It is launched in much the same way as Explorer or the command prompt. First, select **Run** from the Start menu and enter **regedit**. The resulting window will look like Figure 5.16.

Figure 5.16 Regedit Main Window

In the left-hand pane of the window are the five main sections, or *hives*, containing data for several areas of the registry. When the hives are expanded, different keys are shown. When a key is selected, the right-hand pane shows its value. Registry values can be *string* (easy to read and understand text) or *binary* (hexadecimal digits). For this book, we edit both types of data. Although the interface may look complex and confusing, using **regedit** is a straightforward process.

WARNING

Incorrectly setting or deleting registry values can make your computer unbootable.

Tips and Tricks...

Covering Your Tracks by Removing Yourself from the Uninstall Menu

Many software packages leave a reference in the Uninstall menu so that they can be removed. It would obviously be to your benefit to remove any software that you want hidden from this menu. Fortunately, there is a way to remove the programs using the **regedit** tools.

1. Start **regedit**.
2. Go to **HKEY_LOCAL_MACHINE\SOFTWARE | Microsoft | Windows | Current Version | Uninstall**.
3. Find the key that corresponds to the program you wish to remove.
4. Right-click on that key and click **Delete**.
5. When prompted, select **yes** to indicate that you want to delete the key and its subkeys.
6. On the File menu, select **Exit** to close regedit.
7. View the Currently Installed Programs list to ensure that your program is deleted.

Viewing Processes and Services

Processes and services are literally the programs that run on a computer. Anything that is running is a *process*. A *service* is a special instance of a process that can run even when a user is not logged on. Services are programs that the operating system uses to run everyday operations. You can know what is running on your computer by using the listing and viewing processes and services. They will help you verify the installation of your spy software and ensure that nothing is being used to detect and thwart you.

On most Win9x machines (Windows 95, 98, and ME), you can view running programs by pressing the **ctrl-alt-delete** keys simultaneously. You should be then see a dialogue box that lists all of the running programs. However, this list is not comprehensive, because all running processes are not necessarily running programs. What you see is not an all-inclusive view of the system. To get a complete listing of processes, we recommend using Process Explorer (free software that can be obtained from our Web site *www.cyberspybook.com* or from *www.sysinternels.com*).

Running programs can be viewed using the Windows Task Manager on Windows NT, 2k, and XP computers. The Windows Task Manager contains several tabs for programs, processes, and other statistics. Figure 5.17 shows an example of the Windows Task Manager set to view all processes. Like the Win 9.*x* series, Windows NT, 2K, and XP can also use Process Explorer for viewing processes.

Figure 5.17 Task Manager Set to View All Processes

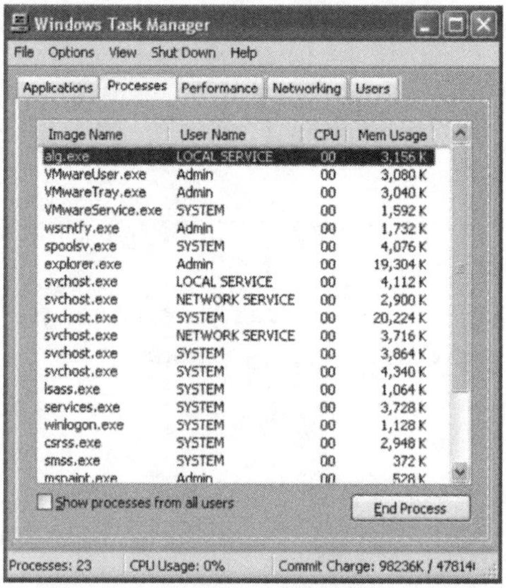

On these platforms, the Service Control Manager (SCM) must be used to view all services and their status. This can be done by clicking **Start** | **Control Panel** | **Administrative Tools**. In the Administrative Tools folder, double-click on **Services**, which will open the SCM. This list shows all of the installed services and their status including their name, a description (if available), their status (started or blank), whether or not they are started manually or automatically, and the user ID under which they are started.

It is necessary to know the aforementioned few tricks for the material presented in this chapter and the rest of this book. As the book progresses, we will make note of other less obvious helpful tricks and techniques.

Software You Will Use

The Web site for this book, *www.cyberspybook.com*, contains links to software that is discussed in this book. In addition, as we find or write new software that we feel is useful for online spying, we will post it on the Web site. Most of this software is released under the GNU Public License (GPL), which means that the software is completely free to use and modify, as long as the people modifying it release the source code showing all of their modifications.

The software we showcase is pretty good (and even better with our modifications), but it may not be the best available. Many different companies offer variations of these same tools for a price. However, we feel that our price (free) is unbeatable, and since you can obtain our software directly from the Web site and download it directly to the computer, there is no paper trail. By downloading our free software there are no credit-card receipts, checks to suspicious software companies, e-mails sent to you, or boxes of spy software showing up at your door. The entire process of getting and using our software is relatively innocuous and straightforward.

That being said, we still encourage you to investigate other software options that may better fit your needs. Our tools are not high-grade government spy software. They won't evade every virus scanner or personal firewall. They are a good start and are designed to evade the average computer user. However, more sophisticated problems may require more sophisticated solutions. A search on *www.google.com* can help point you to the many free and commercial alternatives.

In a few instances, there are not any software solutions available under the GPL that meet our needs. This is the case with personal firewalls and virus scanners, both of which are extremely complex and the result of much research.

In addition, some other small utilities we describe may be freeware or shareware but not necessarily open source. Whenever we can, we try to show a free alternative to any commercial software.

It is important to note that most of the software we ask you to install comes as unsigned code. On operating systems older than Windows XP, this should make no difference. On Windows XP Service Pack 2 and later you will be greeted by dialogue similar to that shown in Figure 5.18.

Figure 5.18 Running Unsigned Software Warning

This is a warning that says the program has not been cryptographically signed by its authors. Select **Run** to install the program.

Utilities

This section describes the tools you will use throughout this book that are not directly used for spying, but are still needed for viewing images, reading files, making archives, and other tasks.

IZArc

IZArc is a freely available compression/decompression utility that handles *zip* and *rar* files, two of the most popular compression schemes for Microsoft Windows as well as many other less popular compression schemes. Unlike the trial versions of other compression software, IZArc never expires. IZArc also offers the best compromise of price (free), functionality, and polish.

If you are installing software on your PC for viewing and handling archives, IZArc is a great choice. If you are installing it on a target's computer, you should first determine if that computer has any software already installed to handle archives. The best way to check is to double-click on an archive and see if a program opens it up. If you see a "Select Program" dialogue, you probably don't have the capability of viewing archives on that computer. You can then install IZArc if you wish (it may be better to handle the archives offline on a separate computer), but you should take steps to make a particularly stealthy install.

Download From

IZArc can be downloaded from www.cyberspybook.com or alternatively from its home site at http://www.izsoft.dir.bg. It comes as a self-extracting executable.

Installation

For the purposes of this book, we assume that you are installing IZArc version 3.4. Begin by double-clicking on the IZArc installation file. You should immediately see a screen asking you to uninstall any previous versions of IZArc and a dialogue asking you to select the preferred language for installation. Now you should see the IZArc Welcome screen.

Click **Next** and accept the following two screens of license information. The default installation location should also be accepted. When you reach the screen asking about creating a Start menu, select the box **Don't create a Start Menu** folder for a stealthier install (Figure 5.19).

Figure 5.19 IZArc Start Menu Folder Dialogue

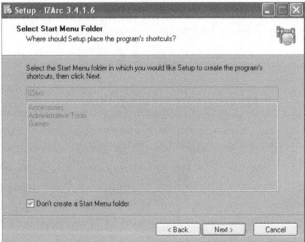

At the next dialogue, the options for a "Quick Launch" and "Desktop" icon are at your discretion. If you are installing on your personal machine it doesn't matter. If you are installing on a target machine, we suggest unchecking both options. Next, there are a few more screens to click through.

After the installation is complete, IZArc asks you to select a language and presents you with a screen similar to that in Figure 5.20. This is where you select exactly what type of archives IZArc will open. We recommend pressing the **Deselect All** button and then checking only the archive types you will need. Assigning IZArc to too many archive types might disrupt previously installed archive software and reveal your presence on the target box.

Figure 5.20 IZArc Archive Type Association Screen

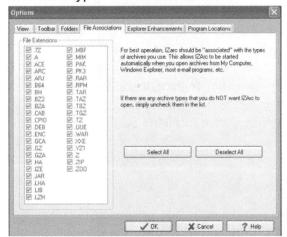

Usage

IZArc is almost self-explanatory in that it is implicitly activated whenever a compressed archive file is double-clicked. It has several icons for file extraction and other common functions.

Kaboodle

Knowing a target machine's Internet Protocol (IP) address enables you to track it on a network so that you can remotely access it. However, because many home networks have dynamic IP addresses (the address can change every time the computer connects), you need a method to locate your target machine as its IP address changes. Kaboodle offers a visual means of mapping out your network and shows representations of different machines on it. By using Kaboodle, you can automatically find out the location of every machine and its IP address. As a bonus, Kaboodle can automatically detect machines running Virtual Network Computing (VNC) and connect you to them.

Download From

Kaboodle can be downloaded from *www.cyberspying.com* or its home site at *www.kaboodle.org*. This file comes as a self-installing executable file.

Installation

Installation of Kaboodle is a relatively straightforward process. You begin by double-clicking on the executable you downloaded. You should immediately be greeted by Kaboodle's Welcome screen. After clicking **Next** you will receive a License Information screen. Agree to the license and click **Next** again. The next screen will ask you where you want Kaboodle installed. Accept the defaults and continue. Kaboodle will finish installing.

Usage

Kaboodle will place an item in your program menu and an icon on your desktop. Clicking on either will start the program. It will immediately scan your network and list all of the computers and network devices it can find, which will be displayed on a screen similar to the one shown in Figure 5.21.

Figure 5.21 Kaboodle's Main Screen

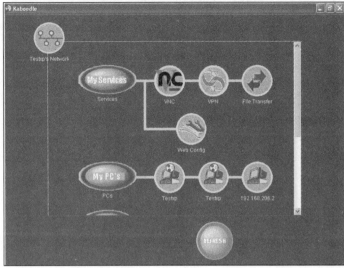

There should now be icons for every computer and device on your network. Double-clicking or right clicking on an icon will give you a dialogue similar to Figure 5.22. This shows the machine's IP address, Media Access Control (MAC) (low level) address, and other information about the computer. With this tool, you can easily discover and track different computers on your home network.

Figure 5.22 Kaboodle Giving More Information About a Computer

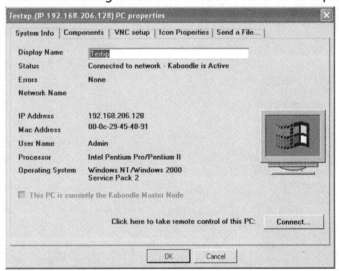

Finding Interesting Stuff

Looking for files of interest on a computer can be like searching in the dark for a needle in a haystack. For example, a typical installation of Windows XP Service Pack 2 with a few typical applications has more than 1,000 folders containing more than 20,000 files. This is a significant amount of data for any one person to look through. To simplify the tasks of searching for meaningful data, we present some basic search tools. This is the software you will use to search for material of interest on your target computer. These are tools that help you comb through the thousands of files that can be found on a typical machine and develop a useful list of "interesting" ones to examine more closely.

MS Search

One of the most powerful tools for searching for information is already installed on your computer. Microsoft has a Search utility built into its operating system that allows you to conduct a variety of searches on the file system. You can search for files based on name, time accessed, and content. When pointed at the C:\ drive (the entire file system), you can conduct a very broad search for anything that may interest you. Search is found on your Start menu by clicking **Start | Search**. Figure 5.23 shows the search dialogue box. (MS Search is covered in more depth in Chapter 6.)

Figure 5.23 Microsoft's Search Dialogue Box

Google Desktop Search

The Google Desktop Search software allows you to search your computer using a Web browser. It will also find e-mails, AOL Instant Messaging Chats, files, and Web caches. The advantage that the Google Desktop Search program has over Microsoft's search program is its ability to classify advanced file types. Being able to display cached Web images and chat logs increases the ease of search and evaluation. In addition, using Google Desktop Search to look for information is a format that most computer users are familiar with.

Download From

The Google Desktop Search tool can be downloaded and installed from *http://desktop.google.com*.

Installation Instructions

Google has made installation of the Desktop Search software as easy as possible. Using your Web browser, go to http://desktop.google.com. Click on the **Agree and Download** button; this will begin the installation procedure. A pop-up window will ask if you want to run or download *GoogleDesktopSearchSetup.exe*. Click **Run**; this will begin the installation procedure. The installation program will shut down any open Web browsers in order to continue installation. Once this has finished, a browser window similar to the one shown in Figure 5.24 will open, indicating successful installation and offering several configuration options.

Figure 5.24 Google Desktop Search's Configuration Page

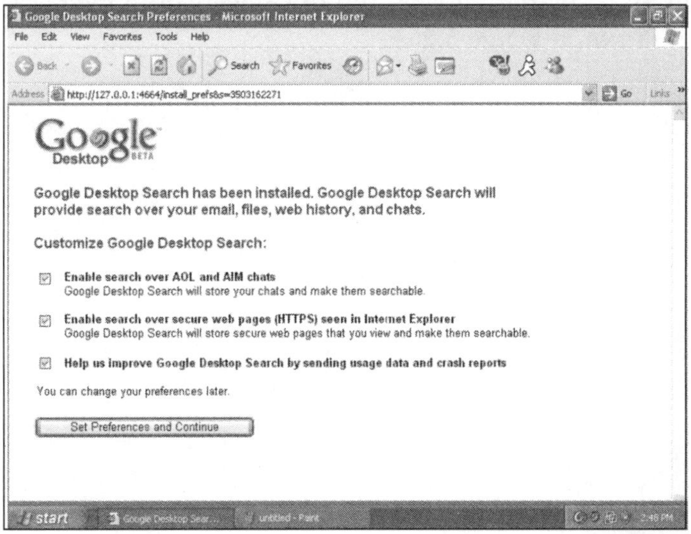

Of the given options, **Enable search over AOL and AIM chats** and **Enable search over secure Web pages** should be set. The option for providing feedback to Google can be set if you wish; however, it has no bearing on the effectiveness of the Google Desktop Search tool's ability to search for information. Once you have set your preferences, select the **Set Preferences** and **Continue** buttons. The next window that appears indicates that Google is indexing your computer, as shown in Figure 5.25.

Figure 5.25 Google Desktop Search's Indexing in Progress Page

Clicking on **Start Searching** takes you to Google's main interface for searching your desktop, as shown in Figure 5.26.

Figure 5.26 Google Desktop Search's Main Search Dialogue

Usage

You can select the desktop icon, or the Google Desktop Search item from the Program Files menu. A window similar to that in Figure 5.26 will appear. From this Web site you can choose to search the Web or follow other Google links. However, as long as desktop is selected, you will be searching from your hard disk. When performing a search, the Google search tool classifies its finds as files, e-mail, images, and chat logs. Any of these are clickable and viewable by whatever application they are registered with.

Collecting on the Computer

Like the tools mentioned in "Finding Interesting Stuff," the software discussed in this section is designed to help you collect information passing through the targeted computer. These tools are used to collect files, e-mails, or events that took place on that computer, but that has left no long-term evidence behind.

PC Inspector

The first type of software we use to collect information that was once (but is no longer) on the computer is a tool named PC Inspector. It takes standard searching techniques one step further by scouring the hard drive to recover files that have been deleted (and long forgotten).

Download From

You can obtain the most recent version of this freeware tool through the *www.pcin-spector.de/file_recovery/UK/welcome.htm* Web site, or with the other archived software on our Web site.

Installation Instructions

The installation process for this application is straightforward. You are not required to make any decisions or selections other than indicating which language the instructions should be displayed in and accepting the license.

Protected Storage Explorer

Next, we expand our search for hidden information to the memory of the computer and the applications that execute on it. In particular, we directly target Microsoft's Protected Storage area with a tool rightfully named Protected Storage Explorer.

Download From

You can acquire this tool either through from *www.cyberspybook.com* or from *www.forensicsideas.com*.

Installation Instructions:

Like the previous tool, installation of the Protected Storage Explorer is straightforward. Double-click on the installation executable that you acquire from the Web site and follow through the menu questions. In addition, we suggest that you ensure that the "Just me" box is checked so that icons are not created on the desktops of other users of the computer (Figure 5.27).

Figure 5.27 Protected Storage Explorer Installation Folder Selection

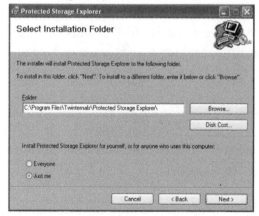

Best Free Keylogger

The searching tools already mentioned in this chapter can look for information that used to be on a computer; now we want to gather new and transient information as it is created. To accomplish this, we rely heavily on an application called Best Free Keylogger (BFK), which is capable of capturing keystrokes and surveillance images of the desktop.

Download From

The BFK is available at *http://bfk.sourceforge.net* and at *www.cyberspybook.com*.

Installation Instructions

The most important aspect of the installation process for this tool is the selection of the **Installation** folder. This is where the images and collection will be stored, so make sure that it has plenty of available disk space (see Figure 5.28).

Figure 5.28 Best Free Keylogger

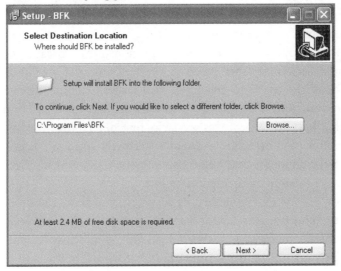

Like many of the others, this is a GNU-licensed application.

Collecting over the Wire or the Air

A lot of the data on computers is evanescent; it is sent to the computer, or passes through it, but never stays there for long. It may be information that originates on the computer, but is not collected by other tools, or it may be data such as an instant message that is sent to the target computer, viewed briefly, and then discarded forever.

The next category of tools we discuss are commonly referred to as *sniffers*. Sniffers enable you to monitor network traffic and collect some of this ephemeral data that can be very interesting and very elusive. A sniffer allows you to capture all of the information that is entering and leaving a computer via the network. A correctly installed and operating sniffer will yield a wealth of information to any cyber-spy. Many valuable protocols such as Internet Relay Chat (IRC [the standard version]), AOL Instant Messenger (AIM), Yahoo, Microsoft Network (MSN), e-mail, and Hypertext Transfer Protocol (HTTP) are transferred across the network in plain-text, meaning they are not encrypted and anyone who captures the packets can view the data in them.

There are basically two different locations that you can sniff from: the target's machine or another machine that can see the traffic. The target's machine is an easy choice if you can get to it. A sniffer on that machine will see all network traffic coming in and out of the machine. When coupled with a remote access tool, a sniffer-implanted target machine is a well-bugged and powerful eavesdropping device. We also show you how to set up your account to sniff for all traffic, even when you aren't logged in. If for some reason you can't obtain access to the target's machine, a different approach must be taken. In that situation, network monitoring has to be done from a remote machine.

There are several options that can be used when trying to capture traffic remotely. In order for remote sniffing to work, the computer you install it on must be able to see all of the traffic to and from your target machine. There are several scenarios where this is possible. An easy and ideal scenario is if all computers are connected with a hub. To test for this scenario, first determine your IP address then turn on your sniffer of choice (to be discussed shortly) and look at the traffic. If any of the traffic has IP addresses that belong to your network but not your computer, your computer is probably connected via a hub.

If you are on a network connected by a switch, you have a couple of other options. The first option is to set your listening computer as a network chokepoint and force all network traffic to pass through it. This would involve putting two network adapters in your machine, configuring it to forward traffic, and placing it in a network chokepoint, as shown in Figure 5.29.

Figure 5.29 Computer Used as a Pass-through for Sniffing

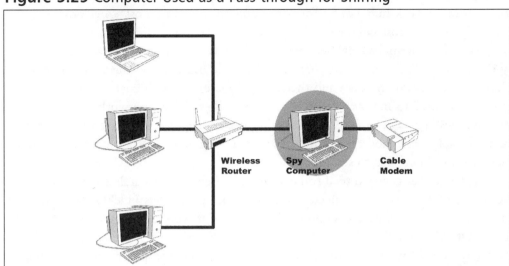

Alternatively, you could acquire a small hub and connect it into a chokepoint. Using the hub creates a much simpler setup. All that is needed is the hub and two additional network wires, one to connect to your listening station, and one to complete the original connection. Figure 5.30 shows how to set up this topology.

Figure 5.30 Using a Hub to Build a Network Tap

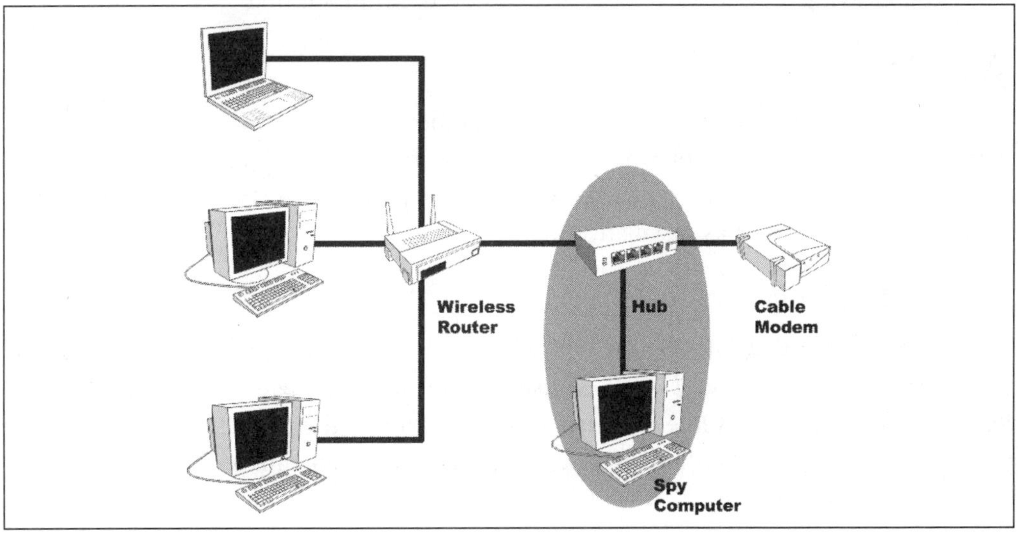

The only difficulty with using a hub is that in this day and age it may be hard to find a true network hub. For performance and cost reasons, most stores now generally only sell low-cost switches.

You may remember that there are two obvious chokepoints: between a router and the cable/DSL modem and between the cable modem and the wall. The connection between the modem and the wall is done either with coaxial cable or phone cable as opposed to network cable. Most people do not have network adapters that can use these types of cable. As a result, the best chokepoint is between the router and the cable/DSL modem. a computer intercepting all of the traffic on the home network would be able to see everything.

One area that is guaranteed to be a broadcast region is a wireless network. If your target's computer is connected to a network via Wireless Fidelity (Wi-Fi), sniffing will be a relatively easy process. Because of its very design, wireless must be broadcast, and a wireless signal can be picked up directly out of the air. There are two ways to sniff wireless traffic. You can sniff with your computer without adding it to the wireless network, which has the advantage of being stealthier. Because your computer has never become part of the network, no one knows if it's there and therefore no one can monitor its traffic. However, if wireless encryption is turned on (i.e., Wireless Encryption Protocol [WEP] or Wireless Application Protocol [WAP]), it is easiest to become part of the network to see the plaintext view of all the packets. Even then it is still extremely difficult to detect if your computer is actually collecting and sniffing traffic.

The following are software tools that can be used for sniffing.

WinPcap

This device driver must be installed on any Windows machine that will be used for network monitoring. It enables different packages to collect or sniff packets on the network. Some popular sniffers come with WinPcap as part of their installation, but most don't, so we cover its installation here.

Download From

The latest version of WinPcap that will work with the tools we use in this book can be downloaded from *www.cyberspybook.com* or from its home page at *http://winpcap.polito.it/*. While it comes in many formats, the best and easiest to use is the WinPcap auto-installer. This is an executable that, when run, installs WinPcap and all of its associated files.

Installation

Installation is straightforward and follows a few simple steps. Unlike most of the other software packages we will be discussing, WinPcap does not have any real configuration options. As a result, installation is done in five easy steps:

1. Using techniques from this chapter's "Basic Skills" section, look for and remove previously installed versions of WinPcap.

2. Double-click on the **auto-installer**.

3. Click **Next** on the Welcome screen to go to the license information.

4. Accept the license information and then click **Next**. You should receive a final screen showing WinPcap was installed.

5. Click **Finish**

Ethereal

Ethereal is a very powerful tool that we will be using throughout the remainder of this book. Ethereal can be used to capture packets and analyze protocols. We will show you how to use Ethereal to examine captured packets, which will allow you to determine what data was passed in the conversation. Ethereal can be used to filter the captured packets and to display selected data. This allows us to capture a large amount of traffic and quickly sift through it for the important information.

Download From:

The latest version of Ethereal can be found *www.cyberspybook.com* or at Ethereal's main site, *www.ethereal.com/download.html*. Ethereal can be obtained either as a self-extracting executable or an archive. For the purpose of this book, we will discuss using the self-extracting executable because it will provide the easiest method of installation.

Installation

Installation of Ethereal is relatively straightforward. However, WinPcap must be installed before installing Ethereal. Installation of Ethereal requires six steps:

1. Double-click the downloaded Ethereal executable. This will create a pop-up window displaying the Welcome screen.

2. Click **Next**; you will be greeted by a license screen.

3. Read and agree to the license.

4. At the Choose Components screen shown in Figure 5.31, select the
    Ethereal Components you want to install. The defaults are usually accept-
    able.

5. Now you should be at the **Choose Install Location** screen. Once again
    the default values work.

6. You will be greeted by a final pop-up window; click **Finish** to finalize
    installation.

Figure 5.31 Ethereal "Choose Components" Screen

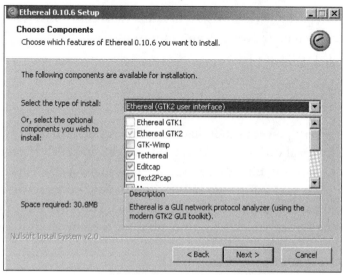

Usage

Ethereal is a relatively easy tool to use. Initially, we only cover its basic capabilities.
Once you've become comfortable with its basics, we will discuss its more powerful
features. This section explains the basics, which focus on using Ethereal as a packet
sniffer.

The first step is to start Ethereal, which can be done either by double-clicking
the icon or from **Start Menu | All Programs | Ethereal | Ethereal**. This brings
up the Ethereal's interface, as shown in Figure 5.32.

Figure 5.32 Ethereal Interface

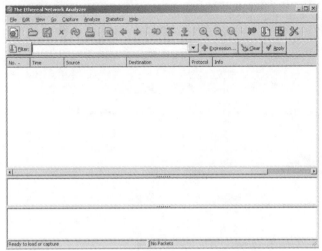

Although the main Ethereal graphical user interface (GUI) may seem a bit daunting, don't become dismayed; using Ethereal is actually very easy.

The next step is to go to **Capture | Start**, which will display the capture dialogue, as shown in Figure 5.33. This dialogue allows you to select various options that will determine what Ethereal captures. If the computer has multiple network interfaces, you can choose to capture on one or all of them. Ethereal can also be set to write collected traffic to a file, which can then be examined at a later date using the Ethereal GUI. An important option to check is **Capture packets in promiscuous mode**, which allows every packet on the network to be collected, not just those intended for the local machine that has Ethereal installed.

Figure 5.33 Ethereal Capture Dialogue

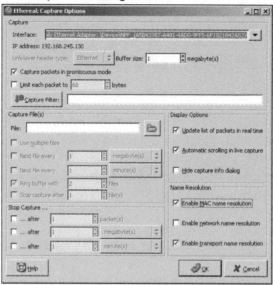

Once you have selected your options, click **OK** to begin packet capture. Ethereal will then display a status dialogue indicating how many packets and of what type have been captured. Packet Capture continues until the **Stop** button is selected. After Packet Capture is stopped, Ethereal displays the captured packets in a manner similar to that shown in Figure 5.34.

Figure 5.34 Ethereal with Captured Packets

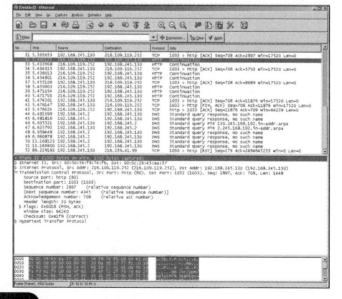

The Ethereal GUI shows all of the captured packets. As shown in Figure 5.34, the GUI is split into three sections: the top section displays all of the captured packets, the middle section displays a single packet's protocol information, and the last section allows the user to examine a raw packet. To select which packet to examine, you simply highlight it in the top section. As you will notice, this causes the highlighted packet to be displayed in the middle and bottom sections as well. Selecting different sections of the packet field descriptions in the middle display causes Ethereal to expand those areas and show additional information about the packet. This also allows you to select which sections of the raw packet you wish to analyze in the bottom display.

One of the most useful features of Ethereal is its capability for filtering out selected packets. You can select a packet, and Ethereal provides the ability to display only the conversation that the packet was a part of. In order to do this, right-click on the highlighted packet and select **Follow TCP Stream**, as shown in Figure 5.35.

Figure 5.35 Selecting the "Follow TCP Stream" Option

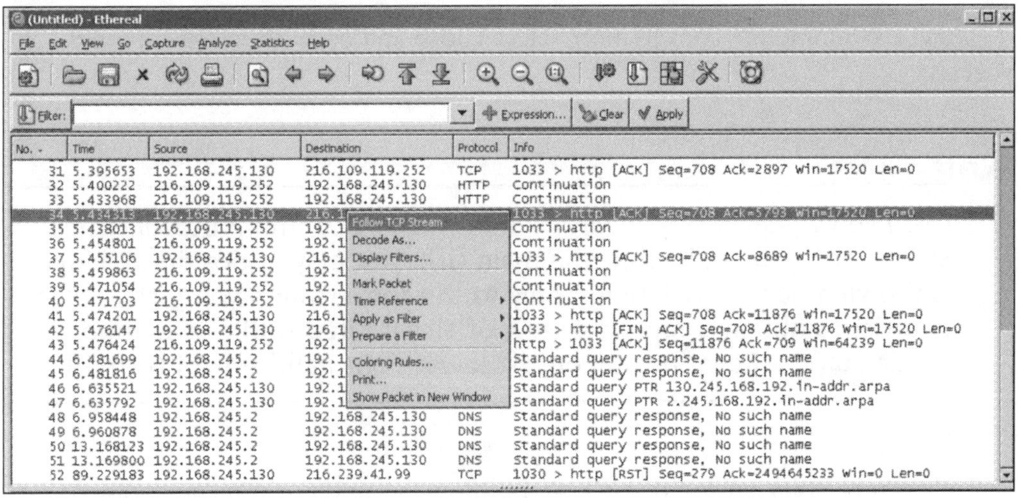

Ethereal then displays the conversation that the packet was a part of, as shown in Figure 5.36. This allows you to easily identify and follow specific conversation streams on a heavily congested machine.

Figure 5.36 Ethereal Showing a Decoded TCP Stream

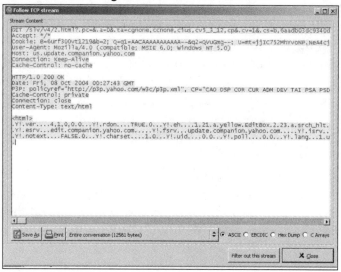

After examining the conversation, select **Close** and go back to the captured packets.

> **NOTE**
>
> Once you've finished following a Transmission Control Protocol (TCP) stream and you are back at the main GUI, you may notice that Ethereal is showing packets belonging only to the conversation you just studied. In order to obtain a complete view of all captured traffic, it is important to click on the **Reset** button on the lower right-hand side of the GUI.

Ethereal is a very powerful sniffer and protocol analyzer. It is recommended that you use Ethereal to capture and examine some of your own packets as practice, to help you learn how to use it effectively.

Packetyzer

Packetyzer is another sniffer package that we recommend. At its core, it is very similar to Ethereal and, in fact, uses the Ethereal Capture engine in order to work. However, the makers of Packetyzer determined that Ethereal did not meet all of their needs. The resulting product, Packetyzer, performs all of the core functions of Ethereal and then some. Notable improvements include a more Microsoft Windows-like interface, its ability to graphically visualize traffic, and the capability to capture and analyze Wi-Fi (wireless) traffic and locate Wi-Fi access points. Some people also find its interface more intuitive than Ethereal's.

Download From

Links to Packetyzer can be found at *www.cyberspybook.com* or at *http://www.network-chemistry.com/products/packetyzer/*. Each site should have a link for downloading the current version of the Packetyzer setup executable.

Installation

Packetyzer installation is relatively easy, and to keep things simple we will be using the default layout and options. Installing Packetyzer requires eight steps:

1. To start installation, double-click on the Packetyzer set-up executable. This will bring up the initial Setup screen.

2. Select **Next** at the initial screen to bring up the license agreement.

3. After reading the license agreement, select the **I accept the agreement** button, then select **Next**. As noted earlier, the GPL license allows you to freely download and use the tool, but restricts repackaging and selling it. Following acknowledgment of the GPL agreement, you will be displayed additional licensing and copyright information.

4. You should now be at the screen for setting up the installation location. Accept the default path and click **Next**.

5. Packetyzer's setup will now ask where to place the Start Menu Folder. Once again, use the default and select **Next**.

6. The next screen (Figure 5.37) prompts for two additional options. The first is to install a desktop icon. Select this option at your own discretion. Although it will make it easier to find and run Packetyzer, it makes it easier for other users to discover it as well. Completely overt installation of a sniffer may clue some users in to your sneaky intentions. The second option is to install the WinPcap driver. If you have not already installed WinPcap, select this option. If you walked through the installation at the start of this section, you should already have the latest version of WinPcap installed. After selecting your options click **Next**.

7. Now that the options are configured, Packetyzer is ready to be installed. Select **Install** to begin the process.

8. After a minute or two, the final screen will appear. Click **Finish**.

Figure 5.37 Packetyzer Options

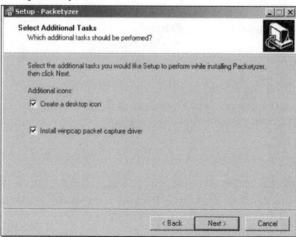

Usage

We will be using Packetyzer as a sniffer and an analyzer. After starting Packetyzer by clicking on the icon or through the menu bar, you will be presented with a **Capture Options** pop-up window (Figure 5.38). This window allows you to set the interface that Packetyzer will collect on, as well as size limits and promiscuous mode. Usually the default interface will work for packet capture. We don't recommend limiting the capture size on each packet; promiscuous mode is a good idea. Automatic scrolling of a live capture is a good feature; it shows you packets on the screen as it captures them. Unfortunately, this option also takes a lot of central processing unit (CPU) time and can slow your PC down to a crawl. The final option limits the size of your total capture to about 10,000 kilobytes, or about 10 megabytes. That is an acceptable default value for some things. If you are on a network where several people are browsing the Web or engaged in other high-bandwidth activities, 100,000 or even 1 million kilobytes might be a better value. After selecting all of your options, click **OK** to continue.

Figure 5.38 Packetyzer Options

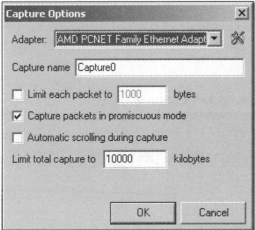

The main Packetyzer window (as shown in Figure 5.39) is now displayed. You can select the **Help** tab to receive further help at any time. Much like Ethereal, the main Window is divided into sections; however, it also has tabs taking you to other screens of interest.

Figure 5.39 Packetyzer Main Window

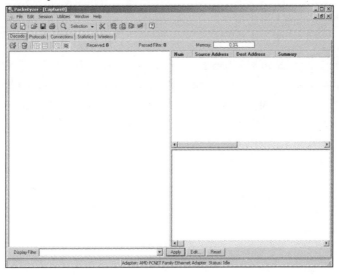

To begin capturing packets you can either go to **Session** | **Start Capture** or press **F5**. To stop capturing packets go to **Session** | **Stop Capture** or press **F6**. In the example shown in Figure 5.40, a browser was started that went to *www.google.com*

as its home page. The captured packets are displayed in three separate sections of the GUI: the top right section shows all of the packets that were captured, the bottom right section shows the raw dump of the highlighted packet in the top window, and the left side shows the protocol of the packet broken out. This is the same basic design as Ethereal.

Figure 5.40 Example Packet Capture

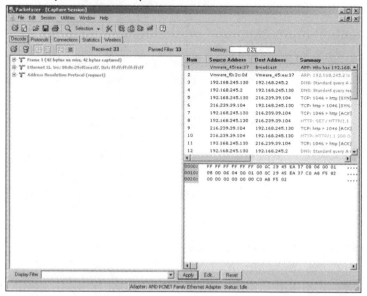

By selecting a packet in the top right portion and right clicking on it, Packetyzer will display advanced options. Packetyzer will automatically follow the TCP stream of a session. Figure 5.41 shows all of the traffic that was sent between the machine and Google's Web server.

Figure 5.41 Captured Traffic for a Web Session

Looking back at Figure 5.39, you may notice that there is a tab labeled Wireless. This tab gives access to Packetyzer's wireless features. If your computer or laptop is equipped with a Wi-Fi card, you can use this section to obtain information about wireless access points available to your machine. Packetyzer has some more advanced features than Ethereal. Feel free to experiment with Packetyzer and explore its capabilities. You may find it is more intuitive to use than Ethereal.

Snort

Snort is an open source Intrusion Detection System (IDS) that has many distinct uses. As an open source project, it benefits from having many people contributing to its evolution. As a result, it has become a very powerful and effective IDS. One critical component of its intrusion detection capability is its ability to capture and store packets. It can also be run as a service, allowing it to collect packets from all users, which is especially useful on a multi-user Windows XP machine. As a service, Snort can run covertly in the background, making it difficult to detect.

Download From

Snort can be found at *www.cyberspybook.com* or at *www.snort.org*. Like most other GPL projects, it comes in a range of formats from source code to archive files to self-extracting executables. A self-extracting executable is the best and easiest choice for our purposes. As with other tools previously installed, WinPcap must already be installed.

Installation

After downloading the self-extracting executable, double-click on it to begin the installation process. The installation of Snort requires five steps:

1. The first step is to read and agree to the license. By this point the GNU GPL should be familiar to you. Click **I Agree** to continue.

2. The next screen is Installation Options where Snort can choose to log its data to a database (Figure 5.42). We will not need to use this advanced option. Click **Next** to continue.

3. The next step is to choose your installation components. As usual, the default components will suffice. Click **Next** to continue.

4. Next choose the installation location. Take note of this location. Unlike most of the other programs that we have installed, Snort does not create an icon or an entry in the Start menu. It must be started from the directory that it was installed into.

5. Click **Install** to begin the installation process. Snort will display a status bar to keep you updated about its progress and a final pop-up window when it has completed.

Figure 5.42 Snort Logging Options

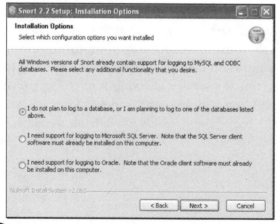

Usage

Snort will be used as the local sniffer, because it can generate traffic log files and examine those logs. Snort must be installed and configured to run as quietly as possible; therefore, it should be installed as a service. This takes several steps that are relatively easy.

1. The first step is to create a directory where the log files will be placed. For our example, this directory will be located where the Snort executable file resides, but it can be put anywhere, and in fact should be put somewhere less obvious. The easiest way to create the log folder is to use Explorer. Go to the Snort directory, right-click **New | Folder**, and change the folder name to **Log**. You can also give it a less obvious name.

2. Once the Log directory is created, you must set up Snort as a service. To do this, use the command line from where the Snort executable resides. At the command prompt enter

    cd c:\snort\bin\Snort.exe \service \install –L C:\snort\ bin\Log –b.

    where the **-L** option indicates where to place the log files. Since there are spaces in the path, the entire path must be placed within parentheses. The **-b** tells Snort in what format to save the log file.

3. Now that Snort has been installed as a service, it must be set to start automatically on reboot. The easiest way to do this is to click **Start | Control Panel | Administrative Tools | Services**. Now all of the services on the machine will be displayed. Find the entry associated with Snort and right-click and select **Properties**. A Properties window will be displayed that will look similar to Figure 5.43. Under the **Startup Type**, select **Automatic** and press the **Start** button to activate Snort.

Figure 5.43 Snort Properties Dialogue

Snort is now installed and activated. To ensure that it is functioning correctly, start up a Web browser and go to a Web site. Check the Log folder; there should be a *snort.log.xxx* file. These are the files that will be examined later to determine the activity on the machine.

> **NOTE**
>
> You can drag your Snort log files into Ethereal or Packetyzer and use these more advanced tools for packet analysis.

OWNS

One-Way Network Sniffer (OWNS) functions like a regular sniffer but goes further in its processing of the information. OWNS attempts to reconstitute the files that it observes passing through the network. This allows you to examine the files that were passed on the network with minimal analysis and no reconstruction on your part. OWNS attempts to break out the Graphics Interchange Formats (GIFs), Joint Photographic Experts Groups (JPEGs), e-mail, and other file types, which are all very useful in determining what someone is doing online. This is a good sniffer to use if you are actively monitoring the person in real time. It is also good for capturing e-mail sent with Microsoft Outlook, Outlook Express, and AOL mail. The biggest downside to OWNS is that it is an older piece of software and no longer updated.

Download From

OWNS can be found at either *www.cyberspybook.com* or at *http://sourceforge.net/projects/owns*. The current version is *own-0.5-win.zip*.

Installation

OWNS uses WinPcap, which should already be installed on the system. Installing OWNS is quite simple and is done by double-clicking on the OWNS archive file and extracting it to a directory of your choosing. It is important to note that this application does not create an icon on the desktop or Start menu, so keep a note of where it is extracted.

Usage

OWNS is very simple to use. To start using it, click on the **Owns.exe** file in the directory that you extracted the application to. Doing so brings up the OWNS interface, as seen in Figure 5.44.

Figure 5.44 Initial OWNS Screen

The **Source** tab allows you to select the sniffer and source that it will collect on. Because we installed WinPcap previously, this option should be selected. You also have the option of using a file or network interface as the source. The file could be a *tcpdump* file from a previous session captured by any of the previously mentioned sniffers. However, for our demonstration we will use the network interface to collect and analyze the files that are viewed by our target. By selecting the **Parameters** tab, the next set of options (Figure 5.45) can be displayed.

Figure 5.45 OWNS Parameters Tab

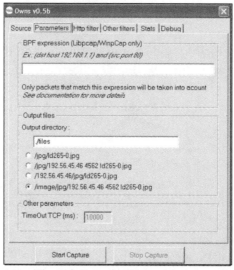

This tab allows you to determine where the output files will go and in what form they will be saved. In the example shown in Figure 5.45, OWNS will create a directory named "files" wherever the executable resides, to store the collected files. After sniffing the network, you can go back to this directory and look at what was found. Clicking on the **HTTP Filter** tab brings up the next set of options (Figure 5.46).

Figure 5.46 OWNS HTTP Filter Tab

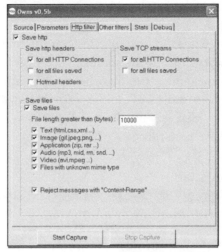

The **Save Files** option allows you to select which types of files should be saved. For our purposes saving them all is recommended. We also recommend lowering the minimum file length for saving. Currently, it is set at 10,000 bytes, or about 10KB. You should lower this setting to about 1,000 or even 500 bytes. This will be important in later chapters because you will discover that some sites, in order to reduce bandwidth, will transmit their Web pages compressed. These compressed Web pages are often well under the 10,000-byte default. Make sure you also check the **For all HTTP Connection** box in the "Save http headers" and "Save TCP streams" sections. Select the **Other Filters** tab for more options (Figure 5.47).

Figure 5.47 OWNS Other Filters Tab

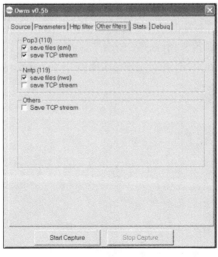

The **Other Filters** tab allows you to select if you want to capture e-mail and news traffic. Once these have been selected, the **Start Capture** button will begin sniffing.

As OWNS works, the **Stats** tab will update with the traffic going by (Figure 5.48). Selecting **Stop Capture** stops the sniffer. Once OWNS is stopped you can go into the files directory and examine the files that were transferred. This makes it very easy to determine what the person was looking at. Additional help on OWNS can be found in the *doc directory* that was installed with OWNS. Double-click on the **index.html** file to view the help file.

Figure 5.48 OWNS Stats Tab

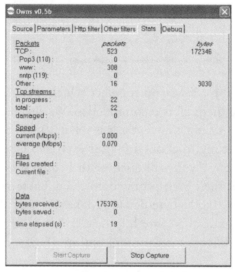

OWNS provides an extremely powerful capability for network traffic analysis. It can break out all of the material flying across the network, making visualization simple and easy. Using OWNS on your Snort log files can significantly reduce the amount of time you spend analyzing them looking for interesting material.

Tips & Tricks...

Live Web Browsing Monitor

You can watch the pictures that fly across your network in real time by opening an Explorer window to your OWNS collection directory and setting your view options to thumbnails. Any pictures that OWNS can see and reconstruct will appear one by one in the directory. You can at any time double-click on one for close inspection by using your installed image-viewing program.

Remote Access Tools

Some tools like Snort are very effective spy software because they run quietly on a target machine. Others like Ethereal, need more intimate access. What do you do if you can't get continual access to the computer? You install a remote access tool.

A remote access tool is a piece of software designed to allow you to control a computer from another box, as if you are physically sitting at the computer. Three very good and easily available options are Back Orifice (2k and XP versions), Microsoft's Remote Desktop, and VNC. In this book, we utilize the program UltraVNC (*ultravnc.souceforce.net*) in our examples.

UltraVNC

VNC comes in several flavors. There is the original VNC or RealVNC (*www.realvnc.com*), an optimized version TightVNC (*www.tightvnc.com*), and the version we will be using, UltraVNC (*http://ultravnc.sourceforge.net*). We believe that UltraVNC is the best choice for several reasons. First, it contains most of the optimizations of TightVNC. Second, it has built-in stealth options, making discovery by your target slightly more difficult. Finally, it also has extra capability for file transfers and other added functionality.

Download

UltraVNC can be downloaded either from our site or from its home page at *http://ultravnc.sourceforge.net*. It comes either as an archive of all necessary files or as a self-installer. For this book, we cover only the self-installer.

Installation

Once you download the self-installer, you can run it by double clicking on the executable. This will launch a Setup screen that will prompt you to ask what components you wish to install (Figure 5.49).

Figure 5.49 Installation of the UltraVNC Remote Access Tool

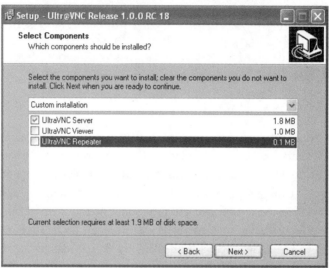

This prompt is very important because it will determine what software is extracted and installed on which computer. Unlike the other applications, you need to install this in two places: (1) on your target's machine and (2) on the remote machine that you are planning on using to access the target's computer. On your target's computer you want to check only the **UltraVNC Server** option and click **Next**. This will also ask you if you want to create a desktop icon; we suggest that you leave this box unchecked. If you want this to restart upon each book, check the **Register UltraVNC Server as a system service**. Next, it will install the software.

Next you can start the server from the Menu bar or from the icon that is created on the desktop tray. The first thing that you need to do is configure a password and other specific options that you desire (Figure 5.50). In particular, we suggest that you check the **Enable File Transfer** box so that you can copy files to/from this computer.

Figure 5.50 Configuration of the UltraVNC Remote Access Tool

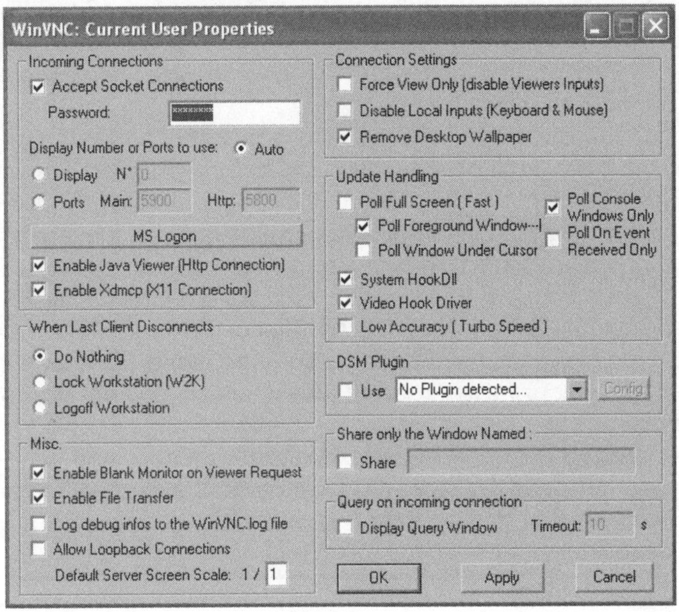

Meanwhile, you need to install the viewer on your computer. To do this follow the same aforementioned steps, but this time check only the box that says **UltraVNC Viewer** in the **Select Components** dialogue box. Once this is complete, you will be ready to remotely access the computer.

Usage

Usage of this tool is covered indepth in Chapter 6.

Tips and Tricks...

Take a Trip Back in Time

Throughout this chapter we have been instructing you to install software on your target's computer. In doing so, we continuously urge you to be as stealthy as possible with making a note of changes and returning the system to its original state when all is complete. However, there is one thing that you cannot prevent when you install software, and that is the presence of new files.

Continued

If you install a keystroke logger on your target's computer, and he stumbles across it, you could be caught. In fact, your target will have found not only the software but also a means of determining when it was installed. Microsoft Windows keeps track of time attributes having to do with file creation time, modification time, and last access time.

One thing you can do to help keep the accusatory fingers from pointing at you is to set the clock back on the computer before you install any software or access any files. For example, if you were out of town last week, and you set the clock back to that date, then when your mark notices the access time, you couldn't possibly be a suspect! This is also an easy way to evade searches done for specific access times. For example, let's say your mark always uses the Microsoft search tool (**Start | Search | All files or folders | When was it modified**) to look for files that have been recently accessed. By changing the date back, you will evade your target's search. But whatever you do, **do not forget to change the time back**.

You can change the time by double-clicking on the time displayed in the bottom right of the computer screen. A calendar and a clock will appear on your screen. Both can be changed by selecting either new dates or a new time and clicking the **OK** button.

Mastering Your Domain

The first steps you must take are to "master your domain." Like a good spy, you must develop knowledge of what you are up against so that you are prepared to operate in it. This involves becoming familiar with the networks, computers, and software you will be monitoring. As with all of our spying endeavors, from now on we will follow the six steps of the SLEUTH methodology to help us accomplish our goals.

In attempting to understand your environment, you should at a minimum try to learn the following information:

- What computers are in your home network?
- What operating systems do they have installed?
- Are they connected to the Internet, and if so how?
- What security software do they have?
- Do you have an account that you can use to install software?
- What access does your account give you?
- What account does your quarry use?

You should also make an effort to determine if and how the computer is connected to the Internet.

- What other objects are on the network?
- Is the computer connected via wireless or wires?
- Do all the computers connect into a hub or switch?

In addition to the *concrete* factors mentioned, you should also study your target and determine how, when, and where they use computers.

- Do they send and receive e-mail from home?
- Do they chat?
- Do they plug in a work laptop to your network?
- Do they leave themselves logged in all day?
- Do they set a password on their account?
- Do they stay up and use their computer late at night?

All of these factors will play a part in how you spy. The techniques you utilize against someone who sends and receives e-mail from a family computer will be different from the ones you use against someone who plugs in a laptop wirelessly. Another problem can arise if your target logs on and off frequently with a password-protected account. Not an insurmountable problem, but one nonetheless. If you are successful, you will have the requisite knowledge needed to develop a more involved spying campaign against your targets.

Despite the apparent simplicity of your goals, they are involved enough to lend themselves to two separate missions. The first is done around the house before you even touch a computer; the second is done at computers of interest. The first determines targets of interest; the second penetrates them and collects the information that you will need for further surveillance against them. Everything so far has been presented as one unified plan; however, in reality, it has two logical parts, which will be executed at two different times. Even though we introduced both parts together, we now break them up into two separate missions, each of which will follow our SLEUTH methodology.

Mission 1: Assess Your Surroundings (Before You Sit Down)

Set Goals

The goals for this mission are to obtain a working knowledge of your home computing environment. This includes all of the computers and peripherals, who uses which machine, when and what for, and how they connect to the Internet. After the mission is completed, you should have a better idea of your targets of interest, and know what computer or computers in your home you would like to run a more involved spying operation against.

Layout a Plan

Now that you have an idea of the information you need, you can develop a plan for obtaining it. Because it will be from and about a computer, the plan is broken into several parts. The first is a general information-gathering plan that will inform you about your home's computing environment and people's usage patterns. It will be used to help you focus your efforts on each computer that is significant to your goals. The second part of the plan will give you a more in-depth picture of your target of interest. It will give you the information you need to develop a deeper and more involved spying campaign against that system.

Before you even sit down at a computer, you can answer a few of the questions asked in the "Goals" section. Walk around your house and count the computers. For each computer, make note of who uses it and for what. Once you have that information you can probably narrow down your collection to those machines of interest.

Before you begin to look at your newly targeted machines, look at your home network. Figure out how it's connected. Is it cable, DSL, dial-up, or something else? Document how it works. Locate and document some of the critical infrastructure pieces. Look for your cable or DSL modem. Find out where it's connected. Is there a router for your home network, a switch or a hub? Locate each of these. At this point, it may help to draw a diagram of your network. It doesn't have to be sophisticated; boxes will do to represent computers, hubs, and routers. Draw in the network wires that are used to connect them. If the computer is connected wirelessly to the Internet, give it a special marking. Now you have a network map. You will use this later on when we address sniffing.

Finally, before you sit down, plan to take some time to look for usage patterns. This can be helpful since the next few steps will require you to spend some time physically at the computers you're interested in. In some cases, you may want to do this covertly, so it's important now to determine when you will have windows of time to fit your spying in. If the computer looks like it will be difficult to access, develop a plan to obtain access to it. For example, if your kids are on the computer nonstop when they're home from school, and you can't get to it when they're in school, work on a plan to get them out of the house while you're home. Send them on an errand or send them on an outing with your partner while you stay home to "catch up on work."

Evaluate Risks

For the first mission, your risks are relatively limited. The information you wish to collect can be obtained easily and with little effort; it can be done by overt observation. The biggest risk is in alerting your target to your interest in computers, which may alarm them if you are not usually uninvolved in the home computer and network. Luckily, your quest for this information can usually be passed off as simple curiosity or obsessive compulsiveness, whichever works for your situation. Another risk to consider is that any notes and diagrams you make can be discovered. Different methods can be developed to address this. For example, you can designate several pages of a "work" notebook for your information. Putting your computer diagrams in the middle of a notebook filled with boring accounting may be one safe place. Other steps would involve physical security of all your documentation. At this point, discovery of any thing you document will be the weakest link in your operations chain. While your activities may be dismissed, the fact you are recording information may be a little harder to dismiss. Develop a method to minimize the risk of your documentation being discovered.

Use Best Judgment to Execute Your Plan

Goals are set, a plan is developed, and the risks are assessed and minimized. It is time to execute your plan. This mission should be relatively simple and straightforward; we foresee few obstacles preventing successful completion. However, make this practice for your future operations. Don't stray far from the SLEUTH methodology and remember the other important spy principles. Don't be greedy in your search for information. Remember, many successful operations take time. Trying to get too much too fast may clue others in to your intentions. Don't modify your behavior too much. Try to get the information you need while making it look like you're not doing anything unusual.

Take in Observations

This is the most crucial step of your first mission. It is important to carefully document the information you've obtained. Below are some of the specific details you should be looking for:

- How many computers do you have?
- For each computer determine:
    1. Where is the computer located?
    2. Is the computer a laptop?
    3. Is the computer connected to network? The Internet? How?
    4. Who uses the computer? What do they use it for? When do they usually use it? What account access do they have?
    5. Can you access the computer?
- What other devices are on the network? Routers, cable modems, and so forth?

Handle the Situation

Now that you've collected your information, it is time to use it. You know your target and now hopefully you know about their computing habits; what machines they use, when the use them, and for what. Basically, you should have a good idea of your target machines and when you can physically access them. This is the information you will need to begin your second mission, a more in-depth collection of information.

Mission 2: Penetrate Your Targets (at the Computer)

Set Goals

The first mission helped you narrow down the computers you will be going after and helped you determine a good time to have physical access to those machines. Now that they have been determined, it is time to gain a deeper knowledge of your targets of interest. The second mission is about obtaining the appropriate information from each machine to be able to carry out more in-depth and remote spying. The specific goals for this mission are to identify the operating system and its users, the passwords or knowledge of how to obtain access, and the security software installed for each computer you have targeted.

Lay Out a Plan

For this mission, you will seek to accomplish the following objectives:

- Obtain access to the machine

- Determine the operating system

- Determine security software

- Create a method for sustained access

The first step you need to plan for is obtaining access to the machine. This requires that you have physical access for a certain period of time; we recommend 30 minutes. All of the procedures can be done in less than one minute, and almost instantaneously by a piece of software; however, it is always good to build in extra time for mistakes and possible errors. Thirty minutes should give you enough time to get into the machine, record the necessary information, and clean up.

The next step is to make sure you can log on to the machine. Many home machines don't have passwords, but some do. If you encounter a password prompt such as the one shown in Figure 5.51, you will have to obtain a password to access the machine.

Figure 5.51 Windows XP Password Prompt

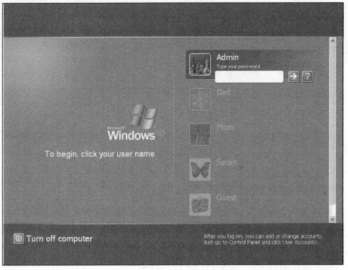

When faced with a prompt you have several choices. If you're an advanced computer user you could boot to a different media and mount the drive, or power down the computer and take its hard disk out to view elsewhere. These techniques, although effective, are involved, take experience, and leave traces. For example, a paranoid user may notice their computer has been reset since they were last on.

Obtaining the password is generally a better solution. You can go about this in several ways. One is to "guess." Guessing generally works in the movies, but we've never had much luck with that method. To improve your chances with guessing, you can look for a password "reminder" lying around. In movies, this is a post-it note stuck to the monitor, and in this case, we actually agree with the movies. Another great place to look for a password reminder is under the keyboard.

Using a keystroke logger offers an alternative to guessing passwords. A keystroke logger is a piece of software or hardware that captures user input at the keyboard. When a keystroke logger is software, it collects the keystrokes and writes out textual interpretations to a file. A hardware keystroke logger can take many forms (see Figure 5.52). It is a small device that fits between a keyboard with a PS/2 connector and the PS/2 slot. It quietly records keystrokes and stores them in its internal buffer. The keystroke logger can then be taken to another computer and its cache of keystrokes viewed. In cases when you can't log on to a computer, a hardware keystroke logger is the best bet for getting the password.

Figure 5.52 Hardware Keystroke Logger

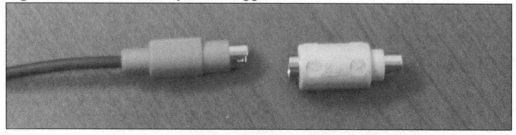

Once you've obtained access, the next step is to determine the operating system. In most cases, this can be done visually, but there are several guaranteed methods that should be used for verification. The **ver** command will reveal the operating system version and can be launched by opening a command prompt and typing **ver.exe**. Figure 5.53 shows the results of running **ver** on a Windows XP machine.

Although this can give operating system version and build information, it does not necessarily do it in an easy-to-understand format. For example, service packs are never clearly stated. An additional way of finding out the operating system version, including service packs, is to open the control panel, find the **System** icon, double-

Figure 5.53 Running ver.exe on a Windows XP Machine

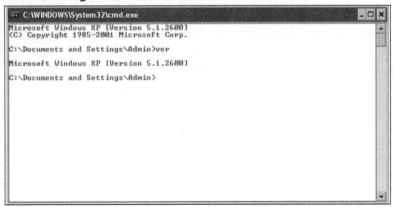

click to open it, and select the **General** tab. You should then see a window like that shown in Figure 5.54, giving the operating system, service packs, and information about the CPU and main memory.

Figure 5.54 Determining OS Version

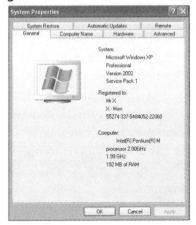

Next, it is time to look for security software, in particularly for virus scanners and firewalls. These are the types of software that can play havoc on spy tools. They are designed specifically to prevent what you are attempting to do. Although most of our tools should bypass virus scanners, it is still good to be aware of them. Firewalls, on the other hand, can prevent some of our tools from working altogether. You can find most of these tools by looking at the small icon bar in the lower right-hand corner of the screen. Hold your mouse over each icon and its title will be displayed. If you are using Windows XP, you might have to click on the arrow that displays

show hidden icons to see all of the running software. Popular virus scanners are made by the Norton and Mcaffee companies. Popular firewalls are Zone Alarm, Norton, and Microsoft's built-in firewall. If you are using Windows XP Service Pack 2, you can go to **Control Panel | Security Center**. This gives you all of the information about installed firewalls and virus scanners.

Finally, it is time to create a method of sustained access. This is how you will have continued access to the computer. In some cases where there is no password and physical access is easy, there is nothing to do. If you had to obtain the password from a hint or a keystroke logger, it is a good idea to leave a keystroke logger and means of remote access in place in case the password is ever changed. If you do not think you will have ample opportunity to physically reach the computer again, it is a good idea to install one of the remote access tools described in the "Software" section. You can use these tools to access the machine remotely, almost as if you were physically sitting at the computer.

If you are going to install remote access software, you need to take the following steps:

1. Install and configure the remote access software.

2. Determine the information necessary for reassessing the machine.

The first step is relatively obvious and follows the procedures mentioned in the "Remote Access Software" section. The second requires that you know three things: the port number you plan to run the software on, the IP address, and whether the firewall will allow it to run. The first of those values, the port number, is easy to determine. Unless you configure your backdoor (assumed to be UltraVNC) to use a different port, it will be 5900. Figuring out the IP address is also a relatively simple process. On older Win9x machines you can run *winipcfg.exe* to get a graphical display of IP address information. The current method is to open a command prompt, as explained in the "Basic Skills" section. At the command prompt type in **ipconfig**. The results should look like Figure 5.55.

Figure 5.55 Running IPconfig

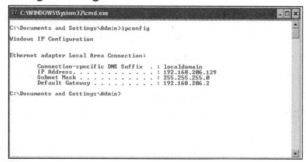

Finally, you need to make sure your remote access software works with the currently installed firewall, if there is one. If the machine is Windows XP Service Pack 2 or greater, Microsoft's firewall will be running by default, but also be prepared to expect Zone Alarm or Norton Firewall. The best way to test for this is to run your software and look for a pop-up prompting about it. Before you permit your software to run, look for an option to make sure it is always permitted. On Zone Alarm this means selecting a **Make This the Default Action**, and in Norton, select the **Always Permit versus the Permit** option.

NOTE

If you are installing remote access software or any software that uses the network, make sure you test it first, and make sure that the firewall allows it. You may have to explicitly tell the firewall to let the software connect and receive connections. When doing this, make sure your choices for allowing the software access become the default action for that firewall. You don't want your user to be prompted by his firewall anytime *you* want to access your target's computer.

Notes from the Underground...

Password Profiling

If you're lucky enough to obtain a password, either through a keylogger or via some other means, make sure you record it. Keep a list of passwords for your targets. After you've compiled some you can begin the process of password profiling. This is the process where you look at passwords and, using your knowledge of your target, look to see how they generated their passwords. In addition, you want to look for any similarities between their different passwords; in many cases, people will use the same password for many different types of accounts.

To begin profiling, start by writing the person's name on a piece of paper. Make sure to include their maiden name, nickname, or any other moniker applicable. Then write down their parent's name, spouse's name, kid's names, pet's names, as many names of those close to your target as you can discover. Now, write down their birthday, anniversaries, license plates, and other relevant numbers. Follow this with a list of all of the passwords you've obtained so far. Now

Continued

begin to look for patterns and similarities. Do they use parts of their names? Any significant numbers? Although people are encouraged to generate strong passwords, most don't. There usually is some weakness and familiarity in what they use. Once you find that you can compile a list of frequently used passwords and a list of possible passwords.

For example, assume we are targeting John Doe. Our profile sheet for him might look like this:

```
Name John Doe

Wife Jane Doe

Child Billy Doe

Dog: Spot Doe

B-Day: 10-10-1959

Anniversary: 6-12-1981

Hobbies: Hunting, cooking, car repair

PC password: johnd59

AIM id: johnd59

AIM password: meandjane81

Yahoo id: johndoe

Yahoo password: meandjane81

MSN id: hunter1959

MSN password: johndkillsit
```

From our example, we see that his "typical" password is *meandjane81*, basically the story of his wedding. Since it's used multiple times, we have a high likelihood of seeing it again for other accounts. We also notice that his password for his PC is his login ID for another account. Finally, we see that he uses words relating to his hobbies and numbers from significant numbers in his life to build his passwords. Most real profiling will not be as easy, but it's a worthwhile exercise.

Evaluate Risk

Like the previous mission, your risk should be minimal, and easily explainable, but it is still present. This time, because you will actually be at a computer, it is important to make sure that you have sufficient time to sit at and work at the computer without being discovered. Make sure that you plan for some "oops" time, as things can go wrong. Have a mission clock and set a make or break time. Once you've reached this point you either continue your operation or give up. It's also good to set a conservative finish point, a time by which you will leave the computer regardless of mission status. Determining these values beforehand will help reduce on-the-fly decision-making and mitigate the risk posed by the "I-just-need-5-more-minutes" problem.

Using Best Judgment to Execute Your Plan

Once again, it is time to actually execute your plan. Hopefully, your prior planning and preparation will pay off allowing you to accomplish all of your goals quickly and without being detected. Remember that you are working in the real world and not a spy book, so expect something to go wrong. Someone may discover or confront you, or the technical steps you so carefully planned may not work out as expected. Be prepared. Have a good story for those that you may encounter, and if the computer is not co-operating, don't panic. Write down what you observe, step backwards, try to unset anything you did, and go back to the planning phase.

Take in Observations

For this mission, you want to have two types of observations. First, collect your targeted information, the stuff you want to learn about each computer. For each machine you target you should note the following:

- **Operating System** This is important. When selecting software in future missions you, will have to make sure that it runs on that operating system. Most software discussed here will have documentation showing what it will run on. Know this before you try to install it.

- **Security Software** Knowing what security software is there helps with planning for your software implants. If you can, get copies of the security software and test your future implants with them. This will help you set things up so that your remote access tool doesn't trip firewall alarms, or your keystroke logger isn't caught by a simple anti-virus program.

All of this will be useful in the future. However, you should also collect some operational intelligence. As you do so, record things that you may or will change so that they can be reset to their original values when you are complete. For example, if you change the View options on Explorer, make sure to change them back. If a certain user was not logged in, make sure you log out completely. Try to leave things exactly as you found them.

Handle the Situation

By now you should have a complete view of your target's computing environment. You have all of the information to begin planning a more in-depth attack against their system. By learning the operating system, user's involved, and connectivity information, you can plan what will or will not work on a computer. Installing persistent access either via means of remote access such as VNC or collected passwords, will allow you to re-enter your target at a future date to conduct further operations.

Summary

This chapter covered a wide variety of topics. It introduced some basic skills and tricks for working with a computer, described the many pieces of software you will be using in depth, and performed two operations. You should have learned the following important lessons from this chapter:

- Covering your tracks is critical to being a successful cyber-spy.

- Explorer and the command prompt give you the ability to closely examine and run little known commands on your target computer.

- Different utilities such as IZArc and Superscan are not necessarily spy software, but they will help with your spying efforts.

- Microsoft's built-in search tool and Google's desktop search tool offer you the ability to look for files of interest on a target computer.

- Sniffers offer an extremely powerful capability to collect information from the network, in some cases even from computers you are not literally sitting at. Ethereal and Packetyzer are great tools for watching traffic on the network. Snort is a great tool for covertly installing on a target's machine. OWNS is a great tool for automatically analyzing and decoding interesting network traffic.

- The first mission had you profile and narrow down your targets.

- The second mission helped you obtain specific information about your targets that will be used to conduct a more sustained spying effort against them.

By now you should have a good idea of proper tradecraft, and how to apply to the SLEUTH methodology to your spying endeavors. Hopefully, you have a good deal of information about your target's computing habits, and their computer systems. Everything you've learned so far, in both collected intelligence and tradecraft, will be necessary and useful in the following chapters.

## Chapter 6

Spying on the PC

"Opportunities multiply as they are seized"
— Sun Tzu

Topics in this Chapter:

- **Mission One: Collect the Basics**

- **Mission Two: Examine the Past**

- **Mission Three: Live for the Present**

- **Mission Four: Prepare for the Future**

- **Mission Five: Look for Hidden Information**

- **Summary**

Introduction

By this point, you should be familiar with almost all that you need to know about the *mechanics* of conducting a successful spy operation using a computer. You know how to act, what to expect, and what you are looking for. Now, you just need the *skills*, and that is what this chapter will teach you. In the following pages, we guide you through basic techniques that will get you started. No matter the intention behind your spying, these scenarios will apply to you. They will be needed to make informed decisions and to proceed with the more pinpointed operations such as collecting e-mail and snooping on Web traffic introduced in later, more advanced chapters.

Techniques in this section are organized by their goals. Mission 1's goal is to collect basic information about your target, which will help you become familiar with your target's computing environment. Familiarization is a necessary step and is why intelligence operatives are sent to intensive courses about a country prior to their deployment to a foreign land. In Mission 2, you must learn about your target's history and examine his or her past by sifting through different information caches throughout the computer. You will be amazed when you discover the types of evidence your target leaves behind after he or she is gone. In Mission 3, you take account of what is being done now, in the present, by identifying what files and applications have been recently accessed. This step allows you to find out the current state of affairs. Present evidence may not lead you to all that you need, so in Mission 4 we introduce you to expanded methods for future collection. This type of collection means covert sustained access; we demonstrate simple ways to do this step. In Mission 5, we cover aspects of forensics and how to recover files that were thought to be permanently deleted.

Together, these steps will introduce you to basic spy techniques on a PC. They will help you identify what a person is doing on a computer and when he or she is doing it. Knowledge of their activities will allow you to determine where to focus next.

As with previous missions, we strongly recommend following the SLEUTH methodology; however, in order to focus on the details of this chapter, we will no longer explicitly spell out its steps.

Mission 1: Collect the Basics

The first step for any good spy operation is to learn about the environment and any potential type of access that already exists. If you were a spy deployed overseas to learn about another country, you would first need to identify the major players and places of the area. This is essentially what you are doing in this mission, but on a smaller scale.

In your case, you have already identified *whom* you are spying on. But in the world of computers and the Internet, this person can go by many names. You need to identify what e-mail addresses and chat personalities your target is using. You also need to size up your "competition" by determining what this person uses the computer for. This means finding out what files have been executed, viewed, and saved, what Web sites have been visited (and how many times they have been visited), and what has gone on in past e-mail communications.

Tips and Tricks…

Unplug or Risk Being Discovered

We live in an *instant* society with connectivity at our fingertips. When spying, however, instant connectivity can be a bad thing. Some clients automatically download e-mail when they are launched, and chat programs such as America Online Inc.'s (AOL's) Instant Messenger can be configured to launch automatically by default following a login. It is a dead giveaway to your target if one of these things accidentally happens.

Imagine what would happen if you decided to carry out your spy operation in the middle of the night, and when you launched Netscape Navigator it started up AOL's Instant Messenger. Everyone who has your target's Instant Message name in his or her "buddy list" will see the name sign on. The next day, someone may make a comment about you "being up late" or something of that nature. Even worse, during the window in which the name signed on and you were able to sign off, someone may have sent a message and become distraught when you did not reply back.

To be safe, before logging into an account or launching an e-mail client on an already logged in account, it is best to disconnect yourself completely from the Internet.

The most common ways to disconnect a computer from the Internet are as follows:

- Physically removing the Ethernet cable (refer to Chapter 3 for a review of hardware components).

- Removing the wireless external Personal Computer Memory Card International Association (PCMCIA) card or disabling wireless access by pressing the wireless button on your laptop if your antenna is internal.

Continued

- Shutting off the cable or Digital Subscriber Line (DSL) modem is effective if you suspect that the computer may be connected via wireless or other means, but you can't identify a wireless card. This should ensure that no traffic leaves your house to the Internet.

- Alternatively, as a last resort, once you log on you can disable network connections from the operating system by clicking on **Start | Control Panel | Network and Internet Connections | Network Connections,** and then right-clicking on each connection listed and selecting **Disable,** as shown in Figure 6.1. Note, however, that this change remains after you log out or the system is rebooted, so be sure to follow the same steps as the previous instructions, but select **Enable** to restart the connection once you are done spying.

Figure 6.1 Disable Network Connections Before Spying to Reduce the Risk of Accidentally Launching an Application with "Auto-Login"

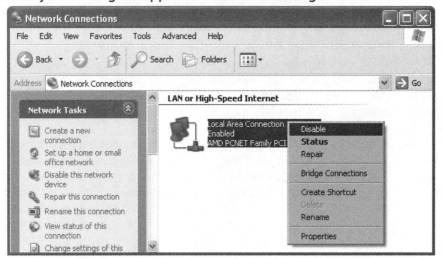

Identifying User Accounts

Uncovering account identities is like locating the targets of a conventional intelligence operation. On the Internet, your 13-year-old daughter Katie can be a 16-year-old named Sarah, or worse, a 21-year-old named Jenn. Identifying accounts, or personas, on the computer will assist you in the targeting needed for later chapters.

E-mail and chat names can be highly descriptive and may alert you to troubling behavior. For example, identities such as "Snorty MicCoke" could indicate that your son has a potential interest in illicit drugs, or hangs out with people online who do.

This next section helps you identify potential access, e-mail, and chat accounts that can be collected upon. We start with access accounts on the computers themselves and end with the more illusive Web mail and chat accounts that provide anonymity and very little attribution.

Access Accounts

Operating systems separate one person's preferences and privileges from another's with user (or access) accounts. As discussed in the previous chapter, when you are *administrator*, you have access to every file on the computer. However, to be successful in targeting and using spying software, you need to determine what other accounts exist on your computer. As administrator, other accounts on the computer can be easily found by selecting **Start | My Computer | Control Panel | User Accounts** (see Figure 6.2).

Figure 6.2 Listing of Users on a Microsoft Windows XP Installation

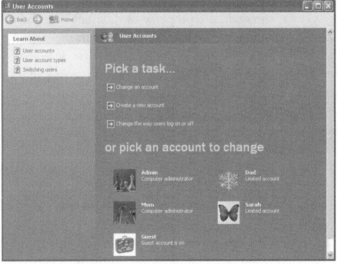

You need to know what account the person you intend to spy on uses. Many of the monitoring programs that you are going to install throughout this book are account sensitive. It is important to be aware of all of the access accounts on the computer and to identify which ones your target is using.

NOTE

Details count when you are spying on others. If you discover a secret account that your children or spouse is using, be careful with your knowledge. The last thing you want to do is forget to log out when you are reading e-mail on that account; carelessness like that will get you caught. If you find that a secret account is being used and you choose to log in and explore it, always leave the computer "untouched" looking when you walk away. This means that if the computer was originally logged into the Administrator account when you sat down, be sure to log out of the secret account and log back into the Administrator account. Otherwise, your spying will change from covert to overt, whether you want it to or not.

E-mail Accounts

Just as operating systems segregate the property of different users by account, so do e-mail servers. E-mail accounts are used to separate which messages belong to which user. There are two categories of e-mail services: those that download e-mail onto your computer and those that store e-mail remotely on the provider's servers. However, in many cases, the line of distinction between the two categories has blurred because many offer flexible options to do either.

As a general rule, your Internet service provider (ISP) has most likely configured your service to be checked and retained by local e-mail clients such as Microsoft Outlook, Outlook Express, or Eudora. E-mail-only services such as Hotmail and Yahoo were designed to be managed by Web browsers. Because clients must be configured and e-mail is stored on the local computer, the first category of service is far less anonymous.

On the other hand, Web-only accounts can be very anonymous because they can be checked from anywhere, anytime with very little evidence left on the machine used to access the mail. Unfortunately, if your target uses good tradecraft, you may be limited to detecting Web mail accounts in the short duration in which your target actually accesses the Web sites. As you should be aware of by now, spying for the purpose of solving a mystery (is person X doing Y?) will probably **not** uncover a smoking gun when you first start your efforts. Instead, think of this as a trail of breadcrumbs, and each detail helps you get one step closer to the knowledge or truth you seek.

NOTE

The username for accounts is almost always part of the e-mail address. For example, the account name is authors in address authors@ cyber-spying.com.

Knowing about an account gives you an important piece of the e-mail puzzle. Passwords to the accounts are the second piece of the puzzle, and they are needed to monitor the e-mail (as discussed in a later chapter). For now, you need to harvest information and identify every e-mail account that you think your target is using. We start the search by collecting account information from Microsoft Outlook, Outlook Express, and AOL's e-mail client. We then address the threat of Web-based e-mail and the anonymity it provides.

Microsoft Outlook Express Accounts

The e-mail client Outlook Express comes with the Microsoft Windows operating system and is the default mechanism for sending and receiving e-mail in standard installations. Because of this, it is a primary focus of our book. It is a versatile client that allows you to separate e-mail into different accounts and send and retrieve Web-based e-mail as if it were no different than what is provided by a standard ISP.

Later chapters explicitly focus on how to collect e-mail, but first you need to learn about your environment by discovering accounts, or as Outlook Express refers to them, *identities*. A listing of all of the identities for an installation can be found by opening that application and selecting **File | Identities | Manage Identities**. As Figure 6.3 shows, identities on this computer are Barbara, David, and the Main Identity for the installation.

Figure 6.3 Microsoft Outlook Express Listing of Identities

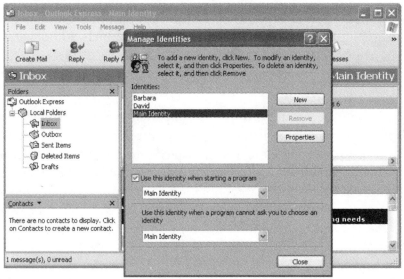

   Identities can be explored by highlighting the name and selecting the
Properties button. Accounts can be password protected; however, the Protected
Memory Viewer tool and keyboard sniffers addressed later can help bypass this
method of protection. Within each identity are one or more e-mail addresses. To
identify an address being used, select **Tools | Accounts**. When you select the **Mail**
tab you will see e-mail accounts configured for the identity. Highlighting any listing
of interest and pressing the **Properties** button will bring up the more detailed
information needed for further collection (see Figure 6.4).

Figure 6.4 Hotmail Account for Jenn under a Microsoft Outlook Express Identity

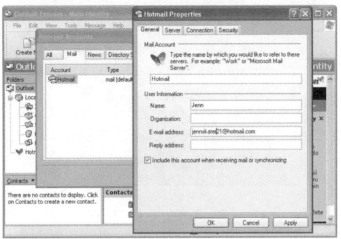

> **NOTE**
>
> It is very important to realize that one option of Microsoft Outlook Express (and many other clients) is to always check for new e-mail automatically as soon as the program is launched. If you launch this program and it downloads e-mail, your target may realize that you are monitoring him or her. Instead, be sure to disconnect your computer from the network so that it cannot reach the mail server and retrieve the e-mail accidentally.

Microsoft Outlook Accounts

If Microsoft Office is installed on the computer, it probably has Microsoft Outlook installed as its default e-mail client. Therefore, we show you the ins and outs of identifying accounts within Outlook. Unlike Express, it does not have different identities, so we go straight to listing e-mail accounts. To access information about the accounts, start the application and select **Tools | E-mail Accounts** (see Figure 6.5).

Figure 6.5 Locating E-mail Accounts in Microsoft Outlook

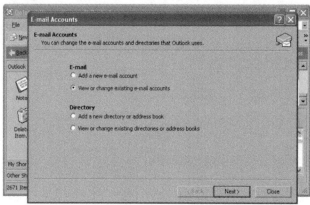

If you select **View or change existing e-mail accounts**, it will display specific account information for each address similar to the details shown by Outlook Express. Note, however, that this will show you account information *only* for the access user that you are logged in under. To identify accounts used by others, you will need to either log in as each access user (i.e., in our case that would mean Mom, Dad, Sarah, Guest, and Administrator) and follow the aforementioned steps or proceed to the more advanced techniques related to scouring the hard drive.

AOL Accounts

AOL is a popular ISP that distributes a specialized client for viewing downloaded e-mail. As shown in Figure 6.6, AOL accounts can be identified by looking at the "Screen Name" bar. As with the others, if your target checked the **Save Password** box, you will be able to access the account easily.

Figure 6.6 E-mail Accounts Configured in AOL's E-mail Client

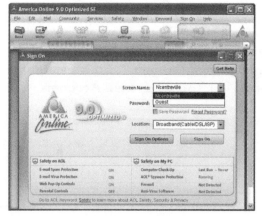

At this point you should have a collection of e-mail addresses configured into the Microsoft Outlook, Outlook Express, and AOL clients on the computer. This gives you a good starting point, but it is not where your search ends. Now we guide you through searching the computer for hints of Web-based e-mail accounts that are being used. To do this, we scour the hard drive.

Notes from the Underground…

Exposing Microsoft's Protected Storage

If identifying the location of the e-mail accounts has whet your desire for collecting data, you can go one step further by accessing Microsoft's protected storage to uncover the passwords to these accounts. There are many commercial applications that do this, but we had great success with a freeware tool called Protected Storage Explorer, which was written by James and Jeremy Pullicino. You can download this tool from *www.forensicideas.com*. Installation of the tool is straightforward, and it creates an entry in the Start menu under *Twinternals*. The tool itself has an interface that is very similar to the **regedit** application that we used previously (see Figure 6.7).

On the left side of the image are categories of elements that have been extracted from memory, and on the right are the values. In this case, Microsoft Outlook account number 01c4c852779500c6 belongs to the Yahoo address of fictional character, Sarah Evans. You can see that the Yahoo mail password we created for her is *fourwheels*. People tend to reuse passwords whenever possible, so utilizing a tool such as this may assist you greatly in your endeavors. It should also be noted that this tool is capable of displaying passwords saved by Internet Explorer as well as other applications that utilize "protected" storage.

Figure 6.7 Protected Storage Explorer in Windows 2000 or XP

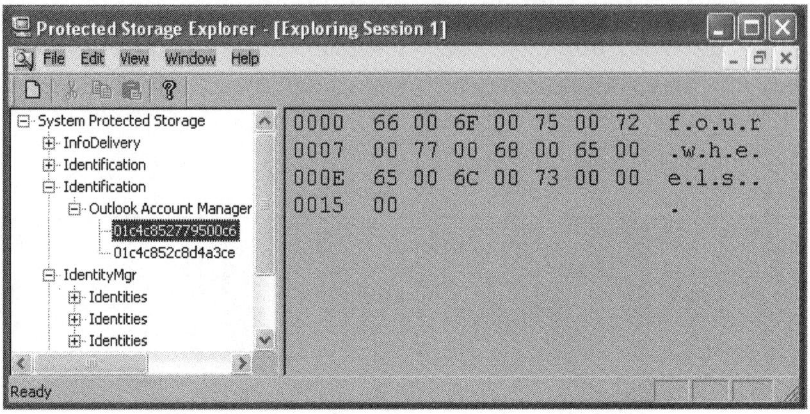

Scouring the Hard Drive

Although our main intention of searching the hard drive is to identify Web-based e-mail accounts, we will also search for other evidence of interest. As we said previously, hard drives are the closets of computers; some are clean and some are dirty. The dirty ones, though, can be very dirty, so make sure that you are ready for what you may find. Information is either intentionally stored on a hard drive, or it is unknowingly placed there by applications. We will search for both types.

Searching for Web-Based E-mail Accounts

Web-based accounts are easy to use, but difficult to track down. If you notice, most of the controversial postings in the previous chapters were done with Web accounts. This is because acquiring an e-mail address requires no true form of identification, and they can be easily used and thrown away.

Popular Web e-mail providers include:

- *www.hotmail.com*
- *mail.yahoo.com*
- *gmail.google.com*
- *www.hushmail.com*
- *webmail.juno.com*
- *www.postmark.net*
- *my.screenname.aol.com*

Some providers such as Hushmail and Yahoo go one step further and download the e-mail compressed or encrypted to the browser, making it significantly more difficult to collect and analyze. First, you must identify which accounts exist before you can determine the best method of collecting on them. Besides methods such as keystroke capturing and network sniffing (discussed later), accounts can be identified through information stored in browsers or files left on the hard drive (such as cookies). We will now scour the hard drive for this evidence.

Automatic Logins

Many browsers offer the ability to store the username and password of a Web site so that users do not have to remember it. If your target has done this, then by all means take advantage of it. To find out if these automatic logins exist, first make sure that you are logged in with the same access account on the computer as they use. Next, launch Netscape Navigator (if it is installed) and go through the following section to identify stored passwords.

Netscape

Identifying both the existence and the value of passwords in Netscape Navigator is easy. From the application select **Edit | Preferences,** expand **Privacy and Security**, click **Passwords**, and press the **Manage Stored Passwords** button. This will list the Web site that uses the password as well as the associated username (see Figure 6.8).

Figure 6.8 Netscape Navigator's Password Manager

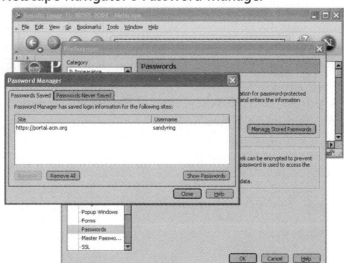

You can go one step further and click the **Show Passwords** button to find out what the usernames and passwords are (see Figure 6.8). Remember, everything is a breadcrumb here. Humans are creatures of habit, and we are willing to bet that your target has used this password on many other sites as well. We suggest making a note of any passwords that you come across, as they may be of significant use later. In addition, for future reference, this same dialog window contains a **Remove** and **Remove All** button that can be used in the event that you accidentally store one on your target's computer.

NOTE

Netscape Navigator started into business working on a browser that had a similar look and feel to the National Center for Supercomputing Applications' (NCSA's) Mosaic program. In fact, two developers who had worked on the browser at NCSA were the developers who formed Netscape Communications Corporation. Interestingly enough, Netscape is said to have been actually codenamed "Mozilla," short for *Mosaic Killer,* during this development period. Years later, an open source project named Mozilla has begun and is the producer of the Mozilla Firefox browser demonstrated throughout this book.

Mozilla Firefox

Mozilla Firefox is another popular browser that is very similar to Netscape Navigator. In most cases, the techniques described for Mozilla will operate in Netscape Navigator and vice versa. Because of this, for the remainder of this book we limit our demonstrations to Mozilla alone (unless there is a significant difference in the behavior of Netscape Navigator). To view the saved passwords in Mozilla, select **Tools | Options,** select **Privacy**, expand **Passwords**, and press the **View Saved Passwords** button (see Figure 6.9).

Figure 6.9 Mozilla Firefox's Password Manager

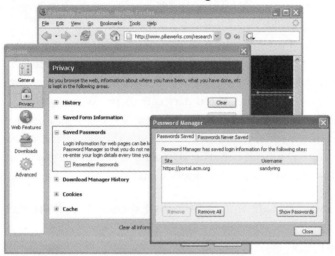

Internet Explorer

Unfortunately for us, Internet Explorer makes things difficult. It provides the capability to "remember" passwords and clear those that have been remembered, but it does not provide an interface to view them once they are stored. One option is to traverse down the lists of possible providers and visit each Web site using Internet Explorer to see if it remembers a password. The big ones to try are Yahoo, Hotmail, and Google's Gmail. If the password has been remembered it will show up as asterisks in the account input section (see Figure 6.10).

Figure 6.10 Example of a Stored Username and Password in Internet Explorer

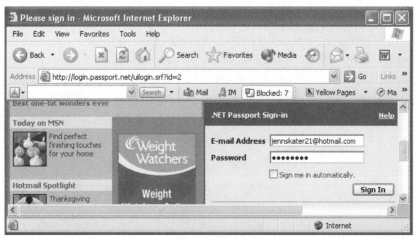

Note that Hotmail has the option to log directly in when the password is remembered; therefore, do not be alarmed if you are immediately greeted with e-mail when you visit *www.hotmail.com*.

Alternatively, the Protected Storage Explorer application demonstrated in the sidebar titled "Notes from the Underground: Exposing Microsoft's Protected Storage" can be used. When you run it, on the left side of the column you will see Internet Explorer as one of the stored data categories. When you expand this tab it lists a Uniform Resource Locator (URL) for each site that has been stored, and when you click on that site, it allows you to view the associated password. As Figure 6.11shows, it can display both the user ID (*sandyring*) and the password (*Gatorade*) for the Association for Computing Machinery's (ACM's) portal site.

Figure 6.11 Internet Explorer Passwords Exposed Using Protected Storage Explorer

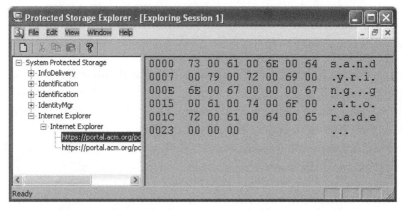

Microsoft Search

So far, we have shown you how to identify Web-based accounts saved in browsers and Hypertext Transfer Protocol (HTTP)-compliant e-mail clients such as Outlook and Outlook Express. Next, we search the hard drive to find cookies and other files that may contain account information. One easy way to do this is to use the searching capability that is directly built into Microsoft Windows. To do so click **Start | Search** and expand **All files and folders**. As a start, we recommend searching for partial addresses such as "@hotmail.com" (see Figure 6.12).

Figure 6.12 Using Microsoft Windows' Searching Capability to Uncover Evidence of Hotmail Accounts

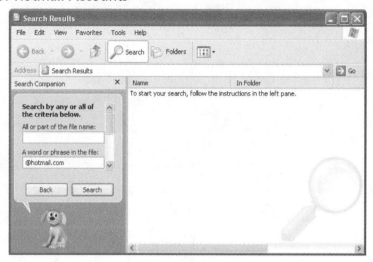

NOTE

Microsoft created the .NET Passport to provide a simple means of signing on to Web sites. Some Web-based mail sites (such as Hotmail) leverage this capability. User names for Web sites that use this type of authentication are stored in cookies from admin@passport. Even though it is not a Web mail provider itself, add @passport to your searching criteria. You may be surprised by the account names that turn up.

Tips and Tricks...

Microsoft XP Search May Ignore Nonregistered Extensions

If your searches using Microsoft XP are not yielding the results that you expected, make sure it is configured to index all files. There is a setting in the registry that controls this option.

Continued

To make sure that it is correctly configured, start **regedit** by clicking **Start | Run,** and entering **Regedit** into the dialogue box. Once this comes up, on the left column click on **HKEY_LOCAL_MACHINE | SYSTEM | CurrentControlSet | Control | ContentIndex** and make sure that **FilterFilesWithUnknown Extensions** is set to 1 (see Figure 6.13).

Figure 6.13 Registry Entry That Allows You to Expand Your Search Capability

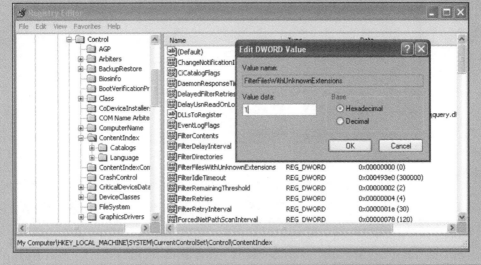

Google Desktop

Another searching option is to use the power of Google Desktop. As with anything, there are positives and negatives to using this tool in your spying endeavor. The positive is that it is very thorough. With this tool you can view all AOL Instant Messenger chats, Microsoft Outlook and Outlook Express e-mails, and Web sites visited by Internet Explorer (including those that use secure connections).

As an example of the usefulness of this tool, a simple search for "Yahoo mail" on our target's computer reveals cached copies of the inbox folder, copies of incoming messages, and copies of messages sent by our target (see Figure 6.14).

Figure 6.14 Using Google Desktop to Uncover E-mail Accounts

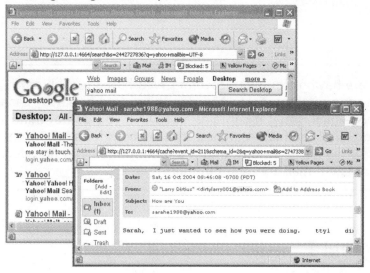

The two biggest drawbacks of using Google Desktop to spy are that: (1) it is always running, and its presence is not covert and (2) by constantly searching the computer for information to cache, it changes the access dates on files. Besides running multiple indexing processes at all times, Google Desktop places an icon on the desktop tray (see the icon to the left of the temperature in Figure 6.15).

Figure 6.15 Google Desktop's Tray Icon

There are many tray icon-hiding applications available on the Internet (including our site) that can take care of this issue. Even so, be cautious; this tool was not built to be covert and running it without your target's permission may alert them. Processes will continue to be shown in the task list and if your target ever clicks the **Google Desktop** link on *www.google.com*, they will be diverted to the tool on port 4664 of their own computer.

The other negative side effect of using Google Desktop is that it is constantly searching files on the computer to update its indexing information. This means that it is continually changing the access time on nearly every file on the computer, and searches that reference "access time" will not reflect the *true* access time of your mark. Instead, they will simply point to when the indexing application last accessed them. If you have this installed, try searching for the modified date instead of the accessed date.

> If you are having trouble uncovering Web-based e-mail information with any of your searches, try to broaden them. One giveaway characteristic of every e-mail is that it contains an "@." If you do not mind sifting through all of the false matches, try searching for a "@" alone. This should bring better results, and is a foolproof way to find documents that contain e-mail addresses in them.

Finding Old E-mail Stored in Mail Clients on the Computer

Besides caching tools such as Google's Desktop, there are two ways that e-mail is stored on your computer. It is either retained in the message database used by your particular client, or it is saved by users when they select **Save As**. Depending on the configuration of the e-mail client, the **Save As** option typically saves the message in Hypertext Markup Language (*.htm*), plain text (*.txt*), Outlook Template (*.oft*), Outlook Message format (*.msg*), or Outlook Express e-mail format (*.eml*). We suggest using either Microsoft Search or Google Desktop to search for all of the potential options, particularly those that are proprietary to e-mail such as *.oft*, *.msg*, and *.eml*.

Outlook Express

With Outlook Express, you can find where messages are stored by going to **Tools | Options** and clicking the **Maintenance** tab. From there, click the **Store Folder** toward the middle of the screen; it will show you the directory where all of the messages are stored (see Figure 6.16).

Figure 6.16 Outlook Express Stored Message Folder Location

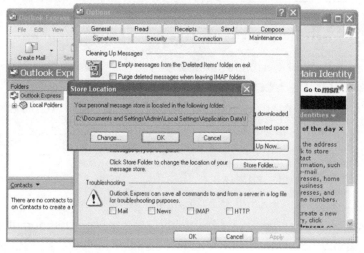

You can copy the contents of this folder onto a CD for later analysis. Note that you need to close the application before doing so. Once you have made copies of the entire folder and loaded it on another computer for analysis (see Chapter 8), make sure that you also browse the **Deleted** and **Drafts** folders.

Microsoft Outlook

Using Microsoft Outlook, databases can be located by selecting **Tools | Options** from the application and pressing the **Data Files** button in the **Mail Setup** tab (see Figure 6.17). Like Express, you should close the application prior to making a copy of these files.

Figure 6.17 Microsoft Outlook Stored Message Database Location

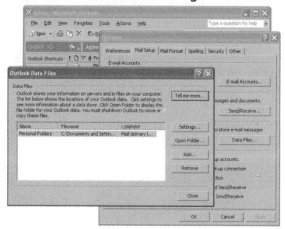

Notes from the Underground...

Use Hard Drive Scouring to Identify Microsoft Outlook and Outlook Express Mailboxes

Now that you have learned what Microsoft Outlook and Outlook Express mailboxes look like, you can specifically search the hard drive to identify them. To help you, here are the names of common files:

Microsoft Outlook Express

Inbox.dbx The main mailbox containing incoming messages

Outbox.dbx The location where outgoing messages are temporarily placed

Sent Items.dbx A folder that contains messages that have been sent

Deleted Items.dbx Previously deleted e-mail

Drafts.dbx E-mail messages that have been written but not yet sent

Save.dbx A folder where messages can be placed and saved

Microsoft Outlook

Outlook.pst The main mailbox containing incoming messages

Archive.pst Archived messages for storage

To make things easiest, bring up the Microsoft search tool and search for all files that end in either *.dbx* or *.pst*. You can do this by going to **Start | Search**, clicking on **All files and folders**, and entering **.dbx** into the **All or part of the file name** input box. Following this, do the same search for **.pst**. These searches will uncover the most common mail message databases as well as any custom folders created by your target.

AOL

AOL's mail client can store messages locally on the hard drive or remotely on AOL servers. To find the location of local messages, expand the **Saved on My PC** line under **My Mail Folders** on the client (see Figure 6.18).

Figure 6.18 AOL Stored Message Database Location

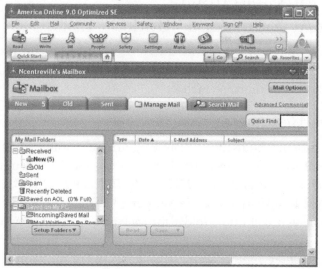

Tips and Tricks...

Expanding Your E-mail
Search Beyond the Local Computer

Finding messages on the local machine can be enlightening. However, finding postings by your spouse or children on the Internet can be truly eye-opening. Once you identify a collection of e-mail addresses and have thoroughly searched the hard drive, expand your search to the Internet. Search engines such as *www.google.com* or *www.yahoo.com* are great at caching Web site and news group message postings for months (or even years).

Remember, each piece of information that you uncover takes you one step closer to your goal. Discovering a secret Web-based e-mail account being used by your spouse or child, and then learning that this account is being used on the Internet to post inappropriate messages, may not be as unrealistic as you think.

Searching for Chat/Instant Messaging Accounts and "Buddy" Lists

Three of the most common chat clients are AOL Instant Messenger, Yahoo Messenger, and MSN Messenger. Identifying accounts on each is slightly different, so we attempt to show a method for each.

AOL Instant Messenger

The Registry Editor can be used to locate a significant amount of information about AOL Instant Messenger accounts. First, you can use it to identify user names. To do this, launch **regedit** and go to **HKEY_CURRENT_USER | Software | America Online | AOL Instant Messenger (TM) | CurrentVersion | Users**. Below this section, you will find a folder for each screen name previously used on this computer. By clicking on the screen name that you are interested in finding more about, you will see another series of folders. One of the more interesting folders is **recent IM ScreenNames**, which contains information about who this person has recently been chatting with (see Figure 6.19). In this case, we learn that this computer has been used under the name *skgirl1988* to chat with someone named *creepychris001*.

Figure 6.19 Using the Registry to Identify IM User Accounts and Contacts

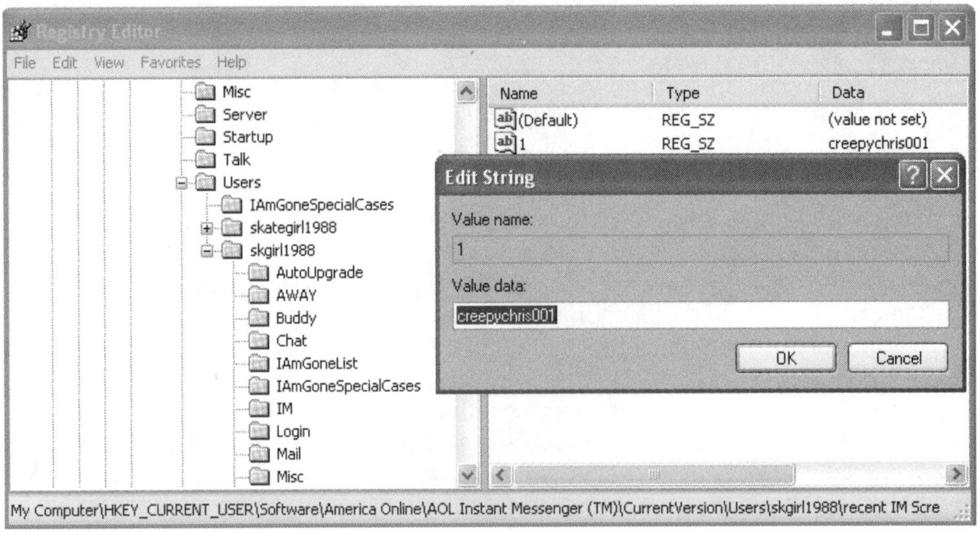

We encourage you to explore each of the folders to learn additional information. For example, you will find that the **Misc** folder contains an entry named

LoginCount, which can tell you how many times this account has been used. This could be a helpful way to determine if your child is using Instant Messenger after you have told them to log out and focus on their homework.

Yahoo Messenger

A Yahoo Messenger account is even easier to locate. Simply open the file explorer and look in **C:\Program Files\Yahoo!\Messenger\Profiles** to obtain a listing of the default installation directory for the application (see Figure 6.20). If it does not exist, try using the Microsoft search tool and query for Messenger.

Figure 6.20 Yahoo Messenger Profiles

In this case, we learn that someone named *sneakyskgurl* has been logging in to Yahoo Messenger to chat.

MSN Messenger

Like other Microsoft services, MSN Messenger utilizes the .NET Passport system as its logon. That means that anyone with a .NET Passport can automatically utilize MSN Messenger without having to create a special account. For example, because Hotmail also uses .NET authentication, any Hotmail account could potentially be used in MSN Messenger. We suggest scouring the hard driving using Microsoft Search or Google Desktop to locate documents that contain references to *passport.net* or *passport.com* to locate potential user names.

Mission 2: Examining the Past

Now that you have identified e-mail addresses and chat accounts of interest, it is time to learn what they have been used for. Start by locating information on previous chat logs that you were able to locate and place special emphasis on uncovering past activities within browsers.

Chat Logs

Sometimes people seem to almost want to get caught; when they do something taboo they save a memento of the occasion. When it comes to chatting or instant messaging, this is generally in the form of either a photograph of whom they chatted with, or a recording of the entire chat session. In the computer world, these recordings are referred to as *logs* because the application essentially logs everything that is sent and received between the parties that chat. Unlike federal laws associated with telephone conversation recording, either party can legally record the other in chat applications.

You can capture these chats using many different techniques. For a start, we help you recover previous sessions. There are essentially two ways that log files can be stored using most chat clients. The first format uses the rich text format (RTF) and is stored within an *.htm* file. In order to read an RTF log, you need to open it using the client itself. For example, using AOL's Instant Messenger, you can do this by first clicking on any one of the "buddies." This opens a second graphical user interface (GUI); you should select **File | Open Saved IM** and select the file that you wish to open. Note that it will probably have either an Internet Explorer or a Mozilla icon associated with it because it ends in *.htm*. The second and probably easier way to open it is to use a word processor that supports this format, such as Microsoft Word. Chat logs can also be stored as plain-text files, which end in *.txt*. This type of file can be opened with most applications, including Mozilla, Internet Explorer, Notepad, and Microsoft Word.

In Figure 6.21, we give you a glimpse of the more advanced Google Desktop techniques, which are covered in more detail later in this book.

Figure 6.21 Using Google Desktop to View Previously Captured AOL Chats

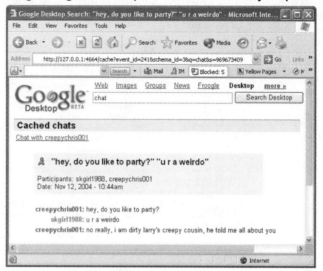

Here, you see that a simple search for "chat" using Google Desktop uncovered previously captured AOL chat logs between *skgirl1988* and *creepychris001*. (Even more interesting are the live chat collection techniques that we show you in Chapter 10.)

Browser Caches

Another interesting way to look into the past activities of your target is to view browser caches. Caches are stored copies of frequently visited Web pages and images that a browser uses to speed up reloading and enhance performance. Luckily, these caches also enhance the performance of your spying! We illustrate how to view them using the two most common browsers, Internet Explorer and Mozilla.

Internet Explorer

First, we examine how to view and increase the cache of Internet Explorer.

Viewing the Cache

The cache of the Internet Explorer browser can be viewed by clicking on **Tools | Internet Options**, selecting the **General tab**, pressing the **Settings** button in the **Temporary Internet Files** section, and clicking on the **View Files** button. This opens an explorer browser that consists of a list of Web pages, images, scripts, and cookies (see Figure 6.22).

Figure 6.22 Viewing Internet Explorer Cached Pages and Images

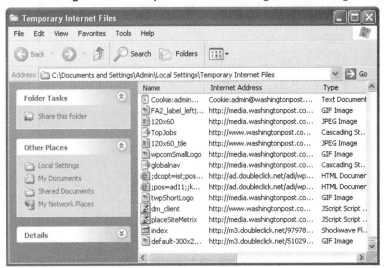

Make sure you select **View | Details** for a full listing. If you scroll to the far right, you will find information on when the image was last accessed, which can be particularly informative.

Increasing the Cache

As you can see, information collected from the cache can be interesting. Unfortunately, the one drawback with caches is that they are limited in size. You can actually increase your likelihood of collecting additional information of value by increasing the cache. When using Internet Explorer as the browser, you can increase the cache by following steps similar to the previous example. From the browser click on **Tools | Internet Options**, select the **General** tab, click the **Settings** button in the **Temporary Internet Files** section, and increase the **Amount of disk space to use**.

Mozilla Firefox

We now show you how to view and increase the cache of Mozilla Firefox.

Viewing the Cache

Viewing the cache in Mozilla is relatively simple and particularly interesting because it allows you to view what is in memory as well as on disk. To do so, type **about:cache** in the address bar as if you were typing a Web site URL (see Figure

6.23). This brings up a page of statistics that lists where the cache is stored as well as how much disk and memory space is in use.

Figure 6.23 Viewing Mozilla Firefox's Cached Entries in Memory and on Disk

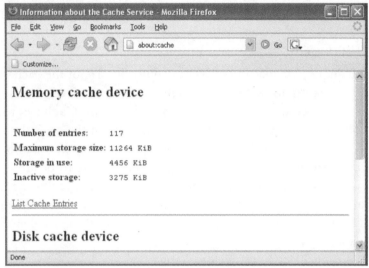

This page also contains a link to **List Cache Entries** for both memory and disk utilization. If you click on this, it will bring you to a convenient listing of all entries. Each entry contains information about the images, as shown in the following example:

```
           Key: https://www.syngress.com/images/logo.gif
     Data size: 67876 Bytes
   Fetch count: 5
 Last Modified: 10/26/04 17:10:39
       Expires: 12/22/04 19:57:01
```

If you click on the **Key** hypertext link, it will bring you to additional details about the object.

```
           key: http://www.syngress.com/images/logo.gif
   fetch count: 5
  last fetched: 10/26/04 17:14:33
 last modified: 10/26/04 17:10:39
       expires: 12/22/04 19:57:01
     Data size: 67876
      Security: This document does not have any security info associated
                with it.
        Client: image
```

If you click on the hypertext link again, it will fetch the image so that you can view it. It also tells you when the image was first viewed and how many times it has been fetched. If you discover that someone is looking at particularly disturbing images, there may be a big difference between one viewing that could have occurred by accident and one that has been fetched several times.

Increasing the Cache

Like Internet Explorer, Mozilla allows you to adjust the size of the cache for performance enhancements. To do so, from the Firefox browser click on **Tools | Options**. On the left column expand **Privacy** and click on **Cache** in the bottom of the right column. Next, you need to increase the size of the cache by typing in a new disk space size. Assuming that your computer is relatively new and has a hard drive of sufficient size, you should be able to increase the size to be around 150,000K. Also notice that just to the right of the cache size specification is a button that says **Clear** (see Figure 6.24). You can use this button for future reference to clear your personal history so that these very spy techniques will not accidentally uncover any of *your* private activity.

Figure 6.24 Increasing the Cache in Mozilla Firefox

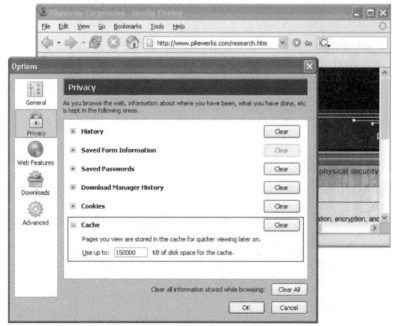

Browser Cookies

Cookies are a good way to find out what sites someone visits and what they do at those sites. As we did with the caches, we show you how to view cookies in both Internet Explorer and Mozilla Firefox.

Internet Explorer

Because cookies are in a sense a type of cache, you can view the cookies in an Internet Explorer browser by following the exact same steps as you did to retrieve the cache files. From the browser click on **Tools | Internet Options**, select the **General** tab, click the **Settings** button, and select **View Files**. To better highlight the files that are cookies, click **Type**, the header of the third column. This ensures that the files are organized by file type versus date, address, or any other criterion (see Figure 6.25).

Figure 6.25 Viewing Cookies Stored by Internet Explorer

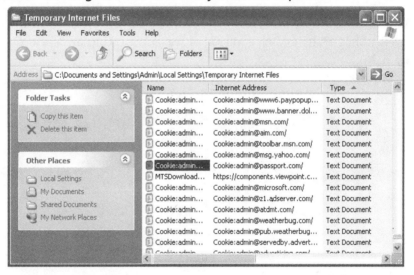

As an example of the type of useful information you can find in a cookie, take the highlighted cookie from the last figure that was set by *admin@passport.com*. If you double-click on the first column, you will be warned about the danger of running a system command (which is not a threat because these are text files) and then the cookie will be opened. In this case, the content of the cookie reveals a Hotmail Web account.

```
admin@passport[1]
MSPPre
sarah_evans687@Hotmail.com
passport.com/
9216
2189574144
32107986
3573644000
29667875
*
```

This cookie tells us that the e-mail account that has been recently registered with Microsoft's *passport.com* service is **sarah_evans687@hotmail.com**. As learned earlier, this also tells us that *sarah_evans687* is a potential user name for MSN Messenger as well.

Mozilla Firefox

When using Mozilla as a browser, you can view cookies by selecting **Tools | Options**, expanding **Privacy**, selecting **Cookies**, and clicking on **View Cookies** (see Figure 6.26).

Figure 6.26 Cookie Stored by Mozilla Firefox

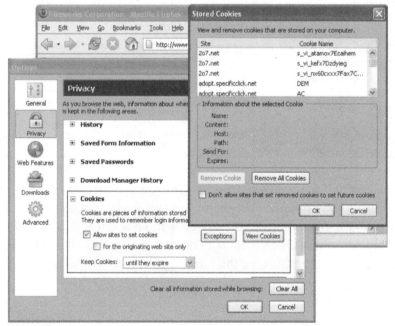

You will notice that this interface provides you with the opportunity to remove your evidence on the computer by clicking either **Remove Cookie** or **Remove All Cookies**, depending on your need.

Browser Histories

Browsers provide a collective view of activity through their *history* mechanism. Please note, however, that this history may not be completely reliable, as it is trivial to remove any entry from the list by highlighting it and pressing the **Delete** key. Nevertheless, it is still a useful place to check, because many people are not aware of this capability.

Internet Explorer

First, we explain how to view and increase the history cache in Internet Explorer.

Viewing the History

The history of what Web sites were visited and when is easy to access when using Internet Explorer. To help you visit sites, Microsoft has created an Explorer Bar. To add this bar and access the history select **View | Explorer Bar | History** from the browser (see Figure 6.27).

Figure 6.27 View the History in Internet Explorer

Doing this creates a column with the left side containing a listing of Web sites that were visited, organized by when they were accessed. Like everything else, make sure you undo this when you are done by closing the History window. Simply closing the browser in its entirety will not remove it, and the next time the browser is launched, the History Explorer bar will open again. Imagine the discovery your target will have made if that happens!

Increasing History Cache

Similar to the steps to increase the cache or cookies, you can increase the number of pages that are stored using this history. This can be done by selecting **Tools | Internet Options** from the browser and from the **General** tab increasing the number of pages in the **History** section.

Mozilla Firefox

Now, we explain how to view the history and increase the history cache in Mozilla Firefox.

Viewing the History

The history of someone accessing the Internet using Mozilla is similar to that of Internet Explorer. To see Mozilla's history select **View | Sidebar | History** or alternatively **Go | History** from the browser. This opens the History window sidebar to the browser that organizes the history by access time (see Figure 6.28). Each specific domain can be expanded to view additional details about when it was last visited.

Figure 6.28 View the History Using Mozilla Firefox

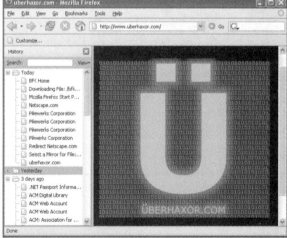

Increasing History Cache

If you find that collecting information about the history provides useful details, it may be useful to expand its collection capability. Just as browser caches can be expanded, so too can history buffers. Using Mozilla, this can be done by selecting **Tools | Options**. Next, expand the **Privacy** icon, and click on **History**. Under **Browser History** you can increase the number of days in which history is collected, which will increase your ability to discover information about Web usage. In addition, for future reference, note that to the right of the input section is a **Clear History** button that allows you to remove all of your browser history evidence from the application.

AOL Browser

It is fair to mention that like the other popular browsers, the AOL software easily allows you to view the history of the Web sites. This can be done by dropping down the arrow to the right of the URL address text box. Notice that AOL includes search keywords in its History bar, which can be especially useful if you discover the terms dating services on your spouse's computer (see Figure 6.29).

Figure 6.29 View the History in AOL's Browser

Mission 3: Live for the Present

When we say "live for the present," we mean identify the applications and files that your target uses on a daily basis. Here is your chance to get into the "mindset" of what your target uses the computer for. We start by identifying frequently accessed programs and end with ways to keep track of recently accessed files. Pay special attention to this section; if you are not careful, snooping on your target's computer may land you on either of these lists.

Recently Used Applications

The Windows Start menu and Registry provides a means of identifying frequently used applications.

Start Menu Recent Programs List

You have probably noticed how, for convenience, Microsoft Windows keeps a list of the most frequently and recently used applications in the top of the Start menu (see Figure 6.30).

Figure 6.30 Applications Listed in the Microsoft Windows Start Menu

This is one of the easiest and best ways to learn what the computer is being used for. As the next couple of sections demonstrate, applications themselves can give away tremendous amounts of information about who is doing what and when.

Some people try to hide their activities by using alternative applications. For instance, if you and your spouse share a common computer, and Internet Explorer is set as the default browser, your spouse may switch to secretly using Netscape Navigator instead to hide his or her history, cache, and cookies. By observing the Start menu, you can watch for behavior such as this because Netscape Navigator will show up as a commonly used program (see Figure 6.30). Likewise, if you install spy software on your target's computer and run it, it will also show up. For example, take the previous figure; it advertises that a portion of the program TightVNC, which could be used for spying, has been recently used.

Tips and Tricks...

Removing the Frequent Programs List

Be cautious that what you are going to monitor is not observable to others. Just as your mark's frequently used applications will show up in the Start menu, so too will yours. There are two ways to prevent this from occurring. The first is to remember to launch several inoffensive applications when you have completed your monitoring so that they show up instead. The buffer of frequently used programs is small, and you can likely clear it by launching five or six others.

Otherwise, if you fear that you may forget to do this you can take the more drastic measure of disabling this list from the Start menu altogether. However, note that by doing this you have created an observable change in the behavior of the computer that may alert your target. If you intend to do this (or want the tip for your own personal privacy) than read on.

On Windows XP the frequently used programs list can be removed from the Start menu by adding the following DWORD values of (0x00000001):

HKEY_CURRENT_USER | Software | Microsoft | Windows | CurrentVersion | Policies | Explorer |

NoStartMenuMFUprogramsList

HKEY_LOCAL_MACHINE | Software | Microsoft | Windows | CurrentVersion | Policies | Explorer |

NoStartMenuMFUprogramsList

Continued

> In addition, you can remove a specific program from the most frequently used list by creating a string value named "NoStartPage" at **HKEY_CLASSES_ROOT | Applications | <the program you want to exclude>.exe**

Registry Entries for Recently Accessed Programs

An extensive list of recently accessed programs can be revealed in the Windows Registry by opening **regedit**, accessing **HKEY_CURRENT_USER | Software | Microsoft | Windows | CurrentVersion | Explorer | ComDlg32 | OpenSaveMRU**, and clicking on the **exe** folder (see Figure 6.31).

Figure 6.31 Using the Registry to Identify Recently Accessed Applications

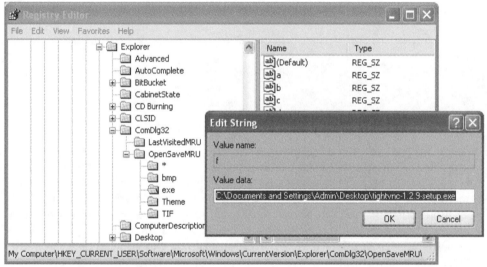

Note that this same method can also be used to view previously accessed files by clicking on folders such as **doc**, **mp3**, **txt**, and so on.

Registry Entries for Recently Run Programs

Directly accessing programs is only one way of launching applications. As we did with regedit and Explorer, applications can also be indirectly started using the **Run** application on the Start menu. You can use the Registry to learn which programs have been recently started using this technique by using regedit to view **HKEY_CURRENT_USER | Software | Windows | CurrentVersion | Explorer | RunMRU** (see Figure 6.32).

Figure 6.32 Using the Registry to Identify Recently Run Applications

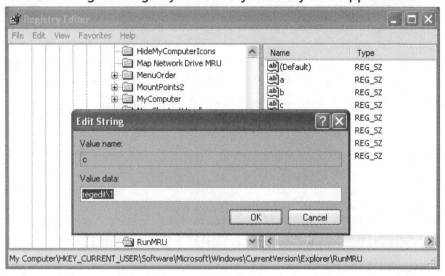

Here, our spy techniques of searching through the Registry are being logged.

Start Menu Recent Documents List

Besides the information stored within the Registry we just showed you, recent documents can be accessed by making a copy of the **Recent Documents** folder when you first log on. To do this go to **C:\Documents and Settings\<*the user*>\My Recent Documents**, where <*the user*> should be the user you are spying on (see Figure 6.33).

Figure 6.33 Opening the "My Recent Documents" List

Double-clicking on this icon will open a folder containing links to files that have been recently accessed. This is also an area that you need to be very aware of in order to cover your own tracks later and ensure that any files you open on your target's computer are not shown. Entries into this list can be deleted easily by right-clicking on the file link you want to remove and selecting **Delete**. Because most people are not aware of the existence of this folder, you are likely to find an unedited version of what files have been recently accessed.

Notes from the Underground...

Applications that Support MRU Lists

An ever-increasing number of applications are enabling Most Recently Used (MRU) list caches. These applications include, but are not limited to, the following:

Audio and Video
Microsoft Media Player
Winamp

Compression
WinZip
WinRAR

Editors
Microsoft Word
Microsoft Wordpad
Microsoft Notepad
Microsoft PowerPoint
Microsoft Excel

Graphics
Microsoft Paint
Microsoft Image Composer
Ultimate Paint

Continued

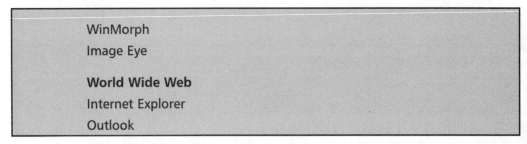

WinMorph

Image Eye

World Wide Web

Internet Explorer

Outlook

It should be noted that there is an alternative method that is not as intuitive, but is more reliable. When files have been purposely deleted from this listing, they can still be found within the registry's listing of recently accessed documents. To uncover these, from regedit access **HKEY_CURRENT_USER | Software | Microsoft | Windows | CurrentVersion | Explorer | RecentDocs** (see Figure 6.34).

Figure 6.34 Uncovering Recently Accessed Documents from the Registry

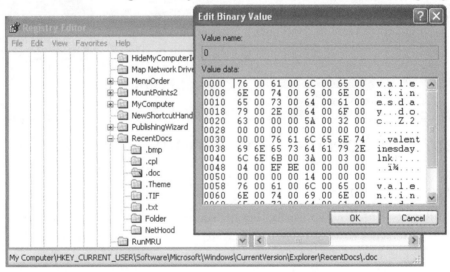

In this example, a link to the file *Valentinesday.doc* has been recently accessed, but no longer appears in the **My Recent Documents** list because it has been purposely removed. Nevertheless, cyber-sleuthing can still identify it in the Windows Registry.

Tips and Tricks...

Disabling All User Tracking

At this point you may be feeling paranoid about how easily you can be tracked on your own computer. You can specify a couple of registry values to prevent some of the techniques discussed in this chapter from being used against you. Specifically, create DWORD entries of one of the following keys depending on your level of paranoia:

HKEY_CURRENT_USER | Software | Microsoft | Windows | CurrentVersion | Policies | Explorer | NoRecentDocsMenu – Completely removes the recent documents menu

HKEY_CURRENT_USER | Software | Microsoft | Windows | CurrentVersion | Policies | Explorer | ClearRecentDocsOnExit – Clears the recent documents list every time you exit the account

HKEY_CURRENT_USER | Software | Microsoft | Windows | CurrentVersion | Policies | Explorer | NoInstrumentation – Disables all tracking

Searching Specific Time Periods

Microsoft Search

One of the best little-known capabilities of Microsoft's built-in Search tool is its ability to search files based on when they were last accessed. This will undoubtedly prove to be one of the most useful capabilities in your cyber-sleuthing. You can follow behind someone on a computer and determine exactly what files he or she has touched and when he or she touched them.

WARNING

The spy world is full of baits and traps. Watch out for this. If the person whom you are attempting to monitor is sneaky and watching you, then he or she may set traps that you unknowingly stumble into. Just as the access time search capability can be an asset, it can also be used against you if you are not careful.

For example, if you search and discover a document named *Secret.doc,* clicking on it to view its contents will update the access time. When your sneaky mark returns home, he or she could use this search against you by also searching for all of the files modified during the last *x* number of hours. This would reveal that you have accessed the file. One way to avoid this is to change the date on the computer before accessing it (we elaborate on that later in the book).

For example, launch **Start | Search** and then click on **All files or folders**. Expand **When was it modified** and select an option such as **Within the last week** (see Figure 6.35). When you are ready, click **Search**.

Figure 6.35 Using Microsoft Search to Uncover Activity During a Specific Time Period

NOTE

Be sure to select **More advanced options** in the Microsoft Search window and make sure that **Search system folders** and **Search hidden files and folders** are both checked.

Tips and Tricks...

Popular Search Terms

One of the best ways to learn about Web sites that have been visited is to learn what keywords are being searched for. With Microsoft Internet Explorer you can enable this by checking the box at **Tools | Internet Options**, selecting the **Advanced** tab, and checking the box that says **Use inline AutoComplete** (see Figure 6.36).

With auto completion enabled, you can easily browse to see what search terms have been used. This is as easy as starting to type the name of commonly used search sites such as *www.google.com*. By the time you get to the second "G" in Google many options appear in the Address bar (see Figure 6.37).

This is another way to view the history that some people find more convenient than searching daily.

Figure 6.36 Turning on AutoComplete in Your Target's Browser

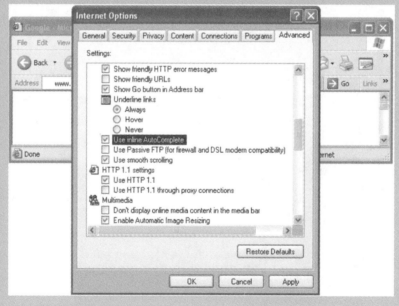

Figure 6.37 Stored Web Sites and Search Terms Revealed through AutoComplete

Mission 4: Prepare for the Future

Some spy operations are more like investigations: you find tidbits of interest but no smoking gun, yet you still suspect that somewhere one exists. It requires patience and a great deal of care not to get caught while spying. We are going to introduce you to some stealthy methods of maintaining secret access and collecting information that may lead you to what you are searching for.

Creating a Means of Access

If the computer that you suspect your target of misusing is yours, and it is normal for you to access it as you like, you are in luck. If not, you need to pay special attention to this section. Each time you access someone else's computer you risk getting caught. We are going to tell you about two remote access tools that you can install , which will enable you to remotely access the data on it secretly.

Virtual Network Computing

There are many popular commercial applications that offer the capability to remotely (and securely) access a PC over the Internet, as well as a handful of so-called hacker community tools such as Back Orifice. The tool that we suggest you use is the freeware tool named Virtual Network Computing (VNC). Like most freeware tools, there are many versions of this, each with minor improvements over the other. The distribution that seems to fit our needs the best is UltraVNC, found at *ultravnc.sourceforge.net*. As the previous chapter demonstrated, installation of this tool is simple, and running it is even easier. Once the VNC server on the target machine has been configured and started, you can connect to it remotely with the viewer. To do so, launch the viewer from the Start menu Application list. This will prompt you with a dialog box asking which server to connect to; this is where you put the IP address of the target's computer (see Figure 6.38).

Figure 6.38 Launching VNC to Connect to Another Computer

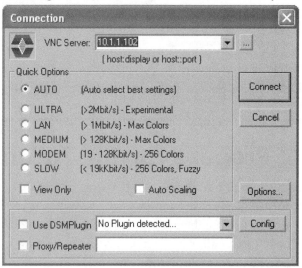

Next, as the connection begins to be established, you are prompted to enter a password (see Figure 6.39).

Figure 6.39 VNC Password Authentication Prompt

Within moments you will be amazed as a live feed image of the desktop is transmitted to your computer for you to observe (see Figure 6.40).

Figure 6.40 VNC Remote Access Tool in Action

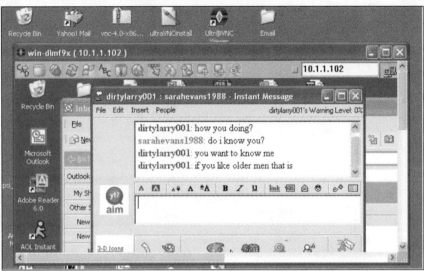

In this live feed, you will be able to observe everything that your target does, as they do it. This means watch as they edit Microsoft Word documents, read e-mail, or chat (see Figure 6.39). But that is not the main reason for teaching you about VNC. We are talking about remote access. As you move the mouse pointer in the VNC window you will actually be moving the mouse pointer on your target's computer. This means that by using this tool you can access the computer as if you were sitting right at the local keyboard. You can send e-mail, create files, read files, delete files, run programs, and so on. Note that there is tremendous danger in this, however. Just as you can watch what your target does, when you take control of the mouse, your target can watch you as well. Imagine your target's surprise if they walked into their room and found their computer mysteriously scrolling through and reading e-mail messages. Remember, just because they are not sitting at the keyboard does not mean they are not in the room.

In addition, the reason we recommend the UltraVNC release above the others is that it comes with a convenient method to transfer files back and forth between the two computers (see Figure 6.41).

Figure 6.41 Using UltraVNC to Transfer Files Between Computers

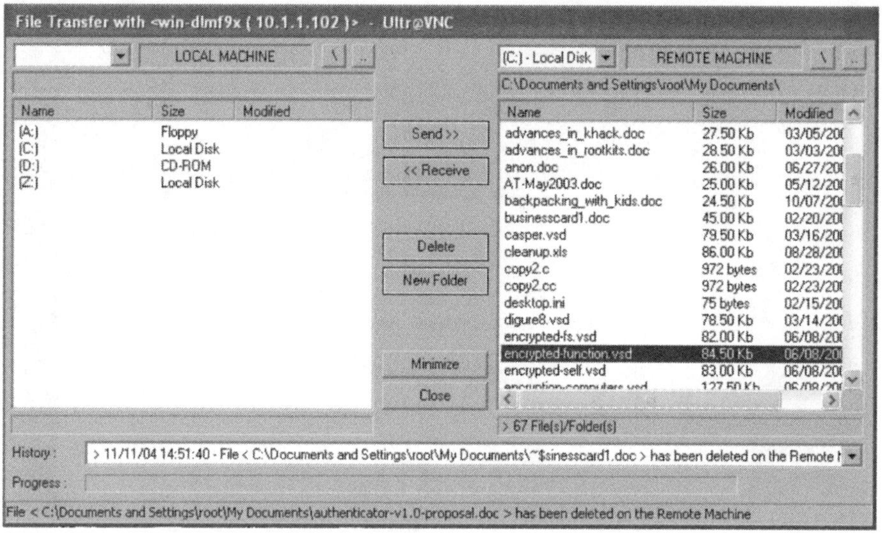

Tips and Tricks...

Can VNC be Used Covertly?

Like most of the tools we have introduced you to, VNC was created to be a remote administration application, and not a tool used by a cyber-sleuth such as yourself. It was been created to explicitly notify the user at the desktop of its presence through a small, but alerting tray icon. Examples of tray icons for the various popular versions of VNC can be seen in Figure 6.42.

From left to right the icons are created by RealVNC, TightVNC, and UltraVNC, respectively (the release we recommend). To make matters worse for you as a spy, when a connection is established to your target's computer using VNC, these icons change color (and in some releases flash). Unless you do not suspect that your target would notice such an alerting behavior, we suggest taking measures to remove this icon.

As mentioned before, there are tools that hide tray icons, but with the version of VNC that we recommend there is a more elegant solution. Using regedit, you need to create a new DWORD value of **1** named **DisableTrayIcon** at **HKEY_LOCAL_MACHINE\SOFTWARE\ORL\WinVNC3** (see Figure 6.43).

Continued

Stop and restart the application, and magically you will notice that it is no longer present in the Desktop tray even though VNC is still running. This needs to be done on the target's machine.

Figure 6.42 Tray Icons for Popular Releases of VNC

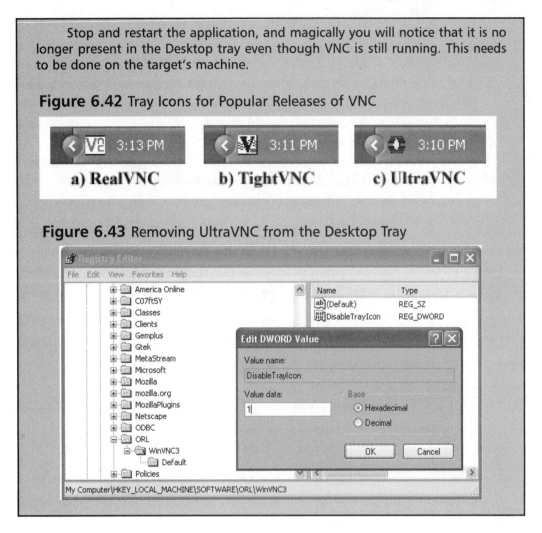

Figure 6.43 Removing UltraVNC from the Desktop Tray

Sharing Drives

If you are not sure that you want to risk the chance of installing remote access tools on your target's computer, you can always take less perilous steps first. One option is to enable sharing of a portion of the hard drive that you want to be able to access remotely. Sharing files or folders across an unprotected network is a security risk. We do not suggest that you do this if your local computers can be directly reached from outside of your network (i.e., if you have wireless access enabled or have actual "routable" IP addresses). If you understand these risks and still want to continue, you can do so by following these steps:

1. Pick the folder you want to share from **Start | My Computer**.

2. Right-click on the icon and select **Sharing and Security**.

3. Under the **Sharing** tab click **Share this folder on the network** and give the folder a name. Make sure to remember this name because you will need it later.

4. It is up to you if you want to provide yourself with the capability to change files on the drive remotely. If you intend to do so, check the **Allow network users to change my files** option. Be warned, though, that doing so is a security risk because potential attackers could also gain access and change files remotely.

5. When you are finished, press the **Apply** button.

Now, go back to your computer, to view the files remotely:

1. Click on **Start | My Network Places**.

2. Select **Add a network place** from the left panel.

3. Highlight **Choose another network location** and press **Next**. Put the IP address of the computer and the share name that you gave it into the dialogue box (see Figure 6.44).

4. Give it a name and click **Next**.

5. Click **Finish**; it will remotely open the folder.

Next, we suggest that you copy the contents of the share over to your local computer to ensure that you do not damage them and reveal your access.

Figure 6.44 Adding a Remote Network Share

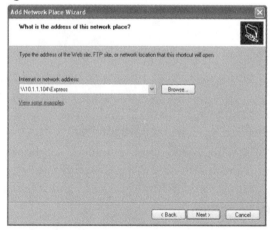

Notes from the Underground…

Using Shared Folders to Access E-mail Remotely

Now that you are aware of how to share folders on your target's computer, we would like to suggest this as a method of remotely accessing their e-mail. You can do this by following the steps outlined in "Sharing Drives." Depending on which e-mail client your target uses, select the location of the shared folder to be the mailbox database directory. In our example we use Microsoft Outlook Express, and the directory is **C:\Documents and Settings\Admin\Local Settings\Application Data\Identities\{6A43D3F5-A97D-4BE4-9BD9-99C8BB A848AA}\Microsoft\Outlook Express**. Selecting a Share folder buried deep in a directory tree will be difficult for your target to casually discover.

Once you have established the connection, create a new folder on your computer to house the contents of the remote e-mail database. Copy the files over and launch the mail client. In the chapter on e-mail collection, we introduce other utilities that can be used to view collected e-mail, but for our demonstration, we used our local copy of Outlook Express. To do so, we changed our store location to point at the folder we created that contains the copy of the target's remote e-mail database (see Figure 6.45).

Figure 6.45 Changing the Location of the Outlook Express Store Directory

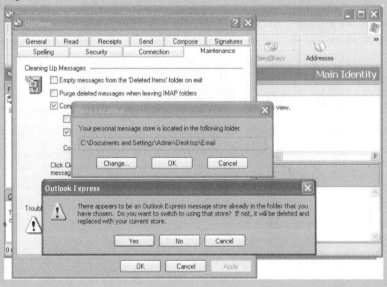

Continued

> Next, we closed and restarted the application, and were able to access the e-mail as if we were sitting on the local computer (see Figure 6.46).

Figure 6.46 Covertly Displaying Our Target's E-mail on Our Computer Remotely

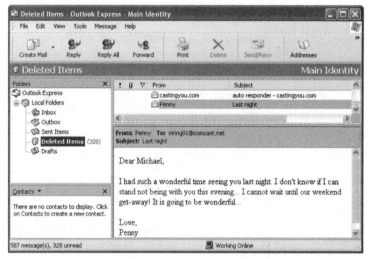

NOTE

If you are having trouble making copies of the folders remotely, it may be because the file is in use by the target's machine. You cannot make copies of certain files such as Microsoft Outlook and Outlook Express databases when they are in use by the application locally.

Keystroke Loggers

Preparing for the future also means using enabling technology such as keystroke loggers. Keystroke loggers can be used to capture every letter that your target types. Because we want you to put these concepts into practice immediately as you read this book, we are going to limit our demonstrations to software-only solutions. However, you should be aware that many powerful hardware solutions exist and are available for purchase on the Internet.

Best Free Keylogger

One option is to download the tool Best Free Keylogger (BFK) from
bfk.sourceforge.net. One of the primary benefits of this tool is that it can be configured
to e-mail its collection periodically to an address that you specify. You can figure this
from the **e-mail** tab on the application (see Figure 6.47).

Figure 6.47 Configuring BFK to Periodically E-mail Collections

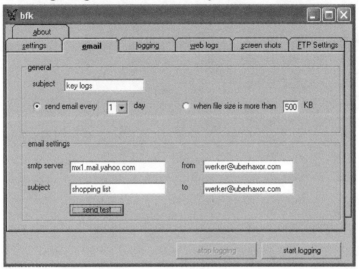

Note, however, that because of problems with spam, many ISPs block outgoing
Simple Mail Transfer Protocol (SMTP) mail to any server other than the ones in
their domain. Be sure to press the **send test** button prior to relying on e-mail as an
acceptable means of acquiring the collected traffic. Once you specify how and where
to send the collection, you must specify exactly what you want collected. This is
done through the **Settings** tab. The most important component of the **Settings** tab
is the designation of **Special keys** (see Figure 6.48).

Figure 6.48 Configuring the Type of "Take" from BFK

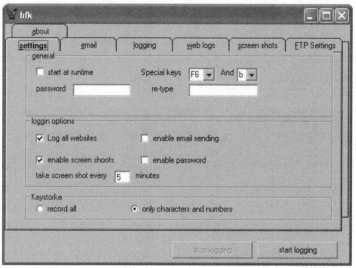

You will need to type these keys anytime that you want to start or stop the monitoring or view the logs manually from the logging, Web logs, or screen shots tabs. You can optionally supply a password (recommended) if you want to protect yourself from your target accidentally by pressing the keys and viewing the collection. In addition, in the login options you can specify what exactly you want to collect. When you are happy with your selection, press the **start logging button** and it will begin.

If your provider does not block it, e-mail will be sent daily to the address you specified with collection details. Alternatively, you can periodically sit at the keyboard (or access the take location remotely through VNC or a shared folder) and view the results (see Figure 6.49).

Figure 6.49 Viewing the Take from BFK

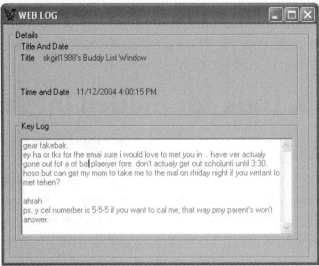

As you can see, keystroke capturing collects typing as it happens and not the finished (polished) product. Because of this, you will see typos and other key events all mixed together. In addition, you will notice that some of the characters that were typed appear to have not made it into the log. In particular, this appears to not capture letters that are repeated (i.e., mall = mal and 555-555-5555 shows up as 5-5-5).

However, this program does have one outstanding quality, which is another reason why we chose it as our example. It is capable of periodically taking snapshots of the desktop to give you a better picture of what is going on (see Figure 6.50).

Figure 6.50 Viewing a Collected Snapshot in BFK

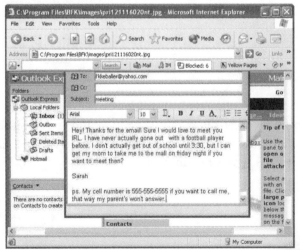

Here, we see one of the recorded snapshots (by default stored in the **C:\Program Files\BKF\Images**). This snapshot shows you the polished version of what the text in the previous collection represents. As apparent by the granularity of the photo, these images are stored with low quality to limit their consumption of the hard drive's memory.

Mission 5: Look for Hidden Information

Easy Stuff

If hard drives are the closets of the computer world, the recycle bin is the closet in the attic where things get placed and later forgotten. Images, documents, and programs that are deleted get placed here and are stored in this folder until they are removed or restored. These files can easily be forgotten (see Figure 6.51).

Figure 6.51 Recovering Forgotten Files in the Recycle Bin

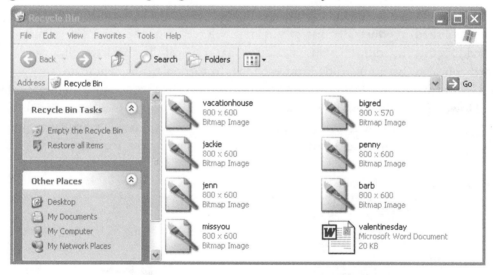

It is not unusual to have thousands of forgotten files in the recycle bin, any of which can be restored by right-clicking on the icon and selecting **Restore**. Make sure that when you are finished copying or viewing the recovered file, you place it back in the recycle bin as it was previously.

Tips and Tricks...

How to Restore the Recycle Bin Icon

Some people prefer not to have the Recycle Bin icon visible on the desktop. This can actually be a blessing in disguise because they may never think to empty it. In this case, the recycle bin still exists and files are still sent to it. The icon is simply not observable any longer.

To browse to the Recycle Bin without using the desktop icon, do the following:

1. Go to **Start | My Computer | Tools | Folder Options | View Tab**.
2. Make sure that **Display the contents of system folders** is checked, **Show hidden files** is checked, and **Hide protected operating systems** (Recommended) is NOT checked.
3. Go to **Start | Run | Explorer**.
4. On the left you should see **Recycle Bin**.

Advanced Stuff

It is possible to go one step beyond recovering files from the Recycle Bin to actually recovering files that have been truly deleted. For speed and overall operating efficiency, files that have been deleted by a user are not actually removed from the hard drive. Instead, pointers, or references, to them within the operating system are removed. There are many tools that take advantage of this situation. One that we will demonstrate is named PC Inspector.

PC Inspector File Recovery

PC Inspector can be used to scan a hard drive to identify files that have been recently deleted and are recoverable. This is useful both as a cyber-sleuth and as general knowledge in the event that you accidentally remove something you later need. To begin, launch the PC Inspector program from the Start menu (or desktop if you created an icon during installation). Answer which language you prefer to use and then press **OK**. Next, the interface for the application will start. To search for recoverable files select **Object | Drive**. Next, highlight the drive you wish to search and press **OK** (see Figure 6.52).

Figure 6.52 Preparing to Scan a Drive for Deleted Files Using PC Inspector

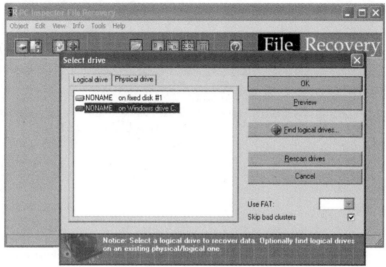

Once the search has completed, you will see another window with two panels. On the left panel is a listing of folders that contain recovered files. Of particular interest is the **Deleted | RECYCLER** folder. When you see a file of interest, right click on it and select **Save to** (see Figure 6.53).

Figure 6.53 Locating and Selecting a File to Recover

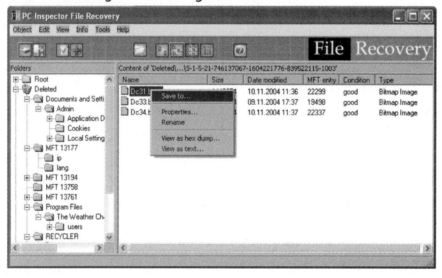

Next, select the directory you want to save it to (Desktop is the default) and click **OK** (see Figure 6.54).

Figure 6.54 Recovering a Deleted File with PC Inspector

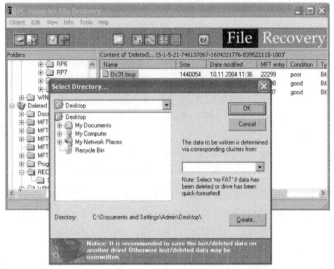

Now that the file has been recovered, either open it for viewing or transfer it elsewhere to open (recommended). Make sure you delete it again when you are finished. *Make sure that when you delete files you don't hold down the* **<Shift>** *key when you either press the* **delete** *key or select* **Delete** *from the menu. This will delete your files directly and prevent them from going into the Recycle Bin.*

Case Study: Expand Your Investigation Beyond the Local Computer

Topic

Slipping grades in school indicate a problem.

Elaboration

Young Christopher was a good student. He always made his teachers proud, but he was awkward among his peers and classmates, who often teased him. Nevertheless, his mother saw only his best side, until the day his report card conveyed that there was a problem. Fearful that he had become involved with the wrong crowd or worst yet drugs, his mother, Sophia, decided to become more involved in his life. As a single parent, she was always wrapped up in her work as the vice president of the local hospital and stayed very busy. However, given the circumstances, she made the time to pay more attention to Chris's activities. She tried talking to him, but he always stated that everything was fine. She tried to get him interested in after-school activities, but all he wanted to do was stay home and play online computer games.

Two weeks went by since his report card, and she still had not found a definitive answer to why his grades were slipping. The only conclusion that she could come up with was that he had been spending far too much time online playing games. She decided that her first step was to move the computer out of his room and into the family room.

Another two weeks went by, and this time a note came home from one of his teachers stating that Christopher had not been adequately completing his homework assignments and on two occasions had not arrived to class on time. Furious, she decided to forbid him from playing games in the afternoon until his homework had been completed. She told this story to a coworker, and he suggested installing some sort of parental lock on the computer so that it could not be used while she was at work. Sophia did not want to be so up front with her lack of trust in her son's adherence to her rules, so she decided to secretly monitor his usage instead.

That night when she got home, she used the Microsoft search tool to identify all of the files and folders that had been accessed over the past 24 hours (when no one should have been using the computer). What she found was a flurry of Internet activity. In particular was a Microsoft .NET Passport cookie associated with the e-mail address *deadshot793@hotmail.com*. She was a little alarmed by the name of the e-mail, but assumed that it was a reference to one of the many videogames he had become so obsessed with. She confronted him, and he seemed embarrassed and repeatedly apologized for not following her rules.

After he went to bed that night she became increasingly bothered by the name on the e-mail address. She decided that she wanted to do a search on the Internet to find out what it was a reference to. What she found was more disturbing than her worst nightmare. Using Google and searching for "deadshot," she came across a number of hateful Web site postings made by her son. The messages were on a wide variety of teen boards, and they all spoke of wanting to do violence against the "preppies and jocks" that "had no idea who they were messing with." There were questions about purchasing weapons, and detailed descriptions about his attempts to use fireworks in his creation of pipe bombs to "teach them a lesson." What she uncovered was a totally different side of her son, one that was deeply troubled and on the path to causing real harm.

All this time he was tormented by the kids in his class (to the point of losing total interest in school), yet he was too embarrassed to tell his successful, high-powered mother. He had been pushed beyond his limit, and despite his sweet personality, was no longer thinking logically about his circumstances. The very next day his mother had a heart-to-heart talk with her little boy, and they openly discussed the pressures of life that everyone (including herself) experiences from time to time. Shortly after that talk, she enrolled him in a new private school along with a counseling program at her hospital to help deal with his problems.

Analysis

It is difficult to imagine what could have happened next if Sophia had not picked up on the early warning sides, as so many parents fail to do. This shows how a computer and the Internet can sometimes become a sort of confessional where people feel the freedom to let their true emotions show in anonymity, and without fear of being judged. This is especially true for young children who are often very fearful of disappointing their parents. Searching the Internet for an e-mail address is no more an evasion of privacy than paying attention to the type of clothing that your child wears. Each is an outward sign meant to make statements. The question is simply if that statement is a cry for help or perhaps a warning of something dangerous yet to come.

Summary

In this chapter, you have begun the active part of your spying. You have assessed the current state of the computer, analyzed past histories, identified current activities, prepared yourself with future access, and identified files that you thought had been deleted. The following list includes some of the key techniques that you will need to remember if you want to be successful throughout the rest of your cyber-sleuthing:

- If an instant message chat session or other interactive online program is not currently open, disconnect the computer from the Internet before you begin spying.

- You can reveal passwords to Microsoft Outlook, Outlook Express, and Internet Explorer (among other programs) using the Protected Storage viewer.

- Microsoft Outlook mail storage databases end in *.pst* and can be copied and viewed on another computer. Likewise, Outlook Express folders end in *.dbx* and can also be copied and viewed elsewhere.

- Web mail accounts such as *Yahoo.com* and *Hotmail* can be identified through careful inspection of remembered browser passwords, cookies, HTTP-capable e-mail clients such as Microsoft Outlook and Outlook Express, browser cookies, and saved messages on the hard drive.

- The Registry contains a collection of recently used applications and file names, even after they have been deleted from the "My Recent Documents" list.

- Google Desktop provides a means to monitor (and search) files, e-mail, Web pages, Web mail, and chats that take place on a computer.

- Remote access programs such as VNC allow you to view and manipulate the desktop of a computer remotely.

- Keystroke-capturing software can be used to covertly collect images and activities on a computer, and e-mail the information remotely.

- Just because a file has been deleted (even those removed from the Recycle Bin), does not mean that the data has been removed from the hard drive. Recover tools such as PC Inspector can restore the files from the drive long after they have been forgotten.

## Chapter 7

Spying on Web Browsing

The printing press is either the greatest blessing or the greatest curse of modern times, sometimes one forgets which it is. — E. F. Schumacher

Topics in this Chapter

- **What Is Web Browsing?**

- **What Can You Get from Web Browsing?**

- **Typical Web Browsers**

- **Collecting Information from Your Target's Computer**

- **Collecting Information about Your Target from the Network**

- **Summary**

Introduction

Like the printing press, radio, and television, Web browsers have revolutionized the way people obtain information. The World Wide Web (WWW) has become the premier information source for most of the world. It offers a faster, more expansive view of the news and other events than most traditional media. In some government-controlled states where all media is "approved," people use the Web to learn about events in the outside world as reported by unbiased (relatively) views. Everywhere else it has been embraced as a quick and convenient method of finding information.

To fully empathize just how powerful and pervasive the Internet has become, ponder these figures from the U.S. Department of Commerce: it took radio 38 years to reach an audience of 50 million, it took television 13 years, and it took the Internet only four. This rapid growth demonstrates just how much this network of computers has become a part of people's lives.

What Is Web Browsing?

To many people, Web browsing *is* the Internet. The advent of the WWW revolutionized how people used and viewed the Internet. It is one of the major factors responsible for the popularity of the Internet. Web browsing has created an easy way for people to publish and view all types of information and has allowed many to share their views and perspectives. Web browsing involves two separate entities: a server that contains the Web pages and a browser that displays them.

A Web page itself consists of two main components: its core information that is to be presented and directions on how to display the information. When you use a Web browser to read a page, your browser starts by sending a "request" to the remote server. The server reads the request and sends the browser a copy of the Web page. This copy is then stored on your machine and displayed by your browser. The Web browser interprets the instructions in the page to display the images, text, and multimedia elements as the designer intended. By having the browser actually interpret the instructions, the amount of information that must be passed between the Web server and your computer is significantly reduced.

Web pages are written in Hypertext Markup Language (HTML), which is a simple text-based representation of the core information and the instructions to display it. As a result, raw Web pages can be viewed in any file editor, such as Notepad or Microsoft Word. On first glance, raw HTML may look odd, as most of it will be the markup commands used to tell the browser how to format and display the contents. If you look carefully, you will find the core or main information that the page is trying to convey.

The first Web pages were completely text based with little markup and no graphics. Over time, capabilities have been added to improve the Web-surfing experience. Modern Web pages can embed Java applications, flash animations, media, and images. Flash animations are embedded in Web pages in such a manner that when the page is retrieved from the server, the animation is shown. The advent of rich multimedia and fast connectivity has allowed the Web to flourish. It has gotten so popular and content rich that it rivals traditional media outlets such as television and newspapers. In fact, many people no longer subscribe to newspapers because they read the content via the Web.

What Can You Get from Web Browsing?

Because Web browsers are the main entrance to the Internet for most people, it is important to know what kind of information you can find when exploiting one. For most people, the online experience starts and ends with a Web browser, which they may use to read Web mail online, shop, bank, pay bills, and search for topics of interest. Being able to monitor a Web browser offers an opportunity to skim vital intelligence from these activities. Several important areas you can collect information from are Web mail, online accounts, sites visited (histories), and multimedia. Using the information from these areas, you can reconstruct a good deal of your target's online activity.

Web Mail

Web mail is currently the trendy way for sending and viewing e-mail. E-mail in its pure form has been around since the dawn of the Internet. In the older days, it was viewed and composed with text-based programs on the servers that people logged into. By the mid-90s, some programs such as America Online's (AOL's) e-mail software, Eudora, and Microsoft Outlook allowed people to download their e-mail from the servers to view and store on their personal computers. Using these same programs, people could write and respond to the downloaded messages and transmit the new mail back through their mail servers. These mail programs had many advantages; people no longer had to log in to difficult mail servers and struggle with UNIX commands to view their e-mail. However, there were also several disadvantages posed by these tools. Because mail was downloaded to a specific application, management became much more difficult.

Viewing e-mail couldn't be done without a computer that had e-mail software. If you wanted to view e-mail from multiple computers, there were coordination problems between the different clients on the different machines.

In the mid to late 90s, Web mail began to appear. Realizing the increasing role of Web browsers in the Internet experience, clever programmers began to develop a Web interface to traditional e-mail. Users could log on to a Web site and view a Web representation of their e-mail box. While initially rather crude and plain, Web mail has improved over the last few years. Current implementations have more advanced features and closely resemble more advanced client-side e-mail programs. Web mail allows people to read and write e-mail with only a Web browser as their client program. Now, you can view e-mail from any machine that has a Web browser. This is great for people who travel or rarely sit at the same computer.

Because e-mail is now combined into the ubiquitous WWW, collection strategies that work against browsers have the opportunity to provide you with your target's e-mail.

Online Accounts

With the rise in the use of Web mail, several other types of online transactions have also risen in popularity. It is not unusual for people to do banking, bill paying, and shopping online. In most of those cases, a person would have an account with the respective institution. There are also other situations where a person would have a virtual online account. They may be a member of different hobby clubs that have their own respective Web sites and message forums. These online accounts are often accessed through Web browsers.

Being able to monitor these activities can be extremely useful. By combining most of a person's economic transactions (shopping, bills, banking) with some of his or her leisure transactions (online forums, and so on), you can build a fairly complete picture of what a person has going on in his or her life. By focusing on and exploiting the common ground of Web browsers, you can collect a lot of information from one location.

Sites Visited

Most browsers keep a history of the sites they have been to. A history can also be obtained from the network by recording all of the HTTP requests for different Uniform Resource Locators (URLs). Although seemingly useless by itself, a list of visited sites can help shine light on people's interests and happenings. Are they visiting the same Web mail site daily? Hourly? If so, they are probably expecting important e-mail. Do they go to the same Personals site continually? Once again, this gives you more information about what a person is doing.

Multimedia

Multimedia can be valuable for a number of reasons. First, it in itself can be directly incriminating. For example, pornography on your family computer, while not necessarily illegal, shows that there is a member of the family with an interest in it. Multimedia content such as images and flash movies can also lead to clues about different sites. Are the images cars, computers, or single eligible women? Do the flash animations advertise for technology companies, promote the virtues of the new Ford Mustang, or tell a naughty story? Close examination of the multimedia material that comes with Web sites can help lead you to an idea of intent without ever having to examine the Web site.

Typical Web Browsers

A browser is used to access Web pages on the Internet. It is an application program on your computer that handles Web content. The Web browser will request, download, and display Web pages as you "surf" the Internet. There are many different Web browsers, with some of the most popular being Internet Explorer; Mozilla and its light version, Mozilla Firefox; and Netscape. There are many other Web browsers available; some are free, and some are available for a small price. Each has its own features, shortcomings, and eccentricities.

Currently, Internet Explorer is the most popular Web browser used; however, Mozilla Firefox is making gains. Regardless of all the bells and whistles that each Web browser advertises, they all have the same basic functionality: bookmarks, a history file, and a cache. These three commonalities are critical locations that can be examined for clues of different activities. As demonstrated in the previous chapter, some Web browsers even have the capability to remember user names and passwords. This feature was designed to enable faster surfing because you don't need to constantly log into a Web site, but it can also be a large security risk that you can take full advantage of.

All Web browsers have the capability to bookmark favorite Web sites that a user visits regularly. By selecting a drop-down menu with a list of bookmarked pages, the user can be taken directly to that page without having to remember the site's Web address. Depending on the browser, bookmarks are sometimes referred to as "favorites." Bookmarks are a good indication of what sites a person regularly visits, or more importantly, has deemed essential enough to remember. Most Web browsers include some of their own bookmarks, but these are generally sites that would not be cause for alarm. Similarly, Web browsers maintain a history. In the previous chapter, we showed you how this history can be used to determine the recent Web activity of a machine.

The cache contains the very sites that the Web browser has recently displayed to the user. When a user browses to the Web site, the Web page is downloaded to the computer and stored in the cache. The browser then displays a copy of the Web page that it has downloaded. After the user has surfed to another page, that copy of the Web page remains in the cache. This is maintained for efficiency in the event that the user returns to the page within a short period of time. The Web browser determines if the Web page on the Web server is newer than the one in the cache, and if it is, the Web page is downloaded. Otherwise, the cached copy is displayed. Most Web browsers can be configured to check for a new version of a saved page every time, never, or only when the browser is restarted. By using a cache, the Web browser attempts to minimize the amount of data that needs to be sent. A cache has a set amount of size that it can utilize. Once this space has been filled up, older Web pages are deleted. Users can also clear out their cache to hide their tracks. A cache is a wonderful part of a Web browser that enables it to serve up Web pages faster and more efficiently, yet can be used to gain an insight into the activities on the computer.

Cookies are small files that are used in Web surfing for a variety of reasons. Many sites configure the Web server to send a cookie, in addition to the requested page, that is stored on your local machine. The next time you go to the Web site, the server will ask if you have a cookie; if you do, that cookie is sent to the Web server. The most common use of a cookie is to save information about you such as your IP address or an assigned ID so that the server can quickly determine who you are. Many Web sites have an option when signing in of telling the server to remember your information. This information is being stored in a cookie. There are many other useful aspects to cookies; however, in the past they have gotten a bad name because some Web sites have taken advantage of them and used them maliciously. As a result of nefarious cookies, most Web browsers allow their users to forbid cookies from being saved on their machine. This option can help prevent some nefarious activities, but most people allow cookies because many legitimate sites use them.

Using the Internet has become an increasingly greater multimedia experience. Web browsers have become more complex, and many have integrated plug-ins to run flash and Java applications. When viewing Web pages, the application files are often embedded directly in the page. The browser automatically loads the correct environment and runs the application. Most Web browsers also contain limited File Transfer Protocol (FTP) capability, which allows a Web server to offer up a file for download. In Chapter 5, we downloaded installation executables; the browser manages the downloading of these files.

Web Browsers

We will now analyze some of the most popular Web browsers and many of the features they implement. Special attention is paid to the information that can be used for exploiting them and making them into effective means of collecting information from your target.

Internet Explorer

Internet Explorer is far and away the most popular Web browser on Microsoft Windows-based computers. A copy of Internet Explorer comes bundled with every version of Microsoft Windows, so convenience plays a big part in its popularity. It is also the most targeted browser by hackers and other nefarious individuals. Before Windows XP Service Pack 2, Internet Explorer came with some default security settings that were absolutely worthless. With more attention being drawn to Internet Explorer's security flaws, Microsoft has made an effective and concerted effort to improve the browser's security profile.

Lucky for you, most of the information that you want is not affected by the new heightened security posture. Most of the information you are interested in is stored on the computer the browser is run from. In Chapter 6, we discussed finding most of this information using the browser. This is a good method, but most of this information can also be found on the file system. This method is also useful for collecting the browser's information. By knowing where it is stored on the file system, you can copy it remotely or copy it to removable media for later examination, all without having to worry about launching the browser and affecting settings. For example, bookmarks are saved under the "Favorites" tag, and come with a number of default sites. They can be collected as an aggregate from *C:/Documents and Settings/<User Name>/Favorites,* where *<User Name>* refers to the account name you are looking for information on. Copy that folder and you have a copy of that user's bookmarks for Internet Explorer. Internet

Explorer history is set to remember Web sites for 20 days. You can view Internet Explorer's history at *C:/Documents and Settings/<User Name>/Local Settings History.* Unlike Favorites, this folder is not as agreeable to copying, so it must be viewed on the disk. If you do copy it, there are certain tools that can decode it that can be found on our Web site, *www.cyberspybook.com.*

Cache files are stored in *C:/Documents and Settings/<UserName>/Local Settings/Temporary Internet Files.* You can also discover the person's cookies in a similar location, *C:/Documents and Settings/<User Name>/Cookies.* This directory has most of the cookie files that Internet Explorer has collected during its time browsing. Figure 7.1 shows the cookie directory for a typical user.

Figure 7.1 Cookie Directory for a Typical User

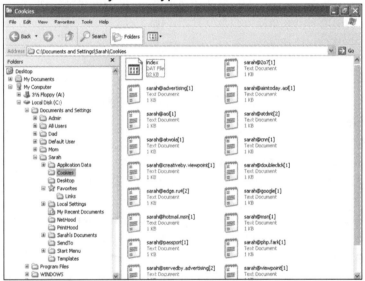

Internet Explorer is the most popular Web browser, and as a result, it is the first place you should look for clues as to what a person is doing online. Now you know where to find a person's history, his or her bookmarks, and the location of the cookies and cache from both the browser (Chapter 6) and the file system.

Notes from the Underground

Super Hidden Files

So far we've taught you how to find Internet Explorer's cache. Clever users, however, probably frequently clear their caches either to save space or to ensure that their caches are not browsed through. Microsoft, however, has a super secret cache that is not cleared out by the browsers' "clear cache" feature. This directory and all of its related files are considered to be "super hidden," meaning that in addition to the built-in hidden attributes they possess, they are also hidden with some additional steps so that they remain invisible even if Internet Explorer is configured to view all hidden files.

For an example of this hidden directory, browse to the cache directory *C:/documents and settings/<current user>/local settings/temporary internet files* for your current user with Internet Explorer. Now in the top menu bar, after the path listed, add the directory *Content.IE5* so that the new path is *C:/Documents and Settings/<Current User>/Local Settings/Temporary Internet Files/Conent.IE5*. You should see something like the screen in Figure 7.2.

This is a "super hidden" folder that has extra cache information. It's very likely that your target doesn't know it is there and has not cleared it. Although not as complete as the normal cache, it should offer you a significant window into that person's Web-browsing habits.

Figure 7.2 Content.IE5 Folder

Mozilla Firefox

The Mozilla Foundation is determined to provide a choice for Internet applications. It produces and distributes a Web browser, Mozilla, along with a stripped-down version, Firefox, and an e-mail application, Thunderbird. As hackers and virus creators target Internet Explorer, Mozilla gains in popularity. A vulnerability in one Web browser does not necessarily indicate an identical vulnerability in another. Mozilla endeavors to provide all of the functionality of Internet Explorer and then add some features to make Mozilla more secure and user-friendly. Mozilla has tabbed browsing enabled and thus allows multiple Web pages to be loaded within the same browser window. A user can switch between the tabs to look at the different pages. This is an alternative to having multiple instances of the browser being open. Another feature of Mozilla is the ability to remember usernames and passwords; this capability is different from using cookies to remember logins. The Mozilla browser allows the user to set the username and password for Web pages that need to be logged into. It even allows for multiple username and password combinations. Mozilla also has other extensions that can be downloaded to personalize and increase the browser's functionality.

Like Internet Explorer, Mozilla has a cache, history file, and bookmarks that can be looked at to determine a person's activities. Mozilla's application information is kept in the Mozilla folder. For instance, data for a person with the username Sarah is found in *C:/Documents and Settings/Sarah/Application Data/Mozilla/Firefox/Profiles/cv4uivs.default.* The last folder may be named differently, as it appears to have a random name for each installation, but it will be under the Profiles folder. As can be seen in Figure 7.3, this folder contains a subfolder titled Cache, which keeps all of the temporary Internet files.

Fig 7.3 Mozilla Firefox Application Folder

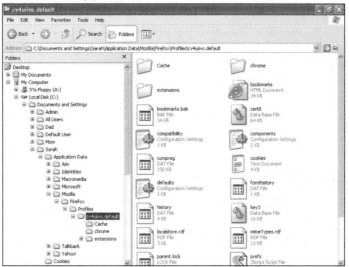

The bookmarks file is stored as an HTML document inside the Profiles folder. If you look closely at Figure 7.3, you will notice a *bookmarks.html* file. This can be double-clicked on and viewed like a normal Web page. There is also a cookies file, which contains the cookies for Mozilla. Mozilla Firefox continues to gain in popularity, and its features easily rival those of Internet Explorer. Once you have determined where Mozilla stores its application data, you can retrieve and look at that data.

AOL Explorer

In the past, AOL has used all types of Web browsers as its standard method of browsing. At one time, it designed its own proprietary browser. Netscape Navigator was the default choice for a while, and finally AOL settled on using Internet Explorer. Currently, AOL users are provided with a slightly customized version of Internet Explorer. This browser is integrated into the AOL application, but for the most part, acts and works like traditional Internet Explorer. From this point on we treat the AOL browser as if it is a standard installation of Internet Explorer.

NOTE

When this book was written AOL's browser was based on Microsoft Internet Explorer. However, during the editing, they announced that they are in the process of converting their browser engine to Mozilla Firefox. While they will continue to support the ability to switch to Internet Explorer as the rendering engine, don't be surprised if in the future the look-and-feel of the AOL browser closely resembles Firefox.

Other Browsers

Many people have used the prevalent Web browsers and found them lacking. Some of these people have even gone so far as to create their own Web browser and distribute it. Features such as tabbing and pop-up blocking are included in many of these browsers. Some of these are free, such as Netscape Navigator, and others like Opera are available for free or for a small price. Advant (*www.advant-browser.com*) is another Web browser that is gaining popularity. These browsers do not have a significant market share, but they are still popular with some users. Many of the innovations in these browsers are replicated in the more popular browsers. Most of these browsers have a history, cache, and bookmarks, all of which can be discovered.

Our Focus

Our focus is on Microsoft's Internet Explorer. Because this is the world's most popular Web browser, learning how to exploit it is a must. The other browser that we focus on is Mozilla's Firefox. This browser is currently gaining in popularity, as many online viruses and spyware applications take advantage of holes in Internet Explorer. A solution to the security flaws of Internet Explorer is to use a different browser. Mozilla Firefox is rapidly gaining market share, so learning how to find its secrets is important. By learning how to find the information from these two Web browsers, using any other Web browser should be an application of the same techniques.

Basic Skills

To succeed at spying on your target's Web browsing, you need to master some basic skills.

Running Programs from Explorer

To maintain a low profile and prevent your target from accidentally learning of your activities, we showed you how to remove a program from the Start menu. This helps prevent your target from discovering your software on his or her machine. However, now you need to use the software. Luckily, there is an easy way to do this using Explorer.

The first step is to start an Internet Explorer window and then browse to the location where the software was installed. This will most likely be in *C:/Progam Files/<software vendor>/<Software application>* or *C:/<software application>*. As shown in Figure 7.4, you must browse to *C:/Program Files/Winspy* in order to run WinSpy.

Fig 7.4 Starting WinSpy Using Explorer

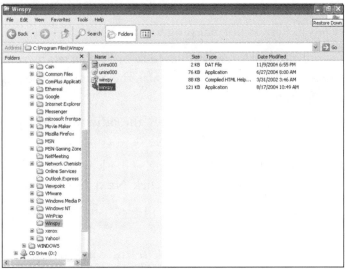

You then start the application by double-clicking on it. This enables you to run the application without having to access it from the Start menu. This is necessary because to covertly install software you should try to minimize all traces of it.

Collecting Information from Your Target's Computer

We now discuss some utilities that are useful in collecting information about a person's computer activities.

WinSpy

WinSpy is a very useful utility that is used to analyze what people are doing on a computer. It aggregates data that reports what URLs have been visited and the addresses in the address bar. It displays the cookies on the machine and reports what documents have recently been opened. It will read the *index.dat* files and display the address contained.

Download

WinSpy is available from *http://www.acesoft.net/winspy*. There is also a link to this site from *www.cyberspybook.com*. Download file *wssetup.exe*.

Installation

WinSpy is installed like most normal programs.

1. Using Internet Explorer, double-click on the ***wssetup.exe*** file. This will begin the installation process. As usual, the Security Warning will pop up; click **Run** to continue.

2. As the Installation Process continues, the official @WinSpy installation window will be displayed. Select **Next** to continue.

3. As the installation proceeds, WinSpy will ask where to place the files. Using the default is acceptable, so click **Next** to continue.

4. The setup program will ask where to place the Start menu folder. Again, click **Next** to continue.

5. Figure 7.5 shows the next window. In this window unclick the box next to **Create A Desktop** icon. This stops an icon from being placed upon the desktop. Select **Next** to continue.

Fig 7.5 Removing WinSpy's Desktop Icon

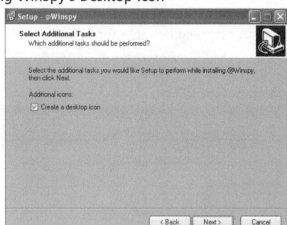

6. The WinSpy setup program now has all of its options. Select **Install** to complete the installation.

7. A final pop-up window will be displayed. Select **Finish** to end the installation program.

WinSpy is now installed and almost ready for use. However, before you continue, there are still a few more steps necessary to decrease your profile. The first is to remove it from the Start menu (discussed in Chapter 5). If you have forgotten how to remove it, go to **Start | All Programs | @WinSpy**. Right-click and select **Delete**. This will remove it from the Start menu, but you can still start it using Internet Explorer. Next, if you want WinSpy to remain on your target's machine, you should remove it from the "Remove Software" list and also ensure that it does not show up on the "Recently Used Programs" list on the Start menu (discussed in Chapter 5).

Usage

WinSpy is very easy to use; however, there is a limitation: WinSpy must be run from the account where the files you wish to analyze are located. The easiest way to do this is to obtain the user's password (if there is one), log on to his or her machine, and start WinSpy using the Internet Explorer window. The main WinSpy window (see Figure 7.6) is displayed. The different buttons at the top cause WinSpy to display the differing information.

Figure 7.6 shows the URL History tab. This window displays the title of the visited URLs and the Web pages' titles. For example, there was a Google search for anorexia. This information could be cause for concern, especially when combined with the Anorexia Nervosa page.

Fig 7.6 WinSpy Reveals Recent URLs

Figure 7.7 shows the Address Bar page. This is similar to the URL History tab, but is a record of all the addresses typed into the address bar. Again, you can see that the user visited the anorexia Web site.

Figure 7.7 WinSpy Reveals Typed-in Addresses

The Cookie tab displays all of the cookie files associated with the user. Sometimes, the cookie resides on the machine even if a user has deleted his or her cache. Next is the Recent Documents tab, which shows all of the files that the user has accessed recently (see Figure 7.8).

Figure 7.8 WinSpy Reveals the Recent Documents

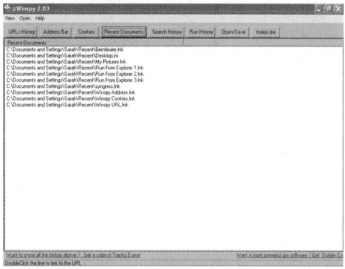

By utilizing the Run History tab, all of the programs started from the run bar can be shown. This information is useful in showing programs that the user started without using Internet Explorer. The Open/Save tab displays all of the recently opened or saved pictures, bitmaps, and text files. This data can be especially useful for finding out what the user has been looking at. Finally, the index.dat tab is where Internet Explorer stores its information. This tab displays all of the Web pages that have been visited. This information is very useful because the Web pages that were just accessed by clicking links from other pages will be displayed. This tab should be explored, because it offers some of the most complete information.

Collecting Information about Your Target from the Network

Now that you have searched the person's Web browser for evidence of his or her past activities, you must determine what your target is doing now. One effective way to do this is to sniff the network and capture all of your target's Web traffic. Once you have the traffic, you can analyze the files to determine what your target has been doing and looking at. Although you probably can get most of the information from the computer and the Web browser, collecting off of the network offers the following advantages:

- Depending on your network's configuration, the location of your listening post, or some advanced attack (see Chapter 10), you can eavesdrop and collect Web traffic from a completely independent computer other than your target's. Thus, you would significantly reduce your footprint on your target's machine and lower your chances of being discovered.

- Most of the information stored on the target is temporary, meaning it is stored in caches or history files. Caches by their very nature are temporary, and the data in them is fleeting. You can never guarantee that the data relevant to you is in the cache. By sniffing, however, you collect all the data as it happens. Nothing can be done to clear this data once you've obtained it. You are guaranteed to have the latest data.

- Information collected on the network can show a temporal relation. When you look at cache and histories, you can get a somewhat good idea of when different sites were viewed. Collecting off of the network can give you a real-time view of events that happen. Watching URLs on the network can show how frequently things happen and give you a more granular view of events. For example, the granularity of most browser's history is down to one day. A network dump can show you at what time and how many times in a day a certain site was visited.

Collecting by Sniffing

To collect information by sniffing, you need to use two tools. In Chapter 5, we discussed using Snort and OWNS as sniffers. In this chapter, we show you how to use them in conjunction with each other to sniff traffic and then analyze it.

The first step is to set up Snort as a service. This will log all of the Internet activity from a machine. If you know that you can sniff the entire network, as is the case with a hub, you can run Snort on your personal machine; otherwise, you must install Snort on the target's machine. Once you have the activity, you can examine it in file *snort.log.xxxxxxxx*. There may be several log files in the directory, and you may need to examine them one by one to ensure that all of the collected traffic is examined.

Now that you have the Snort log file, you must examine it. Fortunately, OWNS is very useful in analyzing a capture file. You only need to set it up to read from a capture file instead of the sniffer. Figure 7.9 shows how to configure OWNS for reading from a file.

Figure 7.9 OWNS Configured to Read from a File

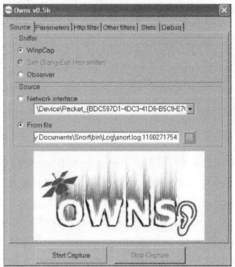

There are a couple of other changes you must make to OWNS before you are ready to begin. First, you need to set the parameters so that OWNS knows to break out the captured traffic by IP address (see Figure 7.10). This way, if you track multiple computers communicating with the network, you can easily narrow down and focus on traffic related to the computer of interest. The other noteworthy thing is the Output directory. In this case, it is ./files, which means that a files directory will be created where the sniffer log is located. This is where OWNS places its output.

Figure 7.10 Setting OWNS Output Directory

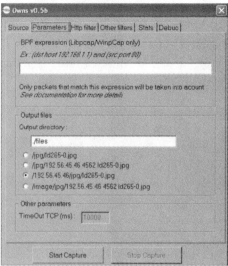

Next, you must select the HTTP Filter tab, where you select what type of files to save. In this case, you select everything. It is easier to disregard extra files, than to miss something important that might have transpired. Once you have set the files, you are ready to run OWNS. Switching to the Stats tab gives you an easy way to see how much data is broken out. Select **Start Capture** to begin breaking out the files using OWNS. This may take some time, but the Stats tab will update everything.

Once this has finished, you can examine the output of OWNS by going into the directory. Figure 7.11 shows that under address 192.168.245.129, which is our machine, OWNS has created several directories. These files include *.cab*, *.gif*, *.html*, *.js*, *.jpg*, and *.swf* directories.

Figure 7.11 OWNS Output Directory

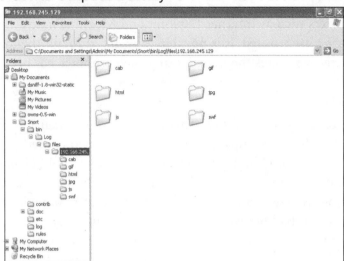

Now you can go into each directory and look to see what you have collected. Some of the directories will be more interesting than others. The .*swf* directory contains all of the shockwave flash objects that were downloaded. Similarly, the .*js* directory is where all of the Java Script files are found. The .*cab* directory has all of the cabinet files, which are a Microsoft-specific type of archive. The .*gif* folder contains all of the .*gif* files that were downloaded. This will give a clue as to what types of Web pages the user is looking at. A quick glance into the .*jpg* directory can reveal what your target has been doing.

The final directory is the .*html* directory where all of the downloaded HTML files are put. This directory may be very large, but will have all of the Web pages that were looked at. Examining these pages will shed some light onto what your target was doing.

Now that you have seen what the person has been doing on the Internet, you can decide what to do next. A good first step is to cover your tracks by deleting all of the contents that OWNS gave you. The Snort log should also be deleted. Using Snort and OWNS together, you can examine your network's traffic and have the contents easily broken out.

Case Study: Browsing for Trouble

Most Web browsers such as Internet Explorer and Mozilla Firefox leave traces of the Web sites they have visited. It is possible to search through the log files and determine exactly what sites the person using the computer has been visiting.

Elaboration

Robbie was a relatively successful information technology manager in a medium-sized health-care company. He had been married to Beth, a wonderful woman whom he met at church, for the past seven years. Robbie and Beth had two young daughters Isabella, 3, and Michelle, 5. They lived in a comfortable house in the suburbs of Washington, D.C. Beth stayed at home with the kids during the day, while Robbie went to work. They found that this was the best arrangement for the kids, even if it stressed the finances of the family. They had to share a car, which Robbie commuted in, every day. From the outside, they looked like a happy family.

Unbeknownst to Beth, the marriage was not so strong as she thought. Robbie was not the devout husband that she believed he was, despite his assurances to the contrary. Beth was busy taking care of their two young children full-time, while Robbie concentrated on his job. Beth had given up her promising career to take care of their children, and had not held a full-time job since she was pregnant with Michelle. Robbie had become less interested in the marriage as time progressed.

Robbie had begun to spend more time at work and spent his free time socializing with his work friends. He had begun to drop hints that everything was not right in the marriage. Robbie's coworkers were aware that he was not being the attentive husband that Beth deserved, but declined to intervene.

As the marriage slowly fell apart, Beth continued to be kept in the dark about Robbie's feelings. Robbie finally decided that he wanted to leave Beth and informed his coworkers of his decision. He told them that he was going to leave his wife and kids because the marriage was not working out. He wanted to be alone.

When Robbie took a step back, he realized that he was not ready to leave the marriage. Although he wanted out, he came to the conclusion that he needed to save up money and get prepared before he left Beth. Robbie wanted to be able to have his own car and apartment when he left the marriage.

Robbie began to save money and began his preparations while keeping Beth in the dark. He even began to ask out coworkers and other women on dates, despite still being married. Robbie for all intents and purposes was single, despite not telling Beth. Robbie was going to leave the marriage when he was ready, and not before then.

Eventually, Beth began to get suspicious of Robbie's activities. Although nobody had told her what was going on, her suspicions began to grow as Robbie became more distant. After she confronted him with her suspicions, and they had several long talks in an effort to get the marriage back on track. However, Robbie's efforts did not match Beth's, and her suspicions grew to where she felt she had to take action. Robbie spent more and more time at work, and when he was home, spent an excessive amount of time on the Internet. Despite her continuous questioning, Robbie never came clean about his actions.

Finally, Beth decided that she had to take action. She spent hours debating what to do about her situation. She considered hiring a detective, but did not want to pay for one, or anger Robbie if he found out. Beth decided that going through his computer and figuring out what he was doing online would give her a clue, without taking any action that was irreversible. After searching his Internet cache, she determined that he was visiting an online bank, among other places. This piqued Beth's curiosity, as they had only one shared bank account. After this, Beth grew more suspicious of her husband's actions.

Over the next couple of months, Beth continued to monitor her husband's actions and tracked his Web activity. She noted that he continued to access the bank's Web site, along with looking at rental property Web sites. There were also links to several used car dealerships in the area. Finally, Beth confronted Robbie with her knowledge of the activities. Boxed into a corner, Robbie finally came clean to Beth, filling her in on the intentions he had voiced to his coworkers months before. They are currently still living together and the situation is unresolved.

Analysis

Beth managed to potentially dodge a life-altering event. Although she was not happy about violating Robbie's privacy, she realized when talking about the situation was not alleviating her suspicions that something had to be done. Beth was still in love with Robbie and did not want to hurt him in any way. She decided to take the least intrusive method available to determine what was happening to her relationship. Beth felt that she had a responsibility to protect herself and her daughters.

The technology that Beth used was not on the cutting edge. By utilizing the Web browsers' history, she determined what sites Robbie was visiting. Because he failed to clear his cache and history after he surfed the Web, Robbie unknowingly left a trail that could be followed. Beth did not have to be technologically competent in order to gain the information that she needed to protect herself. There were more invasive methods that Beth could have used, but she relied on the least intrusive. In this case, the technology Robbie used to help plan his future without his wife ultimately led to the discovery of his activities.

If Beth had not decided to snoop on Robbie's activities, the outcome could have been vastly different. Robbie had planned on leaving her and their children. Beth would have been left unemployed, responsible for two young children and a mortgage, without any safety net.

Summary

The Web browser is the portal to the Internet. As your quarry browses the Internet, he or she leaves tracks that can be examined. The Web browser saves vital information that can be used to your advantage. This chapter addressed the following key points about Web browsers:

- Web browsing has defined the Internet experience for many users. A browser is the only portal and interface to the Internet for most people.

- Exploiting Web browsing can yield a wealth of information, including Web mail, online accounts, lists of visited sites, and other multimedia information.

- Internet Explorer is currently the most popular browser for Microsoft Windows users. It leaves lots of information on the disk about where it has been and what it has been used for.

- Like Internet Explorer, most other browsers have the same few fundamental components, bookmarks, cookies, and caches, all of which give valuable clues to what your target does online.

- Tools like WinSpy allow for easy aggregation of Web browsing information that is left behind on the computer.

- OWNS and Snort combined make an effective system for monitoring and analyzing Web traffic.

The information that you collect from Web browsers, both on the computer and from the network, is an important piece of the puzzle to obtaining total information awareness of your target. If you applied proper tradecraft, followed SLEUTH, and were careful how you approached your tasks, you are now holding a significant amount of information on your target with them being none the wiser. It is now time to proceed and look for more information to round out your collection and fill in the gaps not covered by Web browsers.

## Chapter 8

Spying on E-mail

You Can't Always Get What You Want, But If You
Try Sometimes, Well, You Just Might Find, You Get
What You Need

— The Rolling Stones

Topics in This Chapter:

- Overview of E-mail

- Popular Methods of Viewing E-mail

- E-mail Collection Strategies

- Summary

Introduction

E-mail is the No. 1 application on the Internet. Along with the World Wide Web (WWW), it is largely responsible for the incredible growth and popularity of the Internet. Much in the way traditional mail tied the world together more than a century ago, e-mail has sprung up to offer an information age replacement. As a result, it is one of the most used methods of communication today. E-mail can contain a simple greeting ("hey, let's have lunch"), receipts for an online credit card purchase, or a long diatribe on someone's emotional state. Since the relevance of its content varies from trivial to deeply personal, e-mail, even more than Web traffic, allows you to pry into someone's private business. This chapter explores how to monitor someone's e-mail account and collect and analyze this valuable source of information.

Overview of E-mail

E-mail is an electronic letter sent from one person to one or many people. Just as sending or receiving traditional mail requires a postal address, sending or receiving e-mail requires an e-mail account. E-mail accounts exist on e-mail servers. Users exercise one of several different methods to access their account to view and send e-mail (these methods will be discussed later in this chapter).

First, let's discuss how e-mail is transmitted on the Internet using the account created for this book, "Sarah Evans," or *sarahe1988@yahoo.com*. This address, like all e-mail addresses, consists of two parts: a user name and a domain name. Everything before the "@" is the user name (i.e., sarahe1988), and everything after the "@" is the domain name (i.e., yahoo.com). This is very similar to an address in traditional mail, where the account name is the address and the domain is the zip code. All e-mail that is sent has at least two addresses: a sender and a recipient. Most e-mail messages also contain other unseen data called "headers." Headers are used to help an e-mail message reach its final destination, but are usually invisible to the user. Headers are like the postage markings on a letter that passes through a post office. To better understand e-mail servers, imagine that they are like post offices; each one is responsible for delivering mail to a group of addresses. E-mail is routed from sender to recipient just as traditional mail is. If e-mail is sent from one address to an address nearby, a server merely transfers the outgoing message to the inbox of the other local account. When e-mail must be sent to an address farther away, the e-mail server sends it via Simple Mail Transport Protocol (SMTP) to the remote e-mail server for the domain that matches the domain in the recipient field. This is similar to having a letter sent to the post office that matches the recipient's zip code.

The route that e-mail takes depends on how far it must travel. When a typical message is sent, it first goes from the sender's account to the local e-mail server. In turn, the local e-mail server relays the e-mail to the destination's e-mail server. After receiving the message, the destination's e-mail server places it in the recipient's account. In practice, the e-mail may be passed to multiple e-mail servers before reaching its final destination. Some of these intermediate steps may be delayed, which is why e-mail is sometimes received out of order.

Using the mail analogy again, when you want to send an e-mail (mail a letter), you first compose the letter and then place it in an envelope, address it, and affix postage. You then put it in your mailbox for the letter carrier to pick up. The letter carrier picks up your mail and looks at the recipient's address. When the recipient is served by the same letter carrier (the same e-mail domain), the letter carrier post-marks the mail (adds header information) and places it in the recipient's mailbox. If the mail needs to be sent to another domain, the letter carrier takes the mail back to the post office where it is postmarked and sent to the post office that serves the address requested. There, the letter carrier picks up the mail and delivers it to the recipient. E-mail works by the same principles; however, there are some slight differences, the most important being that the mail is marked at each post office. This is why the headers are so important. Figure 8.1 demonstrates the e-mail process.

Figure 8.1 E-mail Process

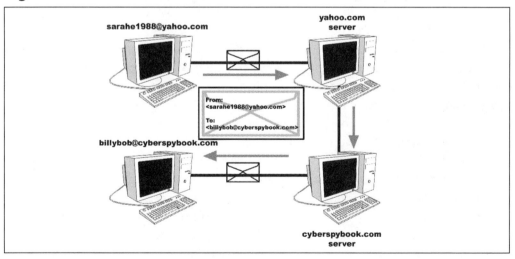

Having originated in the early 1970s, e-mail has significantly evolved in capability during its time. Originally, people would log into time-shared UNIX machines to read their text-only e-mail. The concept of attachments originated when someone realized that binary files could be encoded in text and attached to e-mail messages. This process enabled files such as images and programs to be sent along with text-only messages. While there are still quite a few people who use this method for e-mail, its manual overhead keeps it from becoming popular among home users, particularly those with Microsoft Windows operating systems). Therefore, we do not cover any methods of exploiting these types of users.

The next big revolution was the widespread use of e-mail clients for reading and writing messages from other e-mail clients. E-mail clients are programs that reside on people's personal or work computers. They allow users to download, reply, and send e-mail from their own PCs without having to log into a server. America Online (AOL) was a very popular early e-mail client. Eudora, Outlook, Outlook Express, and Mozilla Thunderbird are other popular e-mail clients. E-mail clients take advantage of SMTP, Post Office Protocol (POP), Internet Message Access Protocol (IMAP), and Hypertext Transfer Protocol (HTTP) for sending and receiving e-mail. SMTP is the mechanism by which an e-mail client transmits outgoing messages to an e-mail server, and POP is the mechanism where a client logs into an e-mail server and downloads messages. Another protocol, IMAP, is similar to POP in that it is used for downloading messages but does not remove them from the e-mail server. This method resembles the older style of e-mail, since a copy of all e-mail is still stored in one central location. This method of e-mail became very popular in offices and business settings. Another important step in the evolution of e-mail was the ability to use Hypertext Markup Language (HTML) and other rich content to send messages that were enhanced beyond plain text. Now, e-mail can contain images, complex fonts and colors, and even hidden scripts in the message body.

The next big revolution in e-mail was the rise in popularity of Web mail. Although using an e-mail client greatly advanced the capabilities of e-mail, it had several limitations. Unlike the time when people logged into central servers to manage their e-mail, using clients tied people down to specific computers. If people did not use the same computer for connecting every time, e-mail box management became extremely difficult as different sent and received e-mail collections were spread out among many computers; there was no one single repository. While IMAP solved the problem somewhat for the receiving side, there was no good solution to unifying sent e-mail folders. Web mail was developed as a new means of sending and receiving e-mail. It is similar to the traditional method, except instead of logging into a remote machine and running an e-mail program, a Web browser is used as the interface, which allows users to check and send e-mail from anywhere. Since the Web browser is a nearly ubiquitous interface, most people's e-mail accounts are highly accessible. Anyone, anywhere with a Web browser, can send and receive e-mail. Because e-mail is stored on the remote server, there is no longer the problem of different mailboxes on different computers.

E-mail's simplicity, familiarity, and extendable sophistication allow it to remain useful and extremely popular despite the arrival of newer technologies. From early account-based e-mail to sophisticated Web mail, all e-mail is based on a set of standards. This allows the e-mail you send on an early 1990s UNIX machine to reach your Hotmail account and receive a response. As a result, regardless of its delivery, e-mail messages have quite a few commonalities, allowing attacks and analysis of one method to work on another.

Popular E-mail Clients

Many people use an e-mail application to read, compose, and store their personal e-mail. Using the application allows users to access saved e-mail even when they are not connected to the Internet, create an e-mail, and send it at a later date. The application connects to the Internet service provider's (ISP's) e-mail server to send and receive messages. Many providers allow you to keep a portion of your e-mail on their server, but set strict limits so that their disk's storage capacity is not overwhelmed. For this reason, most stored e-mail is kept on the user's machine. Many people who use e-mail in their work environment employ specialized local e-mail applications. Some of the most popular ones available are discussed in this chapter, but clients such as Lotus Notes, which are extremely popular in office settings, are very rare in a home environment and are therefore not discussed in this book.

Outlook Express

One of the most used e-mail applications is Outlook Express, which comes installed on every Microsoft Windows machine. Outlook Express has many features and is tightly integrated with the Windows environment. It can be used as an e-mail application and as a newsgroup reader. One neat feature is its ability to manage multiple e-mail accounts, thereby allowing users to connect to all of their accounts. Since Outlook Express is run locally and connects to an e-mail server to send and retrieve e-mail, the e-mail is stored on the computer. As demonstrated in Chapter 6, Outlook Express files can be retrieved and viewed secretly. Outlook Express remains extremely popular despite the fact that it is the target of many e-mail viruses and worms.

Outlook

Outlook is the professional version of Outlook Express. It comes either as a stand-alone product or as part of Microsoft Office. In addition to basic e-mail services, Outlook has functionality for calendars, schedules, notes, and other types of personal information management. It is also very popular for synchronizing with Palm Pilots and other personal digital assistants (PDAs). An Outlook account can be valuable because it may contain all of these types of data.

AOL E-mail Client

This e-mail client is the default that comes with AOL, and is the primary local e-mail client that most people are familiar with. It is closely integrated with AOL's software, but has the same functionality as a normal local e-mail client. One limitation is that it is specifically tied to AOL's service and cannot be used for downloading e-mail from other services. Another significant difference is that although the AOL e-mail client looks like a traditional local e-mail client, it now operates like a Web mail service. It does not use SMTP and POP for sending and receiving e-mail. Most of the techniques described for local e-mail services do not work on AOL clients. Monitoring AOL e-mail should be approached the same was as monitoring a Web mail account.

Thunderbird

Another e-mail application rising in popularity is Thunderbird, a free application from the makers of Mozilla. Like Outlook Express, Thunderbird allows for the control of multiple e-mail accounts. It also allows users to search all of the accumulated e-mail in the user's account. Thunderbird has been gaining in popularity as viruses continue to target its competitors.

According to the usage statistics we studied, Microsoft Outlook, Microsoft Outlook Express, AOL, and Thunderbird are the most popular e-mail clients for traditional non-Web-based e-mail. This is not a comprehensive list, and there is always the possibility that your mark is using a different e-mail client. Luckily, since e-mail is standards based and all clients must adhere to these standards in order to function, the techniques we discuss work with most clients.

Web Mail

Another popular way to access e-mail is Web mail. To utilize Web mail, users use a Web browser to connect to the e-mail server. With this Web interface they can read, compose, and manipulate their e-mail. Any attachments they receive are stored on the remote server, and, at the user's request, are downloaded to the local computer. One advantage of using a Web mail account is that it is accessible from anywhere as long as the computer (or other Internet-accessible device) has an Internet browser and an Internet connection. Many of the original Web mail accounts were free, but came with very little storage space. Additional storage capability was reserved for paying customers. As the price of disk space has decreased and the popularity of online advertising has increased, companies increasingly use free Web mail accounts with large storage capacity to lure users to their sites where they can check their e-mail and access other premium content. Their account is used as the identification (ID) for the rest of the company's services.

Over the years, Web mail has become more popular. Many people use their work-provided e-mail account for work and keep several Web mail accounts for personal use. Because of their anonymity, "disposable" Web mail accounts can be useful in helping protect your identity online and in reducing the amount of spam that is sent to your personal account. Many Web mail services also provide free virus scanning, which helps protect users from malicious programs and viruses.

Using a Web mail account is easy. The first step is to launch your favorite browser and go to the Web mail provider's main page (i.e., *www.hotmail.com* for hotmail accounts). On this page there is an area to login using your user name and password. From here you can compose, save, send, receive, and read e-mail. In addition, most services also have address books to save and sort contacts.

Yahoo

Yahoo offers free Web mail as a way to entice users to the Yahoo Web portal, and is currently one of the most popular Web mail services. You can sign up and access accounts for Yahoo at *http://mail.yahoo.com*. A basic Web mail address from Yahoo currently comes with 100MB of storage. Yahoo also allows users to check other POP accounts from its Web interface. As with most Web mail providers, additional services may be purchased to expand capability (i.e., more storage, POP, and SMTP access to Yahoo accounts, and so on).

Hotmail

Hotmail is a free Web mail service provided by the Microsoft Corporation. Along with Yahoo, it is one of the most popular free Web mail providers and is accessed at *www.hotmail.com*. Basic Hotmail accounts currently come with 250MB of storage space. Like Yahoo, Hotmail accounts can have premium services such as more space and POP and SMTP access added for a fee.

Gmail

Gmail is a Web mail product offered by Google. Originally a search engine company, Google has expanded into many different areas. You have already seen Google's desktop searching tool; its powerful, innovative e-mail interface is another one of its clever inventions. Gmail is still in beta testing and is an invitation-only service; however, Google plans to make it publicly available in the near future. A Gmail account can be found at *www.gmail.com*. This account comes with 1000MB (1GB) of storage and currently offers more free space than any other service. Gmail also provides the ability for users to sort and organize their e-mail using Google-based search engines and techniques. Gmail is also introducing the capability for users to access their accounts with SMTP and POP. However, clever organization that it is, Google forces users to use encrypted versions of both, thwarting would-be packet sniffers. If current trends hold, expect to see Gmail emerge as a dominant force in the Web mail world, possibly overtaking the incumbents, Yahoo and Hotmail.

Other Web Mail

There are many other Web mail services that people are using to communicate on the Internet. Some of these are free and others are pay services, yet they all work on the same principle. By using a Web browser and an Internet connection, a user can access their e-mail service from anywhere. There is even software that allows people to set up their own Web mail servers. It should also be noted that many companies provide a way for their employees to use the Web to check their normal work e-mail when they are away from their local e-mail application.

Collecting E-mail

Now that you have an understanding of e-mail, it is time to focus on collecting it. This section demonstrates a series of strategies to obtain e-mail either via collection from the target's PC or with more crafty means such as sniffing the network and collecting e-mail as it passes from machine to machine.

Target Identification

Target identification is the first step when spying on e-mail. Once you have determined what e-mail service or services are being used, you can plan how to get the information from these messages. E-mail received or sent by your target can be very insightful.

Chapter 6 discussed how to identify all the e-mail accounts known on a computer. Because some computers may yield dozens of accounts, you need to focus and decide which ones to monitor. A person may be using one account to correspond with their conspirators, and another account to keep in touch with family. Of the e-mail accounts you viewed, were some active and some not? Were the ones you thought inactive really that way, or was the e-mail not there, deleted, or something along those lines? Examine each one carefully for clues about its purpose and relevance in your mark's online life.

For example, if you find an AOL e-mail account and the last message stops over a year ago, you may still want to investigate. However, if you know for a fact that your mark no longer uses AOL, you can safely assume that this service is no longer active. Although its contents may be interesting from a forensics and history stand-point, you probably do not need to include this account in your further collection. If you find an account in Outlook Express that has a few messages in its inbox but little other evidence of activity, you may still want to consider monitoring it. Your mark may not save copies of outgoing e-mail and may delete e-mail after he or she reads it, making the account appear to be inactive.

Since the user may have multiple e-mail accounts and may try to hide accounts, the next step is to determine what exactly he or she is doing. There are two ways to do this: (1) sniff the network and analyze the traffic or (2) search the computer for evidence trails. Evidence trails might be in the history of the Internet browser (if they are using Web mail) or in a saved message on the hard drive. References to any Web mail services would be a clue. Another place to look at would be the common e-mail applications; many of them support multiple users.

Collecting E-mail Files from the Target Computer

These methods involve searching for e-mail stored on the target computer. This can be done in many ways, such as locating the stored mailboxes or using the Google Desktop Search tool. (Techniques for doing this are covered in depth in Chapter 6.)

Collecting stored or cached e-mail from a target's computer has many advantages. Depending on how old it is, and how completely it is stored, e-mail can be extremely valuable. This method is also relatively easy; if you know how to search for files on a machine, you can search for e-mail. Once you find it, you can take the e-mail files offline and view them on another computer without your mark being the wiser. Finally, this method also allows you to collect information without having complete knowledge of e-mail accounts and passwords.

Collecting stored e-mail also has several problems associated with it. One is that you may not get all of the e-mail that you want. When looking for stored e-mail, you are looking for anything that a user has explicitly or accidentally saved on his or her machine. Paranoid users may have nothing on their personal computers. Even with the powerful Google Desktop Search tool, the caches you search through may not have the material you are looking for. This method also requires that you have close and continual access to the computer. This may not always be the case. Finally, this method does not work well with all types of e-mail. When a user logs into a remote account with a Web browser, not all of the material on the remote account will be transferred to the user's computer. Valuable information could be sitting on the e-mail server.

While collecting information from a computer is very useful (e.g., address lists, notes, and calendars), it is important to keep the limitations in mind. If you do not seem to be getting new or particularly useful "take," you may want to explorer other options.

Keystroke Logging

Keystroke logging offers another local method of collecting e-mail. Although it is still done on the target's box, it is different enough from collecting e-mail files to warrant mention. This method involves collecting keystrokes from your target's computer using either a hardware or software keystroke logger. The logic behind this method is that every single keystroke your mark types is captured by the keystroke logger. As a result, any e-mail they create on their system will be logged. Its structure will differentiate it from other material being typed in.

Using a keystroke logger also has several other advantages. It can collect from a number of different e-mail accounts without having to adapt a strategy for each one; in fact, you do not even have to know about all of the accounts your mark uses. As long as your target types on his or her PC, the information will be caught. In addition, you do not need to know passwords for either the e-mail accounts or for access to the computer. A wonderful benefit of a keystroke logger is that eventually many passwords will be revealed when your mark types them in.

One of the weaknesses of this method is that keystroke logging captures only data that originates on the target's machine; incoming messages are not logged. Have you ever heard half of a conversation? This is basically what you will get with a keystroke log. You will have your target's original e-mail and his or her replies to messages, but be left guessing at the replies your target receives or messages he or she is replying to. If your mark is using a Web mail account and logs in from remote locations, that e-mail will not be available either. Finally, using a keystroke logger requires close and continual access to your target's machine in order to harvest the keystrokes. Failure to collect the keystrokes in a timely manner could cause your collections to be overwritten as the user types enough to overwrite your keystroke logger's buffer. In addition, keystroke loggers are not limited to collecting e-mail. If your user bounces back and forth between surfing the Web, writing a school paper, chatting online, and typing an e-mail, then you will get a fairly difficult-to-read conglomeration of their typing.

Collecting with a Client

Using a client is a clever way of collecting e-mail from accounts that have or allow POP access. To enable this method of collection, you need several prerequisites:

- The account name

- The account password

- The POP server hostname or IP address

- An "always-on" Internet connection such as a cable modem or DSL

- A local e-mail client

All of this information can usually be collected from e-mail files on the target computer or by sniffing the network. Once you have the necessary information you can set up a "shadow" client. This shadow client will periodically download e-mail from a POP server, but will leave a copy on the server so that the target still receives and reads his or her e-mail.

The following exercise walks you through setting up a shadow client with Outlook Express to collect on a Yahoo account; however, this technique can be done with any local e-mail client on any POP account.

The first step is to obtain the necessary information. For this exercise, we use the "Sarah Evans" account. From searching around on her PC, we have determined that her e-mail account is *sarahe1988@yahoo.com*. Next, using tools covered in Chapter 6 to view Microsoft's hidden storage, we learn that her password is "restless." Finally, by looking at the configuration for her Outlook Express, we see that she downloads her POP e-mail from *pop.mail.yahoo.com*. Now that you have the necessary information, open up Outlook Express and go to **Tools** | **Accounts** | **New** | **Mail**. You will be prompted to choose a display name and an e-mail address. Pick anything; it is not important since you will not be sending e-mail from this client. At the next screen, input the POP or IMAP server you will be collecting from and the SMTP server you will be sending e-mail to. Figure 8.2 shows this dialogue box.

In the top slot, fill out the information on the POP server. In the bottom slot, input completely useless information so that you will not accidentally send e-mail from this account. **This is a very important step for covering your tracks.** Next is the dialogue box for the account name and password, as shown in Figure 8.3.

Enter the account name and password. After clicking **Next**, the account creation is finished and you are taken back to the accounts screen (see Figure 8.4).

Notice that there is now an entry for *pop.mail.yahoo.com*. Now select the **Properties** button on the right-hand side of the Accounts dialogue box. When the Properties dialogue box appears, select the **Advanced** tab and make sure the "Leave a copy of message on the server box" is checked. The dialogue box should look like the example in Figure 8.5.

Figure 8.2 Server Selection Screen

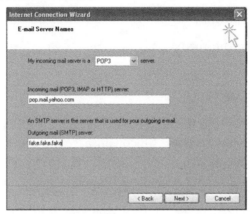

Figure 8.3 Outlook Express Account and Password Dialogue Box

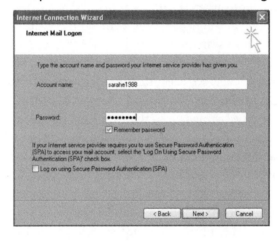

Figure 8.4 Outlook Express Accounts Dialogue Box

Figure 8.5 Advanced Settings for Account Properties

Finally, close the dialogue box and select **Tools** | **Options** on the main Outlook Express window. In the **General** tab, you can modify the "Check for e-mail every 30 minutes" option to a shorter time span. We have found that 7 to 15 minutes are good values. Congratulations. You now have a shadow client set up to collect your target's e-mail.

NOTE

In the spring of 2004, AOL announced Open Mail Access, a policy through which normal standards-compliant e-mail clients could be used for checking AOL e-mail. Using SMTP and IMAP, users can send and receive AOL e-mail through Outlook, Outlook Express, Thunderbird, and other popular e-mail clients. As a result, you now have the power to set up a shadow client for downloading AOL e-mail. Web site *http://members.aol.com/adamkb/aol/mailfaq/imap/* discusses the steps necessary to set up a client for IMAP and SMTP access, although we recommend you skip the steps for SMTP access as you do not want to accidentally send e-mail to your target.

A shadow client is a good covert method for spying on your target; however, it has many advantages and disadvantages, some of which can pose significant risk of discovery. Since it can be run on a remote computer from almost anywhere in the world, it can be incredibly stealthy. A shadow client will allow you to have almost complete access to all of the e-mail your target receives. However, the biggest disadvantage is that you now have the opposite problem of keystroke logging: you have a copy of all incoming/viewed e-mail, but no access to e-mail written by your mark (except in replies). This method also requires knowledge of an account and password, which, if your mark decides to change it, takes away your capability. Also, checking and downloading e-mail marks it as "Read." If your mark uses only a local e-mail application, they will never notice the difference, but if they also log into the Web interface for the e-mail account, the messages in the inbox that you have copied will be marked as "Read" and appear different than truly "New" or "Unread" e-mail. We do not think that the trade-offs are enough to totally discard this method of collection, but instead think it should be used in combination with keystroke logging to collect a complete picture of incoming and outgoing e-mail.

WARNING

It would be ideal to use a different client for other types of e-mail. You do not want to mix your collected intelligence in with your personal e-mail or accidentally reply to some of your take with your personal settings. That is why it is very important to make sure that the client you are configuring for e-mail collection cannot send e-mail. This is easy to do; just make sure that the values for outgoing SMTP servers are set to impossible ones such as "fake.fake.fake.fake."

Tips and Tricks...

Web Mail as a Local Client

This chapter discusses using a local e-mail client as a spy device. While this has many advantages, like people who legitimately use local e-mail clients, you may soon encounter some of its disadvantages. For example, this ties you to one computer for collection, and unless it is a laptop, you are not necessarily able to check your e-mail from anywhere. Downtime for your collection computer means gaps in coverage of your target account. A clever solution exists, however, that combines the power of a local e-mail account with the convenience of Web mail.

Yahoo offers the capability to check POP e-mail boxes from Web-based e-mail accounts. Other Web mail providers may have the same capability. Refer to your specific provider's instructions for setting up this feature. For Yahoo Mail, from the main screen select **Mail Options | Mail** Accounts to go to a series of setup questions. After this, set up POP access just like you would for a local e-mail client. With this capability you can spy on your mark's POP e-mail from your

Web mail account, giving you the flexibility to collect from any machine you can get a Web browser on. You now have the spying capability of a dedicated e-mail client, with the convenience of Web mail.

Using a Password to Log Into Web Mail

Using a password to log into a Web mail account is another method of collecting your target's e-mail. This procedure is necessary when your mark is using a Web mail account, and the messages cannot be collected with a local e-mail client. Since Web mail is a very popular and convenient way of using e-mail, this is becoming a more prevalent scenario. If your mark is using Web mail there are two methods for collecting it. One is to collect the data from the network via sniffing and the second is to log into their account using a captured password.

Chapter 6 demonstrated several methods of collecting passwords, which can be used to obtain access. Once you have logged into a Web mail account, there are several factors to keep in mind as you snoop around. If you are going to read a message in their "Inbox," note whether or not it is marked as "unread." If it is, make sure to reset it as "unread" after viewing the message. Hotmail, Yahoo, and Gmail all have easily accessible commands to mark messages as unread. When browsing through e-mail folders, do not overlook the sent e-mail folder. This holds all of your mark's outgoing messages, which may be a valuable source of information and important in completing your collection mission.

While this is a very effective method for e-mail collection, like the others it is not perfect. It gives you full access to all of the e-mail in the account, but not all accounts have sent e-mail saved, and e-mail that is read and deleted between the time you spy on it will also be missing. Therefore, you must realize that what you see is merely a snapshot, and does not paint the full picture of your target. Even with those shortcomings, it should be considered part of an effective e-mail collection arsenal.

Tips and Tricks…

Call Me

Logging into Web mail accounts is a game of chance. You are always hoping that the e-mail in there is the "freshest" view, in that you are seeing it before you mark has a chance to delete it. One way to stack the odds in your favor is to set up a system to alert you whenever your mark receives new e-mail. Yahoo, Hotmail, and

Continued

Gmail all have different utilities that you can use for message alerts. These utilities allow you to receive alerts in an instant messaging client or even your cell phone. Yahoo's can be found by reading *http://help.yahoo.com* and going to the e-mail section You'll find a description of how to set up the account so that e-mail can be sent to an instant messenger or text message a cell phone. Hotmail allows you to have e-mail sent to a mobile phone. On Hotmail from the e-mail accounts main page select Options | Mobile Alerts. Google provides the Gmail Notifier, a tool that periodically checks a Gmail account. It can be obtained from *http://toolbar.google.com/gmail-helper/*. There are also other notifiers that can serve a wide variety of accounts at once. Some instant messaging clients have notifier plug-ins and will even send you a message notifying you of new e-mail.

Gmail and the premium versions of Hotmail and Yahoo mail also allow their messages to be forwarded to another account. If you are bold enough you can set up a new "dead drop" account for yourself, and configure your mark's Web mail account to send you a copy of their messages. This will guarantee that you get everything they get.

While these tools and methods may provide a convenient "in" for alerting you to your target's e-mail, there are some possible downfalls. When you sign up to for a mobile phone alert or to have e-mail forwarded, your contact information is embedded somewhere in their account, and is a possible means of discovery. While a lot of people rarely look at their settings once their account is set up, it is a possibility. The notifiers are generally the safest method, as they require only an account name and password and should leave little or no trace in the original account.

Sniffing the Network

As seen in previous chapters, sniffing the network can be a very powerful method for monitoring Internet activity, especially because most e-mail is transmitted across the network in plain text. Previous methods discussed usually give only half of the picture. Keystroke logging only captures e-mail typed on a computer, while using a "shadow" client only captures incoming e-mail. On the other hand, Sniffing, when it works, captures all incoming and outgoing e-mail being transmitted on the network. Impressive as it seems, sniffing the network has several drawbacks. For one, a sniffer captures e-mail only on a network that it is installed on. With today's very mobile population, it is unlikely that your target uses only one network for sending and receiving e-mail. A lot of people send e-mail from work and travel, and children use computers from school, libraries, and their friends' houses to read and write messages. The second big drawback of sniffing is that collected network traffic is useful only if the e-mail is in plain text. Encrypted e-mail, or e-mail that travels through Secure Sockets Layer (SSL), such as Gmail's versions of POP and SMTP, can be collected, but are nearly impossible to decrypt.

Sniffing Traditional E-mail

Despite the growing popularity of Web mail and the use of SSL encryption for POP and SMTP, a large amount of e-mail is still sent via unencrypted POP, IMAP, and SMTP standards. This e-mail is very easy to identify and collect with a sniffer. We cover two different methods of doing this; manually through Ethereal or automatically through One-Way Network Sniffer (OWNS). Both require a packet capture file, which can be obtained in many different ways. Our preferred method is by running Snort or some other covert sniffer on your target's computer, although both Ethereal and OWNS can also be run as sniffers.

Once you have your packet capture file, you can drag and drop it into Ethereal. When viewing a packet capture in Ethereal, you can use your knowledge of e-mail protocols to filter out traffic of interest. The easiest way is to type the following phrase exactly as shown (capitalization matters) into the filter bar, as shown in Figure 8.6:

```
smtp or pop or imap
```

Now that the "noise" has been filtered out, you are left only with traffic associated with traditional methods of e-mail. Right-click on any packet and select **Follow TCP Stream** to view relevant messages (see Figure 8.7).

To automate the entire process you can skip using Ethereal and feed your entire packet dump into OWNS. OWNS will automatically sort out all POP messages it can find in a packet dump. While this is a very easy method of collecting messages from a packet dump, OWNS fails to identify and analyze SMTP and IMAP traffic.

Figure 8.6 Filtering Out SMTP, POP, and IMAP in a Sniffer

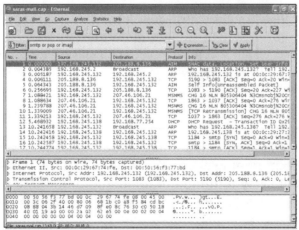

Figure 8.7 Following an SMTP TCP Stream

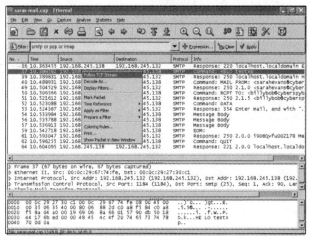

Sniffing Web Mail

Now that you know how to collect SMTP and POP e-mail via a sniffer, it is time to focus on Web mail. Since Web mail is accessed through a browser, collection is a fairly straightforward process; however, there are a few twists that must be taken into account. The procedure for obtaining Web mail by sniffing is nearly identical to the procedure for obtaining Web pages from the network (see Chapter 7). For the following example, we sniff the network with a Snort sniffer installed, which will capture all of the traffic surreptitiously. We will then go back and review it. As with the Web browser traffic, you will run the sniffer log through OWNS to break out the separate HTTP files.

Once you have broken out the files, you can go into the HTML directory and examine the Web pages. There are a couple of different types of Web pages that are important to examine, which will provide you with clues. The first is the Inbox (see Figure 8.8). The Inbox shows recently received e-mail, the sender, and the subject.

WARNING

When we were looking at collected Web mail, we noticed that some browsers, like Internet Explorer (IE), would open the page and then blank out right away as it tried to refresh or connect to something. Finding that annoying, we tried using Mozilla Firefox on our captured Web pages and they displayed just fine. So, as you analyze different captured material, be sure to exhaust all possibilities for viewing it before you discard it as useless. At worst case, most Web pages can be opened up in Microsoft Word or even notepad.

Figure 8.8 A Web Mail Inbox Collected from a Sniffer

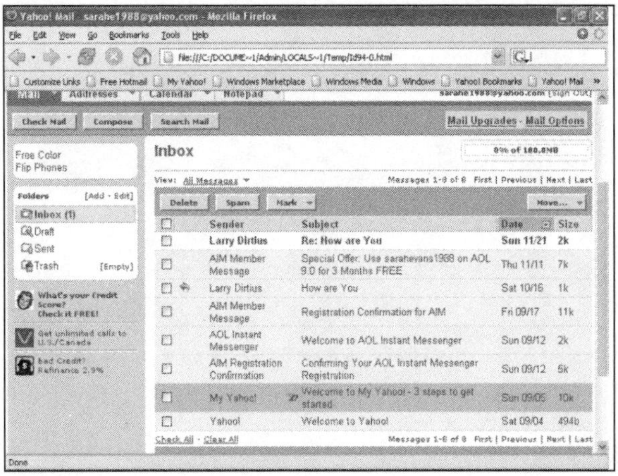

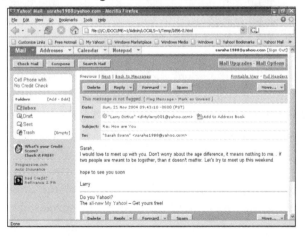

This can be very informative, but remember that many Web mail accounts receive a large amount of spam. Therefore, just because an e-mail has an interesting subject and sender, does not necessarily mean that the mark has requested this e-mail. The more important e-mail to retrieve is the text of the e-mail messages that have been read. The server creates an HTML Web page, when a Web-based e-mail is clicked on. This page is downloaded to the Web browser, which displays the e-mail (see Figure 8.9).

Figure 8.9 A Web Mail Message Collected from a Sniffer

While most Web mail messages appear as HTML files, there are some exceptions. For example, Yahoo compresses the HTML files for a faster transmission so that they appear as archive files that can be opened with IZArc. By clicking on the archive, you can retrieve the Web page in its entirety (see Figure 8.10).

Figure 8.10 Yahoo Web Mail Messages in Gzip Archives

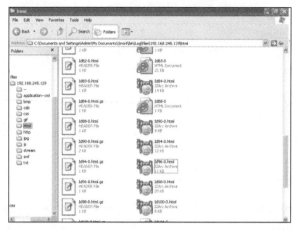

Unfortunately, obtaining the e-mail that is sent from the Web mail accounts is not as easy as obtaining the Web mail that is received and viewed. This is due to the way that e-mail is sent from a Web mail user to the e-mail server. When a user clicks "Send" in their Web browser, the message is transmitted to the Web server, which takes the message and passes it to the e-mail server, which then sends the e-mail.

To collect this outgoing e-mail, we take a different approach than the one used to read and view incoming e-mail. We must look at the actual data being sent by the Web browser. The same Snort log used to retrieve the viewed e-mail can be used to find the sent e-mail.

To do this, begin by loading your Snort file into Ethereal. This will then break up the collection into all the individual packets that were transmitted on the network. In this example, since you want to search for messages sent to Dirty Larry, bring up the search window by selecting **Edit | Find Packet**. You can now search through all the packets looking for the word "Larry." It is important to make sure that the "String" radio button is selected in the dialogue box (see Figure 8.11).

"Larry" was used as an example text stream; however, you can search for any text that you are interested in. Depending on what you are looking for, substitute key words that make sense. Figure 8.12 shows the results of a successful search for a string.

Figure 8.11 Using Ethereal's Search Feature to Find Information in Packets

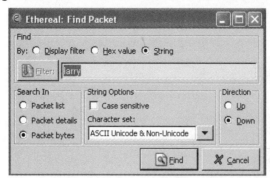

Figure 8.12 Packet Containing the String "Larry" Is Found

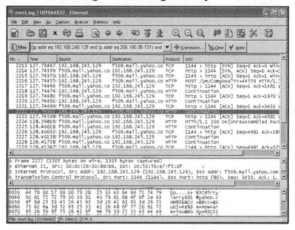

Now that you have located a packet with data of interest, it is time to "break it out" by following the TCP session it belongs to. Do this by right clicking on the packet and then select **Follow TCP Stream**. This brings up a new window with the data from the entire session. Once the session is brought up it will resemble standard Web traffic. The data will be in one of two possible locations. If it is a received message, it will be either HTML, or Gzipped HTML (appears as gibberish but can still be broken out by OWNS). E-mail being sent usually appears as an HTTP Post request, which is how Web browsers send information to the Web server (see Figure 8.13). Outgoing e-mail is difficult to see and read because in a HTTP Post it is URL encoded, meaning that it written so that spaces and other characters are replaced by different values (e.g., a URL-encoded string will have all spaces replaced with a "+." It is not always easy to find and decode outgoing Web mail, but it is there, and it can be done if you feel the information is worth the time and effort.

Figure 8.13 Outgoing E-mail in URL-Encoded HTTP Post

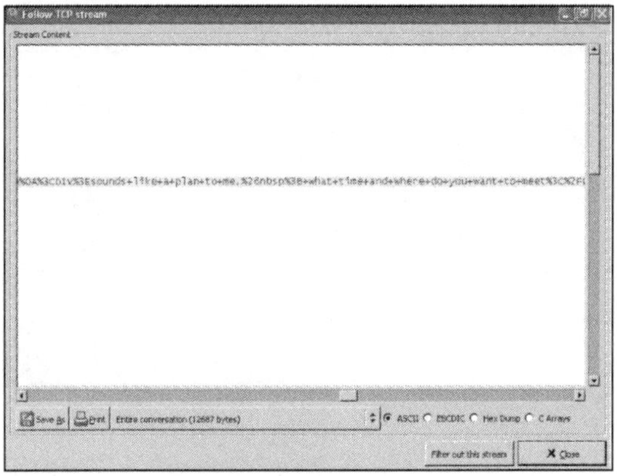

Special Collection Software

If you do not feel that any of the methods we have presented are effective or easy enough, there is always the possibility of using specialty software that is designed specifically for collecting different types of e-mail. While searching on the Web, we found several vendors that provide different software packages designed for e-mail collection. We have not tested or verified any of these packages, and hope that the vendors are not making erroneous claims. However, if after researching you feel a commercial software package is the way to go, happily make that decision. We have no bias against commercial software, and in some cases they are actually very powerful systems. Since we are not supporting any commercial vendors, we will not give evaluations of any packages available.

There are several things to consider when using a commercial spy software package. The advantage you receive with most commercial packages is that they are designed specifically for spying. These applications contain many features not found in the software previously discussed, such as e-mailing reports and alerts and different highly stealthy security settings. These software packages may be designed to specifically avoid firewalls and virus scanners. They may have more full-featured spying options and might automate things that we discussed doing by hand.

However, despite all the apparent advantages of spy software, we do not feel they are the be all and end all for cyber-spying. Before evolving to the point where all of your collection is automated, it is good to have a grasp of spying basics. In many cases this involves performing most spy tasks by hand. Also, software vendors are infamous for making lofty claims and having software fail to live up to those claims. Although many packages are advertised as meeting all of your spying needs, you can never be sure that they will until you have purchased and tested them. By that time it may be too late, or their failure could result in discovery. If using a commercial package, research it carefully and test it out before you actually deploy it so that you are aware of all of its advantages and shortcomings.

As you can see in Table 8.1, there is no perfect way to collect e-mail. Every method has its advantages and disadvantages. You should select the method that best fits your target and access. We recommend a combination of methods. We feel that you should collect as much archival information as possible, using the techniques described in Chapter 6. This provides your base of knowledge and is what you will use to determine how to collect future data. Further collection can be done either with a compromised client, using the password to log into Web mail, or by sniffing the network. All of these are strong methods of continual collection. Be creative; there are probably many other ways of subverting e-mail to your advantage that we have not discussed here. Like most spying problems, start out by looking at what you have and what you need, and then think of a way to connect the two.

Table 8.1 E-Mail Collection Methods Summary Chart

Method	Advantages	Disadvantages
Collecting E-mail Files from the Target Computer	Easy. Files can be taken offline and viewed elsewhere. Does not require knowledge of e-mail passwords.	May not get everything, limited to what the user saves. Depends on access to the computer. Will not work with Web mail.
Keystroke Logging	Does not require knowledge of e-mail accounts or passwords. Will eventually uncover e-mail accounts and passwords. Can be done in hardware without even having complete access to the computer.	Can only collect outgoing e-mail; incoming material is not seen. Limited by capability of keystroke logger, its buffer may fill up before e-mail is collected. Will not collect e-mail that is written somewhere beside the target computer
Using a Client to Download	Very stealthy if done correctly. Can get some e-mail before it is deleted. Relatively simple procedure.	Requires knowledge of e-mail password. Can only collect incoming e-mail; e-mail written by mark will only be seen in replies, if at all. Will not work with Web mail. Will mark e-mail as "read."
Using a Password to Log Into Web Mail	Gives full access to all e-mail in account.	May not have complete pictures as some e-mail may be deleted; sent e-mail may not be saved. Requires knowledge of password. Will only work for old style e-mail or Web mail.

Continued

Table 8.1 E-Mail Collection Methods Summary Chart

Method	Advantages	Disadvantages
Sniffing the Network	Can catch all incoming and outgoing e-mail. Does not require access to the target computer. Can easily be used to obtain e-mail account passwords, which can enable other methods.	Limited to e-mail sent on the network being sniffed.; e-mail written elsewhere will not be caught. Mail in encrypted connections will not be viewable.
Special Collection Software	Tailored specifically for spy purposes. May have extra stealth features and avoid security software.	Purchasing can create a paper trail. May not work as advertised.

Case Study: Return to Sender

E-mail is an important means of communication that many people have embraced. Messages can take on many levels of meaning between different people. Some people prefer the perceived anonymity it provides, and feel safer using it to communicate than voice or other methods. If you are a young person doing something wrong, it is a great way to get in touch with co-conspirators since you do not have to worry about someone "overhearing" you.

Overview

A young girl makes an e-mail mistake that tips her family off to her relationship with an older man. Technical collection allows them to further gather enough evidence to confront her and verify the truth and lies.

Elaboration

Samantha was a bright normal 16-year-old. She was in honors classes, ran track, and had plenty of friends. Like most girls her age, she had a great time dating and hanging out with boys. And, like most girls her age, she thought most of the guys in high school were immature idiots.

When she got home from school, she would plop down in front of her computer, browse the Web, do homework, instant message her friends, and then chat online. One of her favorite rooms was AOL's 20's love. It had the most lively conversations and interesting people. Their teen chat room was way too immature.

This very chat room was where she met Chuck. Chuck was a 26-year-old guy who also liked chat rooms, and found Samantha to be interesting, very interesting. She was a cute and spunky girl who did not have a lot of the jaded and bitter attitude that he felt most women his age had. She was way more mature than most teenagers he knew, and she could carry on a conversation and really "understand" him.

Their online relationship progressed and moved on to the inevitable in real life (IRL) meeting. Samantha thought Chuck was great; he had his own car and apartment, and worked at a real job, so he had money to spend on her, which was cool. None of her friends' boyfriends could do that. Of course, she had to keep this relationship secret from her parents. They would freak out if they knew she was dating an older guy, especially that much older.

Their dating went on during the spring and continued into the summer. Samantha got a job at the shopping mall, so she could walk over to the garage Chuck worked in and see him every day. There was now the perfect excuse (work) to spend time with Chuck, with her parents none the wiser. It was a good summer for Samantha.

Around August it was time for her family's annual summer trip. This year they would be visiting a cousin in California and staying with his family. Growing up she had always loved the family trips, but was she getting too old for that now? Two weeks without Chuck; how would she get by? He could meet and fall in love with someone new during that time.

During the trip, Samantha had a really good time. Who wouldn't in California? Her cousin lived in an awesome house halfway between the beach and the mountains, and she liked the West Coast lifestyle. Even better, he had a high-speed Internet connection in his office, and no one went in there. She had plenty of time to chat with and e-mail Chuck. Things went well and Samantha was able to keep her boyfriend happy by talking to him as much as possible.

When they got home, Samantha was happy about going to work, and having a lot more opportunity to spend time with Chuck completely undiscovered. Everything was perfect, or so she thought. After coming home from work one night, she waved hello to her parents who were sitting downstairs. This time, instead of just waving back and going back to their conversation, they called her back into the room.

"Samantha, come here. There's something we wanted to talk to you about."

Hmm, she wondered, what could they want?

Her parents then presented her with a printout of the first e-mail she had written to Chuck on their trip. Funnily enough it was one he never responded to.

"How did you guys get that?" she asked.

Did you use your cousin's computer to send this guy an e-mail your first night in California? Well, next time you do, make sure you type his address correctly. I bounced back to your cousin had a day after we left. He was surprised to see it, and felt like he should pass it on to us.

"Oh no!" Samantha's heart was beating fast. At least she had not said too much on that particular e-mail, and I guess that explained why he never responded.

"Well, Samantha there's more. After we read this, we asked your cousin if he had anything else. He ran the Google search tool on his computer and was able to come up with quite a few more of your Web mail messages. You have a lot of explaining to do. To start, tell us about this Chuck…."

Analysis

Samantha was in a dangerous and illegal relationship. While the age difference may not be the worst thing in the world, the fact that she kept the relationship from her parents was demonstration of poor judgment. Just like in previous case studies, it was an accidental technical mistake that sent up the first clues that something needed to be investigated more. Samantha's eagerness to send a message caused her to make two mistakes: a mistyped address and using her cousin's mail program. That combination was enough to tip him off, and eventually her parents. Finally, her use of Web mail and Google's ability to search through the cache, allowed her cousin to search for more evidence upon her parent's request. A human mistake and a technical solution allowed for a solid collection of evidence and a quick ending to this case study.

Summary

E-mail is a critical part of gathering computer intelligence on a target. It can lend a very insightful view into someone's life. Since a lot of people have been using e-mail for some time now (the authors' archives go back more than ten years), it can be a very revealing source of intelligence. E-mail, possibly more than any other type of media, gives a very deep perspective on a person, their relationships, and their activity. Several important concepts to remember are:

- E-mail is the Internet's killer application and still the most popular way of communicating online.

- There are many ways to read and write e-mail, including logging onto systems, using an e-mail client, and via a browser through Web mail.

- There are many different ways to exploit e-mail, including copying files from the computer, keystroke logging, using a client, using a password, and sniffing the network.

- No single method offers a perfect means of collecting e-mail. You should use the techniques that best fit your target and target environment. Combine different techniques to help you obtain the entire picture.

By utilizing the techniques we have taught, you can tap into the valuable resource of personal e-mail, which can offer an unparalleled look into someone's private life, giving you more insight and knowledge into your target's mind-set and activity. Successful collection and analysis of e-mail is often all the information you need to confirm your suspicions.

## Chapter 9

Spying on Chat and Instant Messages

Do You Like Older Men?

— Dozens of chat partners

Topics in this Chapter:

- **What Is Instant Messaging?**

- **Types of Chat and Instant Messaging**

- **Collecting Passwords and Buddy Lists**

- **Collecting Chat and Instant Messages**

- **Impersonation**

- **Summary**

Introduction

Chat and instant messaging (IM) are quickly becoming two of the most popular methods of online communication. The convenience of an instant response has helped fill the communication gap left between e-mail and traditional conversation methods such as phone calls. IM has migrated from the computer and become ubiquitous, because it can be accessed from handhelds, cell phones, and pagers. It offers the intimacy of a one-on-one conversation without the pressure of a face-to-face discussion. It is also a good method of meeting new people and widening your social circle. The ambience of a chat room can vary from support group, technical chat, and church group to a singles bar. In each of these situations, a person can enter a crowded room and participate, usually only identified by as much or as little information as they wish to provide. Online chats are amazing phenomena; they are literally conversations with dozens to hundreds of simultaneous participants. A live discussion of this scale is something that is nearly impossible with prior methods of communication.

After entering a chat room, users are exposed to dozens of other chat participants from around the world with whom they can individually engage without any of the complications that would accompany an in-real-life (IRL) meeting. While many people would hesitate to approach a total stranger to discuss intimate details of their lives, it seems to happen quite frequently with IM. The perceived anonymity offered by IM and chat makes people more open about the many topics they will discuss.

Unlike e-mail where the message becomes a record for the sender and receiver, chat and IMs appear evanescent. They are hard to record and their use is difficult to prove. Still, chat and IMs are important parts of someone's online life, and collecting and analyzing them are critical steps in determining a person's profile. This chapter helps readers collect and analyze IMs and chats using different forensic and live collection techniques.

What Is Instant Messaging?

Since the beginning of time, speech (of one form or another) has been one of the most useful forms of communication available. This method is so useful that we have invested billions of dollars to ensure that we have the ability to speak to people anywhere, anytime. The phone industry has sprung up as a result of this effort. While phones have become smaller, more portable, and more convenient, they are not a complete communication solution; they still have several fundamental problems. For example, not every location is appropriate for a phone, and it is still difficult to have a phone conversation with more than a few people.

With the Internet revolution, e-mail promised a new and better way to communicate. It is faster than conventional mail (snail mail) and has much of the same formality and structure, but with more convenience. While it fills a niche as a good substitute for snail mail, e-mail does not completely offer the spontaneity and instantaneous response of talking. It is still mainly a one-way communication system. While someone can send e-mail, feedback depends on the responsiveness of the receiver as well as the mail infrastructure, which can vary depending on the Internet provider. So, while e-mail provided many useful services upon its invention, virtual meetings and conversations were still necessary.

Chat is a development that filled in the gaps between phone conversations and e-mail. It offers many opportunities not available with previous communication methods. One of the earliest chat applications is a program called *Talk* that runs on multiuser UNIX machines. Talk allows two users to send simple text messages back and forth to each other. As the world's personal computing paradigm shifted from logging into a multiuser machine, many new personal IM and chat applications were developed, each adding more functionality and capability. These applications allowed people to simulate being logged into one of the large multiuser systems from a personal computer so that they could talk with other users on the IM network.

As of this writing, there are several different and very popular IM networks. Unlike e-mail, which transmits across a common protocol to seamlessly travel between Hotmail, Yahoo, and so on, today's instant-messaging networks operate in isolation. Communication on a network is in a proprietary protocol, meaning that its method of IM is unique to it. Each messaging service has its own client that users exercise to log onto the network, view other online users, chat in "rooms," and send other users private messages (PMs). The most popular IM networks are AOL's AOL Instant Messenger (AIM), Yahoo's Messenger, and MSN Messenger. While all of these are closed systems with their own protocol, meaning that someone on AIM cannot communicate with someone on Yahoo, there are some programs that allow a user to sign into multiple accounts and multiple messaging systems at one site. We call these *aggregators*, and some good examples are the open sourced Gaim and Cerulean Studio's Trillian and Trillian Pro.

Most of the popular IM software works by the same principles although it may differ in some of the lower-level protocols. When a user starts the IM program, it connects and logs onto a central server with a username and password. The server then passes the messaging program the most up-to-date *buddy list*. A buddy list is a list of all of the accounts that person wants to keep in touch with. By having another person's account in the buddy list, you can quickly send them IMs. The buddy list also gives you a user's status, how long they have been online, how long they have been active, if they are away from the computer, and sometimes their personal "away" messages explaining where they are and what they are doing.

Some IM protocols allow you to add whomever you wish and some require permission from your buddy before they are added to your list. The buddy list is like the high-tech speed dialer of IM except it is stored in the server and not on the end client. This is similar to having your cell phone number directory saved with your wireless provider so that you can use anyone else's phone to access it.

To chat, you either click on a buddy entry to bring up a chat window or enter a chat room. In the bottom of the window is the area in which to type your message. After typing the message and selecting the **Send** button, your text is sent to your buddy. In actuality, with most clients, the messages are not sent directly to your buddy, but to an intermediate server where the message is then relayed. For the most part, this is transparent to the end user and makes very little difference.

Types of Chat and Instant Messaging

For the most part, we cover the big three IM clients: AIM, Yahoo, and MSN. These are the most popular among home computer users. There are two other protocols that are worth mentioning: Internet Relay Chat (IRC) and ICQ (I Seek You). IRC is used mostly by technical people, and ICQ is of historical interest, but both have played a significant role in shaping the chat and IM landscape.

When preparing to spy on someone's IM, it is a good idea to identify which clients they use. Like e-mail, an individual can have multiple IM accounts, one for each service, or multiple accounts for the same service. Correct identification of which clients and which accounts your mark uses is necessary for collecting his or her information.

NOTE

IM clients seem to be in a continual state of flux. They are always being updated because the newest features are quickly integrated. As a result, things are not always where they used to be, and some capability is removed, while other is added. Keep this in mind when you try the commands and menu options we recommend. Since messenger clients change fast, some of the specific directions may be outdated by the time the book is printed. It is more important to keep the concepts in mind, which should remain the same for a long time. Use the Web or other resources to help you find implementation-specific instructions.

IRC

IRC was the first cross-Internet chat system to become popular. It started at the University of Oulu in Finland in 1988. After a few years of growing pains, people in different Internet-connected locations begin using it to chat with each other. While originally started on multiuser UNIX machines, there are IRC clients for Microsoft Windows that allow people to connect to IRC servers and chat. One very popular Windows client is MIRC (*www.mirc.com*).

IRC consists of many isolated networks, each with its own set of rules, guidelines, culture, and dedicated members. Three of the most popular networks are EFnet (*www.efnet.org*), Undernet (*www.undernet.org*), and DALnet (*www.dal.net*). Each network has many channels, which are similar to "chat rooms" found in modern IM clients. Each channel allows dozens of users to join, chat, PM each other, and transfer files. Because of its origins on UNIX bulletin board systems, IRC has a very rich, but somewhat complex command set. In addition, unlike chat rooms on other networks, IRC has implemented a pecking order of sorts on its members. Each room has at least one member with Operator (generally referred to as "ops") status. This person is responsible for maintaining order within the channel by forcibly removing, banning, or filtering disruptive participants. While it is still a very popular method of communication, and the different IRC networks still see substantial amounts of traffic, most people have embraced the more friendly IM clients.

ICQ

ICQ is the clever phonetic spelling of I Seek You. It is the oldest of the PC-based IM networks. Released in November 1996, it has amassed over 180 million users. Unlike the other IM networks, ICQ does not use user names; instead, when people register, they receive a unique ICQ number with which to identify themselves. In 1998, America Online (AOL) purchased ICQ's parent company, Mirabelis. AIM now incorporates ICQ and can communicate with ICQ accounts. You can still go to *www.icq.com* and get a new ICQ account, but it has waned in popularity in comparison with the newer IM clients.

Clients

Clients are the applications that enable you to connect to the different IM networks. While they all work fundamentally the same way (you create an account, log in, populate your buddy list, and either chat with them or enter "chat rooms"), there are a few small differences. Each has the same basic functionality (chat, buddy lists, PMs) and usually the same advanced functionality (Web cams, voice, file transfer), but each works on its own network. AIM clients cannot speak with Yahoo or MSN clients and vice versa. Each of these tools also comes with a raft of add-ons that add tool bars, set your home page, and give you e-mail alerts.

AIM   *www.aim.com*

AIM may be the most popular of all of the messaging protocols and clients. Once accessible just to those who used AOL for their Internet connectivity, it has been opened up for all users. It can now be used on cell phones, palm pilots, and other portable platforms. Like all of the IM services, users create accounts and log into the AIM servers, which store and synchronize buddy lists. When users want to transfer pictures or files they can connect directly to their buddy. AIM also has screen name-linking in which several different online names can be collected and used simultaneously on one account.

Yahoo   *messenger.yahoo.com*

Yahoo Messenger is similar to the other IM networks and includes buddy lists, emoticons, and the ability to hide your status from certain people. Yahoo has also included the capability to send voice via speakers and microphone. As with other IM networks, Yahoo provides the ability to send photos and files. Yahoo Messenger is very integrated with the other services that Yahoo provides, such as Yahoo Mail and the Yahoo Browser Toolbar.

MSN   *messenger.msn.com*

Microsoft's MSN Messenger is the company's entry into the chat wars. MSN Messenger is integrated in Microsoft's other Internet services, such as Hotmail. Like AIM and Yahoo, MSN Messenger also incorporates Web cams and voice so that two people can view each other while chatting. MSN Messenger allows users to set their online status, and, like others, can exclude certain people from knowledge of that status. MSN Messenger is also becoming more integrated with the Windows environment. Despite its placement in the Windows operating system (OS), it still has not surpassed AOL's AIM in popularity.

Aggregators

Aggregators are special IM clients. They do not have their own protocols and servers, but instead allow you to combine your accounts from other IM clients. Multiple accounts from Yahoo, AIM, MSN, and in some cases ICQ can be collected together and treated as one. Your contacts from each messenger are aggregated together into one unified buddy list, which gets around some of the problems previously mentioned. While it does not fix the fact that different types cannot talk to each other (AIM still cannot message Yahoo or MSN), aggregators make it somewhat appear that way.

In addition, the aggregators may be less intrusive than the traditional clients, as they do not install the slew of "extras" that each other messenger comes with. Since the aggregator itself is a complete tool and not trying to promote an Internet portal, they do not come with or install extra search bars, modify your home page, or add programs to your system tray.

Gaim *gaim.sourceforge.net*

Gaim is an open-source program that supports multiple messaging protocols. People who use the Gaim client can access AOL Instant Messaging, Yahoo Instant Messaging, MSN Messenger, IRC, and several other more obscure networks from the same client. Gaim also allows a user to log into a single service with multiple identities. This allows one user to have multiple identities such as both DirtyLarry and DirtyLarry001 on AIM or another service at the same time. More important, it allows for a person to be logged into multiple messaging services at once. Gaim incorporates most of the features of the regular messaging program, but is currently lacking in its ability to handle video, voice, and some of the more advanced capabilities that the IM clients offer. Because it is an open source project, work is being continually done to enhance its capability. For basic chat and messaging on many services, Gaim is an excellent tool to use. It is important to notice if your mark is using Gaim, as this will change some of the ways the collection is carried out.

Trillian *www.trillian.cc*

Trillian and Trillian Pro are products from Cerulean Studios. Like Gaim, it is an IM aggregator. It is currently popular among people with many chat clients, and its power and easy installation also make it a popular choice of users. It comes packaged in a single executable, which requires installing a base executable and several "plug-ins." Because of this, its user base appears to be more widespread in the Windows world than Gaim.

The basic version of Trillian is downloadable for free, and the professional version is available for a small fee. Like Gaim, Trillian can connect to the main IM networks. It can log on with multiple identities to each network at the same time. It can be used to transfer files, and has a rich plug-in system that allows it to do everything from showing the weather to alerting its users to their new mail. Additionally, Trillian can be used to access chat rooms from the many different IM services. Trillian aims to provide every feature that the IM clients provide and add features that enhance the experience. Trillian is popular because it allows one program to take the place of multiple programs and helps simplify a user's workspace.

Tips and Tricks...

Please Hack Me Now!

Determining when a computer is on and when it is not being used are two very important details. For example, you might want to know if someone is away from his or her keyboard if you plan to access his or her computer remotely with virtual network computing or another tool, or if you need to physically get to it to swap out keyloggers. On the other hand, you may only want to turn on your screen-capture software when someone is actually using the computer. All of these scenarios require that you know when your mark is online and ideally also when your mark's computer is left idle or active online.

Thanks to IM, we have a crude form of that capability. Have you ever looked at your AOL, Yahoo, or MSN messenger buddy list? This is a great way to tell if your mark's computer is online. Many people have their instant messenger tools set to "auto start" with their computers. If your buddy is online, you know his or her computer is up. Also, most messengers can let you now if your buddy is idle (has not done anything on the computer for a period of time) or is away (idle for a long period of time). This is great information to have, and can be obtained for free just by putting your mark on your buddy list.

Actually getting your mark on your buddy list may be a slightly more challenging issue depending on the chat network he or she uses. How you do this will depend on what IM clients your target uses. You must first identify the IM client(s) your mark uses and the account ID on each one. It is a good idea to keep track of all of them, in case your mark stops using one particular service (this is where having Gaim or Trillian comes in handy). If your target uses AIM, you are in luck, as it lets you add anyone to your buddy list without your target knowing. Yahoo sends your mark a message saying someone is trying to add him or her to a list and makes it your target's decision whether to let himself of herself be added. In addition, Yahoo has an "invisible" mode, enabling you to appear online to some users and invisible to others. MSN is similar to Yahoo in that it queries your target to ensure that you want your target to add you, and lets you decide if the person adding you can tell if you are online. If you are dealing with one of the trickier messengers, you may have to do some social engineering to get your mark to let you add him or her to your list. Use your imagination and try to create an online identity that would appeal to them, and build up enough of a "relationship" so that your target feels comfortable letting you add him or her to your list. If that does not work, a fake identity may be a great way to learn more about your mark.

Collecting Passwords and Buddy Lists

While there is a lot of information that can be gleaned from IM conversations, there are some situations where just having knowledge of who is on your mark's buddy list may be sufficient. This piece of information alone can shed valuable light onto the composition and nature of your target's online relationships; after all, these are the people your mark feels are worth having only a click away. Also, depending on the messenger service, it can be useful to have block/ignore lists as well. Once obtained, it may be necessary to impersonate your mark to determine some of his or her contacts' relevance and relationship with your mark. This impersonation usually requires your mark's password, another important piece of data to collect. In some cases, the password is hidden and scrambled in registry settings; in others, it sits in a plain text file.

Collecting the Buddy List and Password from AIM

Chapter 6 covered the process for obtaining the buddy list from AIM. Obtaining the password is a slightly trickier procedure. Versions of AIM older than 4.7 stored the scrambled passwords in the Windows registry. Version 4.8 and higher store a *hash* of the password. A hash is the result of feeding the password into a one-way function, meaning that it is mathematically impossible to recover the password from the hash. So, if your mark is using an old version of AIM, there is a chance you might be able to recover the password. To determine the version, go to the AIM window and select **Help | About AOL® Instant Messenger**. A dialogue box should pop up giving numerous tidbits of information, along with the version number. A Google search on AIM password recovery will show several tools that will uncover the password. While this would be a fortunate scenario, it is a highly unlikely one. As of the writing of this book, the current version of AIM is 5.9, and it will most likely be much higher by the time this book is printed. The best bet for actually acquiring a password is to use a hardware or software keystroke logger. In addition to installing one, a good idea is to pull up the client and type in an incorrect password. Since many clients automatically save the last password typed, you need to modify the one stored to ensure that your mark enters the correct one the next time he or she logs on.

Collecting the Buddy List and Password from Yahoo

Like AIM, viewing the Yahoo Messenger's buddy list is covered in Chapter 6. Like AIM, Yahoo passwords are not stored or transmitted in plain text. Similarly, using a keystroke logger is the best advice for collecting this information.

Collecting the Buddy List and Password from MSN

MSN uses Microsoft's .NET passport as the basis for its authentication. Like AIM and Yahoo, the password for MSN is not stored or transmitted in plain text. However, since it relies on .NET passport, access to your target's account is usually enough to get MSN to log on.

Another very useful option of MSN is the ability to save a contacts list By going to **Contacts | Save Contact List.** Using this capability, you can take a list of buddies/contacts from your mark's computer and load them on a different computer for analysis.

Collecting the Buddy List and Password from Gaim

Since Gaim is not distributed by the owners of the IM networks and must interact with more than one network, it is more efficient for Gaim to store its own buddy and password lists. Gaim stores all of its information in easy-to-view *.xml* configuration files. XML files are a type of markup language that is relatively easy to understand and which can be opened by most Web browsers. This is the program you want your mark using. If you have any influence at all, steer your mark this way. There are two files of interest: *accounts.xml*, which has all of the IM accounts and their corresponding passwords and *blist.xml*, which is a copy of the buddy list for each account. There are basically two ways to find the XML files that you are looking for—manually, if you know where they are, or by searching the entire hard drive for them. We discuss both methods along with their trade-offs.

Manual Location of Files

The default location of Gaim's XML files can be found by opening *explorer.exe* and browsing to the following location:

```
C:\Documents and Settings\<Your Marks Account>\Application Data\.gaim\
```

Both files should be there and accessible using Notepad or most any other text-viewing application. This requires one of two things to be true: the user has not marked his or her files as private, which is often the case. Or, if they are marked as private, you must be looking for these files from an administrator account or from the same account as your mark. While this method depends on permissions and is a little trickier than the next one we discuss, it allows you to locate the Gaim configuration directory for your mark, which also contains other useful information. In addition, should the nomenclature for the file names change, you can examine the files in the directory one by one, looking for the correct information.

Automatic Location of Files

Use Microsoft's or Google's search tool and look for *blist.xml* and *accounts.xml*. To broaden your search and find even more potentially interesting files, a search for *.*xml* in Microsoft's tool or *xml* in Google's should produce useful results. Like the previous method, this one also depends on file permissions. Once you have found the files, their contents should be plainly visible. The following example shows the *accounts.xml* file for a Gaim user. As you can see from this example, account names and their corresponding passwords (when stored) are both clearly visible. In this example, the account name is "sarahevans1988," and the password is "gatorade."

```
0' encoding='UTF-8' ?>


<accounts>
 <account>
  <protocol>prpl-oscar</protocol>
  <name>sarahevans1988</name>  <password>gatorade</password>  <settings>
   <setting name='check-mail' type='bool'>0</setting>
   <setting name='server' type='string'>login.oscar.aol.com</setting>
   <setting name='encoding' type='string'>ISO-8859-1</setting>
   <setting name='port' type='int'>5190</setting>
  </settings>
  <settings ui='gtk-gaim'>
   <setting name='auto-login' type='bool'>1</setting>
  </settings>
 </account>
</accounts>
```

In the next example, we show you the type of information that you can retrieve from a stored buddy list. This example shows you the *blist.xml* file for "SarahEvans1988."

```
rsion='1.0' encoding='UTF-8' ?>
<gaim version="1">
      <blist>
            <group name="Recent Buddies">                    <setting
name="collapsed" type="bool">0</setting>
                  <contact>
                        <buddy account="sarahevans1988" proto="prpl-
oscar">
                              <name>dirtylarry001</name>
      </buddy>
```

```
                          </contact>
                          <contact>
                                  <buddy account="sarahevans1988" proto="prpl-
oscar">
                                          <name>chuckypoo100</name>
              </buddy>
                          </contact>
                          <contact>
                                  <buddy account="sarahevans1988" proto="prpl-
oscar">
                                          <name>sk8gurl</name>
</buddy>
                          </contact>
                  </group>
                  <group name="Contacts">
                          <setting name="collapsed" type="bool">0</setting>
                  </group>
          </blist>
          <privacy>
                  <account proto="prpl-oscar" name="sarahevans1988" mode="1">
                  </account>
          </privacy>
</gaim>
```

From this file, we see that Sarah does not have many buddies added. In true life examples, it is not unusual for people (especially teenagers) to have hundreds of entries in the file. Also, besides just learning the names "dirtylarry001," "chuckypoo100," and "sk8gurl," we have learned that each entry is under the group listing "Recent Buddies." Many people categorize their buddy lists into several groups (i.e., "Friends," "Work," "Hookups," and so forth), which can be descriptive in its own way.

Collecting the Buddy List and Password from Trillian

Similar to Gaim, Trillian stores its buddy list on the computer (via the server). You can retrieve this list by browsing to:

`C:\Program Files\Trillian\users\default\Buddies.xml.`

However, unlike Gaim, this list does not contain the password of the user. Instead, the password is stored encoded in an *.ini* file for each service. For the popular ones we are monitoring, the files are:

`C:\Program Files\Trillan\users\global\default\aim.ini`

```
C:\Program Files\Trillan\users\global\default\msn.ini
C:\Program Files\Trillan\users\global\default\yahoo.ini
```

In these files, we are searching for a line similar to password=9447F5AB4BE7BFF7. Instead of encrypting the password, Trillian uses a two-character encoding scheme to scramble them. There are several programs that will break this encoding for you (including one available on our Web site), but to give you a better idea of how they work, we have included Table 9.1, which we can use to break the password in our *aim.ini* file). The top row contains the characters from our file, and the left-hand row contains the decoded plain text. You just need to match up the two character letters from the top row with the correct letter.

Table 9.1 Sample of a Table to Decode Trillian Passwords

Plain Text	84	7	5	AB	4B	E7	BF	F7
a	92	47	E0	A5	58	E7	BA	F3
b	91	44	E3	A6	5B	E4	B9	F0
c	90	45	E2	A7	5A	E5	B8	F1
d	97	42	E5	A0	5D	E2	BF	F6
e	96	43	E4	A1	5C	E3	BE	F7
f	95	40	E7	A2	5F	E0	BD	F4
g	94	41	E6	A3	5E	E1	BC	F5
h	9B	4E	E9	AC	51	EE	B3	FA
i	9A	4F	E8	AD	50	EF	B2	FB
j	99	4C	EB	AE	53	EC	B1	F8
k	98	4D	EA	AF	52	ED	B0	F9
l	9F	4A	ED	A8	55	EA	B7	FE
m	9E	4B	EC	A9	54	EB	B6	FF
n	9D	48	EF	AA	57	E8	B5	FC
o	9C	49	EE	AB	56	E9	B4	FD
p	83	56	F1	B4	49	F6	AB	E2
q	82	57	F0	B5	48	F7	AA	E3
r	81	54	F3	B6	4B	F4	A9	E0
s	80	55	F2	B7	4A	F5	A8	E1
t	87	52	F5	B0	4D	F2	AF	E6
u	86	53	F4	B1	4C	F3	AE	E7
v	85	50	F7	B2	4F	F0	AD	E4
w	84	51	F6	B3	4E	F1	AC	E5
x	8B	5E	F9	BC	41	FE	A3	EA
y	8A	5F	F8	BD	40	FF	A2	EB
z	89	5C	FB	BE	43	FC	A1	E8

If you followed this exercise, you should have determined that 94 = g, 47 = a, F5 = t, AB = o, 4B = r, E7 = a, BF = d, and F7 = e. The result is that we now know that the password for this account is "gatorade." Next, we turn our attention to the collection of the actual communications between chatters.

Collecting Chat and Instant Messages

Collecting information on the chat sessions that your mark is conducting can be done in several ways. Most of the popular chat programs come with the capability to save a log file of the conversation. While some people may enable this to keep a record of their conversations, a lot of people never bother with this setting. This is a great place to keep track of chat, because a thorough log can yield all types of useful information. When logging is not an option, either because the program does not have the capability, or because you cannot physically access the machine, sniffing becomes the other alternative. Most chat is still in plain text and can easily be picked up with sniffers.

Collecting through Logging

Most IM clients can be configured to log all of their traffic. This is an excellent feature that can help you in your spying efforts. Very few users pay attention to the maze of preferences that most clients offer, and turning on logging is generally a very quiet and unobtrusive option that has a low risk factor. Even if someone were to discover that logging was enabled for his or her messenger, it does not immediately point the finger at anyone, or indicate that spying has occurred.

Setting Up Logging with AIM

AIM does not come with a method to log all of the chats. However, there are many extensions and add-ons to AIM that will provide this functionality. If your mark has installed them, it may be possible to log his or her chats. It is also possible (as demonstrated in Chapter 6) to use the Google Desktop Search Tool to log and view AIM chats. Also, several packages such as Parent Tools for AIM <add other packages> offer a logging capability.

Setting Up Logging with Yahoo

The first step is to log into the person's account and start Yahoo Messenger. Then you need to bring up the Preferences menu. This can be done either by selecting **Messenger | Preferences** or **Control + Shift + P**. After the Preferences menu is shown, select the Archives option on the left. After toggling on the Archives option, logging will be activated. You can then exit Yahoo Messenger and log off of the account. Log files are saved for a duration of 10 days as *.dat* files in the following location:
```
C:\Documents and Settings\<Mark's Account>\Application
Data\Yahoo!\Messsenger\Profiles\<Mark's Yahoo ID>\
```

The contents of this directory can be copied to be viewed at your leisure later. Unfortunately, Yahoo does not store the data in clear text and in order to read the files you must use Yahoo's built-in viewer, which requires you to be logged in. Since this is a risky option, we prefer to use a tool called *Archive_Reader.exe*. This tool can be found either at its home site, *www.carbonize.co.uk/Yahoo/archive.php*, or from our Web site. For Archive Reader to work, you must also have Yahoo Messenger installed and the *.dat* files placed in a valid account's log directory.

Setting Up Logging with MSN

Only the newer version of MSN Messenger has the ability to log chat files. If your mark is using Messenger v6 or higher you are in luck. After starting Messenger and logging in, the options can be accessed by selecting **Tools | Options | Messages | Message History**. Select the check box next to "Automatically keep a history of my conversations." MSN Messenger will now log all of the conversations and place the log files in the following location:

```
C:\Documents and Settings\<Mark's Account>\My Documents\My Received
Files\<User ID>\History\sender.xml.
```

Note that the User ID will be the Messenger ID and some additional names. The *.xml* files can be viewed by double clicking on them, or opening them in a word processor such as Notepad or Wordpad.

!WARNING

After you have collected log files, buddy lists, and passwords, you may be eager to immediately view them. Keep in mind that by opening the files on your target's machine you are leaving a history behind. If you open a *.xml* buddy list using Wordpad, the name of that buddy list will be left for the next person that uses Wordpad to see.

Instead, get a small Universal Serial Bus (USB) drive and copy the files to it. Take them somewhere else and view them on a computer that you feel is reasonably secure, or that you can reasonably clean up so that anyone seeing it will have a hard time determining what you have done on it.

Setting Up Logging with Gaim

Gaim logging is very easy to toggle on. Proceed by logging into your mark's account and start the Gaim program. Once the Gaim program is started, select the **Preferences** button on the window, which will pop up a window with menus. Select the **Logging** tab to bring up the logging options. Under **Message Logs**, select the check boxes next to "Log All Instant Messages" and " Log all Chats." You can also select the format it will save them in: *.txt* (view with Notepad) or *.html* (view with a Web browser). Finally, select **Close** to exit the window. Once logging is enabled, it will work for all of the messenger networks. Gaim will automatically log the files under:

```
C:\documents and settings\<Mark's Account>\Application
Data\.gaim\logs\aim\Userid\sender

C:\documents and settings\<Mark's Account>\Application
Data\.gaim\logs\yahoo\Userid\sender

C:\documents and settings\<Mark's Account>\Application
Data\.gaim\logs\aim\Userid\sender
```

In these examples, "Userid" is the name that your target uses to log into the service, and "sender" is the account of the person that they are communicating with. The stored logs can then be copied and viewed at a later date.

Setting Up Logging with Trillian

Trillian, like its counterpart Gaim, can log all of the messages and chats for all of the messaging protocols. To set up the Trillian logging, first start the program. Next, bring up the menu window which is done by clicking on the green globe at the base of the Trillian window. From this menu, select **Preferences** and the **Message History** tab. This will allow you to select what is logged to a file and where that file is to be stored. By default, Trillian stores the log files in:

```
C:\Documents and Settings\<Mark's Account>\logs\<service>\
```

In this example, service is AIM, Yahoo, MSN or whatever IM service your mark is using. Trillian stores its log files as text files, which enables them to be viewed with Notepad.

Collecting through Sniffing

While sniffing may not be able to get passwords for you anymore, it can still obtain most messages and chats, which are still (mostly) done in the clear. Although some clients have encryption built in, it is usually not by default (although this is changing with Trillian). In addition, encryption currently only works between two of the same client.

For sniffing, we recommend using Snort to collect and Ethereal for analysis. Ethereal has many different protocol filters, which are tools that allow it to sort out different types of traffic. AIM, Yahoo, and MSN are all included in its list of protocol filters, and their traffic can easily be isolated for analysis. For example, you can utilize these filters by typing **aim, msnms** for MSN or **ymsg** and **yhoo** for Yahoo in the filter bar, as we did in example Figure 9.1. It should also be noted that you can combine them with the words "and" or "or."

Figure 9.1 Using Ethereal's Filters to Isolate IM Traffic

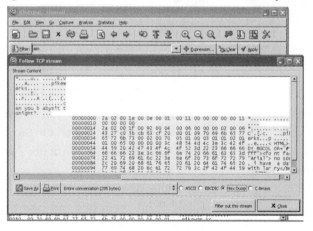

Once you have found a protocol you want to watch, you can more closely examine it by right-clicking on a packet and selecting "Follow TCP Stream." While all of the content is there, most IM traffic is not as straightforward to interpret as e-mail or Web traffic is. As Figure 9.2, demonstrates, the left-hand side of the stream shows the question from Pikewerks to Sarah asking: "Can you babysit tonight?" The right-hand section shows the response where Sarah replies: "No, sorry, I have a date with Larry."

Figure 9.2 Using Ethereal's "Follow TCP Stream" to Analyze an IM

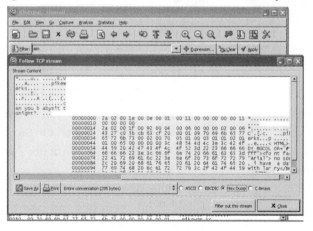

Advanced Collection

Sometimes it is possible to use a new technology in a way that is unintended to help us achieve our goals. One of these is IMSmarter (*www.imsmarter.com*), which is a tool released by Coceve Inc. IMSmarter works with existing IM clients and makes them more useful (or as the name indicates, smarter). It is currently a beta version, which means that the IMSmarter service may change in usability and functionality. The IMSmarter tool allows you to log into a Web page to view copies of your chats, search through your chat histories, and set it up to send you reminders. All of these capabilities, while useful to most IM users, are also very useful to those of us who wish to spy on IM users.

IMSmarter automatically logs IMs. It works by altering the Instant Messenger client's configurations to use the IMSmarter as a proxy. This basically means that when configured, the IMSmarter servers sit between IM clients and their original servers. Because of its convenient location, the IMSmarter server can now see all traffic between a particular IM client and the IM server. This is how the IMSmarter service is able to log all of the IM traffic.

One of the advantages of IMSmarter is that it logs all of the IMs on its Web site, and is accessed by a Web browser. For most IM users, this translates to a convenient place to collect and search through their records should they ever need to recall a previous IM session. For you as a spy, this means you now have a convenient place to collect all of your mark's IM traffic and search through it. Of course IMSmarter was never designed for this type of surreptitious use; it is intended that only the person who actually owns the accounts will have the messages logged.

To set up IMSmarter you first need several prerequisites.

- Access to your mark's computer
- A list of IM clients your mark uses
- The ID and password for each IM client you wish to route through IMSmarter

Once you have this information, log onto a computer and bring up *www.ims-marter.com* in a Web browser. First, you need to create an account for yourself. Select the "Get Started Now" button and answer the questions about the OS and clients you will be attacking. Figure 9.3 shows us selecting to configure AIM, MSN, and Yahoo with IMSmarter.

After you have made your selection, the Web site will give you a Web page explaining how to configure each client. Print them out and take them with you. Now that you have instructions, the next few steps will have to be performed on your mark's computer. Log on and one –by one configure the clients as instructed. After each is configured, the dangerous part occurs. You must log into the IM network for each client; within a minute or two, IMSmarter will send you a message telling you to create an account. Once you are done, you may want to open up the browser history (done through the "History" button on most browsers) and delete the IMSmarter and all related Web sites.

Figure 9.3 IMSmarter Setup Screen

Once you have IMSmarter configured and running, you can log onto the account that you have created and view the logs. Figure 9.4 shows a screenshot of an IMSmarter account. In it, you can search for the messages that have been sent and received with the registered IM clients. You can also see the status of the different accounts; it shows if your mark is currently logged into any of them. Figure 9.5 shows how IMSmarter can be used to search and view chats by different criteria.

> ## WARNING
>
> IMSmarter is a beta tool and so the functionality may change. It was observed that the IMSmarter adds itself to the MSN Messenger buddy list when the user logs on. Therefore, using IMSmarter with MSN Messenger might not be a good idea. However, this behavior may change as it is still a beta version.

Using the IMSmarter service as a means of logging your mark's IMs is one more tool in your arsenal. There are risks in using this as a spy tool because it is fairly easy to discover, merely by having the mark look at his or her client's configuration. IMSmarter service will occasionally send your mark messages in an attempt to be helpful. While a legitimate user of IMSmarter may appreciate that, those of us coercing it to help us spy might frown on this. Hopefully, an unwitting target will dismiss the IMSmarter messages as spam. Finally, if your mark is already a member of IMSmarter, or tries to become a member, the fact that your mark's account names are already registered will produce some problems. If your target creates an account, he or she may be surprised to see that his or her IM accounts are already associated with an IMSmareter account. These risks are all things to keep in mind when considering using IMSmarter as a spy tool. As the IMSmarter service becomes more mature, additional features may be added. In the end, while risky, we believe that this tool has potential and that it can be useful with other means of collection fail.

Figure 9.4 IMSmarter Main Page

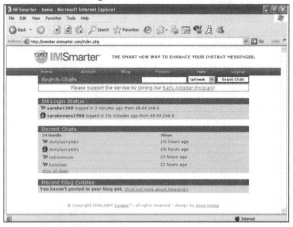

Figure 9.5 IMSmarter Used to Search through Logged Chats

NOTE

Back in Chapter 6, we demonstrated how Google desktop can be used to collect and search IM conversations. Do not forget to include this in your spy arsenal when you are contemplating how to collect this type of traffic. We encourage you to review this section of the chapter to see if it meets your needs.

Impersonation

Sometimes the most successful tactic is to just go for broke and talk to your mark and their contacts. While this usually carries the most risk, it can also reap the highest reward. If you have the mark's accounts and passwords, you have the option of logging onto the Internet as them and interacting with their buddies and contacts. This gives you the option of determining the extent of any online relationship.

The risks of impersonating your mark cannot be understated. They come from all sides; thus, impersonating your mark should not be done without careful application of the SLEUTH methodology. In addition, it is probably a good idea to make sure you have an extremely good understanding of your mark. Know what your target likes and does not like, as well as his or her views on some of the big issues of the day. Since you will be acting like your mark, be prepared to be your target, even if this means expressing views and ideas that you personally find distasteful.

The first and most obvious risk is that you will be found out. If this happens, your whole spy operation is compromised. This can occur if one of your mark's contacts speaks to your mark at a later date about a conversation that the contact "believes" the two had. Depending on how suspicious your mark is, this can be a big red flag showing that something is wrong.

In addition, you should be careful of the timing of your impersonation. It should closely correlate with a time your mark would normally be online. For example, if you log on very late at night, after your mark goes to bed, you run the risk of one of his contacts possibly telling him "you sure were up late last night" the next day at work. You may also want to be sure your mark is not out doing something that all the contacts are aware of. "I thought you played basketball every Tuesday" is an innocent comment that could come from any curious contact and be presented to either you or your mark. If you get this type of question, you might be able to carefully handle it. If your mark gets it, there is another cause of suspicion.

Another risk that must be managed is that your mark could log in from another location. AIM, for instance, would send them a message that they were logged on from another location. While some people would probably discount this with a simple statement such as "Oh, I must have left it on at work/school," it is still a risk factor that you should be aware of.

However great the risks may be of impersonating your mark, it may be the only way to conclusively determine the context of some relationships. Only talking to the mark's buddies will give you the opportunity to elicit information that may not appear in the normal course of spying. It will also give you the opportunity to see who is interested in your mark. Since some messaging clients allow you to send a message as soon as someone logs on, merely logging on will initiate conversation. This could be a good indicator that someone is up to no good. In the course of writing this book, several people added our 16-year-old identity "Sarah" to their buddy lists. Whenever she logs in, they send her messages. This would not be bad except that 30-year-old men have no business picking up 16-year-old girls. The best way to determine if someone is being "cyber-stalked" is to impersonate that person.

With knowledge of some of the known risks, carefully make the decision on whether you want to impersonate them or not. If you decide that the risk is worth the reward, be sure to mitigate them at every opportunity. This means that if you use your target's account and machine to log on, be sure to clean up your tracks. Turn off logging before you chat, or if you forget, make sure to delete any logs that you have created. Do not hold conversations that are too deep or that will be memorable to any of your mark's buddies. And if you are asked a difficult or unusual question, do not be afraid to fake a quick disconnect.

Impersonating your mark provides a unique opportunity to interact with the people whom you are worried about. It is a very high risk versus a reward payoff. In many cases, it gives you the edge and needed information you cannot obtain from collection and analysis. However, since the human factor is involved, and there are many unknowns at play, careless application of this technique can send your entire spy operations tumbling down. Use impersonation as necessary, but use with caution.

Tips and Tricks…

Let's All Get Together

Ok, you plan on using a Trillian or Gaim to impersonate your mark. We recommend that you install and use whichever one you *do not* currently use for personal reasons. Why, you ask? Trillian has a bad habit of merging buddy lists, meaning that all of your buddies could be added to your mark's account. The next time your mark legitimately logs in, his or her list could be populated with all of your friends. This is a

Continued

bad situation. As always in the spy business, caution is the name of the game; make sure to separate your business from your pleasure.

Case Study: Chat

IM has become the way that teens and many other tech-savvy demographics prefer to communicate. Many teenagers no longer spend hours on the phone. Instead, they spend hours in front of their PC chatting away with not one, but usually dozens of their friends at once. With online chat as the place for casual and sometimes not-so-causal conversation, much can be learned about someone while they chat.

Overview

The parents of two high-school-aged girls receive from one the rumor that the other has an eating disorder. Worried about the very serious condition, they use their knowledge to gather information to prepare them to either confront their daughter and handle the problem or comfortably put the rumor to rest.

Elaboration

Ron and Sherry had two girls that they both greatly loved. In their minds, their daughters were both perfect in every way. However, one day they received the shock of their life when Jane, their younger daughter, approached them with a problem.

She had apparently heard from other students at school that her sister, Alison, had a habit of throwing up after meals. Realizing the seriousness of the situation, and the fact she was in no way trained to handle such an issue, she went to her parents immediately.

Both of her parents were also taken aback by the news. While they wanted not to believe it, they also felt that the possibility did exist. After all, Alison was very thin and concerned with her image. Since this was a delicate and dangerous issue, they decided to get as much information as they possibly could first. What they were working with now was a third-hand rumor. If they were going to confront Alison, they wanted hard evidence. Of course, they could just ask her, but if she did have such a disorder it was something she was not even talking to her sister about. They did not want to risk scaring her and driving her to even more secrecy.

They made a plan to obtain as much information as they could and work from there. Alison, like most teenagers spent a lot of time IMing her friends. Both of her parents had her AIM identity added to their Trillian buddy lists. (They were actually using Trillian based on Alison's' recommendations.) The evening they heard the rumor from her sister, while they were doing their personal work, they kept an eye on Alison's buddy icon waiting for it to go idle. Once it did, they knew she was not on the computer, and they would have an opportunity to use her machine. As they walked up the stairs they heard the shower. Good; she was not going anywhere for a while.

After sneaking quietly into her room, they quickly went to her computer, enabled logging on Trillian, and left. Two days later they waited for their daughter to enter the shower again. This time they took Ron's USB drive with them and copied the last couple of days of Alison's chat logs to it. They went back downstairs and loaded them up on their laptops. They quickly turned Microsoft's search tool against the directory of chats, and began to search for different key words, "bulimia," "vomit," "food," "throw up." After a few dead ends they finally came across a chat where Alison touched on the subject:

```
Alison224: So I can't believe Tom really likes me
Carol045: Yeah, but man is Jessica jealous.
Alison224: I know, that b***h. Can you believe she started telling people I
have an eating disorder?
Carol045: She's just jealous; she wishes she could be as thin as you.
Alison045: It's nice and all, but I get teased about that all the time. I
actually wouldn't mind putting on a few pounds just to shut people up.
```

With those few lines of chat, Ron and Sherry felt like they had gotten enough information to make their decision. Since it was extremely unlikely that Alison was aware of their spying efforts, she was most likely speaking candidly and telling the truth. Along with the information from the chat log, they kept a very close eye on Alison over the next week, especially after meals. Failing to find any other evidence of an eating disorder, they dismissed what they heard as rumor, and stopped worrying about it.

Analysis

Since they were dealing with a difficult topic, Alison's parents had to approach it very carefully. Because they had received all of their information third-hand, they felt that they needed to have all the facts straight before they approached their daughter about her alleged problem. A mistake could force her into denial and even more secrecy.

While some people may question the approach that Alison's parents took, it turned out to be effective. While worried about their daughter, they did not want to confront her with such a heavy issue unprepared. They used their knowledge of computer systems to collect some of Alison's candid conversations with friends, to look for clues to the source of the supposed eating disorder. From their secret observations they received enough information to show that the problem was most likely a rumor. They felt secure that their information was correct, since by spying on their daughter without her knowledge, she was in a situation where she would have no reason to alter or hide the truth.

Summary

IM is quickly becoming a popular communication method for young and old alike. In many ways, it is like a telephone because coworkers, friends, and family can use it to communicate interactively and to stay in touch. However, unlike telephones where you can hear the voice of the person you are chatting with, messaging is much less attributable. Many times people speak without reservations on IM about things that they never could bring themselves to discuss in person or over a phone line. Further enabling this anonymity is the way that messaging facilitates anonymous meeting locations (e.g., chat rooms) where these thoughts are shared with absolute strangers. It is these secrets, and the fact that most teenagers will happily tell you that the acronym POS stands for Parent over Shoulder, that brings us to this chapter. The following are some of the key points that you should take away from reading this chapter:

- Messaging services AIM, Yahoo Messenger, and MSN Messenger operate on completely separate and isolated networks. Users on Yahoo Messenger cannot communicate with AIM users and vice versa.

- Aggregator clients such as Gaim and Trillian can be used to combine the account management of many different services into one common client. In addition, because these clients are freeware, you will not be bombarded with the advertising that is present in the other clients.

- If possible, add your target to your buddy list. You can (and should) use the idle time, away notice, sign-on, and sign-off, of your target to track him or her and decide when you can secretly access his or her machine without being detected.

- Most clients provide the option to automatically log all conversations. This is a useful option for you to secretly collect your target's discussions.

- If you cannot access your target's computer, but are located on the same subnet, you can use a sniffer to collect the conversations.

- IMSmarter offers a great method of collecting and searching through chat logs remotely without having to repeatedly go back to your target machine. However, its continual stream of messages make it a rather noisy and dangerous technique.

- When all else fails, you can either try to impersonate your target with a collected password, or you can try and establish communication with your target using an alias. Many law enforcement agencies use tactics like this to gather evidence of wrongdoing. For example, in child pornographer stings, the agents must pose as other child pornographers. There is a fine line between catching someone and coercing them.

## Chapter 10

Advanced
Techniques

Now we are going to knock it up a notch. Bam!

— Emeril Lagasse

I love it when a plan comes together.

— George Peppard as Col. Hannibal Smith of the "A-Team"

Topics in this Chapter:

- **Improving Your Skills**
- **Expanding Your Horizons**
- **Summary**

Introduction

Congratulations, you have made it through the first part of cyber-spy school. By now you should have a basic understanding of the spy process and quite a few tricks to help you pry into people's online lives. You may be feeling computer savvy, and even a little dangerous. Be warned, this is just the beginning. We have given you a few basic tricks and scenarios, which will work most of the time, especially in ideal situations. Of course, one of the most important rules of cyber-spying (all spying, in fact) is that there are no ideal situations.

To be as prepared as possible for these non-ideal conditions, you need to develop skills that will expand your knowledge base and make you as versatile as possible. One major thrust of this chapter is to improve and build upon some of the techniques discussed earlier in this book. We want you to take what you have learned and convert it from basic to guru, so that when you encounter those odd cases, you still have a few more tricks up your sleeve.

Although this book focuses mostly on personal computers (PCs), they are only a small part of the entire cyber-realm. While they are generally most people's gateway to cyberspace, they are not the only area a good cyber-spy should focus on. As cell phones, personal digital assistants (PDAs), and even video game consoles become more advanced, there are more ways to get online and to store and use information. All of these devices can hold clues about how their owner lives. A cyber-spy should not overlook this potential gold mine of information. Harnessing the Internet and its many powerful search engines and online databases should also be a tool in every spy's arsenal. Many people still do things the old-fashioned way—by paper. Detailed credit card statements, phone bills, and other periodic paper documents are a great place for collecting even more information. Viewing the entire picture and collecting and correlating data from different sources is a very important part of spying, and an advanced technique that even professional spies have a hard time mastering.

Tips and Tricks

Take Two

Throughout this book, we have discussed using hardware-based keystroke loggers. In many cases, they are the easiest and only way to get the information you need. If you decide to purchase a keystroke logger for your spying endeavors, we

Continued

strongly recommend that you buy two identical ones. Having two keystroke loggers is extremely helpful when you have to deploy and analyze data from them.

A good spy tries to expose himself as little as possible; for you that means minimizing your time on target. While installing a keystroke logger is a quick and easy task, if you want to take it to any other computer and analyze it, there is a time issue involved. If you only have one, you are forced to install it again after you have dumped the data; hence, there is a window of time when the machine is not being monitored at all.

The situation is improved with two keystroke loggers. When you remove the full one from the back of the target PC, you replace it with the empty one. You now have immediate coverage on the computer. Meanwhile, you can analyze the other keystroke logger on a different machine.

Improving Your Skills

This section is about "taking it up a notch." Many of the basic skills and scenarios presented earlier, while valid, do have problems. Here, we address some advanced techniques to make you a more powerful cyber-spy when encountering realistic complicated scenarios.

Collecting on Switched Networks

As mentioned in Chapter 4, switched networks are becoming very common. For PCs, there is no longer much of a price gap between switches and hubs. In fact, hubs are disappearing from most consumer electronics stores, while switches are being built into cable and Digital Subscriber Line (DSL) routers, making them ubiquitous. Since many of the techniques from the earlier chapters involved sniffing the network, a task made difficult by switched networks, we need to develop a solution to make sniffing a useful endeavor again. We will do this by using a concept known as Address Resolution Protocol (ARP) spoofing. As we will demonstrate, ARP spoofing enables you to use a "Man-in-the-Middle (MITM)" attack against your target.

Notes from the Underground

What Is Spoofing?

Spoofing is the computer term for altering information in a packet in an attempt to hide its true contents. This term is used most often in the context of "spoofing an Internet Protocol (IP) address." In this case, a packet is labeled with an incorrect sender IP address. The receiving computer is deceived into thinking that it is communicating with a computer other than the real sender. Oftentimes, IP addresses are spoofed so that the destination computer cannot respond to the packet.

ARP Spoofing

From Chapter 4, you are familiar with the concepts of an IP address and how it is used to route packets across a network. We will now go a step *lower* to learn about addresses that the hardware itself uses, which are called Media Access Control (MAC) addresses. A MAC address is a 12-digit, 48-bit number that uniquely identifies a hardware adapter (i.e., an Ethernet or wireless card).

Each network adapter in a computer has a unique MAC address. This is how the hardware knows which packets it should retrieve, and which belong to a different adapter (potentially at the same IP address). The first section of each packet is dedicated to the MAC addresses of the sender and receiver. If the MAC address of the packet matches the hardware address of the network adapter, the computer examines it.

To send to a packet with an IP address, the adapter queries the local area network (LAN) for someone who has a matching MAC address. (This is called an ARP request, because you are asking the entire network which MAC address corresponds to the desired IP address.) An adapter that matches responds with an ARP response essentially saying, "Yes, that is my IP address, and my MAC address is 00:0B:DB:1C:00:6C." Because this transaction requires that two packets be sent (a *query* and a *response*), the sending computer tries to reduce future network congestion and stores the response in memory. This table of past responses is called an *ARP cache*. In addition, any other computer that saw the response will store the information. If no one responds, or the IP address is out of the range of the local area subnet, the router or switch that serves the requestor will send a response, which tells the sender that they should send the packet directly to the router to be forwarded to its final destination.

Now, for the danger: there was no mention of *authentication*. It is possible to send spoofed ARP responses to machines on a network to confuse the computers. ARP spoofing can result in a perfect MITM scenario. There is nothing that stops you from shouting out "Yes, that is my IP address, and my MAC address is …" before the legitimate adapter has a chance to respond. That works easily on local area subnets, but what about switched networks? The attacker's computer can proactively send spoofed ARP responses to the gateway router or switch indicating that the attack computer's MAC address corresponds to the target computer's IP address. More spoofed ARP responses are sent to the target computer, telling it that the MAC address of the attack computer corresponds to the IP of the gateway. Having done this, all traffic sent to the gateway from the target computer will be sent to the attack computer, which then examines and forwards the packets to the actual gateway and finally to the target computer. All responses will be sent from the gateway to the attack computer, which can examine them before forwarding them to the target computer (see Figure 10.1).

Figure 10.1 Results of ARP Spoofing/Poisoning

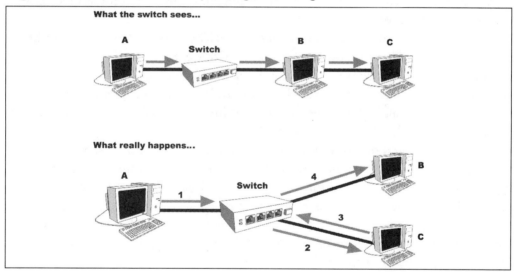

A successful ARP spoofing attack will result in an MITM scenario that is not easily detected by an unsuspecting user. One advantage of being in the middle of a target computer and its gateway is that you can examine and collect all traffic to and from the target computer. In addition, being in this location relative to the target computer and the outside world enables you to attack certain types of encryption, most notably Secure Sockets Layer (SSL). Since their traffic will actually be passed to the Internet through the attacker, the victim will not notice the attack without sniffing the network. Since the ARP caches eventually time out, by stopping to send the spoofed ARP responses, the network will eventually work back into its natural state. It should be noted that this type of MITM attack is sometimes called *ARP poisoning*.

Cain & Abel

Some people create tools to do one thing very well, while others create tools that do many things. Cain & Abel (C&A) v2.5 Beta (released by the owner of *www.oxid.it*) is advertised as a password-recovery tool for Microsoft Windows. C&A is capable of sniffing networks, collecting passwords, and using a variety of cryptographic attacks to crack encrypted passwords. Newer versions of C&A have incorporated methods such as ARP poisoning, to allow for the discovery of more passwords. Although C&A has many exotic and powerful features, we concentrate on some of its more standard features to help expand your current capabilities. We encourage you to download and experiment with this as a tool in your cyber-spy arsenal.

The newest version of C&A can be found at *www.oxid.it/cain.html,* as well as from our site, *www.cyberspybook.com.* In our examples, we use C&A for Windows NT, Windows 2000, and Windows XP.

Installation is a two-step process because a special version of WinPcap must be installed. The first step is to double-click on the C&A executable file and install it as you would any other application. Once installation is complete, it is time to install WinPcap, which has been integrated directly into the installation process (you will be prompted to install it). Since installation of WinPcap was shown earlier, we will not cover it again.

With everything installed, you are ready to use C&A. As with most applications, the first procedure is to configure the tool to your needs. To do this, launch the application and select the **Configuration Dialog** tab (see Figure 10.2). This allows you to select the interface on which to sniff. It is easiest to select the interface by using the IP address as a guide. You can also set the sniffer and ARP to begin on startup, although we do not recommend this. We suggest that you only use C&A when you explicitly want to.

Figure 10.2 Sniffer and General Configuration Options of the C&A Tool

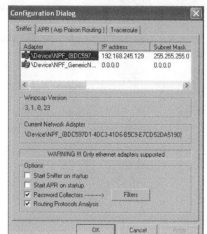

Selecting the **ARP Poison Routing (APR)** tab (see Figure 10.2) brings up the next set of available options. The default options (see Figure 10.3) should be sufficient, but if you are having problems getting the attack to work, you can set the "Poisoning remote ARP caches every 5 seconds" field to poison at a quicker rate.

Figure 10.3 ARP Poison Configuration Options of the C&A Tool

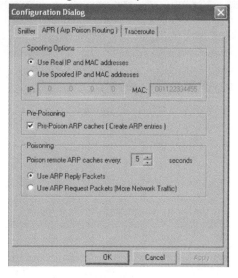

With configuration complete, you are read to begin performing an MITM attack. Double-click on the executable to bring up the C&A window (see Figure 10.4).

Figure 10.4 Main Interface of the C&A

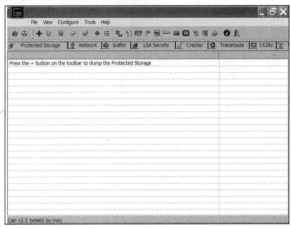

Next, you need to start the sniffer, which can be done by clicking the sniffer button (the far-left icon shown in Figure 10.4). Once the sniffer has started, you can select the **Sniffer** tab in the window to bring up the sniffing suboptions. Right clicking in the window allows us to be aggressive and scan for other machines (see Figure 10.5).

Figure 10.5 MAC Address Scanning Dialogue in C&A

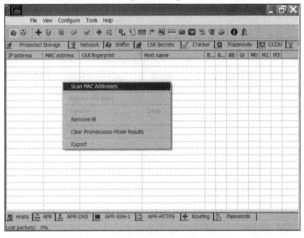

As demonstrated next, C&A can explicitly discover any machine on your network (Figure 10.6 shows the various options that are available). We invite you to explore these options after you download the tool. Since we are going to perform our MITM attack on a small home network, scanning all the hosts in the subnet is enough to bring up all of the computers in our network. If you are on a large network, use a small range to limit the amount of traffic (and potentially alerting noise) that you generate.

Figure 10.6 C&A MAC Address Scanner Options

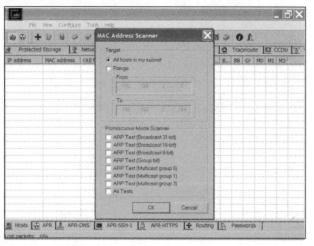

Once C&A has finished its scan of the network, all of the computers it discovers are displayed (see Figure 10.7). In this case, it has successfully discovered all of the machines in our local network. As you can see, the IP address and MAC addresses are both displayed. If C&A determine more information, it will be displayed as well. For example, 192.168.1.1 is most likely a router because the Organizationally Unique Identifier (OUI) fingerprint field says that it is "The Linksys Group, Inc."

Figure 10.7 Results of a C&A MAC Address Scan

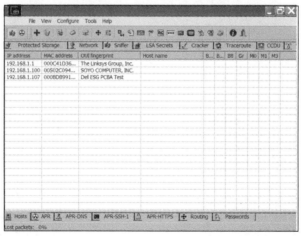

Now it is time to start the ARP poisoning. First, select the **APR** tab at the bottom left of the window. This will bring up the APR interface (see Figure 10.8).

Figure 10.8 C&A APR Interface

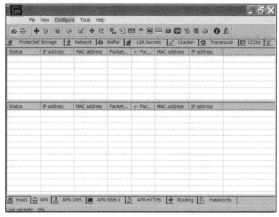

Selecting the "+" button in the upper left corner of the C&A window presents a list of possible machines to ARP spoof. On our network, Figure 10.9 shows the machines that we can poison to mount our MITM attack.

Figure 10.9 C&A Interface to Select New APR

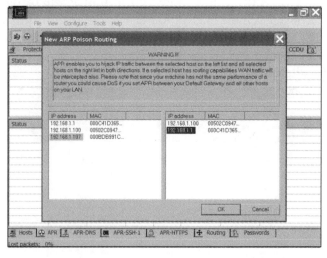

In this instance, we want to poison 192.168.1.107 (the target) and 192.168.1.1 (the gateway). By selecting 192.168.1.107 in the left window, the choices of other machines are displayed in the right window. Selecting 192.168.1.1 and then the **OK**

button sets up the parameters. Because 192.168.1.1 is the gateway for our network, spoofing this connection will redirect all Internet activity from 192.168.1.107 to our machine (see Figure 10.10). At the moment it is idle, so the network is functioning normally.

Figure 10.10 C&A Configured to ARP Poison

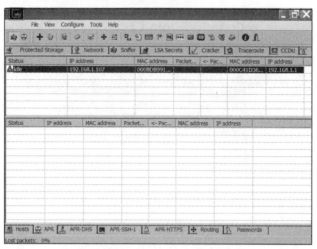

To begin ARP poisoning, select the round yellow and black APR symbol in the upper left corner of the window. This will start the poisoning of all of the caches. C&A will constantly send out ARP responses in order to set up the MITM attack. As the user on the unsuspecting machine uses the Internet, the status of the ARP poisoning is displayed in the windows (see Figure 10.11). We can see where the user on the targeted computer has been browsing. The number of packets passed by the MITM attack is also displayed.

Figure 10.11 Successful C&A ARP Poisoning Attack Example

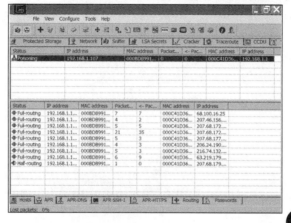

Next, we see the results of our sniffing by selecting the **Passwords** tab in the bottom of the window. Figure 10.12 shows the passwords that we have found. On the top row, we can see Sarah's hotmail password. As seen in the next two rows, not every password can be broken out by this application. Some schemes such as Yahoo transmit unbreakable hashes of their passwords. You can task C&A with attempting to break the hash, but unless the software is extremely lucky, it will not happen.

Figure 10.12 Passwords Collected from C&A on a Switched Network

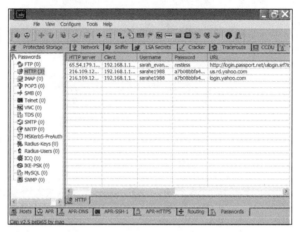

Unfortunately, MITM attacks are not an *unknown* method of gaining access. As a result, Web pages have security certificates and other mechanisms to help secure the Web site (see Figure 10.13). Our unsuspecting victim will get this warning when they browse to a site that uses these certificates. Most people click their way though the security warning, giving free access to their encrypted Web traffic.

Figure 10.13 Certificate Security Warning to Discourage MITM Attacks

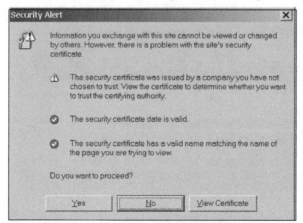

If we are lucky, they will select **yes** to proceed and therefore continue our MITM attack. An MITM attack performed by C&A can be a very useful tool in your arsenal. C&A also has many more functions that can be used to spy on your mark.

Sneaky Web Tricks

This section involves using the information obtained from other methods to help expand access to your online targets. In Chapter 6, you learned to collect e-mail accounts, passwords, and browser histories. In Chapter 7, we discussed how to collect e-mail. The trick here involves combining all of these lessons in order to access other online sites that your target may be using.

For example, many online personal advertisements and dating sites allow users to create accounts where they receive personal messages and other information specific to that site. Depending on why you are spying, this could be information you are interested in.

The first step is to ensure that you have the ability to view your mark's e-mail. Once you have control of the e-mail, the next step is to acquire a browser history and after that, search for sites of interest. Most can be browsed to and viewed; those that cannot may require accounts and passwords. When you encounter one of these sites, the next step is to look (either in protected storage or cookies) for an ID associated with that Web site.

Once you have the target site and account, browse to the site. To log in, you will probably need the password. (If you transfer all of your target's cookies to your computer, you may be able to browse using their session information and not need the password.) While there are many ways to obtain the password, such as logging keystrokes or guessing, most Web sites offer another option: attempt to log in, use anything you want as the password and when you fail, look for a "I forgot my password" button. This usually e-mails the original password, or a new password, to the user's registered e-mail address. Now that you have the password, you can enter the Web site at your discretion.

Another thing to consider is how you are going to handle the e-mail. If you receive a password reminder or a change in password, it is best to delete the message if you can. Although changing the password may be alerting, your mark will most likely follow the same procedure as you and have a new password e-mailed to him. Since you can monitor e-mail, you will also have access to the new password.

A Secret Web Server

Now that you know about the structure and sweet spots (i.e., e-mail boxes and temporary Internet files) of the Windows operating system, you may want to consider installing a tiny Web server on your target's computer. Even when files were hidden, we were able to access them remotely from several Web servers. One such server is freeware application Abyss Web server. You can retrieve this executable from *www.download.com* (search Abyss).

If you want this to remain secret, you must be stealthy in your installation options. We recommend checking only the **Abyss Web Server (required)** box and the **Auto Start** box so that the server is always running (see Figure 10.14).

Figure 10.14 Recommended Abyss Web Server Installation Options

After the Web server has been installed, it is time to configure it for use. The first thing to do is specify an Administrator Login name and password (see Figure 10.15). From a tradecraft perspective, you may want to consider selecting a name like "l33thax0r," which might be the popular choice of a young hacker. Likewise, you could use the name "Mom" if you were trying to overtly convey to your children that you are monitoring them.

Figure 10.15 Configuration of Abyss Web Server Administrator Login Name and Password

The next section must be followed closely; by default, the Web server is tightly configured to be a conventional application serving up .HTML pages. To make things easier, we demonstrate how to do this in a short series of steps.

1. **Serving directory**. Change the default-serving directory to be the folder you are most interested in viewing, by clicking on the **Server Configuration** icon on the left side of the console interface. From there, set the Server Root to be **C:** and the Documentation Path to be **Documents and Settings** (or **Program Files**, depending on your intentions) and change Port 80 to something you will remember (see Figure 10.16).

Figure 10.16 Configuration of Abyss Web Server Root Directory and Port

2. **Disable access log file**. Before you can successfully restart the server, you must remove the logging files. This can be done by clicking on the **Advanced...** button on the left side of the page. This will bring up a new set of icons. Select **Server Parameters**, blank out the value for the "Log File" field (see Figure 10.17), and click **OK**.

Figure 10.17 Removal of Abyss Web Server Log File Storage

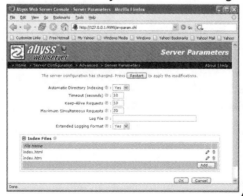

3. **Disable common gateway interface (CGI) capability**. Next, the server will notify you if the CGI Error File does not exist. Since you are not using this in the traditional Web server sense, you do not need this capability enabled. Click on the **CGI Parameters** icon, change "CGI Processing Enabled" to **No**, blank out the "CGI Error File" location, and click **OK**. Your settings should resemble those in Figure 10.18.

Figure 10.18 Disabling Abyss Web Server CGI Capability

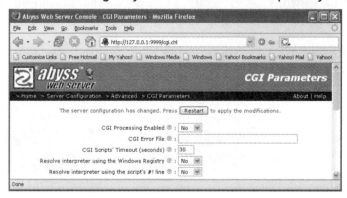

4. **Restart and access**. Lastly, you can press the **Restart** button and access the Web server remotely using a browser pointed at the IP address and port number specified. This gives you full remote browsing access to the root server directory (see Figure 10.19).

Figure 10.19 Browsing to the Abyss Server Remotely

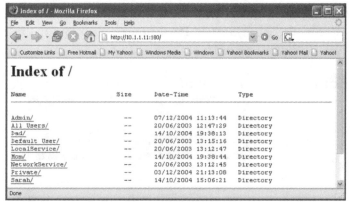

WARNING

Do not install a remote Web server with a root-server directory if you have non-encrypted wireless access on your network, or you do not have a firewall or Network Address Translation (NAT) appliance such as a Linksys router between you and the Internet. If the IP address of the server is routable over the Internet, this is a BAD idea unless you want everyone to be able to access the directory. If you do not have encryption enabled on your wireless access point, a *War Driver* could secretly gain access to your network and access this server as well. If you do not adequately secure your target, you will not be the only one spying on that machine.

You may think that choosing a port other than 80 ensures you are secure, but many "scanning" applications are in circulation that search for the existence of servers just like this.

From a stealth perspective, one problem with this server is that it has an icon visible in the system tray (the far right of the Start menu). As mentioned, applications exist to remove these icons; however, you can also take intermediate measures by hiding options within the menu itself. To access these options, right click on the system tray and select **Properties**. Click on the **Customize** button, which will bring up a list of items. Highlight the **Abyss Web Server** and change the behavior to be **Always Hide** (see Figure 10.20). This trick also works for Google Search and other tools that you may have running on a target computer.

Figure 10.20 Hiding the Abyss Web Server System Tray Icon

While you cannot change or add files onto the remote server, you can browse to it whenever you wish. This is an ideal way to periodically copy e-mail, buddy list information, and temporary Internet files. Unfortunately, this method of access does not lend itself well to retrieving key logging or screenshot takes, because you do not have the means of resetting their file size to be zero. Depending on your technical ability, you can experiment with turning the CGI capability back on and creating CGI executables that are capable of executing small tasks such as this. Likewise, if you enable a CGI command and control interface such as this you can theoretically use it to start and stop other monitoring applications such as the desktop monitoring tool discussed next.

Making Desktop Movies

Desktop movies are recordings of all movements on a desktop and are generally used for tutorials; however, they may also be of assistance in your spying endeavors. There are few free *stealthy* desktop-recording applications available. Most operate by displaying visible "record," "pause," and "stop" buttons. However, it should be noted that commercial versions of this software has been purposefully created to be hidden and stealthy such as "Desktop spy" available at *www.spyarsenal.com*. We do not endorse any commercial products and therefore have not evaluated any of the options, but most (including Desktop spy) give you the opportunity to download them for a free 21-day trial. If you are lucky, you may learn all you need to know in those 21 days. Commercial applications such as this one generally enable you to set certain start and stop times for the captures, which can enables you to know if your spouse wakes up an hour or so before you to access the computer in "privacy."

Another option is to combine the power of virtual network computing (VNC), which was demonstrated in previous chapters, with desktop movie-making software to record movements on your target's computer. Because the desktop monitoring software is located on your computer (instead of your target's), you do not have to worry about a noisy dialogue box. Instead, you merely launch a VNC session and begin capturing data. Figure 10.21 demonstrates how the CamStudio recording box is positioned around a VNC session to make an .AVI movie of the movements on the remote computer. CamStudio, which is freeware, can be downloaded from www.*brothersoft.com/Multimedia_Graphics_Screen_Capture_CamStudio_3944.html*.

There are several freeware desktop movie applications that you may find useful (or more in tune with your needs). Also, it should be mentioned that as of the writing of this book, there are Linux and MacOS versions of VNC recording and playback plug-in applications; however, we were not able to identify any straightforward Windows ports. We encourage you to experiment searching for Windows

VNC viewer-recording capabilities that are built directly into VNC, as they may be more effective. Recording is an option that can be used for proof or confrontation material following an event.

Figure 10.21 Combining VNC and Desktop Recording Software Such as CamStudio Can Enable You to Secretly Store Movies of the Activity on a Remote Computer

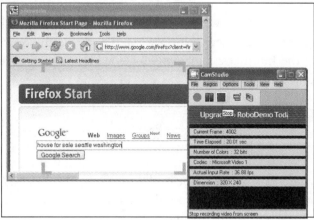

Web Cams

Web cams are difficult to detect and collect data from, not because of technological enhancements that keep them protected, but because of the large (and ever-expanding) number of different clients that are available. Most clients use their own protocol and operate on their own port. Table 10.1 shows a sampling of the various ports used by the different services.

Table 10.1 A Sampling of Ports Used for Video

Description	TCP Port	UDP Port
VDOLive Streaming Video	7000	User Specified
Streaming Real Audio & Video	554, 7070	6970–7170
VocalTec Internet Phone Video	1490, 6670, 25793	22555
Xing StreamWorks Streaming Video		1558
MS NetShow	1755	1755, Dynamic
MSN Messenger Web Cam	5100	
ICU II Video Conferencing	2000–2003	
iSPQ Video Conferencing	2000–2003	
AIM Video Chat	1024–5000	1024–5000
Yahoo Video Chat	5100	

Clients that accompany AIM, Yahoo, and MSN chat clients are some of the most popular for home use. While Snort, Ethereal, and most sniffers collect traffic, there are no good tools for reassembling the video streams from the traffic. Currently, the best we can do is to determine that one is running on our network.

Expanding Your Horizons

For the final part of this lesson, we are going to expand your collection circle from the computers on your home network outward. We start with your home router and end the search on the Internet exploring Google, white pages, and several databases full of information useful for spying.

Small Home Routers

Home networks today often utilize low-end routers such as those produced by Linksys, to share a single Internet connection among several computers. In these circumstances, the router is a choke point in the network that uses NAT to map packets among hosts. Given this responsibility, these devices have access to all of the traffic on the network, and many maintain logs of that traffic.

The first step is to discover where the router is located on the network. This step can be done by identifying which IP address your computer uses as its default router. One method of doing this is to execute **ipconfig /all <ENTER>** from a command prompt (see Figure 10.22).

Figure 10.22 The Default Router IP Address Can Be Obtained by Executing ipconfig from a Command Prompt

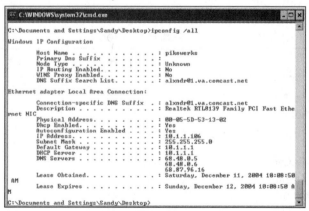

From these results, we see that our IP address is 10.1.1.106 and the address of the default router is 10.1.1.1. Nearly every home router provides a convenient Web

interface for administration and maintenance. The next step is to open a browser and "surf" to this IP address. You will most likely be greeted with a page querying you for a user name and password (see Figure 10.23).

Figure 10.23 Password Prompt from a Linksys Router

If you are lucky, this password may not have ever been set by anyone in your home. Several Web sites such as *www.cirt.net/cgi-bin/passwd.pl* list default passwords and account names on products such as this. Alternatively, you can wait for someone to log in to administer this, and capture the keystrokes. However, note that doing so may take a lot of time because few people need to frequently view or change this information. Given all of the previous password recovery tools discussed in earlier chapters, another option is to try e-mail and Web account passwords that are commonly used by your target. It is very likely they are using one of them on the router.

As a last resort, many of these devices provide a means of "resetting" the system to factory defaults. Doing so completely eliminates the password and enables you to have full access of the system. We recommend only doing this if: (1) no one else in your house is currently accessing the Internet (as it will disrupt the connection, (2) if you have reviewed set-up and configuration information on the manufacture's Web site, and (3) if you have a good cover story/back-up plan in the event that you are not able to re-configure the Internet connection. For example, if you claim that the power went out, flip the switch on the circuit breaker so that other devices appear to also have lost power. This is also a good time to quickly install a keystroke logger on your target's computer so that you can identify what the new password is. Otherwise, if the Internet connection works after you reset it, you should be able to directly access the Web site (after potentially using a default login such as username: admin password: admin). Note, however, that resetting the router will also delete any wireless encryption keys, so be sure that you have considered all of the potential side effects before you take this *extreme* approach.

From this point on, we will assume that you have gained access to the router through one of the means mentioned. For our purposes, the most interesting aspect of the routers is its logging capability. In the Linksys model (see Figure 10.24), you can access the log page by clicking on **Administration | Log**. Your version may differ somewhat; therefore, you should look at the documentation for your particular model for specific directions. In our example, ensure that the "Log" button is checked **Yes** to capture traffic information.

Figure 10.24 Internet Traffic Log Location on a Linksys Router

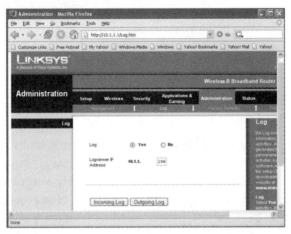

When some time has passed and a log has been collected, you have two options. You can either view the log directly on the router itself through the Web interface, or you can have it sent remotely to a computer where it is stored and updated on the fly. When your computer is shared with your target, you should access the log only from the Web interface; otherwise, your target may stumble across the software and become suspicious. To view the log locally, you must click either **Incoming Log** or **Outgoing Log**. The incoming log maintains a list of traffic that is destined for your home network and the Outgoing Log lists where users in your network are going out. The Outgoing Log will probably be the most useful (see Figure 10.25).

In this figure you can see outgoing traffic information for four different computers:

- 10.1.1.100 is using the AOL Instant Messaging (IM) client (port 5190)
- 10.1.1.101 is surfing to the *www.sony.com* Web site

- 10.1.1.104 is accessing the *www.usatoday.com* site and its associated advertisements

- 10.1.1.106 is also using AOL IM.

Figure 10.25 Outgoing Internet Traffic Log on a Linksys Router

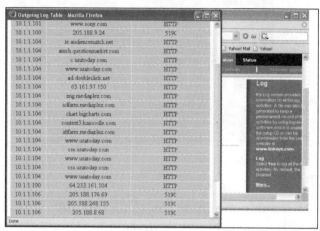

The drawback to accessing information directly on the router is that it has a limited amount of storage space. This means that depending on the amount of traffic, this log may only date back 5 or 10 minutes. If your target was conducting illicit activities while you were at work, you may be out of luck.

To solve this problem, save the log files remotely on a computer that your target does not use. This will enable you to maintain larger amounts of data about the traffic. Most home routers have remote clients such as this for accessing and saving log files. In our example, Linksys provides an application named *LogViewer*, which can be downloaded at *ftp://ftp.linksys.com/pub/befsr41/logviewer.exe*. Once you install this application you must verify that the address entered into the "LogViewer IP address" field is correct (i.e., in our case it is set to 10.1.1.106). As Figure 10.26 demonstrates, the log from the LogViewer application is very similar to what you will view on the Web site. The two biggest differences are (1) larger amounts of access data can be stored and (2) logs are updated in real time so you can literally "watch" this application for an up-to-date view of all Internet activity on the network.

Figure 10.26 Outgoing Internet Traffic Viewed Remotely Using LogViewer

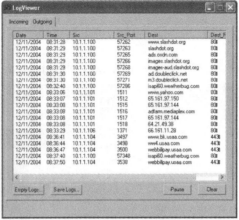

Cell Phones

Cell phones have become a ubiquitous communication device. Modern ones much more closely resemble computers than the traditional phones of 10 years ago. Today, cellular phones have Web cams, still cameras, Internet surfing, e-mail, and IM capability built directly into them. Each new model takes a step closer toward realizing the same communication functionality as desktop computers. With this enhancement also comes a security consciousness, with exploits and viruses aimed at cell phones already in circulation.

Given the wide assortment of carriers (i.e., Cingular, Verizon, NexTel, Sprint, T-Mobile, and so on) in the U.S., there is also a wide selection of phone manufacturers and each manufacturer has a hefty selection of cell phone models. Because it is impossible to cover all of them (and the most current models will likely be updated by the time you read this), we stick to a series of collection recommendations:

1. **Determine the model.** When your target is in the shower or has stepped out for a moment without the phone, physically investigate it to determine what manufacturer and model it is. Most phones have markings that identify them. Given the general interest that many people have with "gadgets," including phones, you can even admire it while they are around and simply ask, "What model is your phone? It is cool." If this does not work, determine which wireless provider they are using by asking them or looking for a bill in the mail. Next, go on the Web and find the provider and then search through all of their available telephone models for one that looks the same.

2. **Read the manual.** In general, people are not keen on reading instruction manuals, but think of this as your opportunity to tune your skills before you even touch the phone. If you cannot find the manual, search the Internet; the manufacturer's site is sure to have an electronic one available (see Figure 10.27).

Figure 10.27 Using a Provider's Web Site to Research a Particular Phone

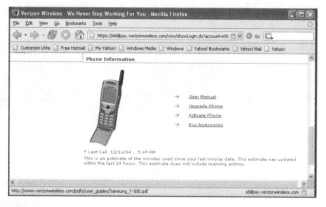

3. **Visit the store.** If this model phone is available for purchase, you may find it useful to visit the store for a demonstration. Request to see all of the "ins and outs" of the phone's functionality. This will help you become familiar with it and give you a chance to experiment.

4. **Scour the Web for features, tips, and tricks.** Before jumping into collection, search online for information about the model. You should be aware of every feature that is available for your exploitation, as well as any exploitation methods for bypassing passwords, and so forth, that have already been posted by others.

5. **Look for histories.** Now that you have done your homework, you are ready to get started. One of the most useful characteristics about cell phones is that, much like computers, they maintain usage histories. At a minimum, this should tell you who has called your mark, who your mark has called, and how long they talked. You can usually access this information without a password.

6. **Look in the address book.** Stored address books can be useful because (1) the phone numbers can be entered into the reverse telephone directories and (2) labels entered into the phone may be extremely descriptive (and sometimes alerting).

7. **Exploit the features.** Many phones today have calendars and camera, video, and Internet access. Search for residual information from any of these. For example, many of the people that use their cell phone for instant messaging stay logged on non-stop. This is an excellent chance for you to retrieve the buddy list (and maybe even password) of your target. Likewise, some forward communication through text messaging using services such as AOL's MyMobile (see Figure 10.28).

Figure 10.28 Using AOL's MyMobile Service to Forward Instant Message Text

NOTE

Consider using mobile forwarding as a means of sending e-mail and text message pager alerts to yourself to notify you that your target is online, signed on to IM, or sending/receiving e-mail.

8. **Billing.** If your target literally has their cell phone on their hip at all times, you may find that your spying efforts have not yielded much success. Never fear, you have one more option. The beauty of phone calls is that they are logged with details on the transaction times, locations, and participants. These bills come in the form of paper listings, or even more popular today, are accessible using electronic accounts. Analyze these carefully, because the information they contain could be your big break in the case (see Figure 10.29).

Figure 10.29 Analyzing the Cell Phone Bill for Activities

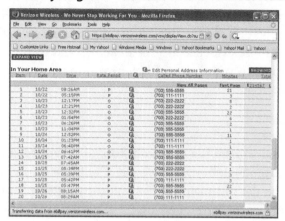

Imagine that 703-111-1111 is your home number and 703-222-2222 is your cell number. You may be curious as to why your spouse is always calling 703-555-5555 for long periods of time. Furthermore, the calls to this unknown number tend to occur first thing in the morning, during lunch, and late in the evening, all times that you are not around. The call on October 23 at 11:04 PM is an especially interesting one. You know that your spouse is always in bed by 10:00 PM. This would mean that your spouse secretly got up to use the phone after you fell asleep.

Likewise, some bills have information about where calls originate from. This can also yield interesting clues (see Figure 10.30).

In this statement, the origin of the call is displayed in the sixth column. Beyond learning whom your target is calling and when, you can learn where they are. If they are highly active on the phone, you can use this as a type of tracking system. For example, say you are monitoring your child who was supposedly spending evenings at "football practice" in Springfield, VA. You may find it highly interesting that on the nights of October 25 and 26 your child was making phone calls from Washington, D.C., shortly after 5:30 P.M.

Figure 10.30 Cell Phone Bill Origination Information

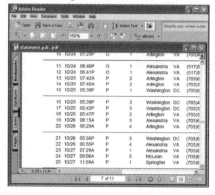

Again, few things beyond a confession by someone bring a concern to closure. Each tip and trick that we have given you can be used to collect a wide assortment of clues that can be pieced together. This combination serves two purposes: first, it helps you gather more evidence against someone, and second, it helps you make sure that you are correct in your concern before you jump to conclusions and make emotional accusations.

Google

The Google search engine is a wondrous tool for cyber-spying. Despite the fact that there are an enormous amount of Web pages online, Google manages to discover, catalog, and cache the vast majority of them for your searching pleasure. As you will see, many of these pages were never meant for public viewing. Furthermore, once a page has been included in a caching engine such as Google, it will be there for a long time (see Figure 10.31).

Figure 10.31 Outgoing Internet Traffic Viewed Remotely Using LogViewer

Imagine that "Larry Dirtius, a.k.a. Dirty Larry" changed his mind about posting to the *www.trueconfessions.book* Web site one day after first posting there. Even if he successfully persuades the site administrator to remove his posting, it will still show up in the Google search. Since the page has been removed from the Web site itself, clicking on the "Dirty Larry: The Real Story" link will give a "404 File Not Found" error. However, thanks to Google, we can click on the **Cached** link, and it will retrieve a copy of the original posting.

Notes from the Underground

Cheat Notes on Google Hacking

The definitive Google hacker is Johnny Long of *Johnny.ihackstuff.com*. Besides being a highly useful forum on the subject, his site contains a database full of useful search terms in Google for uncovering information that no one expected to be made public. For example, Figure 10.32 demonstrates how the tip in his database to search for **"# -FrontPage-" inurl:service.pwd** provides username and password hashes for 121 different Web sites.

Figure 10.32 Google Hacking to Discover Information

Even funnier in our context is a Google search for **"buddylist.blt index –hack,"** which gives you the screen name and complete buddy list for several accounts. It is probably worth putting the name of the person you are searching for in the query just in case their buddy list is being exported. If you are lucky, you will come across one or two others that have that person added as a buddy. We also recommend the book *Google Hacking for Penetration Testers* by Johnny for additional examples and explanations on the subject.

Online Databases

There are several tpes of online databases.

Blogs

Blogs are basically chronological online journals. They are replacing the vanity personal Web pages of the mid to late '90s as the way most people attempt to leave their mark on the Internet. It was estimated by Technorati, Inc. that as of October 2004, there were 4.2 million blog sites online. Also, a 2003 Pew/Internet survey reported that approximately 53 percent of adults in the U.S. had written in a blog. Even Google has a blog at *www.google.com/googleblog* that records the musing of different employee's at Google.

Different people and groups create blogs for varying reasons. Some are parts of projects, others are people's personal thoughts and ramblings. When looking for information on a mark, finding their personal blog, if there is one, is a great discovery. This can yield all sorts of personal information that you can use to support or discredit other information you may have collected on them.

Public Records

Without a doubt, the finest option for public records searches is the renowned LexusNexis service. We encourage you to research the *www.lexisnexis.com* site and determine if this level of service is necessary for what you are trying to accomplish. You should note, however, that there are many free services that are extremely useful as well. One such site is *www.searchsystems.net*. Because available records vary by city, it starts by asking you to select the city and state that you are interested in. In our case, we are curious about "Larry Dirtius," whom we have been reading about, so we search "Richmond, Virginia." Figure 10.33 shows a small collection of the many sites that are returned from our search.

Figure 10.33 Public Record Sites Available from *www.searchsystems.net*

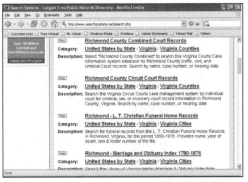

One of the records databases of particular interest was the "Richmond County Combined Court Records." Selecting this brought up a site that we used to search for "Dirty Larry." Figure 10.34 shows an example of this site; most cities have similar sites for their court systems.

Use public-record databases for your area (e.g., marriage records, court records, and driving records) to better investigate your target. Investigations that used to take intensive effort are becoming easily available . As public records become easier to find and access, what once was semi-private information such as housing assessments is available to the intrusive neighbor.

Figure 10.34 Court Records for Richmond, Virginia

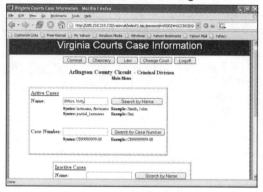

Credit Reports

Thanks to the Fair Credit Reporting Act (FCRA), U.S. consumer reporting companies must provide a free copy of their credit report to individuals once a year. Because the debits of individuals that are married can often be grouped together, this may be a good way to search for hidden credit cards and bank accounts if you suspect financial misconduct on the part of your spouse. You can access this information at *www.annualcreditreport.com.*

Address and Phone Listings

Online phone listings can help in many ways. Remembering that everything is a trail of breadcrumbs they many not gleam a solid "proof", but they can certainly provide useful clues.

White Pages

If you discover the name of an individual that your mark seems to be corresponding with a great deal, you can use search sites such as *www.addresses.com* or *http://phone.people.yahoo.com* to discover both that person's phone number and address (see Figure 10.35).

Searching for Larry Dirtius reveals his 804 area code, phone number, and address in Richmond, VA. If you followed our story about 16-year-old Sarah from Alexandria, VA (in Chapter 6), who we learned is really 13-year-old Katie, you know that her parents should keep her away from any unescorted visits to Richmond. Dirty Larry lives there.

Figure 10.35 White Page Search for Larry Dirtius Yields His Address and Home Phone Number

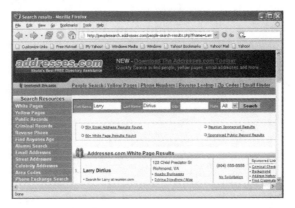

Similarly, you may not have solid proof that your spouse is cheating on you, but you discover a large number of e-mails from a person that has made you suspicious. While we do not condone any type of affair (regardless of online-only or not), there may be a difference between the exchange of lusty e-mails and an actual meeting. Suppose you search for the address and phone of this person and discover that they just happen to live in the town that your spouse has been recently traveling to "for work." This also gives you a phone number to watch for on cell phone caller ID log, which may indicate that there is a potential problem.

Reverse Directories

What can you do if you discover that the same unfamiliar phone number has been listed repeatedly on your child or spouse's cell phone? Make use of the many reverse phone directories available. For example, Figure 10.36 shows how *www.reversephonedirectory.com* can be used to look up phone number 804-555-5555.

Figure 10.36 Reverse Directories Enable You to Identify the Owner of a Telephone Number

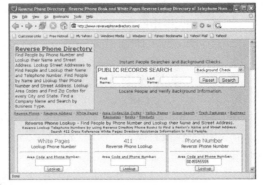

If the number that you are searching belongs to a cell phone, you may receive information stating that it is registered to a provider, but will most likely not receive the actual owner's name.

Social Engineering

We cannot write enough about the power of *social engineering*. Unlike computers that have rules and strict protocols set in code, people adjust their decisions based on *reason*. This reasoning can be internal contemplation, or a choice that can be swayed or altered by outside forces. Like it or not, nearly everything that surrounds us is social engineering to some extent. This book is an example: in approximately 400 pages we have expressed our opinions about many subtleties of computer science that may or may not change the way you think. Every advertisement that you see is a company's attempt to socially engineer you to *think* that you *need* their product. Never discount social engineering as a method to gain access to your target's computer or accounts. What might not be available through technical means may be available by talking to the right person. Why spend effort snooping on a person, when you can get them to give you access?

Many times when tracking our mark we are looking for information that they would not willingly give us. Sometimes it is necessary to use social engineering to approach them and "pump" them for information. Since we have talked a lot about online identities, it would not be a bad idea to create an online identity that you feel appeals to your mark, approach them, and build up a relationship with them. By creating online characters to interact with your mark, you can ask questions they might/would not give to most normal people. In addition, with whatever knowledge you have of your mark, you can tailor your online identity to best match any personal preferences they might have. For example, your teenage son may not want to open up to you, but he might feel comfortable talking to a girl his age. Keep this path in mind in your search for information from your target. While technical collection is powerful, never underestimate the power of social engineering.

Summary

New and advanced techniques help cyber-spies with more difficult "real world" situations. In addition, potential spies should look beyond PCs for other areas where useful information can be collected to help them build a picture of their adversary's activity. Several key topics in this chapter were:

- C&A allows us to automatically sniff a switched network, perform MITM attacks, and collect passwords from targeted machines.

- Techniques from the previous chapters can be combined to obtain difficult-to-find information, or to help deepen access into our mark's online life.

- A Web server is a great means of remote access to a computer. While based on simple and stable principles, they have most of the capability needed to become full-fledged spy tools.

- Personal routers are critical chokepoints in most home networks, and can offer a great deal of information on what goes on inside them.

- The pervasiveness and communication abilities of cell phones makes them an important technology to watch when tracking someone's activity.

- There are a wealth of online resources ranging from Google to public information databases that can be used to collect information about your mark.

- Social engineering is one of the oldest methods of spying, and it is still very important even with all of the technical means available today.

Becoming a good cyber-spy requires plenty of knowledge and lots of practice. Everything we have taught up until now is just a launching pad. We encourage everyone to keep learning about new technology and how it plays a role in your everyday interactions. As more technologies become part of our lives, we open up doors to both newfound utility from the technology, and privacy implications as these new technologies are subverted to become useful spy tools.

## Chapter 11

Counterspy: Are You Being Watched?

"Just because you're paranoid does not mean they're not out to get you."

— *Unknown*

Topics in this Chapter:

- **How to Be Sneaky**
- **How to Tell If You Are Being Watched**
- **How to React If You Are a Target**
- **Identifying Who Is Spying on You**
- **A Note about Spyware**
- **Case Study: Guilt Is for Suckers, Not Spies**
- **Summary**

Introduction

Now that you know how online activities can be collected, you should think about your own vulnerability. As you are collecting your target's Web traffic, e-mail, and instant messages, someone else may be collecting the same from you. As demonstrated earlier, online applications come with little to no expectation of privacy; therefore, unless you take precautions, you are inherently vulnerable to being spied on.

This chapter provides the tools you need to minimize your exposure and make it difficult for others to spy on you. Beyond all of the technological plug-ins that can enhance security, you must recognize that each action you perform on your computer leaves evidence for someone else to analyze. This chapter starts by teaching you how to keep a low profile online, which means avoiding activities either by limiting where you conduct them from or surrounding yourself with secrecy enablers such as encryption and steganography.

Next, we teach you to identify if you are being spied on by pointing out warning signs to watch for; we also teach you about traps that you can set to catch others. Finally, we conclude by helping you prepare in the event that you are the target of someone's spy attempt. Keep in mind that knowing how to protect yourself from those trying to watch you will only help make you a better spy.

How to Be Sneaky

There are many ways to introduce stealth and operational elements into your daily interaction with computers. As with most situations, caution introduces inconvenience. You must decide what level of suspicion makes the most sense for your situation. We begin by suggesting some methods to use to limit your dependence on your home network and then we discuss methods of concealment for when avoidance is not an option.

Limiting Evidence by Limiting Usage

One of the easiest ways to reduce evidence on your home computer is *not* to use it for anything that you do not want discovered. There are three ways that this can be done: the exclusion of media, the exclusion of a network, and total exclusion. We recognize that each of these carries some level of inconvenience; however, keep in mind how minor the inconvenience would seem compared to the agony of being caught.

Exclusion of Media

The exclusion of media ensures that the internal media of your home computer is not used, meaning you never allow sensitive information to touch the hard drive of your computer. Not storing evidence on the hard drive prevents someone from conducting after-the-fact forensics. This can be done with removable hard drives, virtual drives, virtual operating systems (OSes), and bootable OSes.

Removable Drives

One of the easiest and least expensive removable drives is a portable Universal Serial Bus (USB) drive, which is a great place to store sensitive information. USB drives can be purchased for less than $50.00 at any retailer that sells computer accessories. These drives provide up to 1 gigabyte (GB) of data storage; you can also go with a larger drive and purchase a USB hard disk. These drives are essentially laptop hard drives encased in a USB interface and can be purchased for less than $100.00. USB hard disks can hold more than 100GB of data.

One thing to keep in mind is that anything introduced into a scenario must have a legitimate *cover* story. If you begin secretly using your new USB drive, you may draw attention to yourself. Instead, be sure that you have a solid explanation of why you purchased it and ensure that it can be backstopped if investigated. Indicating your desire to maintain "secure backups" of financial information may suffice. Then make sure to actually use the device.

Another option is to utilize a storage device that you may already have connected (e.g., an MP3 player). Very few people think to look on music players for hidden files. Apple's iPod is an appealing option because of the large amount of disk space it offers (up to 60GB). Portable music players are plugged into the computer to transfer music files, so a cover story is already incorporated. Figure 11.1 shows how an iPod can be "explored" just like a removable drive.

Figure 11.1 Exploring and Creating a Hidden Folder on an Apple iPod

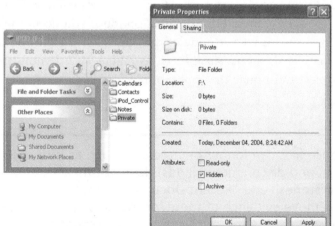

From here, you can create a new folder on the drive named "hidden" to maintain your secret files. (For even more sensitive data, see the file encryption and steganography section later in this chapter.) An ideal scenario to consider is using strong encryption on your sensitive files and, using steganography, implanting them into an existing song on your iPod. This should withstand tremendous interrogation, especially if you have a large number of songs loaded on your player. Even if someone suspected that the file contained steganography, they would have to break the encryption to access the information.

NOTE

The same hiding attributes we suggest for hiding secret files, are used on the iPod to prevent files from being copied. While there may be legal restrictions, copying off of an iPod is technologically feasible. To do so, launch **Start | Run | Explorer**. Verify that you have correctly set your explorer window to show hidden files by selecting **Tools | Folder Options | View**. Make sure that "Show hidden files and folders" is checked and that "Hide protected operating systems files (Recommended)" is not checked, and then use explorer to browse to the iPod mounted on the computer (probably the "F:" drive). Music can then be copied into folders from **iPod_Controls | Music | F00**.

Virtual RAM Drives

A random-access memory (RAM) drive can be created for the temporary storage of files. A RAM drive simulates a regular hard drive, but completely disappears when the computer is powered down. This is a great option if you do not need long-term access to a file. To download a free copy of this application, go to AR Soft's Web site at *www.arsoft-online.com/download/ramdisk.zip*. As Figure 11.2 demonstrates, there is a few options to select from once the application is installed.

WARNING

Just because files can longer be accessed (such as Virtual RAM drives, USB drives, and disconnected iPods) does not mean they will not appear in the ""Histories" and "Recent Documents" lists. Precautions must be taken to remove evidence of these locations, or they may give away your hiding place. Imagine the clues someone investigating would get if they stumbled across the file *F:\Private\Weekendgetaway.doc* knowing that the *F:* drive generally refers to the iPod.

Figure 11.2 Configuring AR Soft's RAM Disk Application

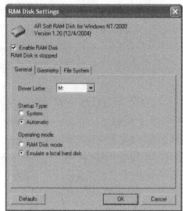

Under the **General** tab, select the drive letter that you wish to have the RAM drive mounted under. Be sure *not* to select a drive that is already in use. Next, select the size (in megabytes [MBs]) of the RAM drive under the **Geometry** tab. Do not make the disk any larger than 100MB unless you have installed additional memory in your computer system.

The **File System** tab allows you to name the volume, give it an ID, and change sector and entry counts. Do not change any of the values in this tab. When finished configuring your drive, click the **OK** button to proceed.

The next step is to open up the RAM drive so that you can save files to it. To do this, launch **Explorer** from the **Start | Run** menu. By default, the RAM drive does not appear on the screen; however, if you enter the drive name into the **Address** box (see Figure 11.3), it will open the disk.

Figure 11.3 Opening Your RAM Disk for Use

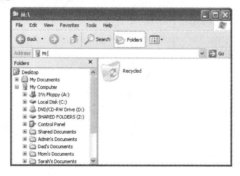

The RAM drive is now ready to store files, folders, and applications as if it were a regular hard drive. This is a good place to store temporary files or executables such as steganography tools that you do not want installed on your regular hard drive. When the computer is powered down, all information on this drive is permanently erased.

Notes from the Underground

Stealthy Installation on Removable and Virtual Drives

Because you select a removable or virtual drive as your installation location does not mean you will not leave traces elsewhere such as system files and registry entries. We encourage you to explore installation-monitoring tools such as InstallSpy, available at *www.tucows.com/preview/337007.html*. This freeware application from 2BrightSparks tracks all changes that occur during software installation. After the installation is complete, you can view a report of the activity. This report helps to identify evidence that you need to remove when you are finished with the software.

If you are confronted about having InstallSpy on your computer, use the fact that it is a great utility for tracking the installation of spyware for your cover story.

Virtual OSes

Another option beyond using a virtual RAM drive is to use a completely virtual OS. A virtual OS is an entire computer with OS and software simulated within a single program. There are several applications that do this; our favorite is the commercial program VMware (*www.vmware.com*). Using VMware you can install one or more virtual machines inside your existing "host" OS. Each machine is completely self-contained and is graphically displayed in its own window (see Figure 11.4).

As can be seen, the virtual machine looks and feels almost identical to a true machine. The prime difference is that the C: drive of this computer resides entirely in a virtual file system located on the host computer. This makes forensics of the hard drive more difficult because the investigator cannot easily extract information directly from the host computer; the virtual computer would have to be started and examined.

Another advantage of using VMware is the *Snapshot* and *Revert* capabilities (see Figure 11.4). You can install a virgin system and take a snapshot of it, thereby saving a copy of the "state" of the machine. This means that when you press the *Revert* button it will appear identical to when you took the snapshot. From an operational perspective, you can take a snapshot of a clean system, access the Internet, and revert to a clean state when you are finished. These steps will completely erase any evidence of your Internet activity from the virtual machine. Likewise, because the entire virtual machine is saved in a file on the host machine, the file can be securely deleted to remove all evidence of the machine itself. Virtual machines such as this provide an excellent opportunity to access the Internet in a stealthy fashion.

Figure 11.4 VMware Workstation Currently Executing Microsoft Windows XP

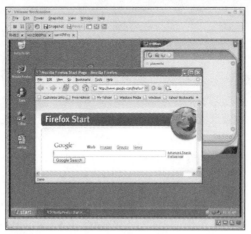

Bootable OSes

Beyond OSes that execute virtually on your host OS, you can use specialized "boot" disks that do not require a hard drive. Because of size limitations, most of these are Linux-based OSes, one of the most popular being Knoppix (see *www.knoppix.net*). After you burn the image to a CD, you have a completely portable, bootable OS that executes without the use of a hard drive. Figure 11.5 demonstrates the "look and feel" of the Knoppix distribution of the Linux OS.

To use Knoppix, place the CD in your player and recycle power; it automatically attempts to configure your Internet connection using Dynamic Host Configuration Protocol (DHCP). By default, Knoppix comes with a Web browser, Instant Message (IM) chat client (Gaim, which is discussed later), and an e-mail client. Figure 11.5 shows Koppix using anonymous Hotmail and IM accounts. Because this entire session resides entirely in memory and not on the hard drive, all evidence will be erased from this computer when the power is turned off. In addition, conducting your Internet activities in a Linux-based environment may give you the edge in anonymity.

Figure 11.5 Linux Bootable Knoppix As an Alternative for Privacy on a Home Computer

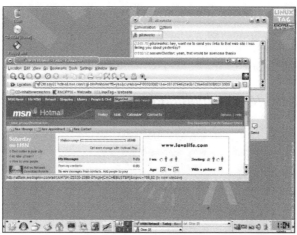

Exclusion of the Network

While not relying on the hard drive helps prevent some actions from being detected, remember that evidence travels across your home network, which leaves you vulnerable to sniffers and other network-based collection mechanisms. The next step is to leverage wireless network services offered by restaurants, coffee shops, hotels, and so forth, so that no evidence of your activity can be collected from your home network. Keep in mind that forensics can still be collected from the hard drive, so be sure that you do not rely on any internal media if it can be accessed by others. In addition, many of these networks restrict activity to Web surfing; consider combining some of the media exclusion methods with network exclusion to enhance your level of protection.

> **WARNING**
>
> While true that using a favorite coffee shop or bookstore to access the Internet makes you safe from snoops on your home network, beware of downright thieves. Public access points are a breeding ground for criminals who watch people enter passwords and credit card numbers that they then steal and use. Most of these free access points use wireless access, which means that the signals are floating around in the air for all to see. Be careful that your transactions are protected via encryption. Even with encryption, be careful with the transactions you conduct. A cleverly executed Man-in-the-Middle (MITM) attack could compromise your encryption.

Total Exclusion

The last step is to take advantage of full Internet access services offered by libraries, business centers, and Internet cafés. Most Internet cafés have automated systems that erase and reinstall the OS of each computer between each session. However, some do not, and it is possible that they could have keystroke loggers installed. Because of this (and other lack-of-privacy issues), do not conduct any banking or other important activities from these computers. Internet cafés do, however, provide a perfect means for the totally anonymous and untraceable sending of e-mail and chat sessions, especially when combined with disposable e-mail addresses such as those available from *www.hotmail.com*, *www.yahoo.com*, and *www.gmail.com* and a disposable chat ID. Many people believe that this is where a lot of Internet Spam is originated from because of its potential for untraceable messages.

Tips and Tricks...

AIM Express

Have you ever wanted to IM someone but did not have the ability to install America Online (AOL) Instant Messenger (AIM) on the computer you were using? AOL recognizes that many schools and businesses do not allow you to install your own software, so it created a program named "AIM Express."

AIM Express is exactly like AIM except you download a Java client from *http://www.aim.com/get_aim/express* and run it without any installation. The look and feel is almost identical to traditional AIM, except that you do not have to worry about leaving a disk and registry trail. Just make sure that you do not accidentally save your password in the browser for others to find.

Limiting Evidence with Secrecy and Stealth

Venturing out of the house every time you want to use the Internet is not always practical, and for many applications, you cannot get away with installing them on removable or virtual drives. For these cases, the best advice we can give you is to use constant vigilance. In other words, *erase what you can, hide what you cannot erase, and encrypt what you cannot hide.*

Erasing Cookies and Internet Files

As mentioned in Chapters 6 and 7, histories, cookies, and caches can be erased using almost the same steps. With Mozilla Firefox, you can access this option by clicking on **Tools | Options |** and the **Privacy** tab. This tab opens up a window that gives you the ability to delete individual components, or you can click on the **Clear All** button (see Figure 11.6).

Figure 11.6 Erasing Cookies and Temporary Internet Files with Mozilla Firefox

The same can be done with Microsoft Internet Explorer by clicking on **Tools | Internet Options |** and the **General** tab. In the "Temporary Internet files" section you can click on the **Delete Cookies** and **Delete Files** buttons. Likewise, in the "History" section you can click on the **Clear History** button. To keep your Web surfing private, be sure to always clear this evidence from your browser.

NOTE

In Chapter 5, we discussed the "super hidden" directory found in *C:\Documents and Settings\<User Name>\Local Settings\Temporary Internet Files\Content.IE5*. In addition to being well hidden, this folder contains cached Web pages and images from Internet Explorer, and it is not automatically cleared out when you clear Internet Explorer's cache. Therefore, if you are clearing out the cache, do not forget to manually browse there (you have to enter the path in the address bar) and delete all of the files.

Erasing History with Tweak UI

One problem with privacy and Microsoft Windows is its lengthy collection of history lists saved for nearly everything. As an option for users that prefer secrecy, Microsoft offers Tweak UI from Windows XP PowerToys. Download it from *www.microsoft.com/windowsxp/downloads/powertoys/xppowertoys.mspx* and search through all of the options for those that fit your needs and preferences. Make sure that **Clear document history on exit** is checked under the "Explorer" settings and that both **Maintain document history** and **Maintain network history** are unchecked. See Figure 11.7 for an example of suggested configuration options.

Figure 11.7 Configuring Tweak UI to Clear Document and Network Histories

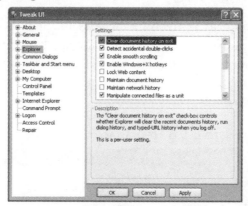

Erasing Files with PGP Wipe Utilities

This section introduces the concept of "secure" deleting. To prevent erased files from being recovered (as demonstrated in Chapter 6), utilize a utility such as the one included in Pretty Good Privacy (PGP) freeware version 6.5.8, which can be downloaded from *http://web.mit.edu/network/pgp.html*. There are newer versions of the software available, but 6.5.8 is the last completely free version with full functionality.

The encryption software included in this package is utilized throughout later sections of this chapter, but for now we will use only its "Wipe" capability. Once the software is installed, you can safely delete a file so that it is not easily recoverable by right clicking on the file (or directory) from the Explorer screen and selecting **PGP | Wipe**. Alternatively, you can use the "eraser" icon on the PGP Tools menu launched from **Start | PGP | PGP Tools**. Once the file to be deleted is chosen, both methods open a confirmation window warning you that the selected files will be permanently deleted (see Figure 11.8).

Figure 11.8 PGP Freeware 6.5.8 Wipe Utility Demonstration

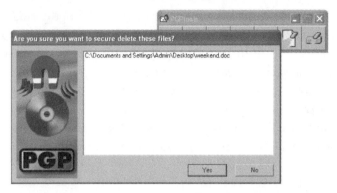

Similarly, this version of PGP freeware includes an application called "Free Space Wiper" (see Figure 11.9) that is designed to cleanse any lingering files that were previously deleted by non-secure means (e.g., the default Windows "Delete" application). "Wipe" every sensitive file you delete from your hard drive so that it cannot be recovered by anyone else.

Figure 11.9 PGP Freeware 6.5.8 Free Space Wipe Utility

At this point, we have illustrated several techniques for excluding and removing sensitive data from being obtained by someone spying on you. However, some things cannot be hidden and must remain in plain sight. For those items, we will teach you methods of encryption and steganography. One problem with using advanced techniques is that if they are detected they indicate that you are intentionally trying to hide something. An intelligence officer traveling overseas on vacation with a digital camera is one thing, but an intelligence officer caught with a secret concealed camera is a completely different circumstance. Be careful using these, and make sure that you are ready to give a well-thought-out cover story if confronted.

> **NOTE**
>
> Consult the latest U.S. export regulations related to encryption at *www.bxa.doc.gov/Encryption* prior to using, posting, or transferring any software containing encryption outside of the U.S.

Encrypting E-mail

There are several encryption possibilities when it comes to e-mail, but the option that we feel is best suited for the casual home user is PGP freeware 6.5.8. In addition to providing the disk-wiping utilities discussed previously, PGP freeware 6.5.8 also provides a robust mechanism for securely sending e-mail that is easy to use. As we will demonstrate, this integrates easily into several e-mail clients such as Microsoft Outlook and Outlook Express.

Generating, Exporting, and Importing Keys

Using encrypted e-mail comes with some initial overhead in the process of key generation and exchange, but the benefits of sending private e-mail far outweigh the minor inconvenience of this process. To make things easier, we have outlined the steps that you need to take to accomplish this.

1. **Download PGP**. If you have not already done so, download version 6.5.8 of PGP freeware from *http://web.mit.edu/network/pgp.html*.

2. **Create a public/private key pair for yourself**. Click **Start | All Programs | PGP | PGPkeys** and accept the default options. Next you will be asked to enter a pass phrase (see Figure 11.10). Make sure that you select something that is easy for you to memorize, as you will *not* be able to recover this (or read *anything* encrypted with this key) if you forget it.

3. **Export your key.** Your key must be exported so that others can use it. This is done using the same PGPkeys program as in the last step. Right click on the entry that belongs to you and select **Export** (see Figure 11.11).

Figure 11.10 PGP 6.5.8 Freeware Key Generation Utility

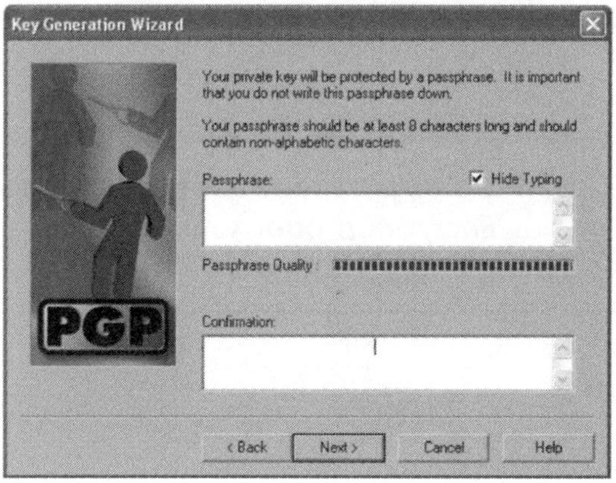

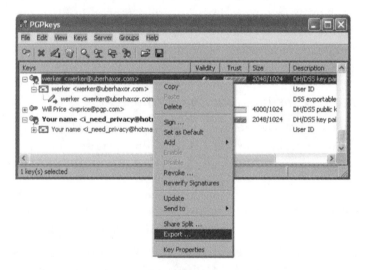

Figure 11.11 Export Your Public Key Using PGP Freeware

4. Selecting Export causes a second window to open, which will ask where you would like the key to be saved. Once your public key has been saved to a file, send it as an e-mail attachment to anyone that you want to use it with. In turn, you must ask that person for a copy of their public key so that you can send/receive encrypted e-mail to/from them. When you receive a key, you can import it by using the same PGPkeys utility. From the top menu select **Keys | Import** (see Figure 11.12).

Figure 11.12 Import PGP Public Keys Received from Others

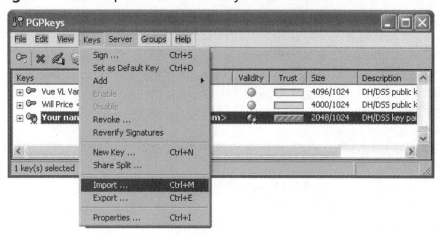

5. If the key you received from the other person is not signed, it is considered invalid and cannot be used to encrypt or decrypt e-mail. In this case, the circle in the **Validity** column will be grayed out for that user. If you are not certain of its validity, ask the sender to digitally sign the key and verify the signature. Otherwise, if you are certain that it can be trusted, you can sign it yourself. To do this, from the PGPkeys menu select **Keys | Sign**. As Figure 11.13 demonstrates, this prompts you with a second window that explains the process.

Figure 11.13 Signing an Imported Key

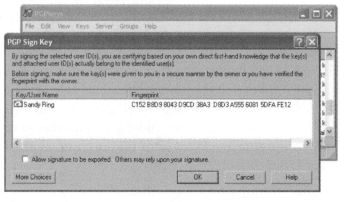

When you click **OK**, a third window appears that will prompt you for your pass phrase so that the key can be signed (and therefore considered valid). Once a key is considered valid, it can be used to send and receive e-mail.

Using PGP Freeware with E-mail Clients

Although there are more recent releases, we demonstrate this version of PGP freeware because of its nearly seamless interface with Microsoft Outlook and Outlook Express. A message can be sent encrypted using this application in nearly the same way as sending a plaintext message. Create the message as normal, but when you are finished select the **Encrypt (PGP)** option from the drop-down tool bar on the right (see Figure 11.14).

Figure 11.14 Encrypting a Message in Microsoft Outlook Express Using PGP Freeware 6.5.8

Once you have done this, click the **Send** button to securely e-mail the message. A window will prompt you to select all of the keys that you wish to include in the encryption (see Figure 11.15).

By default, the window will have an entry for the key that matches the e-mail address of the recipient. However, if you want others to be able to view this message you can also drag their names down into the "Recipient Selection" window. When all of the keys have been included, click **OK** and the encrypted message will be sent to the recipient(s) (e.g., the encrypted version of the ice cream message in Figure 11.14 can be seen in Figure 11.16).

Figure 11.15 Selecting Encryption Keys for Outgoing E-mail in Microsoft Outlook Express

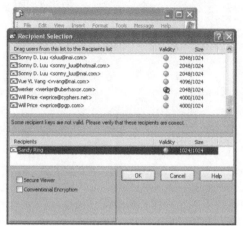

> **NOTE**
>
> Unless you specify otherwise, e-mail messages sent to a recipient are not encrypted using your public encryption key. This means that even though you are the originator of the message, you must also drag your name down into the "Recipient Selection" window if you want to view them in the "Sent" folder.

Figure 11.16 Example of a Message Encrypted Using PGP Freeware 6.5.8

```
-----BEGIN PGP MESSAGE-----
Version: PGPfreeware 6.5.8 for non-commercial use <http://www.pgp.com>

qANQR1DBwE4D0vnWUNPqS98QBACELLxgG8kQ56XTzrBR1evBsypq2GEznjqTiIjo
19n/92g6FHtKi5oTf5Tlugkinzf4Qc19lgryior66234Eoc31/wZ9QInbYDbyfBn
i5cFkJ3mAEgqy5ZOGyO+7WzfRmZdcVkPT6uCJ193rGQZv1tEy8U7rJzTPlR9x94v
GHhvaQP/SpEu7F19v8iTDAllvFPfdSDoUbghf+0w/o0m0CdHoKt/Fos5mdnulF4i
CCL/9g6f+K3gSEFYVkHd7uOgSO8WR56c53mNmB6WExcUTIut9KkfBBsG5Bn8uYad
hNvVoJZ7wYTzhI+JpKDGQGmxbBrcGX2LQ+D4oK9lngp5DaFxFqPJbE3EcEbetw/P
LMHsOlDIrqU4T8BicPUv6S75kdcPVMHZtL+WH70joy4PSEPrqvZcz3PYEwQo8CrY
I6t9VIBJa834kHUmSk+DXV8jaNhQHKZqrSJjew8I+bFXjynB0eaw1FYysxbrvvkM
FNSJ2Q==
=sP4T
-----END PGP MESSAGE-----
```

Notes from the Underground…

History Behind PGP

Philip R. Zimmermann released the first version of PGP on June 5, 1991, from the U.S., which was quickly distributed among several Bulletin Board System (BBS) networks. Soon afterward, he was notified by RSA Data Security Inc. that PGP was in violation of their patented algorithm. Approximately one year later, the next major release of this tool made its way outside of the U.S., which prompted U.S. Customs to launch an investigation because of its alleged violation of the regulation of non-exportable weapons.

In the meantime, Zimmerman sold the rights to the commercial version of PGP to ViaCrypt, which happened to hold a license for the RSA algorithm. This same year (1993), they released ViaCrypt PGP 2.4 for commercial use within the U.S. In 1994, the Massachusetts Institute of Technology (MIT) struck an agreement with RSA and Zimmerman to distribute a freeware version of PGP for non-commercial use, which is demonstrated in this book.

Likewise, you can decrypt e-mail messages in much the same manner. Most e-mail clients send the encrypted message as an attachment that ends with *.asc*. When a message like this arrives, click on the attachment and either **Open** it or **Save** it to disk, depending on your preference. If you choose to **Open** it, you will be prompted to enter your secret pass phrase before you will be allowed to read the message (see Figure 11.17).

Figure 11.17 Receiving and Reading PGP Encrypted Messages in Outlook Express

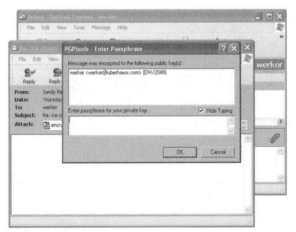

Other freeware versions of PGP exist, including GNU-licensed version GPG, which is available at *www.gnupg.org*. (We encourage you to experiment and decide which version best suits your needs.) Encrypting e-mail is good practice and helps maintain privacy both on the computer itself (if messages are stored encrypted) and across the network as messages are sent.

Encrypting Files with XP

Microsoft Windows XP Professional (not Home Edition) comes equipped with the ability to encrypt files and folders with its default installation. This is done using Encrypted File System (EFS), which operates by marking files that you want encrypted with a special attribute that tells the OS that the file should be stored encrypted. This attribute can be set by right clicking on the file, selecting **Properties**, clicking on **Advanced**, and checking the **Encrypt contents to secure data** box (see Figure 11.18).

Figure 11.18 File Encryption Capability Built into Windows XP Professional

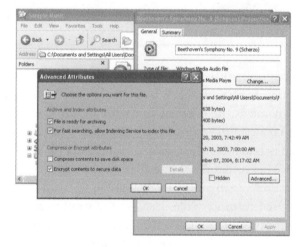

This encryption is based on public key cryptography and only works when the file is on the New Technology File System (NTFS), although it will protect the file even if the disk is mounted remotely or from a different OS. If the file is transferred to another (non-NTFS) system, it will be decrypted. Also, since the ability to encrypt the file is tied to your account, anyone who accesses your account can read your encrypted files. In general, we feel this encryption method is too limiting; we only recommend it if the measures discussed next are not an option.

Encrypting Files with PGP

Another use of PGP freeware is its ability to secure files using strong encryption. Once the PGP application is installed, you can do this by selecting the file you wish to encrypt, right clicking on it, and selecting **PGP | Encrypt** (see Figure 11.19).

Figure 11.19 Encrypting Files Using PGP Freeware 6.5.8

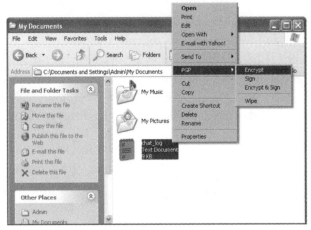

A second prompt appears that asks you to drag the names of the recipients into the bottom window (see Figure 11.15). When you are finished, a second file is generated with the same name as the original, but with an *.asc* extension. In our example, this process creates a file named *chat_log.txt.asc*. It is your responsibility to securely wipe out the original file (*chat_log.txt*) using **PGP | Wipe** (discussed previously in this chapter). This is useful because files can be encrypted using multiple recipients and sent securely as an alternative to encrypting entire e-mail messages. Similarly, this can be used to protect files that are transmitted across networks through other mechanisms such as via Web sites. This type of encryption is also good for files you want hidden and protected on your computer.

Encrypting Storage

Entire portions of a hard drive can be protected with encryption using an application such as the TrueCrypt cryptographic file system (available from *truecrypt.sourceforge.net*). Once installed, TrueCrypt is easy to configure and use. Configuring the application takes place in five straightforward steps.

1. **Specify a volume.** Select a drive letter and press **Create Volume**. This will create a window asking you to enter a location into the field (see Figure 11.20). When you are satisfied, click **Next**.

Figure 11.20 Select a Volume Name, Type, and Location Using TrueCrypt Configuration

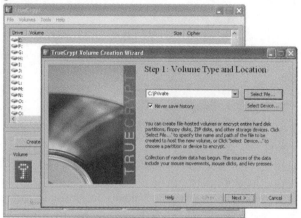

2. **Select an algorithm.** Select an encryption algorithm and click **Next** (see Figure 11.21). Be careful with your selection; some of the algorithms included require a special license prior to legal use. We recommend sticking with the default (Blowfish) encryption.

Figure 11.21 Selecting the Encryption Algorithm

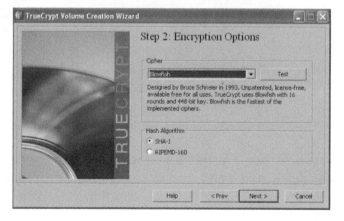

3. **Designate volume size.** Next you must specify the amount of space you want to set aside for the EFS (see Figure 11.22). It is important to note that this is an immediate use of space and not an upper limit. The entire amount of space is consumed when the volume is created, even though you do not technically have files utilizing the space in its entirety. The amount of space that you select is dependent on your anticipated need and the amount of free space that is available.

Figure 11.22 Designating the Volume Size

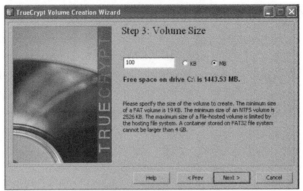

4. **Choose a password.** This password must be between 12 and 64 characters long (see Figure 11.23). When matching passwords have been entered, continue by pressing the **Next** button.

Figure 11.23 Choosing a Password

5. **Volume format.** The final step is to press the **Format** button presented on the next screen. This may take several minutes depending on the size of the file system you selected. In this case, it took less than 10 seconds because of the small volume size.

At this point, the volume named *C:\Private*, which is 100MB in size, has been created and encrypted using the special password. To use this volume, it must be mounted, which can be done using the main TrueCrypt interface (see Figure 11.24).

Figure 11.24 Using a TrueCrypt Partition

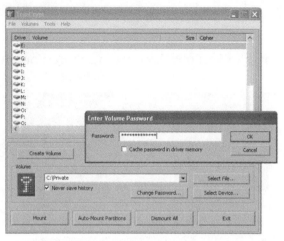

Beyond providing a means of encrypting individual files, this can be used for more robust purposes such as encrypting folders used by e-mail (or banking application) clients. As discussed in Chapter 6, these folders can be identified for each application and changed by selecting Tools | Options | Maintenance | Store Folder. Figure 11.25 demonstrates how you can change your folder for Outlook Express to now be stored in the mounted EFS (drive E:).

Figure 11.25 Configuring Outlook Express to Store E-mail on the Encrypted Drive

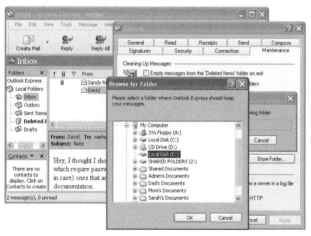

When you are finished accessing the data on the encrypted drive, click **Dismount All** from the TrueCrypt interface, which will prevent others from accessing your data

(see Figure 11.26). In this case, the encrypted drive has been unmounted; therefore, when Outlook Express is launched it is not able to access any of the securely stored e-mail.

Figure 11.26 Attempt to Securely Access Data Stored on an Unmounted TrueCrypt Drive

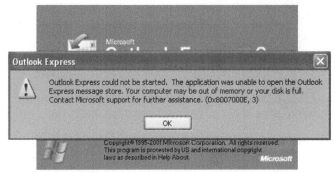

Experiment with which applications that can and cannot operate with encrypted drives. Encrypted drives are a good way to maintain information securely because they do not require the overhead associated with encrypted individual files.

Encrypting Chat

Even though many people divulge some of their greatest secrets during an IM chat session, previous chapters have shown that this is not secure and leaves your messages vulnerable to spying. In most clients, messages are sent in plaintext by default, which means that anyone with a network sniffer between you and the recipient can retrieve your messages. To help prevent this, the following sections demonstrate three available encryption options.

Trillian

Trillian is a multiuse chat client that is available for download at *www.trillian.cc*. Unlike AIM, Trillian can send and receive messages on other networks such as MSN or Yahoo. After Trillian is installed, encryption can be enabled through the "Preferences" menu by checking both boxes in the "SecureIM" section (see Figure 11.27).

Figure 11.27 Enabling IM Encryption in the Trillian Chat Application

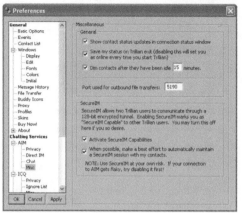

AOL versus Trillian

AOL Attempted to Disrupt Trillian

Despite multiple attempts by AOL to block Trillian traffic from traveling across their network and interfacing with AOL clients, Trillian has repeatedly released new versions that are capable of bypassing disruptions. A past blocking attempt greeted Trillian users with the message:

AOL Instant Messenger: You have been disconnected from the AOL Instant Message Service (SM) for accessing the AOL network using unauthorized software. You can download a FREE, fully featured, and authorized client, here http://www.aol.com/aim/download2.htm.

You can read more of the saga between AOL vs. Trillian at www.geek.com/news/geeknews/2002feb/gee20020218010316.htm.

In order for someone else to communicate with you using Trillian, they must install and enable Trillian SecureIM. Once this is done, both parties can communicate without fear of observers snooping on their communications (see Figure 11.28). Note the lock icon in the bottom center of the chat dialog; this is how Trillian shows that it has established an encrypted session.

Figure 11.28 Trillian Client Demonstrating the SecureIM Capability

Gaim

A second option with a similar look and feel to AOL's AIM client is Gaim. Like Trillian, Gaim is free and can be obtained at *http://gaim.sourceforge.net*. While this application itself does not come with encryption capabilities by default, you can obtain an encryption plug-in for Gaim at *www.sourceforge.net/projects/gaim-encryption*. To use Gaim with encryption, download and install both the client and the encryption plug-in. To configure encryption, from the Gaim client select **Preferences | Plugins**, and check the **Gaim-encryption** box (see Figure 11.29).

Figure 11.29 Gaim Client Encryption Configuration

Once the plug-in is configured, encrypted messages can be sent to and received from users that also have Gaim encryption installed and configured. You can verify

that messages are being sent and received encrypted by the status of the "lock" buttons on the chat dialogue box (see Figure 11.30).

> **NOTE**
>
> Although both Gaim and Trillian clients can communicate using standard IM protocol, Gaim encryption does not operate the same as Trillian encryption; therefore, these two clients cannot be used to securely communicate together. In order to securely chat with someone using Gaim encryption, you must use the same client (and vice versa).

Figure 11.30 Encrypted Chat Dialogue Using Gaim

Skype

Skype provides low-cost long distance telephone calls over the Internet through their client (available at *www.skype.com*) and for noncommercial users, it provides free encrypted IM and voice chat. Skype does not participate with the AOL IM network; therefore, anyone that you want to securely chat with must have a Skype account (see Figure 11.31).

The biggest difference between this client and other chat applications is that if you click on the telephone in the left-hand corner of the chat window, Skype establishes a secure voice connection between the two parties (see Figure 11.32). In addition, there is a commercial Skype plug-in called SkypeOut that allows you to call traditional telephone numbers using Skype. By using Skype, you are avoiding two problems that may plague you if you use a traditional telephone. First, you avoid any traditional phone taps on your side, since you will be using the Internet to make your outgoing phone calls. Even if you use Skype over a dial–up modem, its protocol will make it much more difficult to decipher later. Second, by using Skype in place of a real phone, your call record is modified. Calls that you do not want other people to know about can be done over Skype, where there is absolutely no record. With SkypeOut you merely pay for minutes, so there is no record of the numbers you call.

Figure 11.31 Encrypted Chat Using Skype

Figure 11.32 Encrypted Voice-over-IP (VOIP) Using Skype

Steganography

Steganography is another good way to hide information in files, either over e-mail or in chat. The difference between steganography and encryption is that steganography *hides* information whereas encryption *secures* information. Encrypted files visibly look protected (see Figure 11.16) and steganography hides information by subtly placing it in ways that are not visibly apparent. For example, imagine the following e-mail message.

Hi David. **I'm coming** over to see your new house **really** soon. **Call me** around **two S**aturday **even**ing and we can **set** a **night.**

Even though it does not look protected, it contains the secret message: ***Hi Molly. Call me at seven at night.*** Sound and image files are ideal places to hide information because subtle changes in them are not visible. In addition, because their data is not stored in a human-readable plaintext format, the information stored can be encrypted for additional protection.

Freeware tools such as S-tools, that easily drag and drop secret messages into files, are available at *www.snapfiles.com/get/stools.html*. Most of these tools offer additional security by using password encryption in addition to their hiding capability. However, we recommend that sensitive data be protected with strong encryption (such as the kind demonstrated with PGP) before they are hidden using steganography. Figure 11.33 demonstrates how a password gets added to the image of a boat containing a secret message.

Figure 11.33 Using S-Tools to Secretly Implant a Message within a Photograph

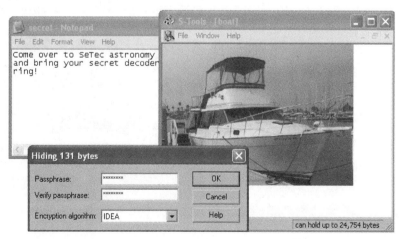

Dragging the secret file into the image causes a prompt to appear asking you to specify a password and encryption algorithm. This password must be known by whomever you want to open the file if you intend to use it as a secret storage mechanism locally on your computer.

The benefit to using steganography over encryption is that it already has a built-in cover story. For example, imagine an e-mail from the owner of this boat with the picture attached. This e-mail could be completely legitimate and contain information such as:

- For Sale: Marina del Rey, CA

- Twin Volvo gas engines, four cylinder 140s with 1050 hrs running

- Auto-pilot

- Hot water heater, electric when dock side and engine heated when cruising

- Battery charger

- Trim-tabs

- Two VHF radios

To the casual (or even well-trained) observer, nothing appears to be unusual or secretive about this message. In Figure 11.34 there are two images that appear to be identical; however, the image on the left is an original and the image on the right contains the secret message from Figure 11.33. Any recipient that knows the password and has a copy of the S-tools can read the secret message from the e-mail.

Figure 11.34 Images of an Original Message and a Steganographic Message

Steganography also lends itself well to a concept referred to in the spy community as "dead drops." Although the secret message is hidden in the boat picture, the

mere act of sending an e-mail directly to another makes a connection between the two parties. If you want to secretly communicate with someone else, consider "dropping" the image at a third-party location such as an online auction, newsgroup, or Web site. The intended recipient could see the picture while searching for boats and secretly decode the message. If done carefully and using a believable cover, catching this method of communication is nearly impossible.

Avoid Keyloggers

One trick to avoiding keyloggers is to not use the keyboard at all. While this sounds impossible, it is indeed doable. The technique for doing this is definitely inconvenient, but it is a useful secret to know in the event that you are confident someone is monitoring your keystrokes. The Microsoft Windows OS comes prepackaged with an application to do this.

1. Click **Start | All Programs | Accessories | Accessibility | On-Screen Keyboard** to launch the application. This keyboard can be used to do anything that the regular keyboard does, but without the worry of being logged in (see Figure 11.35). Instead of touching the keyboard, you use your mouse to "click" on the keys.

Figure 11.35 On-Screen Keyboards that Help Avoid Keystroke Logging

While using this avoids keystroke capturing, keep in mind that many of the logging programs (such as the one demonstrated in Chapter 6) also capture screenshots; therefore, you may not be completely safe from monitoring.

How to Tell If You Are Being Watched

You have learned how to undo and defeat everything that we have taught you. However, we feel that teaching this without teaching counter-spying tricks would be like releasing a deadly virus without an antidote. We want to arm you with the knowledge and ability to defeat every means of collecting information so that you know what to do if you become someone's mark. First, you must determine if you are actually being spied on. The following steps will help give you confidence in determining this, but like many things discussed in this book, there is no 100 percent way to know for certain. In the Central Intelligence Agency (CIA), it was often said that all the bad spies are found, but you will never know about the good ones.

Examine Your Computer

Your computer is the most obvious place to look for evidence that you have been spied on. Most methods of spying leave behind some clues. If you think your computer is being monitored, carefully examine it for evidence of unsavory activity. Treat it like you would treat a machine you are monitoring.

When examining your computer there are several different things you should look for, including but not limited to, hardware keystroke loggers, newly installed software, duplicate files, new accounts, and recently run programs and file lists. Changes in multiple fields can be a strong indication that you are being monitored.

Newly Installed Software

Newly installed software can be an indicator of suspicious activity on your computer. Several of our spy techniques require us to install software on our target's computer; therefore, you can assume that someone spying on you is doing the same. There are three primary places to check for software that has been installed on your computer. The first is the Start menu, where some programs put items for easy access. Only the most amateur spy would carelessly install software that leaves items on the Start menu, but it can happen, and checking is an effortless task. Merely open **Start | All Programs** and look for new software that you do not remember installing. Sometimes, a small dialog box will pop up in the Start menu informing you that "New Software Is Installed."

The next place to look for software is in **Start | Control Panel | Add or Remove Programs**, which returns a list of software that is registered with the OS, and any unusual software that has been placed on your machine. You can also remove the unwanted software from your system at this location.

Finally, open Explorer, browse to your *C:* drive, and look inside your "Program Files" folder, which holds almost all of the programs that are installed on your machine. Examine every folder carefully so that you have a good idea of what is on your machine.

WARNING

As you prowl your computer's hard disk looking for suspicious software packages, carefully study them before you delete them or take any other extreme action. Microsoft Windows and many other legitimate programs sometimes put oddly named executables in unusual places. Before you delete anything, make a quick Google search on the item to see what it is. Odds are that other people have encountered it and posted something about it. Use caution; otherwise, deleting critical system files could render your computer unusable.

Duplicate Files

Duplicate files are an indicator of unusual activity on your computer. Someone who is collecting your e-mail, chat logs, or other documents may be making a backup in case you ever delete the originals. It is a good idea to occasionally search all of your hard drives to look for all *.doc* (Microsoft Word) and *.pst* (Outlook) files.

New Accounts

Another thing to watch for is whether someone spying on you has created a new account, either to covertly install software or to provide them with a method of continual access, should you ever change your password. You can easily take stock of the accounts you have on your computer by checking **Start | Control Panel | User Accounts**. On most machines, there is usually only one account per unique user and a by-default disabled Guest account.

Recent Lists

Recent lists can also yield clues as to what is happening on your computer. The first one to examine is the recent program list, which appears in the left-hand column of the Start menu. This list shows all of the programs that were recently run; anything appearing here that you have not used recently or do not use frequently can be viewed as a warning sign that someone is running software on your computer.

Recent file lists show what files have been recently accessed. The first and most important one to view is on the Start menu, which shows recently accessed documents and other types of files. You should also open up programs like Microsoft Word and Works to see what files were opened up recently. Find every program that can be used to view "interesting" files, and look at its recent list. If the lists contain files that you know you have not accessed recently, there is a chance that someone found the data interesting and viewed it on your machine.

Use Security Tools

There are many security tools available, both commercial and free, that can help you identify and trace a potential spy. Firewalls and virus scanners are invaluable for catching dangerous programs, and they are also good at catching spy software. You can also search the Web and look for companies that offer different products that are designed to locate spy software. Since we have not evaluated many commercial spy software detection packages, we cannot vouch for their effectiveness; however, remember that any single piece of software is just one part of the puzzle, and should not be your only method of checking your computer. Use your best judgment and the other techniques mentioned here to supplement any software you purchase to keep yourself spy-software free.

Spy on Yourself

The same techniques you use to watch your mark can help you find a potential spy when turned against yourself. The more information you have on your personal computer, the more likely you will have information revealing the presence of a spy, if there is one.

Log Keystrokes

A keystroke log is a great tool for sniffing out possible spies and giving an accurate picture of what has occurred on your computer. Occasional review lets you know if there is any unusual activity, since any keystrokes you do not immediately recognize are usually signs of activity on your computer.

While this is a very powerful method, it has several angles that should be considered before adoption. A keystroke log on a typical computer, depending on usage, can become huge. Collecting all of the keystrokes on a machine does no good if you do not take the time to analyze them. Since you are creating a log of all of your activity, you are now doing the spy's job for them by handing them the information they are probably looking for.

Sniff Your Traffic

Sniffing your own network traffic is another good technique. Collect daily logs of all traffic on your machine and occasionally analyze it with Ethereal and OWNS. When examining the traffic, look for unusual Web connections and e-mail messages, which is how many commercial spying implants communicate. They transmit your private data to their operator using e-mail or the Web. It is also a good idea to look for Virtual Network Computer (VNC), Back Orifice, or Norton Remote Desktop connections, which are all methods by which your computer can be remotely controlled.

Similar to keystroke logging, sniffing your traffic can be a double-edged sword. While its collection gives you a wealth of information that can be used to protect yourself, it is also the very information you are trying to protect from others. A packet dump from your personal machine will contain all of your e-mail, Web browsing, IM, and other online activities. Complexity is another issue; while a keystroke log is relatively easy to go through and understand, packet dumps are not as straightforward. It takes quite a bit of training to be able to successfully analyze a packet dump. Even tools like OWNS that can automatically classify traffic from packet dumps are not sophisticated to the point where they make traffic analysis a trivial task.

Treat this as one tool in your arsenal for catching spies. Since it is a difficult method to use, only use it when other methods or signs have aroused your suspicions and you are trying to home in on a specific tool or person. When used correctly, this can be a great technique for discovering how someone is spying on you.

Passive Forensics

To perform passive forensics, select **Start | Search | All files or folders | More Advanced Options** and check **Search files and folders.** Next, click **When was it modified**, specify dates, and change the drop down from **Modified Date** to **Accessed Date** (see Figure 11.36).

Figure 11.36 Searching by Access Dates

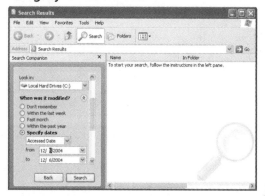

Set Traps

Intelligence agencies such as the CIA have used traps as a means of validating their assets for years. The simplest example is the spymaster who hands his asset a closed briefcase and requests that he take it unopened to a third party; the briefcase is trapped and designed to indicate whether it was opened in transit. An opened briefcase means that the asset did not follow the directions of his spymaster (a career-ending mistake). Even more alarming is the fact that it could mean he is a double agent attempting to gleam intelligence and "methods of operation" from the spymaster. In practice, though, this example has one crucial flaw: *it is not natural*. On a day-to-day basis, how many people do you know that hand their confidential briefcase to a relative stranger for courier?

Setting a trap that is not natural will fail because it is obvious to the targeted party that it is a set up and it divulges your operational intentions. Instead of concocting something new as your trap, draw from subtleties that already exist and are a natural part of your usage.

Internet History Search Trap

The default view of files is very different from the one shown in Figure 11.37. After launching Explorer, select **View | List** to list additional information beyond the name and icon of each entry. Next, click on **View | Choose Details** and check both the **Date Created** and the **Date Accessed** boxes.

Figure 11.37 Access Date on an Application's Binary Indicates When it Was Last Used

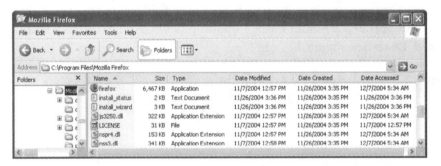

In this case, we are observing the directory for the Web browser, Firefox. You can see that the application itself (the first entry) was last accessed at 5:34 AM on 12/7/2004. This would be particularly interesting if we knew that we were not awake at that time.

Because it is trivial to change the date on Microsoft Windows, an even better experiment is to set a trap. When you have finished using the computer, explore this directory, write down the exact access time, and take it with you. Before launching the application, browse to this directory again and check to see if the time has changed. If it has, someone else has used the browser and may or may not have tried to access cache and cookie information from it.

E-mail Access Trap

A similar trap can be done on directories that contain mailboxes. In the example in Figure 11.35, we saw that the folders for our user account "Admin" in Outlook Express were last accessed at 6:06AM on the same date (see Figure 11.38).

Figure 11.38 Access Date on a Database Can Confirm the Existence of a Spy

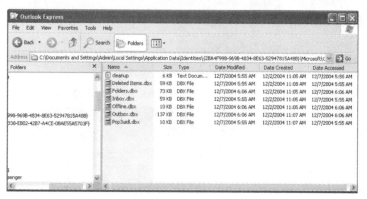

When you have finished accessing e-mail for the day, write down the time and check it when you come back.

Honey Tokens

At this point, you know that legitimate applications can be observed for changes in their access time. Now, consider a slightly different concept: *honey tokens*. The idea of a honey token is to create a file that has the look and feel of a legitimate file, but never access it. For example, using the *Notepad.exe* application, you can create a file that resembles an Excel spreadsheet with relative ease (see Figure 11.39).

This file is populated with what appears to be legitimate information, but is actually a trap. In this case, there are two ways to check the access of this file. The first is to monitor for the file name *Purchases.xls* in Excel's recently used documents list. For example, in Figure 11.40, the file "Purchases" is listed on the right hand side. Since this file was created using Notepad instead of Excel, it should not be listed, which indicates that someone else opened the file. We can now analyze the access date on the file to determine when it was accessed.

Figure 11.39 Honey Tokens Look Legitimate, but Should Never be Accessed

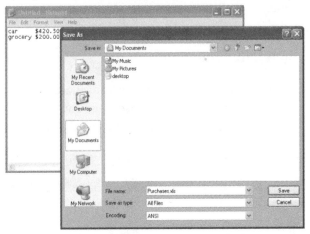

Figure 11.40 Honey Token *Purchases.xls* Created by *Notepad.exe*

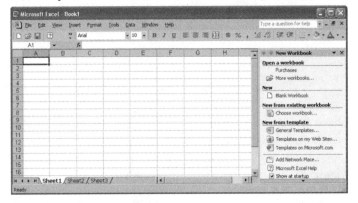

Look for Outside Clues

Someone spying on you may not be doing it through your computer. There are many other signs that can indicate that you are being spied on. This generally works when you have close access to those who you think may be spying on you.

Are your things, especially papers and other documents, always where you left them? Does your spouse "accidentally" open your mail or pick up a phone extension more often than chance would indicate? Are you interrogated at length about numbers on your phone bill or items on your credit card statements? Does your spouse question you about your whereabouts and drop by your office just to see that you are there? These are all behaviors that indicate that you are being closely watched.

In addition to the behavior-based signs, there are also physical clues to look for. What type of material is your spouse or kids reading? Have they taken an interest in computers, spent an unusual amount of time on the family computer, or started reading lots of computer "security" books. Look through credit card statements for unusual purchases, especially those from online companies. When you find them, make sure you go online and check what type of organization a service was purchased from.

Trust Your Gut

You will never know if a really good spy is watching you; however, the previously mentioned techniques will give you a head start into investigating. One of the most important things to do is to "trust your gut." In many cases, "a bad feeling about this" has uncovered a well-planned spy operation. Gut instincts are a spy's worst fear, as they are a very important factor that cannot be planned for or modeled.

While this is the last technique mentioned, it is usually the first one a person uses. A gut feeling is a good start and can lead you to using more complex technical means. Once your suspicions are aroused you can look for other clues, set traps, and spy on yourself to try to find your pursuer. Although we feel your instincts are one of your strongest tools, we also caution you to be careful and not get overly obsessed.

How to React If You Are a Target

Once you discover that you are being targeted, it is time to determine exactly how you will react to their efforts. This is important since it can have a profound effect on their spying operation and your relationship with the spying individual or organization. When you realize that you are being watched you have a multitude of options, but they all boil down to either avoiding your spy, confronting your spy, or maintaining the status quo. Either choice poses many possible issues. Being spied on can be a very emotional and touchy subject, and there is rarely a good way to handle the situation. It is important to pick the action that will result in the best solution for your particular situation.

Avoiding Your Spy

Someone is spying on you and you want to avoid them. Instead of confronting your spy, this choice involves modifying your behavior so that you avoid the spy's techniques. In order to successfully avoid a spy, you must be fully aware of their capabilities and methods. Any mistake on your part when evaluating this can cause you to fail, make you a more suspicious target, and alert your spy that you are on to them.

Once you have identified your spy and their methods, you can practice the age-old technique of feeding them false information. This is a very useful tool in your counter-spy arsenal. You can cause your spy to expend time and effort on as many wild goose chases as you can design.

Maintaining Status Quo

When you decide to maintain the status quo, you are sure that you are being spied on, but since you are not doing anything wrong you choose to neither avoid nor confront your spy. You may choose to do this because you have discovered your spy's methods, and know that they are not catching anything. Forcing a spy to continue their operations, especially when the mark is aware and can control the information, can cause the spy to expend time and energy on a pointless exercise. This option is generally the easiest on your part, as it requires doing pretty much nothing new.

Confront Your Spy

Confronting your spy can result in more dramatic scenarios and will most likely put an end to the spying. During a confrontation, let them know that you know they are violating your privacy and covertly monitoring you. As mentioned, this can be a very dramatic event; several things can play out here. If you are doing something of concern and have been "caught in the act," now would be a good time to handle the issues. Although further denial at this point is generally useless, it is your prerogative (e.g., the CIA will never discuss matters of intelligence or classified documents, regardless of their authenticity or how they were obtained). Changing the questionable behavior that brought someone to spy on you in the first place is also a method of a gentle confrontation. A dramatic change in behavior is likely to alert the spy that something has occurred and that they have been discovered.

If you feel that the spying is unwarranted, a direct confrontation may be more appropriate. In this situation, everything is brought out into the open: your suspicions and evidence of being spied on, and your activity, right or wrong. Accusing someone of spying is a very strong accusation; if you select this path, be prepared for all of the issues that can occur.

Identifying Who is Spying on You

Harder than determining you are being spied on is finding out who is doing the spying; good spies are very difficult to detect. Now that you are fairly sure you are being spied on, it is time to determine by whom. This is a question that may not always be answered satisfactorily, if at all. Many times just knowing that you are being spied on may be enough, but when it is not, there are several steps you can take to narrow down your list of possible suspects.

Make a List of Suspects

Make a list of all of the people and organizations you think may be spying on you, including your spouse, your children, or a private detective. Your spy could also be a hacker or some other complete stranger.

Determine Motive and Means

Now that you have built an exhaustive list of those you think may spy on you, narrow it down by examining each entity and looking for their motive and their means. While some entities on your list may be interested in spying on you, they may lack the means (e.g., your children may not have physical access to your computer or the technology to set up a complete spy operation). Other entities may have the capability, but not the desire.

Search for Evidence

Use the methods we have discussed to search for evidence that you have been spied on. The type of evidence you find should reveal clues as to your spy's capabilities (e.g., you might expect a spouse or child to use a simple homemade or commercial tool, and a company might monitor you with a popular Spyware program).

When looking at your computer you may see that some of your more interesting files, or e-mails have recently been opened and viewed. You may want to stop and consider the cause before you accuse someone of spying. Perhaps your wife was looking in your e-mail to see what you talked with your friends about to better decide your birthday present. Maybe your kids were examining your online calendar, looking for a good day to surprise you at the office. There are generally plenty of relatively innocent reasons for someone to "browse" through your files. Take this into mind before accusing someone of running a spy operation against you.

Build a Hypothesis

Now, try to pull all the pieces together and determine who was spying on you. Was it a simple hack job done by a curious child? Do the software and techniques match the ones in this book, which your wife recently borrowed? Was the software a high-tech spy device that evaded every firewall and virus scanner? In addition, couple your discoveries with your activities. Are you cheating on your wife? Selling drugs, or nuclear power plant blueprints? Does someone have a good reason to be spying on you?

Put together all of the evidence you have collected and correlate it with your list of suspects. Does the evidence match anyone? Does anything you have found support your hypothesis of their desire and capability. Analysis of this data will help determine the most likely suspect.

Act, If You Dare

Now that you have an idea of who is spying on you, it is time to act on the knowledge. We have already discussed many possible actions that you can take when you feel you have been spied on. This step requires some of the most intensive preparation and planning because the actions you take will have an effect on you, your spy, and the relationship between the two of you. As always, confronting your suspect is a possibility, although we would not recommend approaching the U.S. government or the mafia with accusations that they are "watching" you. When your accused spy does talk to you, be open to any excuse or reason they give. As recently discussed, they may have been snooping for totally innocent reasons. Sometimes acting like you have something to hide raises suspicions. Remember: calling someone a spy is a very strong accusation. Do it with caution and be ready for the consequences.

Notes from the Underground...

Be Sure You Are Right

I was chatting with my sister one night, and asked her a question about her and her boyfriend. She was quite taken aback by my question, since it required me to have information she did not realize I had. When she asked me how I knew the information, I decided to play with her; I sent her a link to this book along with the comment "look at what I'm writing." I had actually gotten the information from another sister (in a large family, gossip is the best method of intelligence collection). After seeing the link, my sister thought I was spying on her and logged off in a furor. She then had her computer examined by several savvy friends and found several keystroke loggers on it. I then got an angry phone call and a few days of icy silence as my sister would not speak to me, thinking that I was actually spying on her.

Once everything was straightened out, we talked about what might bee the source of the keystroke loggers and other spy software. Apparently, her ex-boyfriend worked on her computer that previous summer and helped her "set it up." He immediately came up as the number one suspect, who had motive and access. My sister's angry emotional state and desire to explain my surprising

Continued

information caused her to blame a target of opportunity and miss a more obvious suspect. In this case, everything worked out fine and she is never going to let a jealous ex boyfriend touch her computer again. However, in many cases, this type of mistake can have drastic effects. Be careful before you accuse anyone and make sure that you are correct in your accusations.

A Note about Spyware

Spyware is a huge problem with most home computer users. It is usually covertly installed, coming bundled with different free applications or sneaking onto PCs through other insidious methods. Most spyware is set up to collect information on browsing and computer-user habits to help deliver targeted advertising. It may also collect and examine e-mail, keystrokes, and mouse movements.

Unfortunately, since most home computers have spyware, it is hard to determine which spy software was accidentally installed, and what was specifically put there to spy on you. One can argue that all kinds of spyware target you, whether it is a large advertising company or your wife, and they should all be destroyed. However, there is a big difference between having your Web sites monitored by a spyware company for marketing reasons and having your spouse read your e-mail because they think you are cheating on them. Because of that, it is important to be able to sort out what is corporate spyware and what is personal.

Luckily, there are several useful tools for weeding out corporate-sponsored spyware. One popular example is Ad-Aware by Lavasoft, which can be downloaded from *www.download.com* (search ad-aware). An example of this application in action can be seen in Figure 11.41.

Figure 11.41 Lavasoft Freeware Version of Ad-Aware

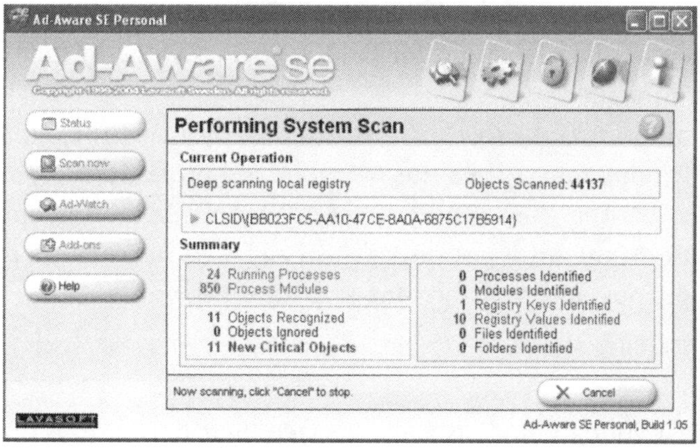

For extra protection, periodically use more than one type of spyware detection and removal system. A second application similar to Ad-Aware, is Spybot Search & Destroy, which can also be obtained at www.download.com (search *spybot*). An example of this application in action is shown in Figure 11.42.

Figure 11.42 Spybot Search & Destroy.

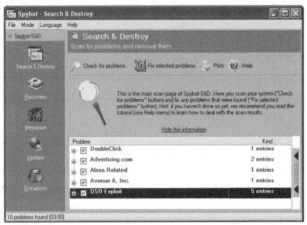

Case Study: Guilt is for Suckers, Not Spies

Spying is a very complex process, both technically and emotionally. Because every case effects all parties in very different ways, it is very important to follow the SLEUTH methodology, plan your actions, and do your best to anticipate the possible outcome. Failure to be prepared for the emotional implications of many scenarios could have disastrous results. When a spy fails to separate their feelings from their mission, they set themselves up for failure. Spying is one of the worst things to do in a haphazard manner.

Another common mistake that many amateur spies make is to underestimate the awareness of their opponent. While not everyone is a professional counter-spy, many people place great trust in their instincts and institution. Many spy operations are discovered because "something just doesn't feel right." It never hurts to expect that your mark is suspicious, and probably one step ahead of you.

Topic

In this case study a young couple is about to face their first serious obstacle. For the first time in almost four years, Greg will be spending the spring and summer apart from Camille. He will be working in a different state while she waits to transfer from her current job. Nervous about his fiancée's party-girl lifestyle, Greg decides to keep a close electronic eye on her.

Elaboration

Together, Greg and Camille are a young, happy couple. They met their junior year of college and become great friends. Between their junior and senior year Greg confessed his love and proposed to Camille. She accepted and they had a wonderful senior year together. After graduation, Camille got a job working in their college town. She got an apartment and they moved in together while Greg looked for work. After about a month of looking, Greg found the perfect job. It had terrific pay, flexible hours, and great benefits. Even better, it was in the same town as the law school Camille wanted to eventually attend. The only complication was that Greg had to start right away, and Camille could not move until after the summer. They would have to spend the next four months two states apart. It was going to be a challenge, but they were a committed couple and would try to see each other every couple of weeks.

Greg was a little nervous about leaving Camille. It would be the first time in three years that they would be apart for more than a few days. He remembered how Camille definitely was a "party girl" before they met. He still cringed a little inside at all the guys around campus that waved and seemed to know her. Perhaps it was due to some of his insecurity or perhaps it was some subtle clues he noticed, but Greg decided to keep an eye on Camille when he was gone, to let him know how she was doing. It would not be any worse than listening to her talk on the phone, he justified it to himself.

So Greg left, and on his visits back he would check his little "friends" that he left on her computers. Things seemed to be going well so far, so there were no worries. He sometimes felt a little guilty about snooping on his fiancée, but his fears won out and he kept watching.

While Greg was away Camille was having a fairly good time. She worked with quite a few young, single, just-out-of-college people, so they were always out partying. She had been with Greg for so long she had forgotten what it was like to be out on the town young, single (relatively), and wild. Even though she was out painting the town red, the thought of straying never crossed her mind, until one night at a company happy hour where her friend Jackie introduced her to her new co-worker, Lorenzo.

Lorenzo was tall, European, and very sexy. He had a great "air" around him; calm, relaxed and confident. When she spoke, he looked deep in her eyes and seemed to be paying close attention to every word she said. Who would not be attracted to that? Knowing that a little harmless flirting would not hurt anybody, Camille spent most of the happy hour talking to Lorenzo, quite a bit of time drinking and laughing with him afterwards, and then the rest of the evening making out with him on the cab ride home.

The next morning, Camille woke with a start, sitting straight up in bed. She immediately grabbed her throbbing head with both hands. "Oh my God I drank way too much last night," she thought, and then the images of the night started coming back to her. "Oh no, I didn't do that!" She looked around quickly;, ok, she was alone, so at least things did not go too far. Her initial feelings of guilt and shock lasted about as long as her hangover. As the day wore on, Camille started thinking about all the things that she had done. "Well it is not like I'm married. He's a cute guy; I'm a cute girl. We didn't hurt anybody." He was not the kind of guy she wanted to marry, not by a long shot. In fact, Greg fit that bill to a tee. But Lorenzo was fun and cute, oh so cute. Would it really be wrong for her to see him again? Just to play around a little bit before she left the dating scene for good? By dinnertime, she decided to send Lorenzo an e-mail thanking him for the wonderful evening and asking him if he would like to have drinks again.

When Camille grabbed her keyboard, she accidentally dropped it, pulling it from the back of the computer. "Well, that's weird," she thought, "It should not be that loose; Greg is always saying how loose it is and reattaching it in the back." So Camille pulled her computer out and reached around. "Hmmm, what is this?" Before she could attach her keyboard, Camille saw a small little tan dongle sitting in the purple keyboard slot on the back of her computer; it looked like it was set up for the keyboard to plug into. "Wait a second! I know what this is!" It was a small hardware keystroke logger. Greg had shown her one a couple of years ago, that he had bought for a computer security class, and had a great time playing pranks on his roommates with it. "Why is this on my computer?" Camille wondered.

Feeling a little nervous, Camille brought her desktop and laptop into the "computer guy" at work. She asked him to check them out and told him she was worried that someone was watching her. When she stopped by that afternoon he told her, "The desktop is clean; it only has the hardware key logger that you pulled, but the laptop has a neat little software key logger that mails out your keystrokes every six hours to a hotmail e-mail address. Do you want me to take it off?" Camille was shocked. Greg was spying on her, which would explain why they keyboard was always loose, wouldn't it? "No, go ahead and leave everything exactly like it is." She could not believe that Greg did not trust her, and even more than that he had the nerve to spy on her. She would make sure he paid for that.

Before she left home, she decided to write an e-mail to Lorenzo. From now on, all of the correspondence with him would be from her work computer. She was pretty sure Greg could not get to that, so she sat down and wrote:

```
Lorenzo,

I had a great time Saturday night. I'd like to hang out with you some more
if you want. Dinner @ my house on Thursday? ☺
```

```
Camille
```

When she got home that evening, she decided it was time to start playing Greg's games back on him. She sat down and wrote:

```
Greg
```

```
I just wanted to let you know how much I think about you and miss you.
Nothing is the same without you, I don't have a minute when you don't
cross my mind. I can't wait until you visit this weekend.
```

```
Love,
```

```
Camille
```

Content in her deception, Camille only communicated with Lorenzo from work. Occasionally, when she need to IM or write him from home, she would temporarily unplug the keylogger, always remembering to put it back when she was done. She did not want Greg to know that she was on to him, yet.

That Wednesday, she had dinner with Lorenzo, drinks afterward, and then they talked and did the things people do after dates. Sometime in the middle of the night, Camille got out of bed and started typing an e-mail to her friend Jackie.

```
        Jackie,
```

```
I can't believe how much in love with Greg I am. He is so amazing, and the
best guy I've ever been with. One of the things I like about him the most
is how he trusts me. Most guys would be uncomfortable with long distance
relationship. He's great and has never doubted me once. Its easy to love a
man like him
```

```
        Camille
```

She did not really send that e-mail to Jackie; she just typed into an empty document. She wanted to make sure that the keystrokes were picked up by Greg's keylogger. The e-mail was not intended for Jackie, but rather for Greg.

As the summer went on, Camille had a great fling with Lorenzo. She also made sure to turn on the sweetness whenever she talked to Greg, and sent several "decoy" messages every day professing her love and devotion for her fiancée. Greg, on the other hand, was having a long guilt-filled summer. He was feeling worse and worse about spying on Camille. She was so sweet to him; everything he collected from her computers confirmed that.

At the end of the summer when Camille came over to Greg's place, he decided it was time to fess up and come clean with her. "Camille, there's something I need to tell you. I've been spying on your computer over the summer because I was worried about you being faithful. But all I ever learned was how wonderful you are and how much you love me."

Upon hearing that, Camille made sure to act angry and disgusted and stormed out of the room in complete anger and disbelief. After he caught up with her, Camille made Greg apologize over and over, beg for forgiveness, and promise never to do it again. In the end she told him that things would be okay, but it would be a long time before she trusted him again.

So, they continued on as a couple and eventually got married. It took a while for Camille to get over being "mad" at Greg, and it took Camille's parents a long time before they trusted Greg again. They could not believe that anyone could have so little faith in their daughter. While their marriage ended up being a relatively normal and happy one, to this day Greg still feels guilty and thinks that spying on his fiancée was the worst decision he has ever made.

Analysis

Greg was wrong, and will have to pay for it for a long time. Camille cheated, and got away with it. Most spy stories do not have happy endings. Greg was worried (and rightly so) about his fiancée's faithfulness. When those fears rose up he had many choices; with those, he somehow felt that keeping an electronic eye on her would be the best idea. He carried out his plans well and did a fairly good job of bugging her computer. Unfortunately, Camille found Greg's spy devices and was able to succeed at cheating, despite his best efforts. In addition, once she knew she was being watched, she was able to play the victim role to her advantage.

Greg made the decision to spy, but he did not think through the outcomes. He fully expected to find evidence of cheating, and when he encountered the apparent longings of a loving girlfriend, his feelings of guilt led to his confession and the collapse of his spy operation. You cannot blame him; most people would have done the same thing in that situation. There were many potential ways that Greg could have come out clean, but emotions and a lot of bad luck ended it.

This just goes to show that the game of spying on loved ones is dangerous and not for everyone. Behind the sexy mystique lies tedious procedures and emotional conflict. As you embark on your amateur spy career, keep this and the other case studies in mind. Be careful what you do, be careful what you look for, be careful what you wish for, and most of all just be careful.

Summary

Being an excellent cyber spy means knowing how to observe others in a manner that cannot be detected. In this chapter, we demonstrated ways to increase the degree of your stealth while increasing your ability to maintain your own personal privacy. While there are many points that you should take away from this, the biggest key to ensuring privacy is to securely delete anything that you cannot afford not to lose; hide what you cannot delete at a location other than your computer, or encrypt what you cannot hide.

- Whenever possible limit your activity on a computer that you suspect may be monitored. Consider using business centers, hotels, or Internet café's for anonymous access.

- Wireless networks in restaurants and coffee shops help you avoid sniffer and router logs on your home network; however, the evidence still resides on the laptop that you used.

- Consider using removable media with a good cover story to hide sensitive documents. USB drives that are also used for financial data backups or MP3 music players such as the Apple iPod, are great examples. Not only are these devices an unlikely location for a spy to look, but they can be easily taken with you when you leave.

- Virtual RAM drives and bootable CD-ROMs can be used for temporary activities. When the power is shut down after using one of these techniques, the contents and history of the activities are completely erased.

- Virtual machines such as those offered through commercial applications such as VMware, can provide an additional layer of obscurity. Anyone spying on you would need to gain access to the local machine, and then know to boot and access the virtual machine to track your behavior.

- PGP freeware is a useful application for securely deleting files, encrypting files, and encrypting e-mail communications.

- TrueCrypt can be used to encrypt entire volumes for the storage of multiple files and/or applications that are password-protected.

- Sometimes, hiding data through steganography can improve privacy because your spy will not know that it is there.

- IM chats are visible for all to see. Make sure you download and configure your chat clients to use available encryption so that your online discussions stay private.

- When you think you have detected a spy, be certain that you have the correct person identified before you confront them. Many times, spies are not around you, but are in a distant location across the Internet that compromised your computer through other means.

Index

Syngress: *The Definition of a Serious Security Library*

Syn·gress (sin-gres): *noun, sing.* Freedom from risk or danger; safety. See *security*.

Inside the SPAM Cartel

For most people, the term "SPAM" conjures up the image of hundreds of annoying, and at times offensive, e-mails flooding your inbox every week. But for a few, SPAM is a way of life that delivers .... orn and the avoidance of .... *Inside the SPAM Cartel* .... dark sub-economy. You'll meet the characters that control the flow of money as well as the hackers and programmers committed to keeping the enterprise up and running.

ISBN: 1-932266-86-0

Price: $49.95 U.S. $72.95 CAN

Google Hacking for Penetration Testers

Johnny Long,

Foreword by Ed Skoudis

What many users don't realize is that the deceptively simple components that make Google so easy to use are the same features that generously unlock security flaws for the malicious hacker. Vulnerabilities in website security can be discovered through Google hacking, techniques applied to the search engine by computer criminals, identity thieves, and even terrorists to uncover secure information. *Google Hacking for Penetration Testers* beats Google hackers to the punch, equipping web administrators with penetration testing applications to ensure their site is invulnerable to a hacker's search.

ISBN: 1-931836-36-1

Price: $49.95 USA $65.95 CAN

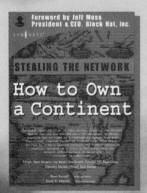

Stealing the Network: How to Own a Continent

Last year, *Stealing the Network: How to Own the Box* became a blockbuster best-seller and garnered universal acclaim as a techno-thriller firmly rooted in reality and technical accuracy. Now, the sequel is available and it's even more contro-versial than the original. *Stealing the Network: How to Own a Continent* does for cyber-terrorism buffs what "Hunt for Red October" did for cold-war era military buffs, it develops a chillingly realistic plot that taps into our sense of dread and fascination with the terrible possibilities of man's inventions run amuck.

ISBN: 1-931836-05-1

Price: $49.95 U.S. $69.95 CAN

SYNGRESS®